Music Techniques in Therapy, Counseling, and Special Education

Music Techniques in Therapy, Counseling, and Special Education

Third Edition

Jayne M. Standley
Florida State University

Jennifer D. Jones
Western Illinois University

American Music Therapy Association, Inc.

Neither the American Music Therapy Association nor its Board of Directors is responsible for the conclusions reached or the opinions expressed in this book.

The American Music Therapy Association is a non-profit association dedicated to increasing access to quality music therapy services for individuals with disabilities or illnesses or for those who are interested in personal growth and wellness. AMTA provides exensive educational and research information about the music therapy profession. Referrals for qualified music therapists are also provided to consumers and parents. AMTA holds an annual conference every autumn and its seven regions hold conferences every spring.

For up-to-date information, please access the AMTA website at www.musictherapy.org

ISBN: 1-884914-19-5

Authors: Jayne Standley
                                Florida State University
                                Tallahassee, Florida

                                Jennifer Jones
                                Western Illinois University
                                Macomb, Illinois

Copyright Information: © 2007 by American Music Therapy Association, Inc.
                                8455 Colesville Road, Suite 1000
                                Silver Spring, Maryland 20910 USA
                                www.musictherapy.org
                                info@musictherapy.org

Technical Assistance: Wordsetters
                                Kalamazoo, Michigan

Cover Design: Angie K. Elkins, MT-BC

Printed in the United States of America

Contents

Preface

The purpose of this book is to provide a systematic, hierarchical approach to the development of leadership skills during music interventions that are intended to function in an educational, therapeutic, or recreational capacity. The book does not, however, deal with the teaching of music as subject matter. Rather, it is intended to be a synthesis and clinical application of research in music and the acquisition of therapy skills. The contents utilize existing knowledge in the field, borrowing liberally from the many persons who have contributed across time to its accumulation.

More than 120 tasks are included, covering a variety of client groups ranging in age from infants to the elderly and incorporating major disability labels used in the allied health fields. Current therapeutic/counseling techniques documented in the literature are emphasized. The interventions are designed for use in actual clinical experiences or with simulated client/student groups and include opportunities for the development of music performance skills and/or the systematic use of recorded music.

All interventions are fully planned and explained with the objectives and procedures given for implementation. They are also sequenced in hierarchical order on a variety of issues: from simple to complex skill acquisition, from single to multiple objectives, and from complete delineation of "how to" information to leader independence in determining how the session should be designed and implemented.

Further, the book is based on a philosophy of leader accountability for the individual client's or client group's response in the session. It stresses the establishment of a priori objectives, the use of documented techniques, and the collection of data for evaluating results. It is also designed for personalized skill development. To facilitate this, interventions are indexed by population, technique, and student objective. These indexes allow selection of an objective to meet an individual student's educational needs.

An extensive, updated bibliography by type of education/therapeutic environment, an updated discography of recorded music titles, and music repertoire lists are provided for use in sessions. These are intended to help students access existing literature and music repertoire as they become independent in planning and designing therapy sessions for specific client groups. This revised third edition includes a section on developing a student's clinically relevant song repertoire. Instructors can use the repertoire development section separately or integrate it with assigned student objectives. Sample role-play instruction cards have been provided to assist instructors in directing simulations to model clinical situations.

The inherent philosophy of this book is that clinical expertise is heightened by awareness of the available research literature in the field and the ability to transfer its findings to applied situations.

Research, in the broadest definition, is a way of thinking, a state of mind. . . . The research attitude represents an objective view of the world, and the finished product is a person who is informed and has the ability to think, that is to analyze, criticize, make transfers, and choose alternatives in the light of all possible evidence.[1]

Activities from Level 2 onward include research and group discussion questions to facilitate the practice of analysis and generalization of information so that the best future alternatives for therapeutic intervention might be chosen and implemented.

Part I

Content and Organization

Introduction

Persons who counsel or teach act upon their own value systems by making many choices for others. Among these choices are determining another's problem, deciding what to teach to promote its resolution, and selecting the most appropriate techniques to use in this endeavor. Many such persons identify professionally with the value system of a particular theoretical approach, as in the Montessori or Springhill educational methods, or the Psychoanalytic, Cognitive-Behavioral Therapy, or Humanistic Psychology approaches to therapy. Others prefer an eclectic label, usually implying adherence to values or techniques borrowed from many approaches on the premise "if it works, use it."

Whatever the value system or theoretical premise underlying the individual's choices, at the level of interacting with the student/client, a technique is utilized. There seems to be an unlimited number of theories or explanations of approaches that have evolved over time, but a finite number of techniques identified to accomplish the therapeutic/educational goal. Many techniques, such as role-playing, focusing of attention, or teaching incompatible responses, seem to be shared or advocated by different approaches. Each system uses virtually the same procedure but interprets differently why it is used and what it is supposed to accomplish (see Silverman, in press).

The actual procedures used with the client or student to implement the selected values are referred to here as techniques. This book is primarily concerned with the skills needed to lead a client or group of clients and with a variety of therapeutic/educational techniques combined with music. It teaches these techniques through the opportunity to demonstrate the skills of planning, implementing, and evaluating results. It also teaches values to the extent these techniques are discussed contextually at the conclusion of the demonstrated activity. Values become apparent as the discussion is guided toward identifying any implied choices inherent in a task and/or comparisons made between therapeutic/educational approaches.

The underlying premise of all activities included here is that the leader accepts responsibility for the client's or group of clients' responses in the session. This establishes a direct relationship between session outcome and the caliber of skill demonstrated and allows the individual to determine personal effectiveness as a leader. Session outcome is, of course, relative to both adequate planning and the ability to adapt quickly to the realities of the interaction. A group of hyperactive children may certainly be more active than normal children, but if the leader fails to control the activity level enough to accomplish at least a portion of the session objective, then the leader has failed to demonstrate a skill. To rationalize by saying the children were too hyperactive for the assigned task would be to abdicate leader responsibility. If a session objective does not match the group's level, then the leader may adapt the planned objective and/or control the children's activity level. The premise of this book for the above example is that the more skillful the leader, the calmer and more on-task the children, and the greater the proportion of session objectives achieved.

This text begins where development of the skill in writing a first lesson or session plan ends. Any such plan must subsequently be implemented with skills other than writing and in reality be adapted immediately to group interaction as it actually occurs. This ability to adapt immediately in response to a group's reactions is a necessary and critical teaching/therapy skill that can be learned only by practice. The skill development may be equivalent to learning to play a musical instrument. One does not become a violinist solely by watching or listening to another play. Neither does one become a virtuoso by reading information on how to play, by writing plans for skillful violin playing, by listening to lectures on same, or by providing correct answers to test questions about violin techniques. One learns to play the violin through many methods, including long hours of actually attempting to play the violin. Similarly, a variety of opportunities to practice teaching/therapy leadership skills would seem to provide the experiential component necessary for development of these requisite abilities. This collection of interventions is organized to maximize such development across many diverse clinical situations.

Text Design

Both a competency-based training program and a collection of indexed music treatment plans, this book is intended for many uses, including the instruction of future music therapists or other group leaders who wish to use music, students seeking assistance with planning interventions for practicum or internship settings, internship directors/practicum supervisors who wish to assign client objectives which can be independently implemented, or practicing therapists who desire a resource for a variety of music applications to diverse therapeutic problems.

More than 120 tasks designed to develop competencies in using music to change behavior, whether for therapeutic, educational, or recreational reasons, are included. They are arranged hierarchically for skill acquisition, from simple to more complex across three dimensions: music skills, leadership skills, and the decision-making skills necessary to plan and analyze effect of group interactions. They are comprehensive across populations with respect to age and label and across current techniques in the allied health fields. They are further designed to acquaint users with the extensive body of research in music and behavior through implementation of documented techniques, discussion of research results and their transfer to applied situations, and provision of extensive bibliographic references. The tasks reflect a philosophical bias of accountability (i.e., the leader is responsible for the *results* of the interaction whether by commission or omission).

The development of skills for leading music interventions includes the leader's music performance abilities, which determine the quality of the musical aspects of the interaction such as singing, accompanying, and conducting, and the skill to engage others, usually nonmusicians, in music activities such as choruses, instrumental ensembles, or dance troupes. This text systematically develops clinical skills while requiring greater musical competence of the leader in the areas of singing, playing, improvising, moving, composing, arranging, and adapting music interventions to meet the needs of specific individuals, whether disabled or diverse in ability, preference, and/or motivation.

For persons not desiring to use the music performance skills in active music participation, tasks are designed to teach the application of recorded music repertoire to health-related objectives and to teach the leadership skills for directing group listening or discussion about music. Some tasks teach the use of selected music as a background for other group techniques to be developed by the leader, such as progressive relaxation, guided imagery, or the stimulation of group conversation.

The leadership objectives progress solely from a consideration of the leader's abilities to the accountability for the group's response in the session and from a single music objective to simultaneous music, group, and individual group member objectives. The tasks are divided into four levels of competency achievement with skills accumulating across levels.

Students learn primarily by leading an individual client or group of clients through one of these interventions as assigned. Clients can be real, as in practicum assignments or internship sessions, or simulated by peers. Progress in community practicum can be assessed and coordinated with additional activities and techniques learned in the classroom through simulation. Students also learn vicariously by being participants during group sessions, observing the leader's techniques, and discussing intent, accomplishment, group response, and alternative methods and procedures.

Student evaluation is accomplished through competency assessments included in the manual, which gradually become more comprehensive in content. Each objective has a recommended *minimum* criterion score on the competency assessment and instructors may, of course, have higher or different criteria for grade differentiation. It is recommended that all sessions be videotaped for subsequent analysis. The student can self-evaluate and compare impressions with those of the instructor.[1] More advanced students can improve observation skills by assessments on peers and learn to give constructive feedback.[2] The assessments function to evaluate progress while also identifying crucial desired skills and specific skill deficits that become future goals for the individual.

Competency Levels

The tasks for competency development are divided into five main levels, each cumulative and requiring increasingly difficult demonstration of skills and abilities.[3,4,5] Level I isolates the development of the leader's music skills and begins with a stated music objective and complete preparation and implementation guidelines. Initially (Level IA), at this level only musical skill, group response to the leader, and accomplishment of the music objective are evaluated. Later (Level IB), tasks at this level add evaluation of music repertoire and personal attributes of the leader (e.g., posture, nervous habits, facial expression—see Competency Assessment 2).

Level 2A moves beyond the music activity to add accountability for achieving a single nonmusic group objective. Objectives at this level are evaluated for the leader's music skill, the leader's personal attributes, and the ability to demonstrate the basic skills necessary for conducting the specified intervention, while also evaluating the effectiveness of the leader to assure the group's accomplishment of the a priori objective. Level 2B introduces labeled populations or client groups with a specific problem to be alleviated by the music session. Again, complete session planning and preparatory instructions are provided.

Level 3 continues the application of music to specific problems of diverse populations while increasing the leader's accountability for the quality of music performance and the presentation and accomplishment of the nonmusic objective by an individual or group. By the completion of this level, the leader has been responsible for multiple nonmusic objectives, has evaluated each objective through collection of group data, and has begun independently making choices about certain aspects of session preparation and planning.

Level 4 is designed to teach the leader to attend to individual problems or objectives within the group while simultaneously directing a music intervention and teaching nonmusic group objectives. Leaders also become independent at this level in planning and preparing for the session. Interventions here require more sustained periods of time in order for the multiple objectives and tasks to be incorporated.

Level 5 provides an opportunity for the spontaneous demonstration of comprehensive competencies learned and allows the assessment of overall skill development and repertoire depth. The student is given a set of specific session demographics, and with only 5 minutes of preparation time is expected to conduct a viable therapeutic interaction. This is intended to be analogous to the real clinical world where one's spontaneity is often tested.

Throughout all levels, each task includes specified assessment and criteria for skill development. Beginning with Level 2, a list of discussion questions is also provided to facilitate generalization or transfer of concepts and techniques demonstrated. These questions are designed to provide information from the research literature, to stimulate thought regarding application to practical situations, to facilitate comparison of demonstrated reactions with literature reports, and to transmit application of demonstrated cause-effect relationships to other clinical situations. Research instrumental in the development of these questions, the activities, and the values expressed herein is cited in the Bibliography.

The following outline provides a concise review of the various areas of hierarchical skill development across levels:

Level 1 Competencies:

Objectives:
    Leader: Music skills (Level 1A)
              Teach music objective (Level 1B)
    Group: Participation

Type of Music:
    Active music participation

Population:
    Peers

Leader Decisions:
    Selection of music according to criteria

Evaluation:
    Leader: Music skills
              Personal attributes (later tasks)
    Group: Responses

Level 2 Competencies:

Objectives:
    Leader: Music skills
              Teach group objective
    Group: Nonmusic objective—health, educational, or recreational context

Type of Music:
Active music participation
Music listening/discussion
Music as background for other techniques

Population:
Peers (Level 2A)
Groups with disability labels (Level 2B)

Leader Decisions:
Selection of music according to criteria

Evaluation:
Leader: Music skills
General leadership skills
Personal attributes
Group: Responses

Level 3 Competencies:

Objectives:
Leader: Music skills
Teach multiple objectives to nonmusic group
Group: Multiple nonmusic objectives

Type of Music:
Active music participation
Music listening/discussion
Music as background for other techniques

Population:
Groups with disability labels

Leader Decisions:
Selection of music
Preparation of activities
Selection of data collection method

Evaluation:
Leader: Music skills
General leadership skills
Personal attributes
Group: Responses
Proportion of group objective achieved according to collected data

Level 4 Competencies:

Objectives:
> Leader: Music skills
>> Teach objectives to nonmusic group
>> Teach multiple, diverse, individual, nonmusic group objectives
> Group: Group nonmusic objective
> Individual nonmusic objectives

Type of Music:
> Active music participation
> Group music listening/discussion
> Music as background for other techniques

Population:
> Groups with disability labels, diverse in age, severity, or type of label

Leader Decisions:
> Specification of problems and procedures
> Selection of music
> Selection of techniques
> Preparation activities
> Selection of data collection method

Evaluation:
> Leader: Music skills
>> General leadership skills
>> Personal attributes
> Group: Responses
>> Proportion of group objective achieved according to collected data
>> Degree of individual objectives achieved according to collected data

Level 5 Competency:

Conduct a music intervention according to specifications received 5 minutes prior to implementation; demonstrate comprehensive music leadership, therapeutic, and/or educational competence.

Individualized Skill Development

The hierarchical arrangement of tasks in this text permits systematic development and accumulation of competencies while also allowing for diversity in student entry level and rate of acquisition. It is designed for highly individualized instruction based on personal assessment of each student, a priori objectives for skill development, directed task assignment, ongoing assessment of competencies, and continuous development through repetition of the process across levels.

For the purpose of this text, the adjectives *teaching* and *therapy* are used interchangeably when describing leadership skills. To the extent that a therapeutic objective and treatment plan are identified a priori and responsibility taken by the leader for its accomplishment, the process of leading individuals through an intervention to achieve the stated objective seems to require relatively the same skills as those of a group music activity to teach subject matter. Since the objective and planning/implementation procedures are specified in each activity, the skills to be developed and demonstrated are generic to many professions. Whether the student aspires to become a music therapist, music educator, or other professional using music activities (special educator, social worker, counselor, psychologist, psychiatrist, etc.), the exercises in this text teach the basic requisite skills and are carefully indexed so that objectives specific to the intended profession may be selected and skills demonstrated in context.[6] This text does not teach the writing of objectives per se since these are preselected. However, specific objectives in observable, measurable terms are modeled, as is content from a variety of educational/therapeutic approaches.

Music Selection

In many interventions all procedural specifications are given for implementation except the specific piece of music to be used. Selection of appropriate music is a basic skill to be demonstrated in every activity. In each case, the selection should be age appropriate for the identified population, as well as from the individual's or group's preferred category or type of music. Major issues to consider when selecting music include the following:

1. Individual client preference seems to be the most important variable for assuring the desired effect of music. Research shows there is no music that is always perceived as sedative or stimulative by everyone. Rather, each individual's preference and past associations will most directly determine his or her response to music.

2. The difficulty of learning new music can be reduced and controlled through careful selection of lyrics, melody, and/or accompaniment. Repetitive words, rhythms, notes, and chords greatly simplify the learning task.

3. Both musical selections and accompanying activities must be age appropriate to function as intended. Many adults resent being given the type of rhythm instruments usually identified with children. Some dances, too, may be identified with children (e.g., "The Hokey Pokey") and may be insulting to older groups.

4. Music meant to facilitate memory must repetitiously pair a melody or melodic phrase with the discrete information to be remembered. Researchers have found familiar music[7] and simple folk-like melodies[8,9] to be helpful. The leader is encouraged to experiment with rhythm and melody when designing music interventions for memory.

Use of Competency Assessments

The competency assessment of music and leadership skills included and used throughout this book was developed from a comprehensive review of research in music to change behavior. There was particular reliance upon items from the following data collection forms: The Behavior Checklist by Furman[10] for assessing guitar-accompanied song leading, the Music Conductor Observation Form by Madsen and Yarbrough,[11] the Behavioral Rating Form for assessing practicum skills of music therapy students by Hanser and Furman,[12] and the Music Therapy Competency Observation Form by Alley.[13] Additional items were drawn from the list of Essential Competencies for the Practice of Music Therapy[14] and from the competency list by Braswell, Decuir, and Maranto.[15]

The initial version of the assessment used herein was field-tested by observing two videotapes of 19 advanced music therapy students. The first shows them conducting song-leading activities with their peers, and the second a year later was with children ages 4–5. Scores on the 100-point assessment in the song with peers ranged 13–78 with an average score of 49.3, and in the song with children ranged 31–93 with an average score of 77.5. These 38 evaluations were compared with two other analyses previously completed on the same teaching interactions.

Following this comparison, the assessment was revised with items added, omitted, or rearranged to comprehensively reflect the primacy and frequency of competencies observed and cited. Additionally, items were weighted for scoring, some on the basis of documented relationship in the research between competencies and effect on clients, some on the basis of frequency of inclusion in other published observation forms, and some on the field-test comparison.

The final version of the 100-point checklist includes 93 items divided horizontally into four major sections on the form: Personal Skills (20 points), General Leadership Skills (40 points), Music Skills (20 points), and Client Responses (20 points). The first three sections list observable therapist skills, while the final section includes observable client responses. Client responses were included and weighted to balance the therapist proficiency score, thereby establishing a relationship among competency evaluation, client achievement, and appropriate behavior.

A basal score in each category functions to weight that section in relationship to the overall evaluation. This is intended to differentiate the special skills that therapists using music demonstrate across all populations and to differentiate music to meet a specific objective from other music interactions with persons needing therapeutic intervention.

The 93 items are further divided vertically into three columns: Deficiencies—behaviors or skills of the leader that are omitted, performed poorly, or undesirable to the extent that they interfere with the effectiveness of the session ($N = 37$); Skills meeting minimum criteria—behaviors deemed essential and basic to every music intervention ($N = 30$); and Skills above minimum criteria—behaviors that indicate more sophisticated abilities ($N = 26$). The final assessment is included in three versions: Competency Assessment 1—music skills only, for evaluation of Level 1A competencies; Competency Assessment 2—music and personal skills for Level 1B competencies; and Competency Assessment 3—the full evaluation of competencies for Levels 2 through 5.

Scoring

Each student's music session is observed for those therapist skills meeting minimum criteria as listed in the center column, and a check is placed by all skills demonstrated. When a minimum criteria competency is not observed in a subset of any category on the form, then that item is left blank, indicating skill omitted, or marked *NA* (not applicable, as in "sings, plays correct in tune pitches" in a session involving only exercising to a record or tape). If a minimum skill item is left blank due to the perception that a skill was omitted, then the deficiencies column immediately to the left of that subset is utilized. Any overt deficiencies noted may be checked there for specific feedback to the leader. When minimum criteria are observed and checked in a subject of any category, the right column is considered. Any additional skills meeting above minimum criteria are checked there.

Section 3.0, Music Skills, provides space for recording those music skills utilized. These items are not included in scoring since therapists use a wide variety of music activities, often in creative or unique ways. The number of music skills or type of skill used (live vs. recorded music) is sometimes less important than the quality of the skill and how it is incorporated into the therapeutic objective. It is considered important, however, to record what music skill was being analyzed in the overall checklist. This allows for comparison across the spectrum of music skills for one individual or for assessment of progress in development of a specific music skill. The competency assessment is scored according to the chart in Table 1.

Criteria

Each intervention includes a specified assessment score to meet criteria for the assignment as a guide for the student and the instructor. (It is recommended that these criteria not be rigidly adhered to but used primarily to establish a reasonable goal.) The criteria scores were set according to results of field-testing across five groups of persons with varying experience and expertise.[16]

Table 2 shows average scores for these groups by skill column: deficiencies, minimum criteria, and above minimum criteria. These scores seem to indicate that the checklist as constructed discriminates expertise and experience primarily through increased scores in the above minimum criteria column: $M = 24.5$ for professional music therapists (MT-BC) and 18.9 for pre-interns music therapy (MT) majors as compared with mean scores of 2.6, 1.9, and 2.2 for the other three groups.

Field-test scores for each group were also tallied across subcategories, for the assessment and as a whole. These results are shown in Table 3. It can be seen that the professional music therapists (MT-BC) scored an average of 91.1 points, the MT pre-interns an average of 81.0 points, the music education (ME) pre-interns and freshmen scored 55.4 and 51.6 points, respectively, and the MT seniors on the baseline task scored 46.4 points. The MT seniors baseline group received the lowest score in almost all categories, even rating lower than freshmen in all areas except client responses. It is felt that this was probably due to the difficulty of the assigned leadership task for this group to use an accompanying instrument. In comparison, no other individuals in groups untrained in music therapy (freshmen or ME pre-interns) elected to use an accompaniment. Otherwise, scores decreased as experience and professional preparation in music therapy decreased.

Table 1

Scoring Chart for Competency Assessment of Music, Personal, and Leadership Skills

All skills meeting minimum criteria and above minimum criteria count 1 point each, except where noted on the form. Deficiencies count –1 each, except where noted on the form. Skills left blank or marked *NA* receive 0 points. Add the basal score* for each category in the category total.

Category		Minimum Criteria Points	Extra Points Above Minimum Criteria	Category Total
1.0	Personal Skills			
1.1	Posture/Stance/Proximity/ Body Language	2	2	
1.2	Speaking Voice	2	2	
1.3	Facial Expression	1	2	
1.4	Eye Contact	2	3	
	*Basal Score 4	7	9	20
2.0	General Leadership Skills			
2.1	Session Planning	4	3	
2.2	Session Preparation	4	1	
2.3	Session Implementation	6	4	
2.4	Session Evaluation	3	3	
	*Basal Score 12	17	11	40
3.0	Music Skills			
	*Basal Score 8	7	5	20
	(All music skills utilized are checked but not included in scoring.)			
4.0	Client Response			
	*Basal Score 8	6	6	
	(In this category all deficiencies count –2 each, all minimum criteria count +3, and all above minimum criteria count +2.)			20

Table 2
Average Group Scores by Skill Columns

	Deficiencies	Minimum Criteria	Above Minimum Criteria
MT-BC (*n* = 13)	0.0	34.5	24.5
MT Pre-Interns (*n* = 25)	1.4	32.5	18.9
ME Pre-Interns (*n* = 25)	3.9	24.9	2.6
Freshmen Music Majors (*n* = 25)	5.1	22.8	1.9
MT Seniors-Baseline (*n* = 25)	8.1	21.5	2.2

N = 113

Table 3
Average Group Scores by Category

	Personal Skills	General Leadership Skills	Music Skills	Client Responses	Total
MT-BC (*n* = 13)	17.7	37.7	16.1	19.5	91.1*
MT Pre-Interns (*n* = 25)	16.6	31.1	15.7	17.4	81.0*
ME Pre-Interns (*n* = 25)	9.4	19.3	14.2	12.5	55.4
Freshmen Music Majors (*n* = 25)	8.2	17.9	14.2	12.5	55.4
MT Seniors-Baseline (*n* = 25)	6.5	16.3	11.3	12.6	46.4

N = 113, *df* = 4, *p* < .001
*Indicates significance from groups without asterisk.

Ongoing Assessment

A Student Progress Form (page 19) is included to assist in evaluating long-term progress for individuals across assignments and skill levels. It is cumulative with entries made after each evaluation of an assignment. A copy can be maintained by the student for recording self-assessment with a second copy maintained by the instructor for course evaluation. Student-instructor conferences to set future objectives and select the next assignment also allow the form to function as a contract between the student and teacher.

Since the tasks are assigned individually and any combination may occur on a given class day, a Class Assignment Form is provided to help the instructor structure the class agenda (page 20). Each task has a recommended time limit to assist the instructor in determining how many interactions to schedule for each class meeting. The form may be replicated and completed for each of these meetings.

Repertoire Development

A section has been added to this text on the development of accompanied song repertoire for use in music therapy. The development of relevant song repertoire can be concurrent with the assignment of objectives or used as a separate section. Lists of songs that are used with different populations in music therapy are provided along with examples of assessment forms. The lists and assessment forms allow for individualized assignments for student repertoire development and evaluation. Additional instructions are provided at the beginning of Part III.

Implementation Procedures

This text is a mechanism for diverse entry levels and rates of acquisition of competencies; for generalization or specialization by population, disability area, or field of endeavor; and for the use of live or recorded music. Its use can coordinate skill development in simulation with skills developed in actual practica or internship settings. It is designed for highly individualized instruction within group and classroom situations.

The following procedures for use with groups of students are recommended:

1. Initial leadership opportunities should be as nonthreatening as possible and designed to desensitize the students to being in front of the group and to being videotaped.

   Some techniques for desensitizing them are (a) the instructor may start a well-known song and have each class member take a turn leading it, with the music continuing as each one stands in place and leads; (b) each person may be given multiple opportunities to lead a predetermined activity without interruption for feedback (which may come at the end of the class and be given to the group, not the individual); (c) everyone may lead the same song, but change it musically in some way. When students begin leading the group without hesitation, they are ready for their first individualized objective. If music skills need to be improved, then objectives at Level 1A would be appropriate. If students are accomplished at functional music skills, then repertoire might be developed through later Level 1B tasks. If students are accomplished in both areas, then Level 2 tasks may be the best starting place.

2. From the outset the class should be taught to be cooperative and supportive of peers in the leadership role.

    This training is crucial for later sessions when difficult client responses may be simulated. If leaders do not feel camaraderie and support from their peers prior to dealing with the pressure of being the leaders for clients with difficult to control behaviors, revenge may become the *modus operandi.* Group members may become very inappropriate clients for subsequent leaders who gave them difficulty in prior simulations. If this happens, the group will become chaotic, uncontrolled, and no longer simulating the specific type of student/client behavior desired. Instructors may establish additional structure by providing students with role-play instructions. A sample of role-play instruction cards is provided in Part II: Competency Tasks (p. 214).

    The following rules are important to teach prior to allowing students to assume the leadership role with individualized objectives:

    - Attendance will be required of students at all class meetings, whether or not they are presenting, so that a group will exist for each leader, and everyone will feel a commitment to effectively role-play the desired client behavior.

    - Each leader will prepare to the best of his or her ability in order to maximize opportunities to learn, realizing that every leadership opportunity will be evaluated.

    - The group will cooperate with the leader at all times unless instructed by the teacher to simulate specific, contrary behavior.

    - If client groups are simulated, their behavior will be role-played exactly as instructed.

    - Only those students instructed to role-play client behavior will do so.

    - All persons role-playing client behavior will respond positively to correct techniques implemented by the leader to deal with the problem.

    - Students will make only positive comments about the leader. Any negative comments will be made and controlled by the teacher.

3. All leadership opportunities will be evaluated.

    Informal evaluation can be used to identify personal assets and deficits, skills demonstrated and not demonstrated. Formal evaluation can be systematic, like counting a specific event or using one of the three competency assessments provided (pages 21–26). Evaluating from videotape is more objective than one's memory and allows both the instructor and student to evaluate at different times.

4. Leadership objectives should be assigned individually and mutually agreed upon in conference between the instructor and student.

   The Student Progress Form may be completed after each conference and a copy maintained by both the student and the instructor. Conferences should be delayed until both the student and instructor have evaluated the previous objective.

5. Objectives should challenge an individual to develop a new skill but not be so difficult as to intimidate or lead to failure.

   Tasks are indexed according to population, techniques, and student objectives and classified according to levels from simple (Level 1) to complex (Level 5). A Class Assignment Form (page 20) completed for each class meeting will help the instructor remember each student's assigned objective.

6. The instructional process remains the same across multiple simulations, though the student's objectives change.

   The process for the leader:
      a. receive assignment
      b. prepare to best of ability
      c. present in class and be videotaped (a videotape of a practicum interaction can also be a presentation)
      d. review tape and evaluate according to instructions
      e. confer with instructor about presentation and identify future objective (indexes may be used to find best activity for objective selected)
      f. repeat process

   The process for the group:
      a. participate in presentation as instructed
      b. respond to all directions and techniques implemented
      c. give positive feedback to leader
      d. discuss session with class instructor for transfer of observations, demonstrations, techniques, etc.

   The process for the class instructor:
      a. evaluate students' previous assignments with appropriate competency assessment by watching videotape or observing live
      b. record results on Student Progress Form
      c. meet with student in individual conferences after he or she has self-evaluated and determine student's awareness of assets and deficits
      d. select next leadership objective by using indexes
      e. make any special assignments for individual to personalize the objectives
      f. record assignment and date due on Class Assignment Form

7. As students become more sophisticated and reach Competency Levels 3 and 4, they will be required to make more decisions about how the session should be structured. They

will also need to acquire some of their own information about techniques and clinical populations.

Bibliographies containing music articles by client group are included to assist with this endeavor. Students can be taught to know and utilize the literature in the field when planning sessions. This can be especially emphasized during the discussions for transfer following each presentation.

8. Decisions regarding selection of music for client discussion groups are crucial.

This task is facilitated by the discography in Part III. Music titles are organized by general discussion topic. Students must decide, however, how the music fits the objective of the group. For instance, Eminem's "Drug Ballad" is listed under the topic Substance Abuse. Under the philosophy of this text, it would be considered a lack of skill for a leader to let the group discussion use this song to justify substance abuse instead of identifying its negative consequences, since justifying deviant behavior is rarely a therapeutic objective.

9. When competencies are acquired, they should remain a part of the person's clinical repertoire.

An effective therapist is able to synthesize knowledge and transfer skills to explicit situation. Level 5 is provided as an opportunity for spontaneous demonstration of skill level. It is a synthesizing task that allows a person to assess comprehensively his or her development.

10. The instructor and students should note that nonreligious music is stressed initially as students select music for education/therapeutic objectives.

Secular music is initially stressed for several important reasons. The objective is to increase nonreligious music repertoire, while sensitizing students to the fact that music from their religious backgrounds will not be appropriate for every client with whom they might work. Once sensitized, the student might later select appropriate religious music from a *client's* faith to meet a therapeutic objective, i.e., as in counseling a terminally ill person with a strong reliance on religious belief. Initially, however, the manual directs the student to secular literature for classroom simulations. There is also an initial emphasis on peer age level and interest that moves to other ages and music preferences. Accurately assessing a client's music preferences and possessing the ability to perform a varied musical repertoire is essential for successful music therapists. Repertoire lists generated from music therapy clinical practice include religious music (See Part III).

11. Each intervention has a recommended time limit. This is merely for class management of simulated opportunities, not the real amount of time required to achieve these same objectives in an actual clinical setting. The instructor should help students acquire clinical perspective by discussion of reasonable time for achieving objectives and necessary opening and closing activities in the same session.

Student Progress Form

Student's Name _____

Objectives	COMPETENCY ASSESSMENT SCORES					Skill Deficits	Skill Assets	Music Used	Future Objectives
	Music Score	Personal Score	Leadership Score	Client Response. Score	Total Score				
Level 1.0 1									
2									
3									
4									
5									
Level 2.0 1									
2									
3									
4									
5									
Level 3.0 1									
2									
3									
4									
5									
Level 4.0 1									
2									
3									
4									
5									

Class Assignment Form

Date: _____

<u>Presentation Order</u>

1. Student Name _____
Objective # _____ Page _____ Time Limit _____
Objective _____
Special Assignments _____
_____
Evaluation _____

2. Student Name _____
Objective # _____ Page _____ Time Limit _____
Objective _____
Special Assignments _____
_____
Evaluation _____

3. Student Name _____
Objective # _____ Page _____ Time Limit _____
Objective _____
Special Assignments _____
_____
Evaluation _____

4. Student Name _____
Objective # _____ Page _____ Time Limit _____
Objective _____
Special Assignments _____
_____
Evaluation _____

5. Student Name _____
Objective # _____ Page _____ Time Limit _____
Objective _____
Special Assignments _____
_____
Evaluation _____

Name _____   Clients _____
Date _____   Objective _____

COMPETENCY ASSESSMENT 1: MUSIC SKILLS

3.0 Music Skills	Deficiencies	Skills Meeting Minimum Criteria	Skills Above Minimum Criteria
Check all used: ____ Voice ____ Autoharp ____ Guitar ____ Piano ____ Percussion ____ Movement: Dance/Exercise, Clapping, or Motions ____ Recorded music	____ Mistakes in voice ____ Mistakes in accompaniment ____ Difficulty starting or continuing music ____ Lack of cues for client participation ____ Uncontrolled variation in beat, tempo, or dynamics ____ Motor activities not matched to music, not sequenced, too easy, too difficult ____ Music not related to objective or ability level of clients	____ Sings correct, in-tune pitches ____ Plays correct accompaniment ____ Music uninterrupted by mistakes ____ Cues group participation in music /motor activity ____ Uses steady beat, appropriate dynamics and tempo ____ Models motor or other tasks adequately ____ Music related to objective and ability level of clients	____ Uses original music or creative adaptation ____ Music skills at exceptional level (+2) ____ Music is obviously enjoyable to client(s) (+2)
BASAL: 8	– _____ Subtotal	+ _____ Subtotal	+ _____ Subtotal = _____ MUSIC TOTAL

4.0 Client Responses	Deficiencies	Skills Meeting Minimum Criteria	Skills Above Minimum Criteria
	____ Clients withdrawn, off-task, nonparticipatory (–2) ____ Objective not achieved by at least 80% of group (–2) ____ High level of inappropriate behavior (psychotic, repetitive, negative, disruptive) (–2)	____ Clients on-task / participatory 80% of session (+3) ____ Objective achieved by 80% of clients (+3)	____ Primary objective achieved by all, secondary obj. achieved by many (+2) ____ Client(s) on-task or participating > 80% (+2) ____ Clients obviously engaged in session (+2)
BASAL: 8	– _____ Subtotal	+ _____ Subtotal	+ _____ Subtotal = _____ CLIENT RESPONSE TOTAL

OVERALL SCORE _____
(music + client response)

Instructions for use on pages 11–13.

Name _____   Clients _____
Date _____   Objective _____

COMPETENCY ASSESSMENT 2: MUSIC AND PERSONAL SKILLS

1.0 Personal Skills	Deficiencies	Skills Meeting Minimum Criteria	Skills Above Minimum Criteria
1.1 Posture/ Stance/ Proximity/ Body Language	____ Chronic slump or restless pacing	____ Stands or sits with proximity and posture appropriate to objective and client(s)	____ Systematically varies posture, stance, proximity to enhance client interaction
	____ Repetitive touching of body, clothing, glasses (tic)	____ Exhibits no distracting mannerisms	
	____ Physical barriers between leader and client(s) or distance too great		____ Uses above for contingent approval
1.2 Speaking Voice	____ Unneccessary words/ sounds (ah, OK, you know); stuttering, hesitations	____ Uses appropriate speech patterns	____ Systematically varies voice to enhance client interaction
	____ Speech too slow or too fast for comprehension	____ Uses comfortable voice volume, speed, and pitch	____ Uses voice for contingent approval
	____ Pitch distracting – too high, sing-song, irritating		
	____ Voice volume inaudible or uncomfortably loud		
1.3 Facial Expression	____ Expression incongruent with verbalizations or objective	____ Has expression generally pleasant or congruent with objective, client, verbalizations	____ Systematically varies expression to enhance client interaction
	____ Expression chronically unpleasant or disapproving (> 20%)		____ Uses expression for contingent approval
1.4 Eye Contact	____ Eye contact reduced or distracted by activity, materials, client placement	____ Maintains eye contact across entire group throughout intervention (+2)	____ Varies eye contact to enhance client interaction
	____ Failure to scan, look at entire group		____ Uses eye contact for contingent approval
			____ Demonstrates high frequency of responses to client behavior
BASAL: 4	–____ Subtotal	+____ Subtotal	+____ Subtotal
			_____ = PERSONAL TOTAL

COMPETENCY ASSESSMENT 2: MUSIC AND PERSONAL SKILLS (continued)

3.0 Music Skills	Deficiencies	Skills Meeting Minimum Criteria	Skills Above Minimum Criteria
Check all used:	____ Mistakes in voice	____ Sings correct, in-tune pitches	____ Uses original music or creative adaptation
____ Voice ____ Autoharp	____ Mistakes in accompaniment	____ Plays correct accompaniment	____ Music skills at exceptional level (+2)
____ Guitar ____ Piano	____ Difficulty starting or continuing music	____ Music uninterrupted by mistakes	____ Music is obviously enjoyable to client(s) (+2)
____ Percussion	____ Lack of cues for client participation	____ Cues group participation in music /motor activity	
____ Movement: Dance/Exercise, Clapping, or Motions	____ Uncontrolled variation in beat, tempo, or dynamics	____ Uses steady beat, appropriate dynamics and tempo	
____Recorded music	____ Motor activities not matched to music, not sequenced, too easy, too difficult	____ Models motor or other tasks adequately	
	____ Music not related to objective or ability level of clients	____ Music related to objective and ability level of clients	
BASAL: 8	– ____ Subtotal	+ ____ Subtotal	+ ____ Subtotal
			= ____ MUSIC TOTAL

4.0 Client Responses	Deficiencies	Skills Meeting Minimum Criteria	Skills Above Minimum Criteria
	____ Clients withdrawn, off-task, nonparticipatory (–2)	____ Clients on-task / participatory 80% of session (+3)	____ Primary objective achieved by all, secondary obj. achieved by many (+2)
	____ Objective not achieved by at least 80% of group (–2)	____ Objective achieved by 80% of clients (+3)	____ Client(s) on-task or participating > 80% (+2)
	____ High level of inappropriate behavior (psychotic, repetitive, negative, disruptive) (–2)		____ Clients obviously engaged in session (+2)
BASAL: 8	– ____ Subtotal	+ ____ Subtotal	+ ____ Subtotal
			= ____ CLIENT RESPONSE TOTAL

OVERALL SCORE ____
(music + client + personal)

Instructions for use on on pages 11–13.

Name _____   Clients _____

Date _____   Objective _____

COMPETENCY ASSESSMENT 3: COMPREHENSIVE LEADERSHIP SKILLS

1.0 Personal Skills	Deficiencies	Skills Meeting Minimum Criteria	Skills Above Minimum Criteria
1.1 Posture/ Stance/ Proximity/ Body Language	____ Chronic slump or restless pacing	____ Stands or sits with proximity and posture appropriate to objective and client(s)	____ Systematically varies posture, stance, proximity to enhance client interaction
	____ Repetitive touching of body, clothing, glasses (tic)	____ Exhibits no distracting mannerisms	
	____ Physical barriers between leader and client(s) or distance too great		____ Uses above for contingent approval
1.2 Speaking Voice	____ Unnecessary words/ sounds (ah, OK, you know); stuttering, hesitations	____ Uses appropriate speech patterns	____ Systematically varies voice to enhance client interaction
	____ Speech too slow or too fast for comprehension	____ Uses comfortable voice volume, speed, and pitch	____ Uses voice for contingent approval
	____ Pitch distracting – too high, sing-song, irritating		
	____ Voice volume inaudible or uncomfortably loud		
1.3 Facial Expression	____ Expression incongruent with verbalizations or objective	____ Has expression generally pleasant or congruent with objective, client, verbalizations	____ Systematically varies expression to enhance client interaction
	____ Expression chronically unpleasant or disapproving (> 20%)		____ Uses expression for contingent approval
1.4 Eye Contact	____ Eye contact reduced or distracted by activity, materials, client placement	____ Maintains eye contact across entire group throughout intervention (+2)	____ Varies eye contact to enhance client interaction
	____ Failure to scan, look at entire group		____ Uses eye contact for contingent approval
			____ Demonstrates high frequency of responses to client behavior
BASAL: 4	– ____ Subtotal	+ ____ Subtotal	+ ____ Subtotal
			____ = PERSONAL TOTAL

COMPETENCY ASSESSMENT 3: COMPREHENSIVE LEADERSHIP SKILLS (continued)

2.0 General Leadership Skills	Deficiencies	Skills Meeting Minimum Criteria	Skills Above Minimum Criteria
2.1 Session Planning	____ Objective not observable ____ Objective above or below client level or not related to identified needs ____ Uses inappropriate material ____ Objective too lengthy or too brief for allotted time	____ Demonstrates specific objective ____ Intervention matches client level and needs ____ Plan fits allotted time	____ Uses task analysis ____ Uses successive approximations ____ Uses criteria-related contingencies
2.2 Session Preparation	____ Room setup not adapted to intervention ____ Extraneous items present hazard, barrier, or distraction ____ Materials require additional preparation; intervention interrupted ____ Clients not in logical position for intervention	____ Sets up room for intervention ____ Clears extraneous items from area ____ Has materials ready for immediate use ____ Places client(s) appropriately for intervention	____ Room setup and client placement arranged to achieve maximum client benefit (i.e. peer tutors, peer modeling)
2.3 Session Implementation	____ Intervention implemented without regard to client response ____ Poor directions (not specific or sequenced, too lengthy) ____ Lack of cues or feedback ____ Pacing too slow or fast ____ Activity interrupted or diverted from original task	____ Adapts intervention to client response (+2) ____ Uses appropriate directions ____ Uses appropriate cueing ____ Uses appropriate feedback ____ Uses appropriate pacing ____ Uses time effectively	____ Gives contingent feedback ____ Demonstrates consistent directions and feedback ____ Shapes primary and secondary client objectives ____ Maintains 4:1 positive ratio of feedback
2.4 Session Evaluation	____ No client criteria evident ____ No client data collected ____ No correction of problems encountered during session	____ Client criteria evident ____ Client data collected ____ Attempted to correct problems in session	____ Individualized client criteria ____ Collected client data on > 1 objective ____ Resolved all problems satisfactorily
BASAL: 12	− _____ Subtotal	+ _____ Subtotal	+ _____ Subtotal
			= _____ LEADER TOTAL

COMPETENCY ASSESSMENT 3: COMPREHENSIVE LEADERSHIP SKILLS (continued)

3.0 Music Skills	Deficiencies	Skills Meeting Minimum Criteria	Skills Above Minimum Criteria
Check all used: ____ Voice ____ Autoharp ____ Guitar ____ Piano ____ Percussion ____ Movement: Dance/Exercise, Clapping, or Motions ____ Recorded music	____ Mistakes in voice ____ Mistakes in accompaniment ____ Difficulty starting or continuing music ____ Lack of cues for client participation ____ Uncontrolled variation in beat, tempo, or dynamics ____ Motor activities not matched to music, not sequenced, too easy, too difficult ____ Music not related to objective or ability level of clients	____ Sings correct, in-tune pitches ____ Plays correct accompaniment ____ Music uninterrupted by mistakes ____ Cues group participation in music/motor activity ____ Uses steady beat, appropriate dynamics and tempo ____ Models motor or other tasks adequately ____ Music related to objective and ability level of clients	____ Uses original music or creative adaptation ____ Music skills at exceptional level (+2) ____ Music is obviously enjoyable to client(s) (+2)
BASAL: 8	– _____ Subtotal	+ _____ Subtotal	+ _____ Subtotal = _____ MUSIC TOTAL

4.0 Client Responses	Deficiencies	Skills Meeting Minimum Criteria	Skills Above Minimum Criteria
	____ Clients withdrawn, off-task, nonparticipatory (–2) ____ Objective not achieved by at least 80% of group (–2) ____ High level of inappropriate behavior (psychotic, repetitive, negative, disruptive) (–2)	____ Clients on-task / participatory 80% of session (+3) ____ Objective achieved by 80% of clients (+3)	____ Primary objective achieved by all, secondary obj. achieved by many (+2) ____ Client(s) on-task or participating > 80% (+2) ____ Clients obviously engaged in session (+2)
BASAL: 8	– _____ Subtotal	+ _____ Subtotal	+ _____ Subtotal = _____ CLIENT RESPONSE TOTAL

OVERALL SCORE _____
(All category totals)

Instructions for use on on pages 11–13.

Part II

Competency Tasks

Level 1 Competencies

Tasks at this level are designed to

    a.   desensitize individuals to being in front of a group, to being videotaped, and to having their leadership skills evaluated.

    b.   assess and improve personal skills in the leadership role.

    c.   teach basic music leadership skills for the activities of singing, dancing, exercising to music, and playing rhythms.

    d.   improve accompanying skills.

    e.   increase accompanied repertoire for sing-alongs.

    f.   sensitize leaders to the necessity for continuously monitoring participants and adapting instruction to client responses.

    g.   introduce the basic instructional techniques of scanning, cuing, modeling, chaining, approving, correcting, task analyzing, fading, signing to music, and collecting data.

    h.   teach appropriate simulation protocol to class members, i.e., participation, cooperation, and active verbal support for colleagues as they perform.

Notes to instructors:

- Level 1A competencies include objectives 1.01–1.03 and are evaluated with Competency Assessment 1.
- Level 1B competencies include objectives 1.04–1.16 and are evaluated with Competency Assessment 2.

OBJECTIVE 1.01

Lead participants in singing a well-known, unaccompanied song.

Participants: Peers

Procedure:

> *Preparation:*
> 1. Select a well-known, nonreligious song.
> 2. Practice and memorize.
>
> *Implementation:*
> 1. State title of song.
> 2. Give starting pitch.
> 3. Cue participants to begin.
> 4. Sing along from memory without pause through entire song.
> 5. Use facial features to encourage participation.
> 6. Scan participants continuously to assess who is singing and enjoying the music.
> 7. At end of activity write down names of people most on-task to music. Give to instructor at individual conference to document scanning skill.
>
> *Note*:   The objective is to lead the song with musical/conducting/facial cues and little or no talking.

Music Specifications:

> 1. Well-known, nonreligious song, appropriate to peer level and interest.
> 2. Song should have at least two verses and chorus (or 12 lines).

Recommended Time Limit: Usually 1–2 minutes

Criteria for Objective:

> Competency Assessment 1:   Music Total   12
>   Client Response Total   13
>
> Music Selection as specified
> Implementation in allotted time
>
> *Note:*   Repeat this objective with different songs until criteria are met on Competency Assessment 1.

Techniques Included: Song Leading
                             Scanning

OBJECTIVE 1.02

Accompany with a rhythm instrument or instruments and lead participants in singing a well-known song.

Participants: Peers

Procedure:

Preparation:
1. Select a well-known, nonreligious song.
2. Practice and memorize accompaniment.

Implementation:
1. State title of song.
2. Play introduction and/or give starting pitch.
3. Cue participants to begin.
4. Sing along and play from memory without pause through entire song.
5. Use facial features or verbal praise during music to encourage participation.
6. Scan participants continuously to assess who is singing and enjoying the music.
7. At end of activity write down names of people most on-task to music. Give to instructor at individual conference to document scanning skill.

Note: The objective is to lead the song with musical/conducting/facial cues and little or no talking.

Music Specifications:

1. Well-known, nonreligious song, appropriate to peer level and interest.
2. Rhythmic accompaniment should include two different ostinati patterns appropriate for song. Each ostinato should last at least 8 beats.
3. Quality rhythm instruments appropriate for adults should be used.
4. Song should have at least two verses and chorus (or 12 lines).

Recommended Time Limit: Usually 1–2 minutes

Criteria for Objective:

| Competency Assessment 1: | Music Total | 12 |
| | Client Response Total | 13 |

Music Selection as specified
Implementation in allotted time

Note: Repeat this objective with different songs until criteria are met on Competency Assessment 1.

Techniques Included: Song Leading
Accompanying – Rhythmic
Scanning

OBJECTIVE 1.03

Accompany with most advanced technique of which you are capable on guitar, Autoharp, omnichord, or piano/keyboard and lead participants in singing a well-known song.

Participants: Peers

Procedure:

Preparation:
1. Select a well-known, nonreligious song.
2. Practice and memorize accompaniment.

Implementation:
1. State title of song.
2. Play introduction and/or give starting pitch.
3. Cue participants to begin.
4. Sing along and play from memory without pause through entire song.
5. Use facial features or verbal praise during music to encourage participation.
6. Scan participants continuously to assess who is singing and enjoying the music.
7. At end of activity write down names of people most on-task to music. Give to instructor at individual conference to document scanning skill.

Note: The objective is to lead the song with musical/conducting/facial cues and little or no talking.

Music Specifications:

1. Well-known, nonreligious song, appropriate to peer level and interest.
2. Song should include at least I, IV, and V^7 chords.
3. Song should have at least two verses and chorus (or 12 lines).
4. Use most advanced accompaniment techniques of which you are capable on guitar, Autoharp, omnichord, or piano/keyboard.

Recommended Time Limit: Usually 1–2 minutes

Criteria for Objective:

Competency Assessment 1:   Music Total   12
                            Client Response Total   13

Music Selection as specified
Implementation in allotted time

Note: Repeat this objective with different songs until criteria are met on Competency Assessment 1.

Techniques Included: Song Leading
                            Accompanying – Harmonic
                            Scanning

OBJECTIVE 1.04

Accompany with most advanced technique of which you are capable on guitar, Autoharp, omnichord, or piano/keyboard and teach participants to sing a *new* song.

Participants: Peers

Procedure:

Preparation:
1. Select a nonreligious song that is probably unknown by peers.
2. Practice and memorize accompaniment.
3. Practice giving starting pitch, singing, and accompanying each line, then chaining lines together.

Note: The technique described below is chaining. It will also be used in future objectives.

Implementation:
1. Sing one verse of song with accompaniment for participants.
2. Make eye contact with all members and assess those who appear to be listening. If members appear bored, change something you are doing, i.e., speak more softly, speed up pacing, move closer to participants, etc.
3. Tell participants that you will sing one line while they listen, and then they will sing along with you.
4. Say "Listen" and sing the first line.
5. Give starting pitch, cue participants' entry, and lead them in singing first line.
6. Repeat Steps 4 and 5 until 80% of participants are accurate.
7. Nonverbally encourage singing, participation, eye contact, etc.
8. Sing first line with participants, say, "Listen" and continue singing second line.
9. Say, "Sing," give starting pitch and entry cue and lead participants in singing second line.
10. Repeat singing second line until 80% of participants are accurate. Continue scanning participants to assess accuracy, enjoyment, and participation.
11. Say "Beginning," give starting pitch, first word of song, and entry cue, lead participants in singing lines 1 and 2 together. Repeat until accurate.
12. Teach each subsequent line using this chaining procedure until entire song is learned. Correct any musical inaccuracies by singing correctly for participants followed by their repeating your modeling.
13. Encourage participation, eye contact, enjoyment, etc., throughout teaching phase.

Note: The objective of the above technique is to teach quickly and efficiently while maintaining a high level of interest and musical accuracy. Little or no talking should be required, and occasions of stopping the flow of music should be reduced to a minimum.

Music Specifications:

1. Song should be appropriate to peer level and interest but probably new to majority of participants.
2. Song should include at least I, IV, and V^7 and one additional chord.
3. Song should have at least two verses and chorus (or 12 lines).
4. Use most advanced accompaniment techniques of which you are capable on guitar, Autoharp, omnichord, or piano/keyboard.

Recommended Time Limit: Approximately 5 minutes

Criteria for Objective:

Competency Assessment 2:   Personal Total   9
                                Music Total   12
                                Client Response Total   13

Music Selection as specified
Implementation in allotted time

Techniques Included: Song Leading
                             Accompanying
                             Scanning
                             Modeling
                             Chaining

OBJECTIVE 1.05

Select the instrument (guitar, Autoharp, omnichord, or piano/keyboard) on which you consider your skill to be second best and accompany and teach a *new* song to participants.

Participants: Peers

Procedure:

Preparation:
1. Select a nonreligious song that is probably unknown by peers.
2. Practice and memorize accompaniment.
3. Practice giving starting pitch, singing, and accompanying each line, then chaining lines together.

Implementation:
1. Sing one verse of song with accompaniment for participants.
2. Make eye contact with all members and assess those who appear to be listening. If members appear off-task, change something you are doing, i.e., talk more softly, speed up pacing, move closer to participants, etc.
3. Tell participants that you will sing one line while they listen, and then they will sing along with you.
4. Say "Listen" and sing the first line.
5. Give starting pitch, cue participants' entry, and lead them in singing first line.
6. Repeat Steps 4 and 5 until 80% of participants are accurate.
7. Nonverbally encourage singing, participation, eye contact, on-task, etc.
8. Sing first line with participants, say, "Listen" and continue singing second line.
9. Say, "Sing," give starting pitch and entry cue, and lead participants in singing second line.
10. Repeat singing second line until 80% of participants are accurate. Continue scanning participants to assess accuracy, enjoyment, and engagement.
11. Say "Beginning," give starting pitch, first word of song, and entry cue, lead participants in singing lines 1 and 2 together. Repeat until accurate.
12. Teach each subsequent line using this chaining procedure until entire song is learned. Correct any musical inaccuracies by singing correctly for participants followed by their repeating your modeling.
13. Encourage participation, eye contact, enjoyment, etc., throughout teaching phase.

Note: The objective of the above technique is to teach quickly and efficiently while maintaining a high level of group interest and musical accuracy. Little or no talking should be required, and occasions of stopping the flow of music should be reduced to a minimum.

Music Specifications:

1. Song should be appropriate to peer level and interest but probably new to majority of participants.
2. Song should include at least I, IV, and V^7 and one additional chord.
3. Song should have at least two verses and chorus (or 12 lines).
4. Use most advanced accompaniment techniques of which you are capable on second best instrument (guitar, Autoharp, omnichord, or piano/keyboard).

Recommended Time Limit: Approximately 5 minutes

Criteria for Objective:

Competency Assessment 2:   Personal Total   9
                              Music Total   12
                              Client Response Total   13

Music Selection as specified
Implementation in allotted time

Techniques Included: Song Leading
                            Accompanying
                            Scanning
                            Chaining
                            Modeling

OBJECTIVE 1.06

Teach participants to accompany a well-known song on Autoharp.

Participants: Peers

Procedure:

Preparation:
1. Select a well-known, nonreligious song.
2. Practice and memorize Autoharp chord changes for accompaniment.
3. Practice teaching procedure in implementation, especially Step 14.
4. Acquire enough Autoharps for participants and place on floor in front of chairs prior to beginning activity.

Note: The technique described below is a ***systematic task analysis*** of how to teach someone to play the Autoharp and accompany a well-known song. Task analysis will be used in future objectives.

Implementation:
1. State task in one sentence.
2. Instruct participants to pick up Autoharps but not to play them.
3. Quickly and briefly approve specific individuals as they follow instructions.
4. Show the participants correct position of Autoharp on lap. Scan participants, correcting any who require it.
5. Direct participants to place left hand on the three buttons needed for song by specifying each finger and button name (or color) in sequence. Scan participants, correcting any who require it.
6. Direct participants to press finger 1 on button _____ (name or color) and to reach right hand across and strum once across all strings. Model these steps as you say them. Correct anyone who made an error.
7. Say "Listen" and demonstrate four strums on this chord in rhythm of song while nodding head in rhythm.
8. Say "Press button _____ and strum four times in rhythm with me; ready, begin," and use strum hand for entry cue.
9. Approve those who are correct and who stop after four strums, etc. Repeat if there were errors.
10. Say "This time we will strum four times on button _____, then four times on button _____. I will cue you when to change fingers. Press button _____ and strum four times in rhythm with me; ready, begin." Use head and strum arm for entry cue. As participants begins strum four, say "Change to button _____" and use head and arm cues to maintain the rhythm of the next four strums. Praise those who are correct. Repeat and correct if there were errors. Encourage those who are trying, watching, listening, following directions, making music, etc.

11. Use procedure in Step 10 to direct participants in strumming four times each on the three chords of song while maintaining rhythm.
12. Use cuing procedure described in Step 10 to strum chords in the sequence used in the song.
13. Repeat Step 12 at tempo appropriate for song.
14. Tell participants that you will sing while they accompany and that you will cue changes. Say "Press button_____; ready, begin," and give head and arm entry cues while beginning to sing song. Cue each chord change.
15. Ask participants to sing along. Use all cuing procedures for beginning, maintaining rhythm, and chord changes.
16. Encourage participation, following specific directions, singing, correct chord changes, accurate rhythm, stopping, etc.

*Note*s:
- All approval should be age appropriate.
- If there are not enough Autoharps for each person in the group, have those persons without an Autoharp simulate one by practicing the same procedures on their laps. Transfer Autoharps after Steps 6, 7, 10, 12, 14. Persons without Autoharps should continue to practice each step in simulation.

Music Specifications:

1. Well-known, nonreligious song should be appropriate to peer level.
2. Song requires only I, IV, and V^7 chords.
3. Song should have at least two verses and chorus (or 12 lines).

Recommended Time Limit: Approximately 5–7 minutes

Criteria for Objective:

Competency Assessment 2: Personal Total   9
                          Music Total   13
                          Client Response Total   13

Techniques Included: Song Leading
                            Teaching from Task Analysis
                            Autoharp
                            Cuing
                            Modeling
                            Approving
                            Correcting

OBJECTIVE 1.07

Teach participants to perform a melody by following cues.

Participants: Peers

Procedure:

Preparation:
1. Select a well-known, nonreligious song.
2. Memorize melody.
3. Determine best arrangement of notes to facilitate melody (scale, melodic position, chord, etc.).
4. Practice cuing individual notes of melody in sequence and in rhythm.
5. Acquire single note, pitched instruments such as choir chimes, boom whackers, or resonator bells and mallets if necessary.

Implementation:
1. Inform participants that they will perform a melody together by following cues.
2. Give participants the instruments in your selected order and ask them not to play them.
3. Briefly demonstrate how to play the instruments for the participants..
4. Show the participants your cues.
5. Have participants follow cues to play in different rhythms and tempos.
6. Praise participants who are following cues accurately.
7. Cue participants that the next sequence of sounds will be the melody. Challenge the group to name the tune at the end of the melody.
8. Cue each note in the melody in sequence and rhythm.
9. Correct any performance errors.
10. Repeat steps 8 and 9 until the entire melody can be performed without errors.
11. Ask the participants to name the melody.
12. Praise participants.

Note: All approval should be age appropriate.

Music Specifications:

1. Well-known, nonreligious song.
2. Song should be diatonic and cover at least an octave in range.
3. Song should have at least two verses and chorus (or 12 lines).

Recommended Time Limit: Approximately 5–7 minutes

Criteria for Objective:

Competency Assessment 2:	Personal Total	9
	Music Total	13
	Client Response Total	13

Techniques Included: Cuing
Approving
Correcting

OBJECTIVE 1.08

Compose a "hello" song appropriate for the participants' age and interest level. Teach the song to participants while accompanying it.

Participants: Peers

Procedure:

Preparation:
1. Compose a "hello" song of at least four lines with an original melody and prepare an accompaniment.
2. Practice and memorize song.
3. Practice chaining procedure below.

Implementation:
1. Sing one verse of song for participants.
2. Make eye contact with all members and assess those who appear to be listening.
3. Tell participants you will sing one line while they listen, and then they will sing along with you.
4. Say "Listen" and sing first line.
5. Give starting pitch, cue participants' entry, and lead them in singing first line.
6. Repeat Steps 4 and 5 until 80% of participants are accurate.
7. Nonverbally encourage singing, participation, eye contact, on-task, etc.
8. Sing first line with participants, say, "Listen" and continue singing second line.
9. Say, "Sing," give starting pitch and entry cue, and lead participants in singing second line.
10. Repeat singing second line until 80% of participants are accurate. Continue scanning participants to assess accuracy, enjoyment, and engagement.
11. Say "Beginning," give starting pitch, first word of song, and entry cue, lead participants in singing lines 1 and 2 together. Repeat until accurate.
12. Teach each subsequent line using this chaining procedure until entire song is learned. Correct any musical inaccuracies by singing correctly for participants followed by their repeating your modeling.
13. Encourage participation, eye contact, enjoyment, etc., throughout teaching phase.

Music Specifications:

1. Compose a song that functions as a greeting, contains at least four lines, and has an original melody and accompaniment.
2. Song uses at least I, IV, and V^7 chords.
3. Song is appropriate to participants' age, interests, and vocal range.
4. Use most advanced accompanying techniques on guitar, Autoharp, or keyboard.

Recommended Time Limit: Approximately 5 minutes

Criteria for Objective:

Competency Assessment 2:	Personal Total	9
	Music Total	14
	Client Response Total	14

Music selection as specified
Implementation in allotted time

Techniques Included: Composing
Song Leading
Accompanying
Chaining
Modeling
Scanning

OBJECTIVE 1.09

Compose a "good-bye" (closing) song appropriate for participant's age and interest level. Teach the song to participants while accompanying it.

Participants: Peers

Procedure:

Preparation:
1. Compose a "good-bye" song of at least four lines with original melody and an accompaniment.
2. Practice and memorize song.
3. Practice the chaining procedure below.

Implementation:
1. Sing one verse of song for participants.
2. Make eye contact with all members and assess those who appear to be listening.
3. Tell participants that you will sing one line while they listen, and then they will sing along with you.
4. Say "Listen" and sing first line.
5. Give starting pitch, cue participants' entry, and lead them in singing first line.
6. Repeat Steps 4 and 5 until 80% of participants are accurate.
7. Nonverbally encourage singing, participation, eye contact, on-task, etc.
8. Sing first line with participants, say, "Listen" and continue singing second line.
9. Say, "Sing," give starting pitch and entry cue, and lead participants in singing second line.
10. Repeat singing second line until 80% of participants are accurate. Continue scanning participants to assess accuracy, enjoyment, and engagement.
11. Say "Beginning," give starting pitch, first word of song, and entry cue, lead participants in singing lines 1 and 2 together. Repeat until accurate.
12. Teach each subsequent line using this chaining procedure until entire song is learned. Correct any musical inaccuracies by singing correctly for participants followed by their repeating your modeling.
13. Encourage participation, eye contact, enjoyment, etc., throughout teaching phase.

Music Specifications:

1. Compose song that functions to end a therapy session, containing at least four lines, an original melody, and accompaniment.
2. Song uses at least I, IV, V^7 chord changes.
3. Song is appropriate to participants' age, interests, and vocal range.
4. Use most advanced accompanying techniques on guitar, Autoharp, or keyboard.

Recommended Time Limit: Approximately 5 minutes

Criteria for Objective:

Competency Assessment 2:	Personal Total	9
	Music Total	14
	Client Response Total	14

Music selection as specified
Implementation in allotted time

Techniques Included: Composing
Song Leading
Accompanying
Chaining
Modeling
Scanning

OBJECTIVE 1.10

Teach a new round to participants.

Participants: Peers

Procedure:

Preparation:
1. Select a simple round of four lines.
2. Practice teaching it according to chaining procedures described in Objective 1.03.
3. Practice Step 4 below with a friend to be sure you can sing the second part.

Implementation:
1. Teach song according to chaining procedure.
2. After song is learned, encourage and cue participants to sing it loudly. Fade your participation (singing along) midway and cue participants to continue. Approve participants for singing without you.
3. Direct participants to sing song without you. Cue entry and drop out, cue participants to continue.
4. Say, "Again," cue entry; at appropriate place begin softly singing second part of round by yourself while using cue for participants to continue. Use facial features to encourage continuation. If participants successfully continue, approve them and go to Step 5. If participants stops, tell them their task is to continue when you come in and repeat Step 4, singing very softly and exaggerating continuation cue.
5. Label this a "round" and say, "This time I am going to pick a couple people to help me. Everyone else will continue." Give starting cue to participants. At appropriate point in song, move to two people on one side of group (Group 2), look at them intently, say "Sing," give only these two an entry cue and begin singing second part. If unsuccessful, correct and repeat. If successful, continue procedure, enlarging Group 2 until it is one half the total group.

Note: All approval should be age appropriate.

Music Specifications:

1. Use new round probably not known to majority of participants.
2. The round contains only four lines.

Recommended Time Limit: Approximately 5–7 minutes

Criteria for Objective:

Competency Assessment 2:	Personal Total	9
	Music Total	15
	Client Response Total	14

Music selection as specified
Implementation in allotted time
Approval is age appropriate

Techniques Included: Chaining
Cuing
Fading
Approving
Correcting

OBJECTIVE 1.11

Teach a rhythm-reading task of at least 16 measures.

Participants: Peers

Procedure:

Preparation:
1. Select 16 written measures of rhythm and prepare poster large enough for entire group to read.
2. Practice playing rhythm accurately while maintaining a steady beat.
3. Assess the most difficult measures that might be problematical to learn and plan how to correct them.
4. Select kitchen implements for creation of a rhythm band: pots, pan lids, strainers, glasses or bottles of water, silverware, timer, etc.

Implementation:
1. Hand out instruments and show people how to play them.
2. Teach rhythm two measures at a time using modeling and chaining (Objective 1.03). Scan participants to assess persons having difficulty. Correct any inaccuracies.
3. When entire rhythm is learned, divide group into parts, letting each part begin on a different measure. Direct participants; cue entry and accurate rhythms.
4. Encourage on-task, following directions, accuracy, enjoyment, etc.
5. Maintain efficient teaching and reduce necessity for stopping and talking.

Music Specifications:

Example should have 16 written measures of rhythm, including rests and at least three different note values. Do not make rhythms so difficult that task cannot be learned in allotted time.

Recommended Time Limit: Approximately 7–10 minutes

Criteria for Objective:

Competency Assessment:	Personal Total	9
	Music Total	15
	Client Response Total	14

Music selection as specified
Implementation in allotted time

Techniques Included: Group Leadership-Rhythm Ensemble
Cuing
Chaining
Modeling

OBJECTIVE 1.12

Engage participants in solo and group drumming.

Participants: Peers

Procedure:

Preparation:
1. Compose a foundational 8-beat ostinato for low drums, a supporting 8-beat ostinato for mid-pitched drums, woodblock, or tambourine, and an 8-beat "fill" ostinato for shakers (i.e., maracas, shaking eggs, cabasa). The three parts should work together and be ease to repeat.
2. Memorize these three parts.
3. Practice playing these parts on respective instruments.
4. Learn to teach these parts by rote without musical notation or musical language. One method of teaching by rote is using a verbal chant.
5. Acquire appropriate ensemble instruments. Identify solo instrument.

Implementation:
1. Display instruments and demonstrate how to play them.
2. Designate one instrument (preferably a large or unique drum) as the solo instrument. Set it aside without a player.
3. Teach the foundational ostinato to the all of the participants by having them clap the rhythm.
4. Select a portion of the participants who are correctly clapping the foundational rhythm to play in on low-pitched drums. Have the foundational ostinato continue.
5. Cue the remaining participants to stop clapping and listening.
6. Clap the fill ostinato in rhythm with the drumming.
7. Select a portion of the participants who are correctly clapping the fill rhythm to play shakers. Have both rhythms continue.
8. Use the same procedure to teach the remaining participants the supporting ostinato. Transfer these participants to the remaining instruments.
9. Allow all three parts to play several repetitions of the 8-beats.
10. Stop the rhythm following the eighth beat. Cue the participants to count in time for 8 beats of silence.
11. Cue all of the parts to enter together.
12. Practice 8 beats of playing and 8 beats of silence until the group can successfully transition from playing to silence without cues.
13. Move to solo instrument. During the silence play a solo.
14. Select a new soloist during the ensemble 8 beats and direct him or her to play during the silence.
15. Continue with solos as time allows.

Music Specifications:

Three 8-beat ostinati for ensemble portion of drumming. The foundational ostinato should use predominantly quarter and half notes with minimal syncopation. The fill ostinato should use subdivided notes with some rests. The supporting ostinato will provide interest and fill in where other parts are silent.

Note: A similar structure can be used with Orff instruments (i.e., xylophones, glockenspiels, metallophones).

Recommended Time Limit: Approximately 7–10 minutes

Criteria for Objective:

Competency Assessment:	Personal Total	9
	Music Total	15
	Client Response Total	14

Rhythm construction as specified
Implementation in allotted time

Techniques Included: Group Leadership – Rhythm Ensemble
Improvising
Cuing
Chaining
Modeling

OBJECTIVE 1.13

Teach sign language to a simple well-known song.[1]

Participants: Peers

Procedure:

Preparation:
1. Select song and signs for major words in song. (See Specifications below.) Choreograph signs.
2. Practice and memorize song and signs.
3. Videotape yourself signing to music and assess choreography and difficulty. Revise signing task to improve smoothness and rhythmic accuracy.*

Implementation:
1. Lead participants through song according to Objective 1.01.
2. Use modeling and chaining to teach signs.
3. Cue rhythmic accuracy of signs.

Music Specifications:

1. Choose a well-known, nonreligious song of four lines with highly repetitive words.
2. Use at least six different signs.

Recommended Time Limit: 10 minutes

Criteria for Objective:

Competency Assessment 2:   Personal Total   9
                           Music Total   15
                           Client Response Total   14
Music selection as specified
Implementation in allotted time

Techniques Included: Song Leading
                           Chaining
                           Modeling
                           Cuing
                           Signing to Music

*Optional step

OBJECTIVE 1.14

Teach eight different exercises (no more than eight repetitions each) synchronized to music.

Participants: Peers

Procedure:

Preparation:
1. Select exercises that fit peer participants' age and level of physical ability.
2. Select recorded music with probable appeal to participants and strong beat. Synchronize exercises so they fit rhythmically and are not too strenuous to complete. (No more than eight repetitions each.)
3. Practice and memorize routine.

Implementation:
1. Teach each of the eight exercises with verbal cue to identify each. (Use modeling and correction.) Ensure that each exercise is practiced at tempo of recorded music to be used.
2. Turn on music and lead participants through routine using cuing. Scan continuously to assess errors or nonparticipation.
3. Encourage participation, enjoyment, and rhythmic accuracy.

Music Specifications:

Recorded music of at least 64 measures, with strong beat at tempo appropriate to physical abilities of participants and of interest to them.

Recommended Time Limit: 5–7 minutes

Criteria for Objective:

Competency Assessment 2:	Personal Total	9
	Music Total	15
	Client Response Total	14

Music selection as specified
Implementation in allotted time

Techniques Included: Group Leadership – Exercise
Cuing
Scanning

OBJECTIVE 1.15

Teach a simple dance of at least 10 different sequential steps.

Participants: Peers

Procedure:

Preparation:
1. Select music and dance steps, synchronize steps with music, and design cues for each step. Use chaining procedure to teach routine. (See Objective 1.03 for chaining procedure and adapt to dance task.)
2. Practice and memorize dance and chaining routine.
3. Design data collection form that allows recording number of persons making an error in each of the dance steps in performance. Compute the percentage of overall error using formula:

$$\frac{\text{Total \# of errors on all steps}}{\text{\# of people in group x \# of dance steps}} = \% \text{ of error}$$

Implementation:
1. Teach a dance using cuing, chaining, and correction. Scan participants continuously to assess those who require assistance. Correct.
2. Encourage participation, enjoyment, and rhythmic accuracy.
3. Ensure that tempo of dance matches that of recording during practice.
4. Turn on music and perform dance.
5. Train a colleague to collect data on the number of group errors during performance to evaluate teaching effectiveness. Calculate percentage of errors with formula above.

Music Specifications:

Recorded song, moderate tempo, obvious beat, of probable interest to peers. (Optional – Perform dance to live music.)

Recommended Time Limit: 10 minutes

Criteria for Objective:

Competency Assessment 2:	Personal Total	9
	Music Total	15
	Client Response Total	14

Music selection as specified
Implementation in allotted time
Less than 20% error of group on total dance

Techniques Included: Group Leadership – Dance
                                         Cuing
                                         Chaining
                                       Evaluating/Data

OBJECTIVE 1.16

Conduct a sing-along.

Participants: Peers

Procedure:

Preparation:
1. Select 10 well-known, nonreligious songs. Selected songs should represent a variety of genres. Prepare a list of the songs.
2. Practice and memorize accompaniment for all 10 songs.

Implementation:
1. Hand out lists while stating you will conduct a sing-along.
2. Ask participants which song they would like to sing first. Determine if there is consensus for songs suggested. If not, lead participants in negotiating until consensus is achieved.
3. Sing any three songs selected by participants for which there is consensus.
4. Accompany each, cuing entry and using facial and verbal encouragement for participation.
5. Scan participants continuously to assess participation, enjoyment, etc.

Music Specifications:

1. Choose 10 well-known songs appropriate for peer group; make list with multiple copies for participants.
2. Accompany with most advanced techniques in guitar, Autoharp, or piano/keyboard.

Recommended Time Limit: 7–10 minutes

Criteria for Objective:

Competency Assessment 2: Personal Total   9
                          Music Total   15
                          Client Response Total   14

Music selection as specified
Implementation in allotted time
Extra credit for use of more than one accompanying instrument

Techniques Included: Song Leading
                           Accompanying
                           Using Repertoire

Level 2 Competencies

Tasks at this level are designed to

a. help students maintain and improve personal skills in the leadership role.
b. teach students to adapt music interventions to the needs of various clients while maintaining basic music leadership skills. The basic goal is to teach students to use music to achieve a nonmusic objective for peers (Objectives 2.01–2.13) and, then for a variety of simulated client populations (Objectives 2.14–2.62), including the following:

- Adolescents with behavioral and/or emotional disorders
- Adults of advanced age including persons in long-term care and assisted living settings
- Adults with chronic and acute psychiatric illness
- Children, adolescents and adults with cognitive impairments
- Children and adolescents with behavior disorders
- Children and adults with cerebral palsy
- Children and adults with visual impairments
- Families in counseling
- Families of persons who have become organ donors
- Infants with developmental disabilities
- Medical patients including those persons who are undergoing surgery or have stress-related disorders
- Parents of children with disabilities
- Parents who abuse their children
- Persons with catastrophic illness
- Persons with terminal illness and their families
- Students with hearing loss
- Students with specific learning disabilities

Note: See page 277 for specific objectives by population.

c. teach students to design procedures to achieve the desired group objectives and to evaluate their effectiveness.
d. teach simulation protocol for role-playing client groups, including controlled, specified deviant behavior and compliance responses to leader attempts to deal with them.

e. promote transfer of ideas, techniques, materials, and skills to other situations for generalized learning.

f. increase awareness of research literature and its clinical applications.

Notes to instructors:

- Level 2A competencies include objectives 2.01–2.13 and are evaluated with Competency Assessment 3.

- Level 2B competencies include objectives 2.14–2.62 and are evaluated with Competency Assessment 3.

- For the majority of the objectives following Objective 2.22, music specifications have been omitted allowing students to make music intervention decisions.

OBJECTIVE 2.01

Use music to maintain group eye contact with you.

Note: Instructor will assign two or three members of group to look away occasionally.

Participants: Peers

Procedure:

Preparation:
1. Select a well-known, nonreligious song.
2. Practice and memorize song and accompaniment.
3. Practice stopping and starting randomly throughout song.
4. Develop data collection form for assessing eye contact.

Implementation:
1. Engage participants in singing song while accompanying them.
2. Use starting pitch and cuing for entry.
3. Start singing when eye contact is established. Scan participants continuously to monitor eye contact.
4. Stop singing when any person loses eye contact with you. Begin again as soon as that person looks at you.
5. Do not use cues such as "Look at me" or "Watch me" to maintain eye contact, only stopping and starting music.
6. Give only directions about singing.
7. Use facial features and pointing to encourage participation, starting, stopping, and eye contact.
8. Continue procedure and song until music is uninterrupted and eye contact is 100%.
9. Have colleague collect data on eye contact to evaluate your technique.

Music Specifications:

1. Select well-known song that contains at least two verses and chorus (or 12 lines), I, IV, V^7 chords, and at least two additional chords.
2. Accompany on guitar, Autoharp, or piano/keyboard.

Recommended Time Limit: 5 minutes

Criteria for Objective:

	Minimum Scores	
Competency Assessment 3:	Personal	10
	Leader	29
	Music	15
	Client Responses	14
	Total	68

Percentage of group eye contact in last verse of song = 95%

Techniques Included:
Song Leading
Maintaining Eye Contact
Scanning
Evaluating/Data

Discussion for Transfer:

1. Research shows music interruption can extinguish in appropriate behavior. Did it in this situation?
2. Typical music rehearsal techniques can be very negative if there is frequent stopping. How can a leader restructure a music rehearsal to enhance pleasure and reduce negative feedback?
3. Why is eye contact important between leader and group? How does this importance vary with different types of groups?
4. How was eye contact evaluated? Discuss alternative ways to evaluate eye contact.

OBJECTIVE 2.02

Eliminate talking in the group.

Note: Instructor will assign two or three people to occasionally speak out inappropriately.

Participants: Peers

Procedure:

Preparation:
1. Select adult action song. Memorize song and motions and practice them.
2. Practice stopping and starting song at random places in order to approve participation, and responses incompatible with talking.
3. Practice a variety of verbal statements which specifically approve participation and which are appropriate for adults.
4. Develop data collection sheet to assess talking per minute.

Implementation:
1. Lead participants in adult action song.
2. Scan continuously to assess participation and talking.
3. Approve persons participating who are not talking.
4. If talking occurs, immediately select person not talking who is closest to the talker, and approve for participation.
5. As soon as talker stops talking and begins participating, approve that individual.
6. Continue until talking ceases and participation is 100%.
7. Ask colleague to collect data on talking to evaluate effectiveness of your technique.

Music Specifications:

Select adult action song that will allow enough repetitions to fill 5 minutes.

Recommended Time Limit: 5 minutes

Criteria for Objective:

Competency Assessment 3:   Minimum scores in each category
Overall minimum score = 70
Percentage of no talking in last repetition = 95%

Techniques Included: Song Leading
Scanning
Approving Incompatible Responses
Evaluating/Data

Discussion for Transfer:

1. How did the selected music intervention function in this situation? What aspects of the music versus the actions versus the leader skills most affected this situation?

2. Discuss the data collection form utilized. How else can talking in a group be evaluated?

3. What are the benefits of identifying a response that is incompatible with one that you, the leader, deem inappropriate?

OBJECTIVE 2.03

Use music to achieve appropriate peer touching. Increase touching 25% over baseline taken 5 minutes prior to beginning of session.

Participants: Peers

Procedure:

Preparation:
1. Specifically define "appropriate peer touching" by observing colleagues prior to planning session.
2. Select music intervention that is structured to elicit touching.
3. Select and practice music.
4. Practice verbal statements that specifically approve touching without using that word.
5. Develop data collection form to assess touching.

Implementation:
1. Lead selected intervention and scan continuously to identify touching.
2. Approve all appropriate touching without using the word "touch."
3. Ask colleague to observe and record touching.

Music Specifications:

Select music intervention of appropriate length that requires frequent touching.

Recommended Time Limit: 5–7 minutes

Criteria for Objective:

Competency Assessment 3:   Minimum scores in each category
Overall minimum score = 70
Increase touching 25% over baseline

Techniques Included: Structuring Music to Elicit Specific Response
Approving
Scanning
Evaluating/Data

Discussion for Transfer:
1. What is appropriate touching and how does it vary within different types of groups?
2. How did selected music intervention function in this situation? What aspects of the music versus the actions versus the leader skills most affected this situation?
3. Were the participants aware touching was being taught?
4. How else can touching, physical proximity, body language be evaluated?

OBJECTIVE 2.04

Use music to create 100% on-task, defined as all participants consistently maintaining eye contact and no talking.

Note: Instructor will assign two or three people to look away and talk occasionally.

Participants: Peers

Procedure:

Preparation:
1. Design music intervention of interest to peers.
2. Design and coordinate rhythmic activities with music. Practice these in follow-the-leader format to structure looking and paying attention.
3. Develop data collection form to evaluate on-task.

Implementation:
1. Direct adult rhythm intervention in follow-the-leader format.
2. Approve incompatible responses at least every 20 seconds including looking, following leader, participating, watching, etc.
3. Ask colleague to collect data on on-task per minute.

Music Specifications:

Option 1: Use recorded music of interest to peers and appropriate for follow-the-leader rhythm playing (clap, stomp, snap, pat knees).

Option 2: Provide group with rhythm instruments and improvise follow-the-leader rhythm playing.

Recommended Time Limit: 5 minutes

Criteria for Objective:

Competency Assessment 3: Minimum scores in each category
Overall minimum score = 70
Percentage of participants on-task in last minute of session = 90%

Techniques Included: Approving Incompatible Responses
Evaluating/Data

Discussion for Transfer:

How does approving an incompatible response affect inappropriate behavior? How frequently does such approval need to be given? How does this approval rate vary across client populations?

OBJECTIVE 2.05

Use music to teach an academic task. Compose a song to teach the meaning of the 10 words listed below:

Dithyramb	Plinth
Gibbous	Speedwell
Hong	Tebbad
Monodont	Torose
Orach	Zoril

Participants: Peers

Procedure:

Preparation:
1. Compose song, plan accompaniment, practice, and memorize both.
2. Practice chaining procedure.
3. Develop form for vocabulary posttest.

Implementation:
1. Use chaining and cuing to teach song to participants while accompanying.
2. Give paper/pencil posttest to evaluate vocabulary learned.
3. Encourage participation and remembering the words to the song.

Music Specifications:

1. Compose song to teach meaning of ten words above. Melody may be original or adapted from existing song.
2. Accompany on guitar, Autoharp, or piano/keyboard using most advanced techniques.

Recommended Time Limit: 10 minutes

Criteria for Objective:

Competency Assessment 3:   Minimum scores in each category
Overall minimum score = 70
90% or above accuracy per individual on posttest

Techniques Included: Composing
Song Leading
Chaining
Cuing
Evaluating/Data

Discussion for Transfer:

1. Research shows music can teach academic information. Did it in this case? How did the music function: reduce boredom of repetition, convey information, and enhance memory?
2. How difficult was this task for the participants? How much information can different types of group learn in a specified period of time? How many repetitions are needed? How did the melody function to enhance memory?
3. Were chaining and cuing effective techniques to teach this particular information?
4. How else can academic learning be evaluated?

OBJECTIVE 2.06

Use music to teach paired responses listed below:

ba—mto	pru—coz
gen—ti	frl—haj
ov—ler	sim—qyv

Participants: Peers

Procedure:

Preparation:
1. Compose a song that uses melody and words to pair the nonsense syllables above.
2. Practice accompaniment.
3. Practice and memorize song and accompaniment.
4. Practice chaining technique.
5. Prepare posttest form.

Implementation:
1. Use chaining and cuing to teach song.
2. After song is learned, fade cues and your singing and have group supply the second half of each pair of syllables.
3. Encourage group for participation and remembering pairings.
4. Use paper/pencil posttest by presenting half of each paired response in random order; have students identify other half of the paired response.

Music Specifications:

1. Compose song to teach the paired nonsense syllables above.
2. Accompany on guitar, Autoharp, or piano/keyboard.

Recommended Time Limit: 10 minutes

Criteria for Objective:

Competency Assessment 3:   Minimum scores in each category
Overall minimum score = 70
90% accuracy per individual on posttest

Techniques Included: Composing
Chaining
Cuing
Fading
Evaluating/Data

Discussion for Transfer:

1. How difficult was this task? Is learning a paired relationship easier or more difficult than learning a series of facts?
2. How might paired relationships/associations be used in therapy? How might music facilitate such objectives?
3. If participants had difficulty with this memory task, for what other skills might they have been approved?

OBJECTIVE 2.07

Use music to teach pronunciation of the three words listed below:

> Yttrium
> Opisthognathous
> Gastroenteritis

Participants: Peers

Procedure:

Preparation:
1. Use dictionary to ascertain correct pronunciation.
2. Compose music that emphasizes and teaches correct pronunciation.
3. Prepare accompaniment.
4. Practice and memorize song and accompaniment.
5. Practice chaining techniques.
6. Develop individual test procedure.

Implementation:
1. Use chaining and cuing to teach song.
2. After song is learned, use fading of cues and require participants to sing and pronounce words alone.
3. Encourage participation and remembering the pronunciation.
4. No modeling or repetitive practice concerning the correct pronunciations may be used other than that in musical teaching techniques.
5. Use individual posttest to evaluate song's effectiveness.

Music Specifications:

1. Compose song that emphasizes correct pronunciation of three words.
2. Prepare accompaniment on guitar, Autoharp, or piano/keyboard.

Recommended Time Limit: 10 minutes

Criteria for Objective:

Competency Assessment 3:   Minimum scores in each category
Overall minimum score = 72
80% accuracy per individual on posttest

Techniques Included: Composing
Chaining
Cuing
Fading
Evaluating

Discussion for Transfer:

1. Did music function to teach pronunciations? Was singing the word easier than saying the word?
2. Is an individual test procedure more threatening than a group one?
3. How difficult or easy was it to determine the correct pronunciation while singing?

OBJECTIVE 2.08

Use music to teach foreign language vocabulary.

Participants: Peers

Procedure:

Preparation:
1. Select at least 10 words from a foreign language that are used in greeting someone.
2. Set these words and their definitions to music.
3. Practice and memorize words, music, and accompaniment.
4. Develop evaluation form to assess correct usage and pronunciation.

Implementation:
1. Use chaining and cuing to teach song.
2. After song is learned, fade cues and require participants to sing and pronounce words alone.
3. Encourage participation and remembering the pronunciation.
4. Have participants role-play meeting someone who is from the country of the language selected and use vocabulary learned.
5. No modeling or repetitive practice concerning the correct pronunciations may be used other than that used in musical teaching techniques.
6. Use individual posttest to evaluate song's effectiveness.

Music Specifications:

1. Compose song that teaches words, meaning, and pronunciation.
2. Accompany on guitar, Autoharp, or piano/keyboard.

Recommended Time Limit: 15 minutes

Criteria for Objective:

Competency Assessment 3:   Minimum scores in each category
Overall minimum score = 72
80% accuracy per individual on posttest

Techniques Included: Composing
Chaining
Cuing
Fading
Evaluating/Data

Discussion for Transfer:

1. Did music function to teach foreign vocabulary?
2. Could participants use the vocabulary in conversation? Is this a different task from singing? How could the singing skill be adapted to transfer the vocabulary to a conversational skill?

OBJECTIVE 2.09

Use music to teach relaxation.

Participants: Peers

Procedure:

Preparation:
1. Prepare relaxation routine using alternating tension/relaxation of parts of body from feet up to head (4 minutes) followed by focused attention task such as imagining floating through space, lying in sun on the beach, etc. (4 minutes).
2. Select appropriate music, and place selected segments onto one uninterrupted music recording that is synchronized with #1 above.
3. Develop form for recording pulse—pre- and posttest.

Implementation:
1. Have each participant take and report his/her pulse rate before relaxation procedure. Record each participant's pulse rate.
2. Direct participants to lie on floor in relaxed position and close eyes. Reduce light in room as much as possible.
3. Turn on music at moderate volume and slowly reduce the background level.
4. Direct planned relaxation routine.
5. Speak in calm, smooth, relaxed style.
6. Encourage "thinking relaxed thoughts" and relaxed body language. Do not call participants by name since you wish them to focus on music and relaxation content.
7. Have each participant take and report his/her pulse. Record each participant's pulse rate.

Music Specifications:

1. Recorded music played at low enough volume to allow you to easily be heard over it (background level), which is instrumental (nonverbal) and probably perceived by peers as "quiet" music.
2. Uninterrupted music recording prepared and synchronized as specified.
3. Use of music player that provides quality playback for size of room and setting.

Recommended Time Limit: 15 minutes

Criteria for Objective:

Competency Assessment 3:   Minimum scores in each category
Overall minimum score = 72
Reduction in individual pulse rates of 5%

Techniques Included: Structuring Music to Yield Relaxation
Directing Relaxation Routine—differentiating tension/relaxation
and focused attention
Evaluating/Data

Discussion for Transfer:

1. Why might selected music not have enhanced relaxation?
2. Why might directions to think specific thoughts (focused attention or imagining) not enhance relaxation?
3. What was the function of the tension/relaxation routine as a form of enhanced body awareness or biofeedback?
4. What was the range of pulse rates and their increase or decrease? What relationship would there be to the pulses of various client groups?
5. What effect did speaking voice and leadership style have on participant's response?
6. Contrast types of relaxation procedures and their applicability to clinical situations.

OBJECTIVE 2.10

Use music to teach participants two action steps to deal with disappointment in their lives.

Participants: Peers

Procedure:

Preparation:
1. Select and specify action steps focusing on potentially positive outcomes of situation, i.e., extinguishing blame, anger, grief; thought stopping; perceiving situation as growth opportunity; putting situation in perspective by identifying far worse problems in life; etc.
2. Select or compose music to introduce the concepts in the selected steps.
3. Practice and memorize music if it is to be performed or acquire recording and quality playback equipment.
4. Prepare a slip of paper for each participant that contains a disappointing situation that might possibly be encountered by peers.

Implementation:
1. Direct people to read slips of paper and assume the role.
2. Perform or play recorded music.
3. Have brief discussion about disappointment and how it is possible to learn to deal with it. State that the task is to practice some possible techniques (2 minutes).
4. Pair participants and have each quickly describe his disappointment to others.
5. Describe selected Action Step 1 and give an example.
6. Direct pairs to help each other apply this step to their own situations by eliciting options and consequences, being supportive, and helping each other reach closure on selected option.
7. Repeat steps 5 and 6 for Action Step 2.
8. Play music again and lead entire group in discussion about how their perception of the problem might have changed.

Music Specifications:

Music to be performed or played that conveys concepts of the action steps selected. (See Discography by Counseling Topic for possible titles.)

Recommended Time Limit: 15 minutes

Criteria for Objective:

Competency Assessment 3:   Minimum scores in each category
Overall minimum score = 72

Techniques Included: Role-Playing
                             Teaching Action Steps

Discussion for Transfer:

1. Research shows that music can establish or change an emotion. Did it in this situation? Did it function to motivate taking the action step? If so, when? At the beginning or end of session?
2. What specific behaviors did participants use to support and motivate each other?
3. How these behaviors differ from simply telling a person what to do to solve the problem?

OBJECTIVE 2.11

Shape a unanimous group decision within a 10-minute time limit.

Participants: Peers

Procedure:

Preparation:
1. Select six songs of equal difficulty, familiarity, popularity, etc. Memorize songs and accompaniment.
2. Prepare list of songs.

Implementation:
1. Tell participants that the objective is to select one song to sing from this list but that the decision must be unanimous.

Note: Instructor will select one of the songs before the session and leader must shape participants to select that one.

2. Open floor for suggestions. Elicit disagreement or alternate suggestions following all songs named except the one desired. Elicit agreement or positive reactions to the suggestion of that song.
3. Continue eliciting discussion until majority of participants seems to be responding positively to desired song, then vote. Do not allow participants to vote until consensus seems apparent.
4. Sing unanimously selected song whether it is the desired one or not.

Music Specifications:

1. Six songs of equal difficulty, familiarity, popularity, etc.
2. Accompaniment on guitar, Autoharp, or piano/keyboard.

Recommended Time Limit: 10 minutes

Criteria for Objective:

Competency Assessment 3:   Minimum scores in each category
Overall minimum score = 72

Techniques Included: Shaping a Group Discussion
Accompanying

Discussion for Transfer:

1. Were the participants aware they were being shaped to a predetermined point?
2. How is shaping a group discussion or decision to a predetermined point different from leading an open-ended discussion? When is this appropriate/inappropriate for the leader? How does this relate to the concept of directive versus indirective therapy techniques?
3. How might participation in this intervention in either the leader or group-member role benefit other types of groups?

OBJECTIVE 2.12

Use music to introduce the topic of drugs/alcohol; then, lead the participants in a discussion about the use of drugs or alcohol, resulting in formulation of guidelines.

Participants: Peers

Procedure:

Preparation:
1. Select music with specified content. If it is to be performed, practice and memorize it. If recorded music, acquire quality playback equipment.
2. Formulate five basic guidelines that would probably be acceptable to peers. Memorize them.
3. Review shaping techniques in Objective 2.11 Implementation and plan how to apply them to this task.

Implementation:
1. Perform or play recorded music.
2. Introduce topic and elicit group discussion about how it relates to them.
3. Shape the participants to formulate the predetermined five guidelines for advice to peers about use of drugs and alcohol.
4. Encourage every member of group to participate, using verbal or nonverbal techniques.

Music Specifications:

Music that conveys concepts about use of drugs and alcohol that references the guidelines to be formulated.

Recommended Time Limit: 15 minutes

Criteria for Objective:

Competency Assessment 3:   Minimum scores in each category
Overall minimum score = 72

Techniques Included: Leading a Group Discussion
Shaping a Group Discussion

Discussion for Transfer:

1. Were participants aware they were being shaped to formulate predetermined guidelines?
2. Why might a therapist not wish to let a group have an open-ended discussion about guidelines for substances that are commonly abused?

3. How might participation in this intervention in either the leader or group-member role benefit other types of groups?

4. How would guidelines differ for various groups?

5. Did selected music convey desired concepts? Does some music encourage "inappropriate" substance use? If so, which music? Should this music be censored with certain groups? If so, which ones?

OBJECTIVE 2.13

Use music to convey the emotions happy, sad, angry, and scared.

Participants: Peers

Procedure:

Preparation:
1. Find musical excerpts that clearly convey happy, sad, angry, and scared.
2. Prepare a recording with the musical excerpts.
3. Identify musical elements (melody, tonality, rhythm, tempo, dynamics, timbre, orchestration) that support the expression of the identified emotion.
4. Prepare index cards with the emotion words written clearly.
5. Locate a variety of musical instruments and bring them to session.

Implementation:
1. Prepare music instruments by placing them on a table or the floor.
2. Ask the participants to write down the emotions expressed by the excerpts you play.
3. Play recording on quality playback equipment.
4. Ask participants to reveal the emotions. Ask participants to describe how the music conveys the emotion.
5. Inform participants that they will play a "guess that emotion game" by listening to a volunteer improvise music to represent the emotions written on cards.
6. Ask for a volunteer to play music to represent emotion.
7. Follow up participants' guesses with discussion of how the music conveyed the emotion or how it misled guessers.
8. Repeat steps 6 and 7 as time allows.

Music Specifications:

1. Recorded music excerpts that convey happy, sad, angry, and scared prepared on a single recording.
2. Music playback equipment.
3. Music instruments capable of conveying the four target emotions.

Recommended Time Limit: 15 minutes

Criteria for Objective:

Competency Assessment 3:   Minimum scores in each category
Overall minimum score = 72

Techniques Included: Structuring Music to Convey Emotion
Music listening
Leading a Group Discussion
Improvisation

Discussion for Transfer:

1. Did all of the participants accurately guess the target emotion from the recorded music? What were the differences among the guesses? How accurate was the leader in decoding emotion in music?
2. Which target emotion was the most easily performed? Which target emotion was the most easily guessed?
3. Which client groups might benefit from this intervention?

OBJECTIVE 2.14

Use music to teach the spelling concept "i before e except after c." Include five words that follow the rule and five words that are exceptions to the rule.

Client Population: Fifth-grade students with SLD* (spelling)

Procedure:

Preparation:
1. Compose song, plan accompaniment, practice, and memorize it.
2. Practice chaining procedure.
3. Develop form for posttest.

Implementation:
1. Use chaining and cuing to teach song to group while accompanying.
2. Give paper/pencil posttest to evaluate spelling learned.
3. Encourage participating and remembering the words to the song.
4. Solicit individual responses for memorizing rule and spelling words.
5. Encourage singing the spelling of words to facilitate memory.

Music Specifications:

1. Compose song to teach objective above. Melody may be original or adapted from existing song.
2. Accompany on guitar, Autoharp, or piano/keyboard using most advanced techniques.

Recommended Time Limit: 10 minutes

Criteria for Objective:

Competency Assessment 3:   Minimum scores in each category
Overall minimum score = 72
90% accuracy on spelling test

Techniques Included: Composing
Song Leading
Chaining
Cuing
Evaluating/Data

*SLD – Specific learning disability

Discussion for Transfer:

1. Research shows music can teach academic information. Did it in this case? How did the music function to reduce the boredom of repetition, convey the information, and enhance memory?
2. How difficult was this task for students with learning disabilities? How much information can be learned by different types of groups in (a) a specified period of time, (b) by a specified number of repetitions, and (c) using the same melody?
3. Would this music be easily remembered to function as an ongoing memory aid across time for SLD students with spelling problems?
4. How else can academic learning be evaluated?

OBJECTIVE 2.15

Use music to increase reading fluidity, comprehension, and pleasure in reading.

Client Population: Third-grade students with SLD (reading)

Procedure:

Preparation:
1. Select reading paragraph appropriate to age and ability level.
2. Compose song that replicates paragraph. Plan accompaniment, then practice and memorize it.
3. Prepare two charts for group reading: one that replicates selected paragraph and one that changes the paragraph by using the same words in different combinations.

Implementation:
1. Teach song paired with a pointing cue to each written word on the chart when sung. Begin with slow tempo. Approve watching and singing.
2. Increase tempo of song until it is as fast as desired reading speed for fluidity. After each line is sung, have the group speak the line.
3. Approve reading smoothly and all pleasure responses.
4. Allow students to read individually while each one points to the words on the chart.
5. Evaluate results of intervention by having group read second chart with words rearranged.

Music Specifications:

1. Compose song to teach above objective. Melody may be original or adapted from existing song.
2. Accompany on guitar, Autoharp, or piano/keyboard using most advanced techniques.

Recommended Time Limit: 10 minutes

Criteria for Objective:

Competency Assessment 3:   Minimum scores in each category
Overall minimum score = 72

Techniques Included: Composing
Song Leading
Cuing
Approving
Evaluating/Data

Discussion for Transfer:

1. Research shows music can teach academic information. Did it in this case?
2. How could this intervention be adapted to increase reading speed?

OBJECTIVE 2.16

Teach a circle dance to 15-year-old students who have moderate cognitive impairments with emphasis on simple, clear, concise, specific directions. Use chaining and cuing.

Client Population: Students aged 14–16 years who have moderate cognitive impairment *

Procedure:

Preparation:
1. Select 10 sequential steps for a circle dance.
2. Do a task analysis to determine most concise, descriptive direction, effective cues for each, and number of beats necessary to complete step (examples of task analysis: Objectives 1.06, 2.19).
3. Memorize task analysis.
4. Develop data collection form to evaluate direction following.

Implementation:
1. Teach dance using chaining, cuing, and correcting.
2. Scan continuously to determine persons needing additional cues and respond accordingly.

Music Specifications:

Recorded instrumental music appropriate for dance.

Recommended Time Limit: 15 minutes

Criteria for Objective:

Competency Assessment 3:   Minimum scores in each category
Overall minimum score = 72
90% of clients followed dance directions

Techniques Included: Chaining
Cuing
Task Analysis
Evaluating/Data

*Includes students with educable mental handicap, autism spectrum disorders, severe learning disabilities, and other developmental delays.

Discussion for Transfer:

1. Discuss whether difficulty of dance matched client capabilities.
2. Discuss additional cues or ways to further simplify the dance and directions for those with lesser abilities.
3. If the leader talked excessively in directing the intervention, discuss and model ways of reducing this.

OBJECTIVE 2.17

Therapist will teach choral performance skills to student with moderate cognitive impairments including song, stage entry, posture, smiling, bowing, exit.

Client Population: Students aged 15–18 years with moderate cognitive impairment

Procedure:

Preparation:
1. Plan systematic way to teach skills. Use modeling, cuing, and fading.
2. Select song that would probably be familiar to group.

Implementation:
1. Teach song and rehearse it to achieve most musical sound possible.
2. Teach performance skills listed in objective. Use chaining, cuing, and fading.
3. Scan group for those needing assistance and for inappropriate behaviors that require correction. Use approval of an incompatible response for correcting.

Note: Instructor will assign some persons to behave inappropriately (e.g., off-task, refusal to cooperate, inappropriate affect).

4. If some persons are exhibiting low affect, exaggerate bowing and smiling cues and teach high-affect behaviors. If group is exhibiting hyperactivity, teach low-affect behaviors.

Music Specifications:

Song consisting of one verse and chorus that would probably be familiar to group.

Recommended Time Limit: 15 minutes

Criteria for Objective:

Competency Assessment 3:   Minimum scores in each category
Overall minimum score = 72

Techniques Included: Modeling
Cuing
Fading
Approving Incompatible Responses

Discussion for Transfer:

1. Discuss performance standards for music ensembles of persons with developmental disabilities and importance of social skills in audience perception. How can leader ensure audiences admire rather than pity group?

2. Discuss benefit of the above skills taught to persons with cognitive deficits in situations other than performance.

3. Discuss effect of modeling and cuing on the learning that occurred. Which was more effective? Did some people need both?

OBJECTIVE 2.18

Use a music intervention to teach adults with mild to moderate cognitive impairments manners appropriate for an adult social occasion.

Client Population: Adults aged 40–55 with mild to moderate cognitive impairments

Procedure:

Preparation:
1. Select three skills to be taught, e.g., shaking hands, introducing self, response to introduction.
2. Do task analysis to determine all aspects of each behavior to be taught, i.e., physical proximity, intensity, speed, eye contact.
3. Plan modeling and cuing techniques to implement task analysis.
4. Compose music that teaches at least one of the three skills.
5. Develop form to evaluate social skills learned.

Implementation:
1. Teach the three skills using music, modeling, and cuing. Have each person practice with leader.
2. Pair clients and have them practice with each other.
3. Scan clients constantly to determine those needing additional help.
4. Approve all correct responses. Point out individual styles that are socially effective.
5. Correct inappropriate behaviors such as rocking, hugging, loud laughing, etc.
6. Evaluate client responses.
7. Be sure that your responses to clients are on an adult level.

Music Specifications:

Music composed to teach a social skill as specified.

Recommended Time Limit: 15 minutes

Criteria for Objective:

Competency Assessment 3:   Minimum scores in each category
Overall minimum score = 72
80% accuracy on evaluation form

Techniques Included: Composing
Teaching Social Skills
Modeling
Cuing
Evaluating/Data

Discussion for Transfer:

1. Discuss how skills can be taught systematically but with enough variability that learned responses do not seem stereotyped.
2. Discuss importance of treating adults with impairments as adults even though interaction by necessity must be simplified.
3. Discuss other social skills that would be important to teach this group.

OBJECTIVE 2.19

Use color-coding system to teach 10- to 12-year-old children with moderate cognitive impairments to play two chords on the guitar.

Client Population: Children (at least 3) aged 10–12 years with moderate cognitive impairment

Procedure:

Preparation:
1. Prepare guitars for students and yourself with red dots (numbered 1, 2, 3) on frets for finger placement of D chord and numbered blue dots on frets for A^7 chords.
2. Practice teaching procedure in Implementation, especially Step 11.
3. Place guitars on floor in front of chairs prior to beginning.

Implementation:
1. State task in one sentence.
2. Instruct group to pick up guitars but not to play them.
3. Quickly and briefly approve specific individuals as they follow instructions.
4. Show the group correct position of guitar on lap. Scan group, correcting any who require it.
5. Direct group to place left hand on the three red dots by specifying each finger and numbered dot in sequence. Scan group, correcting any who require it.
6. Direct group to press all fingers on dots and to reach right hand across and strum once across appropriate strings, modeling these steps as you say them. Correct anyone who made an error.
7. Say "Listen," and demonstrate four strums on this chord in rhythm of song while nodding head in rhythm.
8. Say "Play and strum four times on this chord in rhythm with me; ready, begin," and use strum hand for entry cue.
9. Praise those who are correct and who stop after four strums, etc. Repeat if there were errors.
10. Repeat Steps 5, 6, 7, 8, and 9 for blue dots.
11. Say "This time we will strum four times on red, then four times on blue. I will cue you when to change fingers. Press red and strum four times in rhythm with me. Ready, begin." Use head and strum arm for entry cue. As group begins strum four, say, "Change to blue dots" and use head and arm as cue to maintain the rhythm of the next four strums. Praise those who are correct. Repeat and correct if there were errors. Encourage those who are trying, watching, listening, following directions, making music, etc.

Note: The technique described above is a systematic task analysis of how to teach someone to play the guitar using a color-coded system.

Hint: If there are not enough guitars for each person in the group, have those persons without a guitar simulate one by practicing same procedures. Transfer guitars after Steps 9 and 10. Persons without guitars always continue to practice each step in simulation.

Music Specifications:

D and A^7 chords

Recommended Time Limit: Approximately 10 minutes

Criteria for Objective:

Competency Assessment 3: Minimum scores in each category
Overall minimum score = 72
Music selection as specified
Implementation in allotted time

Techniques Included: Teaching from Task Analysis
Cuing
Modeling
Approving
Correcting

Discussion for Transfer:

1. Discuss a learning problem that a structured lesson plan with successive approximations might permit.
2. Under what circumstances might such a plan need major revision?

OBJECTIVE 2.20

Use music to teach children to follow two-part directions.

Client Population: Children aged 3–5 years with mild cognitive impairments

Procedure:

Preparation:
1. Select three two-part directions, e.g., "Pick up the toy and put it in the box."
2. Compose separate songs to teach each pair of directions.
3. Review chaining and cuing techniques.
4. Acquire any materials necessary for selected tasks.

Implementation:
1. Teach songs while modeling task.
2. Guide each child with physical assistance to complete the task while singing songs.
3. Sing a song and allow all children to perform task at same time. Evaluate those needing further assistance.
4. Approve following directions, waiting turn, sitting quietly, listening, etc.

Music Specifications:

Three short songs, each composed to teach a two-part direction as specified.

Recommended Time Limit: 15 minutes

Criteria for Objective:

Competency Assessment 3:   Minimum scores in each category
Overall minimum score = 72

Techniques Included: Composing
Chaining
Cuing
Guided Assistance

Discussion for Transfer:

1. Discuss how the selected two-part directions varied in difficulty. Could children with mild cognitive impairments learn three directions in one session? What would a realistic timeline be for this group to learn one of these tasks?
2. Discuss function of music. Was it effective in teaching skill? Would children with mild cognitive impairments also need cues and guided assistance in addition to music?

OBJECTIVE 2.21

Use music to teach one aspect of the concept of honesty to children with cognitive impairments.

Client Population: Children aged 12 years with mild cognitive impairment

Procedure:

Preparation:
1. Define one specific aspect of honesty that is clearly differentiated from dishonesty, e.g., "take only your own objects."
2. Acquire any materials necessary.
3. Compose, practice, and memorize music.

Implementation:
1. Use modeling and music to teach specific concept selected.
2. Approve and label correct responses as "being honest."

Music Specifications:

Music composed to teach selected aspect of honesty.

Recommended Time Limit: 15 minutes

Criteria for Objective:

Competency Assessment 3:   Minimum scores in each category
Overall minimum score = 72

Techniques Included: Composing
Modeling
Approving

Discussion for Transfer:

1. Discuss various definitions of honesty and how these other honesty concepts might be simply taught.
2. Discuss learning problems of children with mild cognitive impairments and realistic timelines for them to acquire ideas such as honesty, responsibility, etc. How many different examples would be needed before a concept is formed?
3. Was the music simple enough for children aged 12 with cognitive impairments?

OBJECTIVE 2.22

Use music to teach one language-development task.

Client Population: Children aged 8 years with severe/profound cognitive impairments

Procedure:

Preparation:
1. Select a language-development task appropriate to the age and population.
2. Decide how to use and prepare music.
3. Develop evaluation form.

Implementation:
1. Teach task using music and cuing.
2. Approve correct responses.

Music Specifications: Student's choice

Recommended Time Limit: 15 minutes

Criteria for Objective:

Competency Assessment 3:   Minimum scores in each category
Overall minimum score = 72
80% group accuracy on evaluation form

Techniques Included: Cuing
Approving

Discussion for Transfer:

1. Discuss characteristics of this client population including realistic language goals.
2. Discuss techniques demonstrated.
3. Was pacing of this demonstration matched to responses of the clients? Was it too fast or too slow?

OBJECTIVE 2.23

Use music to teach one color.

Client Population: Children aged 6 years with severe/profound cognitive impairment

Procedure:

Preparation:
1. Select a basic color to be taught.
2. Decide how to use and prepare music.
3. Develop evaluation form.

Implementation:
1. Teach task using music and cuing.
2. Approve correct responses.

Music Specifications: Student's choice

Recommended Time Limit: 15 minutes

Criteria for Objective:

Competency Assessment 3:   Minimum scores in each category
Overall minimum score = 72
80% group accuracy on evaluation form

Techniques Included: Cuing
Approving

Discussion for Transfer:

1. Discuss techniques demonstrated.
2. Discuss how the concept of color can be differentiated from the object, e.g., blue versus blue crayon or blue paper.

OBJECTIVE 2.24

Use music to teach responses to three types of stimulation: one physical stimulus, one auditory stimulus, and one visual stimulus.

Client Population: Infants aged 3 to 8 months with multiple disabilities

Procedure:

Preparation:
1. Specify stimuli—physical (touch or guided movement); auditory (name of child); and visual (brightly colored balloon). Determine multiple responses desired (moving, smiling, vocalizing, visual tracking, head turning toward stimulator and/or source of sound). Plan stimulation routine designed to elicit these responses.
2. Select appropriate recorded music or compose simple, repetitive songs and synchronize it with routine.
3. Develop form to evaluate infant responses.

Implementation:
1. Pair group into stimulator/infant teams with infants lying on floor and stimulators sitting beside them.
2. Demonstrate each stimulation technique used in routine and identify desired responses. Demonstrate use of stroking, vocalizations to encourage desired responses.
3. Begin music and routine.
4. Move around group and encourage stimulators who are using appropriate techniques. Reverse roles and continue.
5. Use form to evaluate responses.

Music Specifications: Student's choice

Recommended Time Limit: 15 minutes

Criteria for Objective:

Competency Assessment 3: Minimum scores in each category
Overall minimum score = 72
80% group response to stimuli

Techniques Included: Infant Stimulation
Evaluating
Composing if opted

Discussion for Transfer:

1. Discuss characteristics of the group.
2. How did music function? Did it have a function for the child as well as the stimulators?
3. How would general stimulation activities become more focused over time to evolve into a specific training task?
4. In what ways might music inappropriately stimulate persons with severe disabilities? Discuss uninhibited primary reflexes, e.g., startle and seizure activity.
5. Would talking to clients during this intervention be desirable?

OBJECTIVE 2.25

Use music to teach body parts.

Client Population: Children aged 4 years with visual impairment

Procedure:

Preparation:
1. Plan which body parts are to be taught and how music is to be used.
2. Plan a teaching strategy that avoids visual cues.
3. Acquire necessary materials.
4. Develop evaluation procedure.

Implementation:
1. Bring blindfolds for each group member to simulate visual impairment.
2. Teach task using cuing and approving with emphasis on specificity of verbal feedback.
3. Evaluate results.

Music Specifications: Student's choice

Recommended Time Limit: 15 minutes

Criteria for Objective:

Competency Assessment 3:   Minimum scores in each category
Overall minimum score = 72
80% group accuracy on evaluation form

Techniques Included: Cuing
                           Approving

Discussion for Transfer:

1. Discuss characteristics of the population and learning challenges.
2. Discuss verbal versus physical cuing.
3. Discuss any techniques demonstrated.

OBJECTIVE 2.26

Use music to teach two grooming skills to children with visual impairments while reducing inappropriate, stereotyped behaviors.

Client Population: Children aged 8 years with visual impairments

Note: Instructor will assign some persons to have inappropriate, stereotyped behaviors.

Procedure:

Preparation:
1. Specify two grooming skills that would be appropriate for this disability and age level.
2. Do task analysis to teach grooming skills, omitting visual cues while using verbal and physical cuing (task analysis example: Objective 2.19).
3. Determine use of music. Prepare and memorize selected or composed music.
4. Develop evaluation procedure to determine whether grooming skills meet criteria.
5. Bring blindfolds for group.

Implementation:
1. Blindfold group.
2. Direct intervention, cuing and approving correct responses and eliminating inappropriate, stereotyped behaviors by using approval for incompatible responses.
3. Evaluate grooming skills and reduction in inappropriate responses.

Music Specifications: Student's choice

Recommended Time Limit: 15 minutes

Criteria for Objective:

     Competency Assessment 3:   Minimum scores in each category
     Overall minimum score = 72
     80% group accuracy on evaluation form

Techniques Included: Cuing
                                         Task Analysis
                                         Approving Incompatible Responses

Discussion for Transfer:

1. Discuss inappropriate mannerisms of persons with visual impairments, e.g., rocking, finger pressing on eyes, inappropriate laughing, facial grimacing, and/or constant smiling. How might these best be monitored and eliminated? Would using the hands for sensory input be inappropriate?
2. How can persons with visual impairments monitor their personal grooming and hygiene? Discuss issues of cleanliness, attractiveness, and changing styles.

OBJECTIVE 2.27

Use music to extinguish pity-seeking behaviors and "I can't do that" responses in adults with recent visual impairment while teaching a mobility task.

Client Population: Adults aged 20–30 with visual impairment

Procedure:

Preparation:
1. Specify possible pity-seeking behaviors that persons with a recent impairment might develop.
2. Develop directions designed to eliminate as many "pity-seeking" behaviors as possible. Also, identify environmental cues that can help the person feel secure in movement across the room.
3. Select music that can be used to cue authoritative (rather than tentative) mobility from one point in room to another.
4. Develop data collection and evaluation procedures.
5. Acquire blindfolds for participants.

Implementation:
1. Blindfold participants.
2. Instruct clients about desired movement using directions designed to eliminate "I can't do that" responses and successive approximation of movement across entire room.
3. Play selected music. Tell group you will stop music if mobility is too tentative or if danger is evident, e.g., walking into something.
4. Let each person practice individually.
5. Approve specific authoritative movements, like head-up, length of stride, etc.
6. Evaluate mobility.

Music Specifications: Student's choice

Recommended Time Limit: 15 minutes

Criteria for Objective:

    Competency Assessment 3:   Minimum scores in each category
    Overall minimum score = 72
    Increased mobility
    Extinction of pity-seeking behaviors

Techniques Included: Mobility Training
        Cuing
        Evaluating/Data
        Successive Approximation

Discussion for Transfer:

1. Research shows that discontinuing the music can function as feedback. Did it in this situation?
2. How could authoritative mobility discriminations become more discrete on the part of those with visual impairments and the leader? What is the final goal? How is this determined?
3. What environmental cues were used? How many were present and simply needed to be identified as opposed to those added by the leader as an assistive device?

OBJECTIVE 2.28

Teach signs to a well-known recorded song. (Reference: *The Joy of Signing*. See Objective 1.13.)

Client Population: Students aged 10–12 years with severe/profound hearing loss

Procedure:

Preparation:
1. Select song and signs for major words.
2. Practice and memorize signs for song and instructional direction and feedback.
3. Videotape yourself signing to music; assess choreography and difficulty. Revise signing task to improve smoothness and rhythmic accuracy (optional step).

Implementation:
1. Use signs paired with verbalizations for all instructional information.
2. Model the song with signs for the clients.
3. Use modeling and chaining to teach the sequence signs.
4. Cue rhythmic accuracy of signs.
5. Videotape group signing and assess overall ensemble effect (optional step).

Note: To simulate hearing loss, the leader can listen to the song through headphones, reduce the volume of musical playback, or provide the participants with earplugs.

Music Specifications:

1. A popular, nonreligious, recorded song with some repeated words.
2. Use at least 20 different signs.

Recommended Time Limit: 10 minutes

Criteria for Objective:

Competency Assessment 3:   Minimum scores in each category
Overall minimum score = 72
Music selection as specified
Implementation in allotted time

Techniques Included: Signing to Music
Chaining
Modeling
Cuing
Evaluating (optional)

Discussion for Transfer:

1. How rhythmically accurate were signs? Were all people signing in the same direction?
2. How could choreography be improved? What cues are needed for rhythmic accuracy?
3. How could persons with hearing loss be incorporated into a sign choir with hearing persons? What social objectives would be important with such a group?
4. Was the leader's sign proficiency adequate for instructional purposes?
5. What other types of clients might enjoy or benefit from signing to music?
6. Did the leader remember to talk while signing? Why is this important?
7. Discuss conditions under which the Deaf community may resent signed songs.

OBJECTIVE 2.29

Teach a rhythm-reading task of at least 16 measures.

Client Population: Students aged 12–15 years with hearing loss

Procedure:

Preparation:
1. Select 16 written measures of simple rhythms and prepare poster large enough for entire group to read. Use only half, quarter, eighth notes, and rests.
2. Practice playing rhythms accurately while maintaining a steady beat.
3. Assess the most difficult measures that might be problematic to learn.
4. Select rhythm instruments or Orff instruments with best potential for resonance/vibration.
5. Pair each note value and rest value with a different physical manipulation of the instrument.
   Example: quarter = strike; half = rub for 2 beats; rest = hands apart for one beat

Implementation:
1. Hand out instruments contingent upon appropriate social behavior and show people how to play them.
2. Teach rhythm two measures at a time using modeling and chaining. Scan group to assess persons having difficulty. Correct any inaccuracies.
3. When entire rhythm is learned, divide group into parts with each part beginning on a different measure. Direct and cue entry and accurate rhythms.
4. Encourage on-task, following directions, accuracy, enjoyment, etc.

Note: Providing participants with earplugs can simulate hearing loss.

Music Specifications:

Sixteen written measures of rhythm including rests and at least four different note values.

Recommended Time Limit: 7–10 minutes

Criteria for Objective:

Competency Assessment 3:   Minimum scores in each category
Overall minimum score = 72
Music selection as specified
Implementation in allotted time
Extra credit given for ability to use signs with teaching instructions

Techniques Included: Group Leadership – Rhythm Ensemble
Cuing
Chaining
Modeling

Discussion for Transfer:

1. How does a person with a hearing loss learn the concept of duration of sound? How do the paired physical manipulations in this intervention help teach that concept? After this concept is learned, could the hearing-impaired person play varying rhythms without the paired physical manipulations?

2. Did the leader hand out instruments contingent upon social behavior or just go around the room in seated order? Why would the social contingency be important in a therapy group? If a social contingency was not used, model and practice this technique until it is mastered.

OBJECTIVE 2.30

Use music to teach an auditory discrimination task to children with hearing loss, i.e., sound vs. no sound or vocal versus instrumental sound.

Client Population: Children aged 5 years with hearing loss

Procedure:

Preparation:
1. Select discrete auditory discrimination tasks and appropriate music.
2. Plan simple directions and learn signs for them.
3. Learn signs to approve correct responses.
4. Develop data collection and evaluation form.

Implementation:
1. Use signs paired with verbal directions to conduct music intervention approving correct responses.
2. Exaggerate body language and facial expressions.

Music Specifications: Student's choice

Recommended Time Limit: 15 minutes

Criteria for Objective:

> Competency Assessment 3:   Minimum scores in each category
> Overall minimum score = 72
> 80% accuracy on evaluation form

Techniques Included: Signing
Auditory Discrimination
Evaluating

Discussion for Transfer:

1. Discuss characteristics of the population and subsequent learning problems.
2. Discuss ways in which music can function with children who have hearing impairments.
3. Were the leader's facial cues and body language exaggerated enough to function well for children with hearing impairments?

OBJECTIVE 2.31

Use music to support range-of-motion exercises appropriate for children with cerebral palsy (CP).

Client Population: Children aged 10 years with CP

Procedure:

Preparation:
1. Learn three range-of-motion exercises and their individual purposes.
2. Select music and synchronize it with exercises.
3. Develop evaluation procedure.

Implementation:
1. Pair up participants in teams with one role-playing a child with CP and one as the child's aide who will assist with exercises.
2. Conduct music intervention and teach exercises.
3. Explain function of each exercise.
4. Emphasize client independence.
5. Switch roles in teams and repeat.
6. Evaluate.

Music Specifications: Student's choice

Recommended Time Limit: 15 minutes

Criteria for Objective:

> Competency Assessment 3:   Minimum scores in each category
> Overall minimum score = 72

Techniques Included: Range-of-Motion Exercises
                            Evaluating

Discussion for Transfer:

1. Discuss characteristics of the population and necessity for physical therapy.
2. Discuss uninhibited primary reflexes and how they can be controlled through training. How can music be detrimental in this process? What musical adaptations can be made to avoid detrimental effects?

OBJECTIVE 2.32

Use music to stimulate group interaction.

Client Population: Adults aged 30–45 with moderate cognitive disabilities and cerebral palsy

Procedure:

Preparation:
1. Specifically define "group interaction," i.e., asking question, listening, answering question, eliciting participation, etc.
2. Develop music interventions to teach selected skills.
3. Develop evaluation procedure.

Implementation:
1. Place clients in circle with leader outside. Move around circle to cue looking at others and talking.
2. Conduct planned music intervention. Be sure to teach group to talk to other group members, not leader.
3. If spontaneous interactions begin, withdraw and let them develop. If they subside, move closer and begin cuing.

Music Specifications: Student's choice

Recommended Time Limit: 15 minutes

Criteria for Objective:

Competency Assessment 3:   Minimum scores in each category
Overall minimum score = 72
80% of clients are interacting per evaluation form

Techniques Included: Stimulating Group Interaction / Socialization
Evaluating

Discussion for Transfer:

1. Discuss special physical and verbal problems of those with cerebral palsy that tend to discourage social interaction.
2. How can these problems be overcome through learning new techniques?

OBJECTIVE 2.33

Use music to teach parents the skills of reinforcement and positive feedback.

Client Population: Parents of children with developmental disabilities

Note: Instructor will pair group members and give them role-playing assignments to which leader should react.

Procedure:

Preparation:
1. Select simple concepts to teach, e.g., immediacy of feedback; contingencies, physical/verbal approval; modeling/cuing.
2. Select simple tasks that children with developmental disabilities might need to learn and select music to teach them, e.g., a color, the concept of up/down.
3. Develop evaluation procedure.

Implementation:
1. Introduce topic and use positive techniques to get parents involved in simulated training sessions.
2. Use ignoring techniques (quickly approve persons positive about child, ignore those making negative statements, watch those being ignored for improved statements, then approve them immediately) with parents verbalizing negative statements about their child.
3. Encourage positive statements and commitment to training.

Music Specifications: Student's choice

Recommended Time Limit: 15 minutes

Criteria for Objective:

Competency Assessment 3:   Minimum scores in each category
Overall minimum score = 72

Techniques Included: Approving
Ignoring
Parenting Techniques
Evaluating

Discussion for Transfer:

1. Discuss problems of parents of children with disabilities. How do these contribute to the high divorce rate in such families?
2. What is the role of the music therapist in parent training?
3. How did the music function in this situation? What other functions could it have?

OBJECTIVE 2.34

Lead a group discussion on appropriate parenting techniques for dealing with problems of children with disabilities. Use music to introduce the topic.

Client Population: Parents of children with developmental disabilities

Procedure:

Preparation:
1. Select one problem to discuss.
2. Plan some role-playing situations to demonstrate the problem.
3. Select or compose music to introduce topic.
4. Develop evaluation procedure.

Implementation:
1. Play music.
2. Lead group discussion.
3. Position all parents to participate without calling on them. Use eye contact, facial expression, body language, pausing, etc.
4. Set up role-playing situations by written out instructions and giving them to members of the group simultaneously.
5. Evaluate.

Music Specifications: Student's choice

Recommended Time Limit: 15 minutes

Criteria for Objective:

Competency Assessment 3:   Minimum scores in each category
Overall minimum score = 72
80% accuracy on evaluation form

Techniques Included: Leading Group Discussion
Parenting Techniques
Role-Playing
Evaluating

Discussion for Transfer:

1. In a group discussion, it is often important for everyone to participate. What is the effect of nonparticipation in such a situation?
2. What techniques can a leader use to elicit and encourage participation?

OBJECTIVE 2.35

Use music to reduce hyperactivity in a group of 8-year-old students with behavior disorders while increasing an incompatible response.

Client Population: Children aged 8 years with behavior disorders

Procedure:

Preparation:
1. Select an incompatible response that reduces the probability of a wide range of hyperactive behaviors, e.g., sitting in chair with hands in lap reduces the probability of running around the room, hitting self or others.
2. Plan music intervention that requires selected incompatible response.
3. Develop form to assess reduction in hyperactivity.

Implementation:
1. Use modeling and cuing to get clients engaged in selected incompatible response. As soon as everyone is responding appropriately, start music.
2. Stop music when any one client deviates from selected response.
3. Approve correct responses frequently—about every 10–15 seconds.
4. Evaluate.

Music Specifications: Student's choice

Recommended Time Limit: 15 minutes

Criteria for Objective:

> Competency Assessment 3:   Minimum scores in each category
> Overall minimum score = 72
> Increased incompatible response
> Demonstrated reduction in hyperactivity

Techniques Included: Reducing Hyperactivity
Modeling
Cuing
Teaching Incompatible Response
Approving
Evaluating/Data

Discussion for Transfer:

1. Discuss characteristics of population and subsequent learning problems.
2. How can very frequent, specific approving become less frequent and more generalized? What is a realistic time for this to occur with this population?

3. How did the music function in this situation? What procedural changes would be necessary with actual children with behavior disorders?

4. What music activities would be more fun for these children than the inappropriate behaviors they usually engage in?

OBJECTIVE 2.36

Use music and approval/disapproval to teach on-task behavior defined as eye contact, no talking, and following directions.

Client Population: Adolescents aged 13–15 with emotional disturbance

Procedure:

Preparation:

1. Select music intervention that is structured to require the above on-task behavior.
2. Plan evaluation procedure to assess on-task behavior of groups and to count approvals and disapprovals of leader.

Implementation:

1. Use approving and disapproving in a 4:1 ratio while leading music intervention. Give feedback at least once per 15 seconds. Maintain 4:1 ratio.
2. After 5 minutes, eliminate approval/disapproval and continue music intervention.
3. Evaluate.

Music Specifications: Student's choice

Recommended Time Limit: 10 minutes

Criteria for Objective:

Competency Assessment 3:   Minimum scores in each category
Overall minimum score = 72
Feedback given once per 15 seconds
Maintenance of 4:1 ratio of approval to disapproval

Techniques Included: Approving/Disapproving in 4:1 Ratio
Evaluating/Data

Discussion for Transfer:

1. Research shows a 4:1 ratio of approval to disapproval is most effective in maintaining behavior. Discuss how the procedure functioned in this situation with emphasis on contingent approval/ disapproval and frequency.
2. What happened in the second half of the intervention? Were appropriate behaviors "learned" so that the music structure maintained them? Why or why not?
3. Were approval/disapproval statements appropriate for age level/sophistication of adolescents? If not, what revision would be necessary?
4. Were the participants able to identify when approvals/disapprovals were not contingent? Do you think a actual adolescents with emotional disturbance would identify this?

OBJECTIVE 2.37

Use music to teach adolescent clients to accept responsibility for their actions.

Client Population: Adolescents aged 15–18 with behavior disorders in juvenile detention

Procedure:

Preparation:
1. Select two or three action steps that demonstrate acceptance of responsibility, i.e., no excuses, attaching consequences to action, no blame, etc.
2. Select or compose a song that expresses these concepts.
3. Plan some role-playing situations with incidents in which adolescents would have to accept responsibility for some action they had taken.
4. Develop evaluation plan.

Implementation:
1. Play music.
2. Lead group discussion.
3. Position each person to participate.
4. Set up role-playing situations in pairs to practice action steps for accepting responsibility. Provide brief written instructions for "actors" in role-plays.
5. Lead evaluation discussion with group on degree of satisfaction with the assigned roles and problem resolutions.

Music Specifications: Student's choice

Recommended Time Limit: 15 minutes

Criteria for Objective:

Competency Assessment 3:   Minimum scores in each category
Overall minimum score = 72

Techniques Included: Leading Group Discussion
Role-Playing
Evaluating

Discussion for Transfer:

1. Discuss actions demonstrating versus verbalizations responsibility. How can verbalization contribute to the manipulative abilities of clients? Is this a potential problem with adolescents?
2. What special problems do adolescents have participating in a group discussion? What skills can a leader use to deal with these?

3. What was the function of music in this situation? How could it have been used earlier or later in the session? Was this music current and likely to be preferred by teenagers? How would a music therapist know the "in" music for any given period? How often would this need to be updated to remain current?

OBJECTIVE 2.38

Teach a complex rhythm to adolescents while reinforcing the rules.

Client Population: Adolescents aged 13–15 with behavior disorders

Procedure:

Preparation:
1. Define three rules appropriate for adolescents with behavior disorders.
2. Plan a complex rhythm using a highly structured format that requires rule following.
3. Develop evaluation procedure.

Implementation:
1. State rules quickly and simply and start enforcing them immediately.
2. Conduct intervention. Approve rule following frequently and equally to all three rules. Keep music going.
3. Be sure approvals are appropriate to adolescents.
4. Evaluate.

Music Specifications: Student's choice

Recommended Time Limit: 15 minutes

Criteria for Objective:

>Competency Assessment 3:   Minimum scores in each category
>Overall minimum score = 72
>80% of clients following rules

Techniques Included: Use of Rules
Approving
Evaluating

Discussion for Transfer:

1. Adolescents sometimes fail to respond to approval of adults. How can a leader deal with this problem?
2. What was the function of music in this situation? How can continuing the music contribute to the interaction with problem students?
3. Would adolescents prefer the music presented?

OBJECTIVE 2.39

Use a music intervention to teach an adolescent group to control the emotion "anger."

Client Population: Adolescents aged 13–15 with emotional disturbance

Procedure:

> *Preparation:*
> 1. Specifically define anger and some action steps to control it, e.g., interruption, deep breathing, counting to 10, etc.
> 2. Develop a music intervention that requires the group to control anger, not express it.
> 3. Develop evaluation procedures.
>
> *Implementation:*
> 1. Model your specific definition of anger and its control; shape clients to imitate it in musical intervention. Encourage overcompensation of anger control.
> 2. Lead a group discussion on how to deal with anger in one's lifestyle.
> 3. Evaluate.

Music Specifications: Student's choice

Recommended Time Limit: 15 minutes

Criteria for Objective:

> Competency Assessment 3:   Minimum scores in each category
> Overall minimum score = 72

Techniques Included: Controlling Anger
Leading Group Discussion
Overcompensation
Evaluating

Discussion for Transfer:

> 1. What are the techniques for anger control? When should they be used? How is controlling anger different from expressing anger?
> 2. Persons with chronic anger-control problems may benefit from learning overcompensation techniques. Discuss what these are and how they could be taught.

OBJECTIVE 2.40

Use music to teach adolescents two specifically defined techniques for establishing a nonsexual relationship with the opposite sex.

Client Population: Adolescents aged 15–18 with emotional disturbance

Procedure:

Preparation:
1. Select two action steps for establishing a relationship, e.g., initiating friendliness, finding out about another person, listening attentively, etc.
2. Define parameters of a nonsexual relationship.
3. Select music that demonstrates these concepts.
4. Develop evaluation procedure.

Implementation:
1. Play music and introduce topic.
2. Teach the two techniques for establishing a relationship.
3. Use role-playing and keep the entire group participating.
4. Help each person plan one additional action step in this area and implement it.
5. Encourage commitment to try action step.
6. Evaluate.

Music Specifications: Student's choice

Recommended Time Limit: 15 minutes

Criteria for Objective:

Competency Assessment 3:   Minimum scores in each category
Overall minimum score = 72

Techniques Included: Establishing Relationships
Teaching Action Steps
Role-Playing
Evaluating

Discussion for Transfer:

1. Why might adolescents need to be taught how to establish relationships? Why nonsexual relationships? Would this be a threatening or nonthreatening task for adolescents with emotional instability?
2. Was the music chosen likely to be captivating to teenagers?

OBJECTIVE 2.41

Use music to teach adolescents to resist peer pressure.

Client Population: Adolescents aged 13–17 with behavior and/or emotional problems

Procedure:

Preparation:
1. Select action steps that adolescents could use to resist peer pressure (assertively saying no, reversing pressure, leading rather than following, use of humor, etc.).
2. Prepare role-playing situations in which adolescents might encounter peer pressure: taking drugs, riding with intoxicated driver, shoplifting, etc.
3. Select music that expresses these concepts.

Implementation:
1. Play music.
2. Begin role-playing situations.
3. When pressure is resisted, encourage group to signal recognition of this by group-designed cheer for team members. Approve creativity in dealing with those applying pressure.
4. Lead group discussion on "winning" at resisting peer pressure.
5. Evaluate.

Music Specifications: Student's choice

Recommended Time Limit: 15 minutes

Criteria for Objective:

Competency Assessment 3:   Minimum scores in each category
Overall minimum score = 72

Techniques Included: Role-Playing
Approving
Evaluating

Discussion for Transfer:

1. Discuss problems of resisting peer pressure. What are some techniques that might be effective?
2. Can teenagers be taught a value for resisting pressure? Why are action techniques probably more effective than lecturing techniques?
3. How could adolescents' propensity for group cohesiveness be used to help them resist inappropriate pressure?
4. Were music and group encouragement techniques age appropriate?

OBJECTIVE 2.42

Use music to teach three Reality-Orientation (RO) objectives.

Client Population: Geriatric clients aged 65–80 with memory loss

Procedure:

Preparation:
1. Select three RO objectives, e.g., day, time, place, current event, season.
2. Compose a song or songs to teach each objective.
3. Review cuing techniques.
4. Prepare visual materials to facilitate objectives (clock, calendar, newspaper, etc.).
5. Develop evaluation procedure.

Implementation:
1. Teach objectives through songs and paired visual materials.
2. Solicit individual feedback on selected objectives.
3. Approve remembering information.
4. Encourage spontaneous discussion of selected issues.
5. Evaluate.

Music Specifications:

1. A song or songs composed to teach three selected objectives.
2. Accompaniment on preferred instrument.

Recommended Time Limit: 15 minutes

Criteria for Objective:

Competency Assessment 3:   Minimum scores in each category
Overall minimum score = 72
80% accuracy on evaluation form

Techniques Included: Composing
Cuing
Evaluating

Discussion for Transfer:

1. Discuss how the selected objectives varied in difficulty. Could older adults with memory loss learn three objectives in one session? What would a realistic time line be for such a group to learn one of these tasks? How many repetitions? Would responses vary from day to day? How did individual responses vary? What can a leader do about these individual differences?

2. Discuss the function of music. Was it effective in teaching a skill? Would geriatric clients also need cues in addition to music? Was the music appropriate for the age and probable preference of geriatric clients? What does the research show to be the music preference of older adults?

OBJECTIVE 2.43

Teach eight different exercises synchronized to music.

Client Population: Geriatric clients aged 70–90 some of whom use wheelchairs for mobility

Procedure:

Preparation:
1. Select exercises that fit client age, level of physical ability, and need to exercise all parts of the body.
2. Select recorded music with probable appeal to this group that has a strong beat, then synchronize the exercises so they fit rhythmically and are in a sequence that is not too strenuous to complete.
3. Practice and memorize routine.
4. Develop evaluation procedure.

Implementation:
1. Teach each of the eight exercises with verbal cue to identify each. Use modeling and correction. Ensure that each exercise is practiced at tempo of recorded music to be used.
2. Turn on music and lead group through routine using cuing. Scan continuously to assess errors or nonparticipation.
3. Encourage participation, enjoyment, and rhythmic accuracy. Use physical proximity for encouragement.
4. Evaluate.

Music Specifications:

Recorded music of at least 64 measures, strong beat at tempo appropriate to physical abilities of group and of interest to them.

Recommended Time Limit: 5–7 minutes

Criteria for Objective:

Competency Assessment 3:   Minimum scores in each category
Overall minimum score = 72
Music selection as specified
Implementation in allotted time

Techniques Included: Group Leadership – Exercise
Cuing
Scanning
Evaluating

Discussion for Transfer:

1. How can exercises be adapted to varying degrees of physical disabilities?
2. What music would best stimulate exercise participation with elderly clients?
3. How would the accoutrements of exercise function in such a group, i.e., sweatbands, running shoes, stop watches, sweat shirts, etc.?
4. What precautions should the leader take in leading exercise groups with elderly persons?

OBJECTIVE 2.44

Use music to enhance social interaction.

Client Population: Geriatric clients aged 65–85

Procedure:

Preparation:
1. Specifically define "social interaction," i.e., asking question, listening, answering question, eliciting participation, looking at or smiling at another member, touching.
2. Develop music intervention to teach selected skills.
3. Develop evaluation procedure.

Implementation:
1. Place clients in circle with leader outside. Move around circle to cue looking at others and talking.
2. Conduct planned intervention. Be sure to teach clients to interact with other clients, not leader.
3. If spontaneous interactions begin, withdraw and let them develop. If they subside, move closer and begin cuing interaction again.
4. Evaluate.

Music Specifications: Student's choice

Recommended Time Limit: 15 minutes

Criteria for Objective:

> Competency Assessment 3:   Minimum scores in each category
> Overall minimum score = 72
> 80% accuracy on evaluation form

Techniques Included: Stimulating Group Interaction / Socialization
                             Cuing
                             Evaluating

Discussion for Transfer:

1. Discuss special geriatric problems that tend to dissipate group interaction.
2. How can these problems be overcome through learning new techniques?
3. What problems could groups attempt to solve that would stimulate interaction?

OBJECTIVE 2.45

Assist older adults to plan a musical performance that can be videotaped and sent to their families as a present.

Client Population: Retired adults residing in assisted living or retirement community

Procedure:

> *Preparation:*
> 1. Select a music intervention as warm-up for the group.
> 2. Plan group discussion and feasible activities that might be suggested.
>
> *Implementation:*
> 1. Conduct music intervention as warm-up.
> 2. Lead group discussion on topic.
> 3. Ensure that everyone participates and has a definite role in plan.
> 4. Select one intervention to begin practicing.

Music Specifications: Student's choice

Recommended Time Limit: 15 minutes

Criteria for Objective:

> Competency Assessment 3:   Minimum scores in each category
> Overall minimum score = 72

Techniques Included: Leading a Group Discussion
Conducting Musical Warm-Up / Socialization

Discussion for Transfer:

> 1. Why might a videotape function as a very special gift to families? How could each individual be spotlighted?
> 2. Could an audio recording serve the same function if it were an individual vs. group project?

OBJECTIVE 2.46

Use music to increase positive interactions between nursing home clients and their caretakers.

Client Population: Residents (65+) in a long-term care facility

Procedure:

Preparation:
1. Select music that expresses appreciation for a special person.
2. Prepare "Appreciation Medals" for each client to award.

Implementation:
1. Sing song. Teach it if it is not already known.
2. Introduce topic of appreciating special people and use group discussion techniques to get clients involved in discussing positive staff interactions.
3. Help each person identify a staff member whom they sincerely appreciate.
4. Ensure that clients choose a variety of staff by suggesting people at all administrative levels and in different departments.
5. Lead clients through facility, strolling and singing selected song while clients make awards to selected staff.
6. Evaluate.

Music Specifications: Student's choice

Recommended Time Limit: 15 minutes

Criteria for Objective:

> Competency Assessment 3:   Minimum scores in each category
> Overall minimum score = 72

Techniques Included: Approving
Leading Group Discussion
Song Leading
Positive Interactions
Evaluating

Discussion for Transfer:

1. Discuss problems of long-term care residents and their relationship to caretakers.
2. What is the role of the music therapist in a long-term care facility? Should it include enhancing relationships with the staff?
3. How did the music function in this situation? What other functions could it have to enhance positive interactions?

OBJECTIVE 2.47

Teach presurgical patients the use of music listening and focused attention to deal with postoperative pain.

Client Population: Presurgical patients aged 18 or above

Procedure:

Preparation:
1. Select music that is probably of interest to clients.
2. Select short relaxation routine that moves quickly to focus attention on a musical element (listening for a particular instrument, counting crescendos, etc.).
3. Synchronize relaxation routine with music.
4. Develop evaluation procedure.

Implementation:
1. Play music and implement relaxation routine.
2. Teach focused attention task.
3. Help each person select personal music for surgery.

Music Specifications: Student's choice

Recommended Time Limit: 15 minutes

Criteria for Objective:

Competency Assessment 3:   Minimum scores in each category
Overall minimum score = 72

Techniques Included: Focused Attention
Music Listening
Evaluating

Discussion for Transfer:

1. Research shows that the individual patient's preferred music is probably the most effective in reducing pain. How can this be dealt with in a group situation?
2. Clients may develop their own focused-attention task. What should the leader do if this is reported?

OBJECTIVE 2.48

Use music and relaxation to teach stress reduction.

Client Population: General hospital patients with heart disease, high blood pressure, ulcers, or other medical condition exacerbated by stress (e.g., epilepsy)

Procedure:

Preparation:
1. Review Objective 2.09 tension/relaxation procedures. Review information about stress and its physiological effects.
2. Plan tension/relaxation routine that emphasizes awareness of biological signs of tension/stress versus relaxation—muscle tension, fatigue or pain, pulse rate, breathing, etc.
3. Select music and prepare uninterrupted tape synchronized to routine.
4. Develop evaluation procedure.

Implementation:
1. Tell group they are role-playing persons with medical diagnoses related to stress.
2. Conduct relaxation intervention to music as per Objective 2.09.
3. Have clients sit up, then practice achieving immediate relaxed state in response to music being turned on. After five repetitions of this, have clients achieve immediate relaxed state while imagining the music.
4. Lead group discussion about effects of tension/stress on medical problems and use of music to implement immediately relaxed state.
5. Evaluate.

Music Specifications:

1. Recorded music played at low enough background level of volume to allow you to be easily heard over it, which is instrumental (nonverbal) and probably perceived by clients as "quiet music."
2. Uninterrupted recording prepared and synchronized as specified.
3. Use of music player that provides quality playback for size of room and setting.

Recommended Time Limit: 15 minutes

Criteria for Objective:

Competency Assessment 3:   Minimum scores in each category
Overall minimum score = 72

Techniques Included: Teaching Relaxation Techniques
Evaluating

Discussion for Transfer:

1. Discuss relaxation procedures in general. (See Objective 2.09.)
2. Discuss how achievement of "immediate relaxed state" might be evaluated other than through patient report.
3. Discuss how imagining the music might facilitate #2 above and how many repetitions might be necessary to master the ability.

OBJECTIVE 2.49

Demonstrate "realistic life goals" by leading a group discussion on modification versus realization of desirable life goals. Use music to introduce positive perspective.

Client Population: Patients with a catastrophic illness/injury

Procedure:

Preparation:
1. Select music as specified.
2. Plan ways to elicit discussion from members who might be angry.
3. Use empathetic listening—repeating what client said back to the individual.
4. Develop evaluation procedure.

Implementation:
1. Play music.
2. Lead group discussion. Approve members for participation.
3. Elicit participation from everyone by demonstrating empathetic listening.
4. Try to shape discussion toward indicators of positive acceptance of terminal illness.
5. Evaluate.

Note: Instructor will assign nonparticipatory roles to participants.

Music Specifications: Student's choice

Recommended Time Limit: 15 minutes

Criteria for Objective:

Competency Assessment 3:   Minimum scores in each category
Overall minimum score = 72

Techniques Included: Leading Group Discussion
Empathetic Listening
Evaluating

Discussion for Transfer:

1. What are the indicators that someone has accepted the reality of his or her illness or injury?
2. How can group members be taught by the leader to be supportive of each other?
3. How can a leader accept all types of participation while shaping toward a specific goal?
4. How does empathetic listening function in this situation?

OBJECTIVE 2.50

Use music to assist persons with catastrophic illness to select one action step to deal with their diagnosis.

Client Population: Patients with terminal illness who have entered hospice care

Procedure:

> *Preparation:*
> Select inspirational, nonreligious music as background for intervention.
>
> *Implementation:*
> 1. Play music.
> 2. Have clients make a list of things they want to do.
> 3. Assist each person to select one thing from list that can be done today and make a commitment to it.
> 4. Elicit feedback about commitment.
> 5. Evaluate.

Music Specifications: Student's choice

Recommended Time Limit: 15 minutes

Criteria for Objective:

> Competency Assessment 3:   Minimum scores in each category
> Overall minimum score = 72

Techniques Included: Teaching Action Steps
Evaluating

Discussion for Transfer:

1. Discuss protection of client privacy in group situations. Would this topic be an important one on which to maintain privacy?
2. How can commitment to a task be discerned and evaluated?

OBJECTIVE 2.51

Use music to enhance relationships between family members.

Client Population: Support group for families who have a member with a terminal illness

Procedure:

Preparation:
1. Select two techniques for enhancing a family relationship, e.g., initiating closeness, exploring another person's feelings, speaking openly, listening attentively.
2. Select music that incorporates or demonstrates these concepts.

Implementation:
1. Play music and introduce topic.
2. Teach the selected techniques for enhancing a relationship.
3. Break participants into "families" and use role-playing to practice techniques. Keep everyone participating.
4. Help each family work out one additional action step to implement at home.
5. Encourage commitment to try action step.
6. Evaluate.

Music Specifications: Student's choice

Recommended Time Limit: 15 minutes

Criteria for Objective:

Competency Assessment 3:   Minimum scores in each category
Overall minimum score = 72

Techniques Included: Establishing Relationships
Role-Playing
Evaluating

Discussion for Transfer:

1. Why might families need to be taught how to enhance a relationship with a member with a catastrophic illness? Could this be a threatening task?
2. How did the music function in this intervention? What other ways music could be used with this objective?

OBJECTIVE 2.52

Use music to teach families of organ donors how to be positive about their decision and to deal with probable negative confrontations from others.

Client Population: Families of organ donors

Procedure:

Preparation:
1. Select inspirational music that promotes the concept of sharing the gift of life and that is nonreligious.
2. Review group discussion techniques in Objective 2.49.
3. Develop evaluation procedure.

Implementation:
1. Separate participants into several family units.
2. Play music and lead discussion on positive aspects of the decision.
3. Have each family discuss among themselves the person most likely to feel negative about their decision.
4. Have each family role-play this person, verbally confronting them on this topic.
5. Lead group discussion on most effective ways of handling such problems. Role-play these action steps.
6. Play music again and have members be supportive of each other's decision.
7. Evaluate.

Music Specifications: Student's choice

Recommended Time Limit: 15 minutes

Criteria for Objective:

Competency Assessment 3: Minimum scores in each category
Overall minimum score = 72

Techniques Included: Empathy
Role-Playing
Teaching Action Steps
Evaluating

Discussion for Transfer:

Next of kin must give permission for organ donation. What pressure does this place on the deciding individual with the rest of the family? Are such decisions usually unanimous?

OBJECTIVE 2.53

Develop a music intervention dealing with identifying roles of family members in a group interaction.

Client Population: Families in distress

Note: Instructor will divide participants into families and give them role instructions.

Procedure:

Preparation:
1. Identify possible roles of family members: authoritarian, dissenter, victim, facilitator, etc.
2. Collect a variety of rhythm instruments.
3. Select recorded music to be used with rhythmic activity.
4. Develop evaluation procedure.

Implementation:
1. Make available groups of instruments to each family.
2. Have clients select instruments and work out group-coordinated accompaniment to music.
3. After playing accompaniment, have family self-analyze their roles. Ask them if each likes the role he or she played. If not, repeat the activity by having the family design a new accompaniment while each person plays the role selected.
4. Lead discussion on how the family interaction changes as the roles change.
5. Evaluate.

Music Specifications: Student's choice

Recommended Time Limit: 15 minutes

Criteria for Objective:

> Competency Assessment 3:   Minimum scores in each category
> Overall minimum score = 72

Techniques Included: Leading Group Discussion
Role Analysis
Family Counseling
Evaluating

Discussion for Transfer:

1. What are the possible roles in family interactions? Which are beneficial and which are detrimental?
2. How could the family work toward permanently changing its interaction patterns?
3. What was the function of music in this situation?

OBJECTIVE 2.54

Use music to teach clients to control anger with children.

Client Population: Parents who abuse their children

Procedure:

Preparation:
1. Specifically define anger. Develop tension routine to help clients identify physiological sensations that precede anger.
2. Select an anger-control action step, e.g., leave room and implement relaxation routine, then make nonviolent plan to deal with problem, and music application.
3. Do not allow persons to engage in music behaviors that act out anger (like beating drums), since this is what you wish to inhibit.

Implementation:
1. Model your definition of anger and its control; shape clients to imitate. Conduct music intervention.
2. Role-play situations with children and let members practice control. Lead a group discussion on how to control anger with one's children.
3. Evaluate.

Music Specifications: Student's choice

Recommended Time Limit: 15 minutes

Criteria for Objective:

Competency Assessment 3:   Minimum scores in each category
Overall minimum score = 72

Techniques Included: Anger Control
Role-Playing
Parenting Techniques
Evaluating

Discussion for Transfer:

1. How can people with anger-control problems learn to censor violence when angry?
2. What might be a detrimental effect of substituting anger responses such as drum beating versus child beating?

OBJECTIVE 2.55

Develop a music intervention to help family members enhance their positive interactions.

Client Population: A family in distress.

Note: Instructor will divide participants into families and give them role instructions.

Procedure:

Preparation:
1. Write a short, simple rap about family membership.
2. Develop a data-collection procedure to assess positive interactions.

Implementation:
1. Teach clients to rap using the Family Rap you wrote.
2. Break groups into families to rehearse rap for performance. Move among clients and approve positive interactions.
3. Have families perform. Stimulate enthusiastic applause from audience.
4. Have each family write a new rap verse about themselves. Use form to observe interactions.
5. Have families perform new verses in sequence interspersed with entire group doing rap chorus.
6. Have families talk among themselves about how they felt while interacting to plan the rap and make a plan to try interacting this way at home on a short, 5-minute, preselected task.

Music Specifications: Rap as specified above.

Recommended Time Limit: 15 minutes

Criteria for Objective:

> Competency Assessment 3: Minimum scores in each category
> Overall minimum score = 72
> 80% positive family interactions

Techniques Included: Composing
Rapping
Approving
Leading Group Discussion
Evaluating/Data

Discussion for Transfer:

1. What positive roles were observed in the family interactions?
2. How could a family work toward permanently changing its interaction patterns?
3. What was the function of music in this situation?

OBJECTIVE 2.56

Teach a square dance to clients using more outgoing members as tutor partners for more withdrawn members.

Client Population: Persons aged 25–60 with chronic mental illness

Procedure:

Preparation:
1. Select 10 sequential steps for a simple square dance.
2. Do a task analysis to determine most concise, descriptive directions, effective cues for each, and number of beats necessary to complete step.
3. Memorize task analysis.
4. Plan ways to cue tutors to stimulate participation in their partners.
5. Develop evaluation procedure.

Implementation:
1. Teach dance using chaining, cuing, and correcting.
2. Scan continuously to determine persons needing additional cues and respond accordingly.
3. Approve all spontaneous participation and spontaneous interactions between partners.
4. Evaluate.

Music Specifications:

Recorded music, instrumental, appropriate for dance.

Recommended Time Limit: 15 minutes

Criteria for Objective:

Competency Assessment 3:   Minimum scores in each category
Overall minimum score = 72
90% directions followed

Techniques Included: Chaining
Cuing
Task Analysis
Peer Tutoring
Approving
Evaluating

Discussion for Transfer:

1. Discuss whether the difficulty of the dance matched probable clients capabilities.
2. Discuss additional cues or ways to further stimulate participation and interaction.
3. Discuss behaviors that persons with chronic illness might exhibit which would be socially inappropriate, i.e., rocking, not participating, dancing alone. How would the therapist handle these behaviors?

OBJECTIVE 2.57

Use music to teach social interaction in a music rehearsal.

Client Population: Persons aged 25–60 with chronic mental illness

Procedure:

Preparation:
1. Specifically define appropriate "social interaction," e.g., asking question, listening, answering question, and eliciting participation.
2. Develop music intervention in a performing ensemble structure to teach selected skills. (Ensemble suggestions: chorus, choir chimes/hand bells, drum circle)
3. Develop evaluation procedure.

Implementation:
1. Place clients in ensemble rehearsal format.
2. Conduct planned intervention. Be sure to teach clients to interact with other members, not leader.
3. If spontaneous interactions begin, withdraw and let them develop. If they subside, move closer and begin cuing.
4. Evaluate.

Music Specifications: Student's choice

Recommended Time Limit: 15 minutes

Criteria for Objective:

Competency Assessment 3:   Minimum scores in each category
Overall minimum score = 72
90% client interaction

Techniques Included: Stimulating Group Interaction / Socialization
Evaluating
Cuing

Discussion for Transfer:

1. Discuss special problems of chronic psychiatric patients that tend to reduce group interaction.
2. How can these problems be overcome through learning new techniques?
3. What problems could music groups be given to solve that would stimulate interaction?
4. When would the music interfere with interaction?
5. How could this be structured?

OBJECTIVE 2.58

Use a music intervention to facilitate reality-based verbalizations.

Client Population: Persons with acute psychiatric disturbance

Note: Instructor will assign some participants to exhibit psychotic behavior (delusional thinking, paranoia, pressured speech, flat affect, etc.).

Procedure:

Preparation:
1. Write a simple rap that incorporates facts about clients and setting.
2. Plan evaluation procedure.

Implementation:
1. Teach clients the reality rap.
2. Have clients discuss the "here and now," the reality of where they are, with whom, and for what reason.
3. Ignore hallucinatory, delusional, or nonfactual statements. Verify all reality statements.
4. Evaluate.

Music Specifications: Rap as specified above.

Recommended Time Limit: 15 minutes

Criteria for Objective:

Competency Assessment 3:   Minimum scores in each category
Overall minimum score = 72
80% appropriate, reality-based client behavior

Techniques Included: Leading Group Discussion
Ignoring
Approving
Rapping

Discussion for Transfer:

1. What are the differences among hallucinations, delusions, paranoia, non-reality-based thoughts and perceptions?
2. How can music function to stimulate awareness of the present reality? What music activities might stimulate non-reality-based thought?

OBJECTIVE 2.59

Use music to teach clients two realistic action steps to begin resolving a problem in their life.

Client Population: Persons hospitalized for long-term depression

Procedure:

Preparation:
1. Select and specify action steps focusing on potentially positive outcomes of a situation while extinguishing blame, anger, and grief. Possible positive techniques include thought stopping, perceiving situation as growth opportunity, putting situation in perspective, making and implementing a decision, etc.
2. Select or compose music to introduce the concepts in the selected steps.
3. Practice and memorize music if it is to be performed or acquire recording and quality playback equipment.

Implementation:
1. Perform or play recorded music.
2. Have brief discussion about disappointment and problems and how it is possible to learn to deal with them. State that the task is to practice some possible techniques.
3. Describe selected Action Step 1 and give an example.
4. Have group role-play and practice the technique in simulated problem situations.
5. Have each person apply this step to a personal situation by writing out a short plan.
6. Repeat steps 3, 4, and 5 for Action Step 2.
7. Play music again and lead group discussion on how the perception of the problem might have changed.
8. Evaluate, using plans written by each person.

Music Specifications:

Music to be performed or played that conveys concepts of the action steps selected.

Recommended Time Limit: 15 minutes

Criteria for Objective:

Competency Assessment 3: Minimum scores in each category
Overall minimum score = 72

Techniques Included: Role-Playing
Teaching Action Steps
Evaluating

Discussion for Transfer:

1. Research shows that music can affect mood. Did it in this situation? Did it function to motivate taking the action step? If so, when—at beginning or end of session?
2. What specific behaviors did leader use to elicit, support, motivate, etc., the clients?
3. Do these behaviors differ from "simply telling a person what to do to solve the problem"?
4. Fifteen minutes is too short a period of time in which to conduct this session in a real, clinical situation. If it were extended across an hour, how would it be conducted?

OBJECTIVE 2.60

Plan a facility-wide special occasion dance (e.g., Valentine's Day) with entry criteria to increase social skills.

Client Population: Persons in residential facility with chronic mental illness

Procedure:

Preparation:
1. Determine minimum social criteria for dance entry that is slightly above that usually exhibited by client group. Consider dress code, attending with partner or guest, participation in dance preparation, etc.
2. Develop evaluation procedure.

Implementation:
1. Lead and focus group discussion to set entry criteria. Insure that predetermined criteria are included.
2. Play recorded dance music and help group practice (role-play) selected social skills.
3. Help clients plan what to wear and how to organize preparations.
4. Evaluate.

Music Specifications:

Dance music preferred by client group.

Recommended Time Limit: 15 minutes

Criteria for Objective:

Competency Assessment 3:   Minimum scores in each category
Overall minimum score = 72

Techniques Included: Leading Focused Group Discussion
Teaching Social Skills
Role-Playing
Evaluating

Discussion for Transfer:

1. Discuss how social skills can be taught with music as a contingency.
2. Discuss importance of treating adults with mental illness as adults even though interaction by necessity might be simplified.
3. Discuss other social skills that would be important to teach these clients.

Level 3 Competencies

Tasks at this level are designed to

a. maintain and improve students' musical, personal, and group leadership skills.
b. increase students' expertise in utilizing music to achieve primary therapeutic objectives with a variety of client groups, including:

-   Adolescents with hearing loss in an inclusive setting
-   Adults in counseling including the treatment of passive aggressive tendency and agoraphobia
-   Adults with acute mental health crises including depression and suicidal ideation
-   Adults with chronic mental illness
-   Adults with cognitive impairments
-   Children and their abusive parents
-   Children who have autism spectrum disorders with typical peers
-   Children with emotional disturbance
-   Couples in counseling for communication problems
-   Parents of newborns in the Neonatal Intensive Care Unit
-   Patients receiving hospice services
-   Persons recovering from strokes including the treatment of motor and communication impairments
-   Persons who are abusing substances or are chemically dependent and their treatment staff
-   Preschoolers in early intervention
-   Preschoolers with developmental disabilities in an inclusive setting
-   Students with disruptive behaviors
-   Older adults with emerging dementia

c. teach students to design and conduct music activities that meet the multiple needs of a clients by incorporating two or more objectives while quantifying responses for evaluating effectiveness.

Note: Time limits are kept short (15–20 minutes) to facilitate multiple simulations in one class period. They may not be realistic for true clinical situations; discussion of each simulation should include appropriate opening and closing activities and pacing for these sessions. At some point, the instructor may wish to give each student an assigned time limit of 40–45 minutes to demonstrate more comprehensive leadership skills.

OBJECTIVE 3.01

Use music to teach assertiveness in expressing emotions (including anger).

Client Population: Adults with passive-aggressive tendencies

Procedure:

Preparation:
1. Specifically define at least two assertive behaviors to be taught.
2. Identify two emotions to express in addition to anger.
3. Plan role-playing situations in which these behaviors can be demonstrated.
4. Plan "spontaneous" transfer intervention for end of session in which level of assertiveness can be measured.
5. Develop form to assess assertiveness.
6. Select or compose music.

Implementation:
1. Discuss traits of passive-aggressive reaction to problems. Use negative modeling to give examples.
2. Describe and demonstrate two assertive behaviors.
3. Involve clients in role-playing the demonstrated techniques to express the identified emotional responses. Alternate with negative modeling of passive-aggressive reaction to same situation.
4. Teach discrimination of appropriate behavior.
5. Conduct transfer intervention and evaluate assertiveness.
6. Use song at end of session to motivate people to try these techniques when encountering their next problem.

Music Specifications: Student's choice

Recommended Time Limit: 15 minutes

Criteria for Objective:

Competency Assessment 3:   Minimum scores in each category
Overall minimum score = 75

Techniques Included: Action Steps for Assertiveness
Anger Control
Role-Playing
Negative Modeling
Evaluating/Data

Discussion for Transfer:

1. When does assertiveness become aggression? How can the leader assure that clients discriminate the difference?

2. In what situations would a person with passive-aggressive tendencies have the most difficulty being assertive? Could these be structured as role-playing assignments?

3. How can the leader get feedback on how effectively the client applies these newly learned action steps when in the "real" world of his or her everyday environment?

OBJECTIVE 3.02

Use music to teach the benefits of music therapy for persons recovering from substance abuse/dependence.

Population: Staff members of an in-patient drug and alcohol rehabilitation center (e.g., administrators, physicians, nurses, social workers, substance abuse counselors, etc.)

Procedure:

Preparation:
1. Investigate rehab facilities structure, clientele, philosophies, and clinicians.
2. Identify two clinical goals that are addressed in rehab toward which you will direct your music therapy intervention as a part of the presentation
3. Plan a brief introduction to music therapy, an intervention(s) to achieve identified clinical goals, and enough remaining time for brief question/answer session
4. Create a one-page informational handout on music therapy services. Make copies of the handout for attendees.
5. Locate necessary music equipment.

Implementation:
1. Begin presentation with short music intervention.
2. Distribute handout and present introduction to music therapy.
3. Conduct intervention.
4. Discuss progress attendees made toward clinical goals.
5. Answer questions asked by attendees.

Music Specifications: Student's choice

Recommended Time Limit: 15 minutes

Criteria for Objective:

    Competency Assessment 3:   Minimum scores in each category
    Overall minimum score = 75

Techniques Included: Inservice presentation
                                  Evaluating

Discussion for Transfer:

1. How did beginning the inservice with music influence the outcome?
2. Did the presenter select essential information about music therapy? If not, what was omitted?
3. What would need to be changed about the intervention presented if it were conducted with actual persons in recovery?

OBJECTIVE 3.03

Use music to reduce inappropriate behavior in the lunchroom by letting disruptive students
    a. formulate guidelines
    b. select music
    c. enforce the contingencies

Client Population: Disruptive 7th and 8th grade students

Procedure:

Preparation:
1. Develop a priori guidelines.
2. Develop role-playing situations.
3. Identify possible music resources that probably would be preferred by teenagers and acquire quality equipment for playback.
4. Develop form to assess accuracy of contingency enforcement.

Implementation:
1. Lead discussion on lunchroom problems.
2. Propose use of music and its contingent interruption to improve situation.
3. Let students select music (radio station, recordings).
4. Focus discussion to formulate guidelines for appropriate behavior and operation of the music contingency.
5. Involve students in role-playing to train them to enforce the guidelines.
6. Approve all instances of correct enforcement and indicators of commitment toward implementation.
7. Have students assess whether contingencies are enforced.

Music Specifications: Student's choice

Recommended Time Limit: 15 minutes

Criteria for Objective:

    Competency Assessment 3:   Minimum scores in each category
    Overall minimum score = 75

Techniques Included: Music Interruption
                                  Focused Group Discussion
                                  Approving
                                  Self-Evaluating Data

Discussion for Transfer:

1. Research shows music interruption can function to decrease inappropriate behavior. How did it function in this situation?
2. Why would letting disruptive students set the guidelines function to improve lunchroom behavior?
3. How would self-evaluation of contingency enforcement function in this situation?
4. Research also shows that peer punishment is usually more severe than that of authority figures. How would focusing discussion toward a priori guidelines prevent teens from being too strict?

OBJECTIVE 3.04

Use music intervention within the SCERTS Model to teach joint attention and decision making.

Client Population: Three children aged 2–4 with autism spectrum disorders (ASD) and two typical peers (aged 2–4)

Procedure:

Preparation:
1. Read research article—Walworth, D. (2007). The use of music therapy within the SCERTS model for children with autism spectrum disorder. *Journal of Music Therapy, 44*(1), 2–22.
2. Develop a music intervention that requires all children to focus on a single object, person, or event. Song composition or arranging will likely be necessary.
3. Develop a music intervention that allows decision making.
4. Prepare systematic musical transitions between interventions.
5. Develop evaluation tool for children with ASD.

Implementation:
1. Set up space for session by defining setting area with chairs or mats and placing equipment in an area accessible to the leader that does not distract children.
2. Direct music interventions and transitional music.
3. Reinforce children individually for joint attention and choosing in an age appropriate manner.
4. Evaluate.

Music Specifications: Student's choice

Recommended Time Limit: 15 minutes

Criteria for Objective:

     Competency Assessment 3:   Minimum scores in each category
     Overall minimum score = 75

Techniques Included: Song Composing / Arranging
                                    Decision Making
                                    Focused Attention
                                    Transitioning
                                    Evaluating

Discussion for Transfer:

1. Which objective was the easier to achieve through music?
2. How did the transitional music function? Was it effective?
3. What music interventions would achieve the same goals for children with ASD who are over age 10? For adults over age 20?

OBJECTIVE 3.05

Use a regularly scheduled facility-wide dance as a reinforcer to encourage and teach reality-based, appropriate social behavior.

Client Population: Persons with chronic psychiatric illness and staff in mental health facility

Procedure:

Preparation:
1. Plan entry criteria for dance (dress, hygiene, price of admission, which might be a ticket earned in a therapy session that week).
2. Plan guidelines for dancing (must have partner, must face partner while dancing, no rocking, etc.).
3. Plan instructions for staff in attendance to monitor and reinforce appropriate behavior.
4. Plan dance music, refreshments, decorations.

Implementation:
1. Assign Axis I diagnoses to participants using the current edition of the *Diagnostic and Statistical Manual of Mental Disorders (DSM)*.
2. Implement entry criteria, cue staff to assist.
3. Begin dancing. Cue staff to assist in approving and maintaining guidelines.
4. Approve staff for assisting and clients for appropriate social behavior.
5. Evaluate effect of intervention on appropriate social behavior.

Music Specifications: Student's choice

Recommended Time Limit: 15 minutes

Criteria for Objective:

Competency Assessment 3:   Minimum scores in each category
Overall minimum score = 75

Techniques Included: Using Music as a Reinforcer
Cuing
Approving
Evaluating

Discussion for Transfer:

1. Why would staff traditionally believe that dealing with problems (emergencies, fights, seizures) was their only responsibility at a dance? How could this attitude be changed over time? What would be the payoff for staff to change this belief?

2. Why might a dance with no entry criteria or no restrictions on "appropriate" dancing actually allow persons with chronic mental illness to further habituate their symptoms?

3. What is the responsibility of the music therapist to teach facility staff how music can best be used in a treatment plan?

OBJECTIVE 3.06

Use music to teach clients with depression an action behavior to reduce the depression.

Client Population: Patients who are depressed patients in a short-term facility

Procedure:

Preparation:
1. Select several action steps to reduce depression that cover cognitive, emotional, and physiological issues.
2. Select a music intervention to teach one or more (exercising to music, thought stopping through music listening, etc.).
3. Select music needed.
4. Develop form to assess effect of intervention.

Implementation:
1. Teach the action step, as well as when and how to use that action to reduce depression. Role-play implementation.
2. Have each client select one additional action step that could be taken to reduce depression.
3. Assess effectiveness of intervention.

Music Specifications: Student's choice

Recommended Time Limit: 20 minutes

Criteria for Objective:

     Competency Assessment 3:   Minimum scores in each category
     Overall minimum score = 75

Techniques Included: Teaching Action Steps
                                  Role-Playing
                                  Evaluating/Data

Discussion for Transfer:

1. Why would depressed persons need a plan of action that covered physiological, cognitive, and emotional issues? How could music be effectively incorporated into all these areas?
2. Research shows that medication is most effective immediately in reducing depression, while counseling or therapy is more effective in maintaining stability across the long term. How would this intervention as described maximize the both immediate and long-term effects?

OBJECTIVE 3.07

Use music to teach two or three academic concepts while shaping individualized social behaviors for each member.

Client Population: Preschoolers (aged 3–5) with cerebral palsy (2 or 3) in an inclusive setting with typically developing children aged 3–5

Procedure:

Preparation:
1. Select two or three academic tasks at the preschool level (colors, numbers, identifying letters, etc.). Select music for each. See Repertoire List, PreKindergarten Songs (p. 234).
2. Plan a different individual social behavior to be taught to each client (waiting turn, speaking softly, keeping hands in lap, etc.).
3. Develop form to assess both academic and social behavior.

Implementation:
1. Assign roles to participants with each having a specific social problem.
2. Direct music activities and teach academic tasks while shaping individual social behaviors. Cue each member to use appropriate behavior and approve those who do.
3. Evaluate effect of intervention on academic and social behaviors.

Music Specifications: Student's choice

Recommended Time Limit: 15 minutes

Criteria for Objective:

Competency Assessment 3:   Minimum scores in each category
Overall minimum score = 75

Techniques Included: Cuing
Approving
Ignoring
Evaluating

Discussion for Transfer:

1. Why would the ability to individualize instruction be important for preschoolers, especially those with cerebral palsy?
2. Why would it be important to teach these children in a group setting vs. one to one? Is MT a good technique for grouping such clients?

3. How can a leader acquire the skill of attending to the needs of individuals while implementing the intervention in a group setting?

OBJECTIVE 3.08

Use music to teach client to establish a relationship with others in the group.

Client Population: Clients with suicidal ideation

Note: Instructor will assign some participants to simulate clients with suicidal ideation and some to be therapy assistants.

Procedure:

Preparation:
1. Select music intervention to best help people establish a new relationship.
2. Review procedures in Objective 2.11 on how to lead a focused group discussion.
3. Develop means to assess effect of intervention.

Implementation:
1. Direct clients in intervention. Use supportive, approving techniques to help members initiate relationships.
2. Lead focused group discussion to help members verbalize commitment to each other and therapy.
3. Help members verbalize commitment to initiate a relationship outside the session. Help each develop a plan to accomplish this.
4. Assess the effects of this session.

Music Specifications: Student's choice

Recommended Time Limit: 20 minutes

Criteria for Objective:

> Competency Assessment 3:   Minimum scores in each category
> Overall minimum score = 75

Techniques Included: Teaching an Interpersonal Skill
Leading Focused Group Discussion
Teaching Action Steps
Evaluating

Discussion for Transfer:

1. Why might commitment to others help a person contemplating suicide maintain stability from one week to the next? Why might it not?
2. Why might initiating relationships be an initial goal for all members of such a group? Would this be the terminal goal for such clients?
3. With whom should such clients try to establish a relationship?

OBJECTIVE 3.09

Lead a focused group discussion on the negative consequences of drug abuse emphasizing harm to significant others.

Client Population: Clients who abuse substances and clients who are chemically dependent

Procedure:

Preparation:
1. Acquire and learn facts about substance abuse (incidence, amounts, frequency of typical abuse, age of most abusers, etc.).
2. Select relevant music for use before, during, or after discussion.
3. Review procedures for focused group discussion (Objective 2.11).

Implementation:
1. Lead discussion and shape the clients to focus on the assigned topic. Contribute facts about abuse as appropriate and use music at some point in the discussion. Have clients monitor and eliminate denial responses.
2. Approve clients for participation by nonverbal means.
3. Ensure that all clients participate.
4. Evaluate your effectiveness as a leader.

Music Specifications: Student's choice

Recommended Time Limit: 15 minutes

Criteria for Objective:

   Competency Assessment 3:   Minimum scores in each category
   Overall minimum score = 75

Techniques Included: Leading Focused Group Discussion
                            Nonverbal Approving
                            Evaluating

Discussion for Transfer:

1. What are the benefits of denial monitoring by the clients?
2. What was the effect on the discussion of the leader inserting specific facts about abuse? Should therapists know such facts about the disorders with which they deal?

OBJECTIVE 3.10

Use music to help couples learn appropriate techniques for improved communication.

Client Population: Couples in counseling with communication problems

Note: Instructor will assign a few participants to be resistive or hostile.

Procedure:

Preparation:
1. Define specific techniques of effective communication (initiating, responding, listening, giving feedback about what is heard, etc.).
2. Develop a music intervention to teach the above. Select appropriate music.
3. Develop form to assess communication skills of each couple.

Implementation:
1. Divide class into couples.
2. Use music to teach basic guidelines/techniques for effective communication. Identify resistive and hostile clients and shape them in more positive, participatory behaviors.
3. Give couples time during the session to practice communication skills in a variety of situations, e.g., expressing affection, solving a serious problem.
4. Evaluate.

Music Specifications: Student's choice

Recommended Time Limit: 20 minutes

Criteria for Objective:

　　Competency Assessment 3:   Minimum scores in each category
　　Overall minimum score = 75

Techniques Included: Teaching an Interpersonal Skill
　　　　　　　　　　　　　　 Evaluating

Discussion for Transfer:

1. Are effective communication techniques situational (expression of affection versus problem solving)? What communication skills are common to all interactions?
2. What is communication? What is the goal? How do you know if it is good or bad? If you have good communication, do you have a good relationship?

OBJECTIVE 3.11

Use music to improve gait and ambulation abilities.

Client Population: Patients with residual stroke symptoms

Procedure:

Preparation:
1. Select music to match these three gait problems: use of walker, shuffling with minimal stride length at fast tempo, and limping with one normal and one short stride due to one dysfunctional leg.
2. Plan instruction to correct stride with physical and verbal cues for each.
3. Develop form to assess improvement in stride.

Implementation:
1. Divide participants into three diagnoses specified. Work with one client at a time while others evaluate and give positive feedback to their peers.
2. Use music, cues, and instructions about walking to regulate rhythm and stride for each client. Approve trying, continuing, and improved gait.
3. After each client begins to improve, cut off music volume for a few seconds and encourage clients to continue, then resume music. Continue intermittent interruption for longer periods of time.
4. Evaluate effectiveness of intervention.

Music Specifications:

Music matched to three gait problems: use of walker (3/4 time), shuffling with minimal stride length (2/4 or 4/4 time), and dysfunction of one leg in shortened stride on one side (2/4 or 4/4 time).

Recommended Time Limit: 20 minutes

Criteria for Objective:

Competency Assessment 3:   Minimum scores in each category
Overall minimum score = 75

Techniques Included: Gait Training
Approving
Intermittent Interruption of Music
Evaluating/Data

Discussion for Transfer:

1. Research shows music can be effective in regulating stride width, length, and rhythm. Was it applied to all these areas in this intervention?
2. How can progress in all these areas be assessed?
3. How did interruption of music affect gait? How long could a person sustain good gait initially without the music to provide structure—seconds or minutes?

OBJECTIVE 3.12

Conduct range-of-motion exercises to music while teaching alternative communication for basic daily needs.

Client Population: Patients with residual stroke symptoms (i.e., motor and communication)

Procedure:

Preparation:
1. Identify at least 5 basic needs that a patient would need to communicate (eat, drink, bed pan, sit up, hot/cold, etc.).
2. Develop an alternative communication system (pointing, sign language, pictures, etc.) for these 5 needs.
3. Analyze the motor skills needed use alternative communication system. Develop range-of-motion or other exercises to support the motor skills. Select music to fit the exercises.
4. Incorporate alternative communication system into motor exercises.
5. Develop means to assess use of signs.

Implementation:
1. Divide participants into clients and therapists.
2. Provide teams with necessary materials.
3. Start music and instruct therapists in conducting exercises and use of communication system. Physically demonstrate and verbally cue each routine. Give feedback to therapists.
4. Evaluate clients' ability to use communication system.

Music Specifications:

Music matched to exercise/communication routine.

Recommended Time Limit: 20 minutes

Criteria for Objective:

Competency Assessment 3:   Minimum scores in each category
Overall minimum score = 75

Techniques Included: Range-of-Motion Exercises
Sign Language (Alternative Communication)
Using Visual Aids
Evaluating

Discussion for Transfer:

1. Why might sign-language instruction be necessary for stroke victims? Who would have to be trained in addition to the clients?
2. How can a person who conducts daily range-of-motion exercises with a client be sensitive to any motor rehabilitation that might be occurring?
3. How do motor impairments affect communication?

OBJECTIVE 3.13

Use music to assist parents in recording a lullaby for their newborns.

Client Population: Parents of ill newborns who will be in NICU (neonatal intensive care) for days/weeks

Procedure:

Preparation:
1. Review music resource for lullabies and music used with infants.
2. Prepare a small songbook of songs with accompanying chord progressions.
3. Rehearse music.
4. Prepare recording and playback equipment. Prepare CD burner (optional).
5. Develop means of reinforcing parent(s) who are timid singers.

Note: This objective can be implemented in 1:1 situation.

Implementation:
1. Explain to classmates that they are parents of newborns who have no musical training. Their infant must remain in the NICU after the mother is discharged.
2. Meet with parent(s) and assist in the selection of a song to record.
3. Rehearse song with parent(s).
4. Record song. Play back for parent. Burn CD (optional).
5. Verbally process emotional issues that the parent(s) express.
6. Evaluate effectiveness of intervention for parent.

Music Specifications:

Songbook of suggested songs to present to parents. Ability to perform parent-chosen music.

Recommended Time Limit: 15 minutes

Criteria for Objective:

Competency Assessment 3:   Minimum scores in each category
Overall minimum score = 75

Techniques Included: Decision Making
Accompanying
Infant Stimulation (Infant-directed singing)
Evaluating/Data

Discussion for Transfer:

1. How would this intervention benefit parents? Infants?
2. Would the music therapist need to be present when the recording is played for the infant? What protocols would be necessary to protect the infant's sensitive auditory system?

OBJECTIVE 3.14

Use music and sign language to increase social interaction.

Client Population: Inclusive setting of adolescents, some with hearing loss or deafness

Procedure:

Preparation:
1. Select songs and signs. Practice according to procedures in Objective 2.28.
2. Plan ways to increase social interaction opportunities between clients, e.g., breaking into small groups and letting students practice together and tutor each other; giving clients opportunities for decision making.
3. Develop form to assess interaction between the two groups.

Implementation:
1. Teach songs and signs.
2. Ensure opportunities for social interaction between persons with hearing impairments and those with normal hearing.
3. Approve all spontaneous positive, social interaction between hearing and nonhearing persons.
4. Evaluate results of intervention.

Music Specifications:

Song with signs that would be of interest to adolescents.

Recommended Time Limit: 20 minutes

Criteria for Objective:

Competency Assessment 3:   Minimum scores in each category
Overall minimum score = 75

Techniques Included: Approving
Signing to Music
Teaching Social Interaction / Socialization
Evaluating

Discussion for Transfer:

1. What would be the probability of increasing social interaction between hearing and nonhearing adolescents using this intervention? What kind of music or decisions would increase this probability?
2. How could adolescents be motivated to continue such social interaction outside the music class?

OBJECTIVE 3.15

Use music to help adults with intellectual disability learn to make decisions by planning a group leisure activity.

Client Population: Adults with moderate cognitive impairments who are co-residents in a group home

Procedure:

Preparation:
1. Select music and intervention to teach decision making: defining the problem, identifying options, identifying pros and cons of each option, arriving at consensus on one option, implementing decision.
2. Develop form to assess decision making.
3. Gather information about leisure opportunities and transportation in the community, e.g., newspaper ads with dates, times, costs, bus routes.

Implementation:
1. Direct music intervention and teach decision-making skills.
2. Introduce topic of deciding on a group leisure activity.
3. Cue clients to use decision-making skills.
4. Approve all spontaneous use of these skills.
5. Review formulated plan and cue issues clients might have omitted.
6. Assess decision-making skills.

Music Specifications: Student's choice

Recommended Time Limit: 20 minutes

Criteria for Objective:

Competency Assessment 3:   Minimum scores in each category
Overall minimum score = 75

Techniques Included: Cuing
Approving
Teaching Decision Making
Evaluating/Data

Discussion for Transfer:

1. Why might planning a leisure activity be highly motivating to these clients? What type of music intervention might be attractive to these clients as an affordable leisure endeavor?

2. What issues would need to be considered besides date, time, cost, and transportation? Are there activities that the community would view as inappropriate for persons with cognitive disabilities? Should a therapist help plan such activities?

OBJECTIVE 3.16

Use music to help parents have a positive interaction with their children.

Client Population: Children and parents with tendency to abuse their children

Procedure:

Preparation:
1. Select task with high frustration potential for parents (high probability of children's failure, very messy, high probability for children to engage in inappropriate behavior, etc.).
2. Select music intervention to teach positive, controlled parenting techniques: positive touching and verbalization, correction without punishment, being proactive through structure rather than reactive to inappropriate behavior.
3. Develop means of evaluating intervention.

Implementation:
1. Divide participants into parents and children.
2. Conduct music intervention and teach positive, effective parenting techniques: controlled, positive verbalizations; controlled, positive touching; correcting without punishing, etc.
3. Direct task with high frustration potential and cue parents to use positive, controlled techniques. Stop any interactions in which frustration begins to develop and have parents leave the room. Teach these parents it is good to leave *before* becoming frustrated.
4. Approve parents who are using techniques and remaining calm.
5. Evaluate effectiveness of intervention.

Music Specifications: Student's choice

Recommended Time Limit: 20 minutes

Criteria for Objective:

Competency Assessment 3:   Minimum scores in each category
Overall minimum score = 75

Techniques Included: Cuing
Approving
Parenting Techniques
Evaluating

Discussion for Transfer:

1. Why would parents need to practice new parenting techniques in the presence of the leader prior to trying them alone?
2. How can parents be motivated to walk away from correcting their child rather than to lose their temper?
3. If the parents knew how to prevent problems from developing, there would be no need for coping techniques. How could the intervention be structured so that the children are less likely to engage in inappropriate behavior?

OBJECTIVE 3.17

Use a rhythm instrument playing to teach creativity, social interaction, and rhythmic skills.

Client Population: Adults aged 70–85 with emerging dementia attending a day health program

Procedure:

Preparation:
1. Select rhythm or percussion instruments with excellent musical sound that are age appropriate.
2. Plan rhythms to accompany a selected favorite song of these clients.
3. Develop form to assess creativity, social interaction, and rhythmic skill.

Implementation:
1. Pass out instruments and teach how each is played.
2. Sing song and let each person play along.
3. Divide clients into sections and teach each a different rhythm.
4. Teach clients to play softly and let individuals take turns doing a solo, dancing, singing, etc.
5. Approve creativity, rhythmic accuracy, and all spontaneous interactions.
6. Assess these three areas.

Music Specifications:

1. Favored song of clients.
2. Quality instruments.

Recommended Time Limit: 15 minutes

Criteria for Objective:

Competency Assessment 3:   Minimum scores in each category
Overall minimum score = 75

Techniques Included: Approving
Stimulating Creativity
Evaluating

Discussion for Transfer:

1. Might older adults feel demeaned by toy-like rhythm instruments?
2. Would adults over 65 need "permission" or prompting to express their creativity or to perform a solo?

OBJECTIVE 3.18

Use music to teach clients to extinguish inappropriate, stereotyped mannerisms, to wait for a turn, and to identify their written name.

Client Population: Children with autism spectrum disorders (ASD)

Procedure:

Preparation:
1. Select music intervention that requires taking turns.
2. Review approving and ignoring techniques.
3. Develop form to assess specified behaviors.
4. Select incompatible responses for stereotyped behaviors.
5. Prepare cards with each person's name.

Implementation:
1. Assign stereotyped behaviors to each person.
2. Direct music intervention and teach name recognition.
3. Approve incompatible responses, correct name recognition, and waiting for a turn.
4. Ignore inappropriate behavior.
5. Assess effect of intervention.

Music Specifications: Student's choice

Recommended Time Limit: 15 minutes

Criteria for Objective:

Competency Assessment 3:   Minimum scores in each category
Overall minimum score = 75

Techniques Included: Approving
Ignoring
Teaching Incompatible Responses
Evaluating

Discussion for Transfer:

1. How did teaching an incompatible response affect the stereotyped behaviors?
2. Could music interruption be incorporated into this intervention?

OBJECTIVE 3.19

Use music and the isoprinciple to:

    a. engage a resistant patient
    b. calm and focus a restless, agitated patient

Client Population: Hospice patients, one age 45 and one age 65

Procedure:

Preparation:
1. Select sequence of songs (at least 3) within the patient's preferred music that move from excitable/engaged to calm/relaxed.
2. Practice and memorize the music. Prepare several different accompaniment patterns and chord progressions to increase your ability to move the client from an undesired to a desired state.
3. Determine what physiological and psychological patient attributes will inform you of the patient's state.
4. Plan for ongoing evaluation of patient's state.

Implementation:
1. Meet with patient and rapidly assess state (resistant or agitated).
2. Communicate your goal to the patient.
3. Begin music. Continue music without stops until patient reaches desired state.
4. Provide closure to the intervention.
5. Assess outcome.

Music Specifications:

Music that is appropriate for a patient age 45 and one aged 65 that can be sequenced to follow the isoprinciple.

Recommended Time Limit: 15 minutes

Criteria for Objective:

Competency Assessment 3:   Minimum scores in each category
Overall minimum score = 75

Techniques Included: Isoprinciple
                            Accompanying
                            Using Repertoire
                            Evaluating

Discussion for Transfer:

1. How was the music changed to bring out the desired patient state? Was this effective?
2. Could this intervention be conducted with recorded music? How?
3. Discuss the value of an extensive repertoire for work in hospice or medicine.

OBJECTIVE 3.20

Use music to teach adults with a fear of leaving the house (agoraphobia) one action step leading to the reduction of this fear.

Client Population: Adults with agoraphobia

Procedure:

Preparation:
1. Learn a relaxation routine (Objective 2.09) and plan desensitization imagery for leaving house on a short trip (grocery store, mall).
2. Select music.
3. Plan role-playing situations.
4. Develop feedback forms.

Implementation:
1. Direct relaxation routine followed by imagery. Use music.
2. Have clients role-play going on selected trip in imagery routine.
3. Motivate clients to attempt this trip during the week.
4. Hand out feedback forms so clients can fill them out after the trip and bring back to therapy next week.

Music Specifications: Student's choice

Recommended Time Limit: 20 minutes

Criteria for Objective:

   Competency Assessment 3:   Minimum scores in each category
   Overall minimum score = 75

Techniques Included: Relaxation
                            Imagery
                            Role-Playing
                            Client Self-Evaluating Data

Discussion for Transfer:

1. Self-evaluation is often an effective way to get explicit information about how a client feels about an experience. What are the problems with relying solely on self-report data? What other types of data collection would be desirable?
2. How could persons with agoraphobia be helped to generalize relaxation techniques to a variety of situations?

OBJECTIVE 3.21

Use music to teach at-risk/early intervention preschooler the following basic skills:

   a. Body skills – gross motor, fine motor, body parts
   b. Communication skills – vocal sounds, gestures
   c. Social/Cognitive skills – following directions, turn taking

Client Population: At Risk/Early Intervention Preschoolers aged 3–5

Procedure:

Preparation:
1. Develop music interventions to address basic skills areas and subareas. Interventions that target more than one area are preferable to maximize the interest and attention of young children.
2. Develop visual aids for at least one intervention. Acquire music instruments.
3. Practice and memorize music interventions and equipment management.
4. Prepare transitions.
5. Determine evaluation.

Implementation:
1. Establish space for session by setting up chairs or floor mats.
2. Begin music interventions. Approve children who make progress on body, communication, and social/cognitive skills. Encourage children who are approximating skills.
3. Transition between interventions.
4. Evaluate progress.

Music Specifications: Student's choice

Recommended Time Limit: 20 minutes

Criteria for Objective:

   Competency Assessment 3:   Minimum scores in each category
   Overall minimum score = 75

Techniques Included: Approving
                             Cuing
                             Incorporating Visual Aids

Discussion for Transfer:

1. Play is work for young children. Were the music interventions both enjoyable and efficacious?
2. What other basic skills are expected of children upon entrance into kindergarten? How can music therapy achieve these skills?

OBJECTIVE 3.22

Use rhythm instruments playing to improve standing balance, weight shifting, and crossing midline.

Client Population: Post-coma adolescents (aged 12–15) recovering from head injuries

Procedure:

Preparation:
1. Identify music interventions that involve rhythm instruments that require the patient to stand up, shift weight side to side, and cross the midline of the body.
2. Be certain the music interventions are appealing to teens.
3. Acquire rhythm instruments. Prepare adaptations to instruments if necessary.
4. Prepare means of evaluating success.

Implementation:
1. Identify 2 or 3 classmates to be therapy assistants. The remaining classmates will be patients.
2. Distribute rhythm instruments to patients and/or assistants.
3. Briefly explain how to play the instrument and the intervention.
4. Begin music intervention. Assure safety of all patients by monitoring fatigue and exertion, stability of balance, etc.
5. Complete all interventions.
6. Evaluate.

Music Specifications: Student's choice including rhythm instruments

Recommended Time Limit: 20 minutes

Criteria for Objective:

>   Competency Assessment 3:   Minimum scores in each category
>   Overall minimum score = 75

Techniques Included: Mobility Skills
Composing/Adapting Music
Inservicing / Coaching Paraprofessionals
Evaluating

Discussion for Transfer:

1. Would rhythm instrument playing motivate moving differently than traditional physical therapy exercises?
2. Consider the interventions presented. What other populations would benefit from these skills? Would additional modifications be needed?

Level 4 Competencies

Tasks at this level are designed to teach

    a. the ability to plan music activities to achieve multiple group objectives for a variety of client populations.

    b. the development of an extensive music repertoire for a variety of therapy activities.

    c. adapting a planned intervention in response to specific problems of individual clients within the group.

    d. the ability to evaluate success in achieving group objectives.

See Index by Technique (page 299) for assistance with specific interventions.

Notes to instructors:

- The instructor should assign participants individual roles prior to the class.
- Time limits may be extended for more realistic pacing of techniques.
- Students are responsible for all music choices *and* implementation decisions.

OBJECTIVE 4.01

Teach dialysis patients to use music and relaxation techniques to reduce the discomforts of dialysis, e.g., boredom, pain, nausea, and blood pressure fluctuations.

Client Population: Kidney dialysis patients; at least one will be critically ill, another will be severely depressed

Procedure:

> *Preparation:*
> 1. Plan relaxation routine to music.
> 2. Plan adaptation for critically ill person.
> 3. Plan intervention for depressed person.
> 4. Plan evaluation for group and individual objectives.

> *Implementation:* As planned

Music Specifications:

> 1. Provide a list of 50 music selections (10 in each of five categories of different types of music) from which patients may select preferred music for use during the four hours of each dialysis session.
> 2. Relaxation routine to music.

Recommended Time Limit: 20 minutes

Criteria for Objective:

> Competency Assessment 3: Overall Score = 75 or above
> Evaluation of group objective and two individual objectives

Techniques Included: Relaxation
Music Listening
Others by Student's Choice
Evaluating

Discussion for Transfer:

> 1. In dialysis situations, what would be the role of the therapist vs. the music? Could the music be available and independently selected by each patient with no therapist present?
> 2. What techniques would be necessary in this situation to deal with people as individuals?

OBJECTIVE 4.02

Teach peers to empathize with the role of a client in group therapy.

Client Population: Peers

    a. One will be verbally domineering
    b. One will be withdrawn
    c. One will be hostile to situation

Procedure:

Preparation:
1. Plan to have each student describe a personal situation that was very embarrassing.
2. Plan to deal with the group members who were assigned to be problematical through approving incompatible responses.
3. Plan to lead a focused group discussion to have students describe how they felt discussing intimate events in public. Make transfers to clients in group therapy.
4. Plan use of music.
5. Plan evaluation of your leadership skills.

Implementation: As planned

Music Specifications: Student's choice

Recommended Time Limit: 20 minutes

Criterion for Objective:

    Competency Assessment 3: Overall Score = 75 or above

Techniques Included: Use of Incompatible Responses
    Leading Focused Group Discussion
    Empathy
    Others by Student's Choice
    Evaluating

Discussion for Transfer:

1. Did the group reveal the most embarrassing, intimate details about themselves or were these censored? What degree of trust would it take for each to reveal censored details? How did the group deal with embarrassment—laughter/lack of eye contact/blushing/ hostility?

2. How was this situation like one that a client in group therapy might experience? What skills would a group leader need to establish trust within the group?

3. Under what circumstances should a leader not encourage a client to make public disclosures in the group?

OBJECTIVE 4.03

Use music and art to help patients deal with their feelings.

Client Population: Persons with terminal illness

a. One will be uncommunicative
b. One will be angry

Procedure:

Preparation:
1. Select music to evoke emotion.
2. Plan for patients to draw to music.
3. Plan to lead a focused group discussion of a positive objective using content of pictures. Decide before discussion starts what the objective of the discussion will be. Make plans to deal with persons with problems.
4. Plan to evaluate your skills as leader and whether objectives were achieved.

Implementation: As planned

Music Specifications: Student's choice

Recommended Time Limit: 20 minutes

Criterion for Objective:

Competency Assessment 3: Overall Score = 75 or above

Techniques Included: Drawing to Music
Leading Focused Group Discussion
Others by Student's Choice
Evaluating

Discussion for Transfer:

1. What effect did the music selection have on the drawing? How would other types of music have functioned in this situation?
2. Was the discussion resolved in a beneficial way, indicating some acceptance of the illness? What were the indicators of this?
3. How was leader effectiveness evaluated?

OBJECTIVE 4.04

Teach a music task using signs and demonstrate differential feedback to 5-year-old children with hearing loss.

Client Population: Children aged 5 years with hearing loss

Procedure:

Preparation:
1. Plan to approve the following:
   a. Child 1—approve for following directions
   b. Child 2—approve for speaking in two-word phrases
   c. Child 3—approve for reduced hyperactivity
   d. Child 4—approve for eye contact
   e. Other clients—approve for correct musical responses
2. Learn signs necessary for teaching the musical task.
3. Practice teaching the task with signs.
4. Prepare evaluation form for assessing your feedback.

Implementation: As planned

Music Specifications: Student's choice

Recommended Time Limit: 20 minutes

Criterion for Objective:

Competency Assessment 3: Overall Score = 75 or above

Techniques Included: Signing
Approving
Evaluating

Discussion for Transfer:

1. How does a leader's skill in differential feedback affect the ability to individualize instruction within a group?
2. Why would preschoolers with hearing impairments require as much individualized instruction as possible?

OBJECTIVE 4.05

Teach a music task to the clients and teach an incompatible response to each of the persons with the problems listed below.

Client Population: Adults with autism spectrum disorders (ASD)

    a. One will be withdrawn
    b. One will be socially inappropriate
    c. One will give incorrect answers to questions

Procedure:

    Preparation:
    1. Plan music task and teaching procedures for those with ASD.
    2. Review procedures for teaching an incompatible response (Objective 2.02).

    Implementation: As planned

Music Specifications: Student's choice

Recommended Time Limit: 15 minutes

Criterion for Objective:

    Competency Assessment 3: Overall Score = 75 or above

Techniques Included: Teaching Incompatible Responses

Discussion for Transfer:

    1. An incompatible response is an appropriate valued response that is mutually exclusive of the specific inappropriate behavior in which the person has been engaging. Were the selected, taught responses in this situation incompatible?
    2. Were expectations readily apparent to the individual?
    3. How did the leader prompt or cue the desired responses?

OBJECTIVE 4.06

Use music to teach personal responsibility for one's actions and willingness to follow rules.

Client Population: Adolescents with behavior disorders

    a. one will be hostile

    b. one will constantly interrupt

Procedure:

Preparation:

1. Develop a musical game with specific rules. Musical games should be motivating to clients while still challenging them. The game should be as original as possible.
2. Plan how rules will be explained and reinforced.
3. Plan to deal with clients with behavior problems.
4. Plan to lead a brief group discussion on accepting responsibility for one's actions and how the rules influenced the game/clients.
5. Determine if and how the "winners" will be rewarded.

Implementation: As planned

Music Specifications: Student's choice

Recommended Time Limit: 20 minutes

Criterion for Objective:

    Competency Assessment 3: Overall Score = 75 or above

Techniques Included: Decision Making
    Leading a Focused Group Discussion
    Following Rules
    Evaluating

Discussion for Transfer:

1. How could you evaluate the ability to accept responsibility?
2. In what other ways could acceptance of responsibility be taught?
3. What was the effect of "losing the game" upon the clients? Is this detrimental?

OBJECTIVE 4.07

Use music to teach patients with psychoses who have been in facility 3 days to select and implement a self-shaping project.

Client Population: Persons with psychoses in crisis-intervention setting; one will begin hallucinating

Procedure:

Preparation:
1. Plan a psychiatric diagnosis for each participant. Plan techniques to deal with the potential problems of each diagnosis and the person with hallucinations, i.e., say name loudly to startle, then approve for being on-task.
2. Plan to have each member select one behavior to self-shape.
3. Plan to teach clients how to implement a self-shaping program for their objective: specify objective, measure it, consequate it, and evaluate results.
4. Plan to get clients to take first action step in implementation of their individual program.
5. Plan use of music.
6. Develop evaluation procedures.

Implementation: As planned

Music Specifications: Student's choice

Recommended Time Limit: 20 minutes

Criterion for Objective:

Competency Assessment 3: Overall Score = 75 or above

Techniques Included: Teaching an Action Step
Evaluating

Discussion for Transfer:

1. What kind of follow-up would be necessary to assist persons with psychiatric illnesses in actually implementing their plan?
2. How could a self-shaping project provide transition between facility and home after discharge?
3. What skills would a therapist need to motivate each person to select an objective with significant impact upon his or her overall problem?

OBJECTIVE 4.08

Use music in a desensitization program for animal phobia.

Client Population: Children aged 8 to 12 with animal phobia

    a. One will hyperventilate at beginning of approach to animal
    b. One will refuse to participate

Procedure:

Preparation:
1. Select music, relaxation routine, and specific animal to which clients will be desensitized.
2. Plan how to deal with person who refuses to participate.
3. Plan desensitization hierarchy for physical proximity to animal following relaxation training and adaptation for person who will hyperventilate.
4. Plan imagery to maximize pleasure following approach to animal.
5. Develop evaluation procedures.

Implementation: As planned

Music Specifications: Student's choice

Recommended Time Limit: 20 minutes

Criterion for Objective:

    Competency Assessment 3: Overall Score = 75 or above

Techniques Included: Relaxation
                                  Desensitization
                                  Imagery
                                  Evaluating

Discussion for Transfer:

1. How would this technique vary for other specific phobias or for generalized phobias such as agoraphobia or panic attacks?
2. What is the function of (a) music in this situation, (b) the relaxation routine, (c) the desensitization hierarchy, and (d) the imagery?
3. Was the procedure age-appropriate? How was this accomplished?
4. How would a leader help the clients move from cognitive rehearsal to action?

OBJECTIVE 4.09

Conduct a music intervention to stimulate socialization between older adults and youth.

Client Population: Adults aged 75+ persons in senior center or retirement community and 4th– 6th graders who are experiencing school difficulties (academic and/or social) involved in a cross-age mentoring program

    a. One of the senior adults will be hard of hearing
    b. One of the senior adults will use a wheelchair
    c. One of the students will be withdrawn
    d. One of the students will be verbally negative

Procedure:

Preparation:
1. Plan music intervention to address socialization and establish pairs for the mentoring program.
2. Plan a method for pairs to determine goals for themselves (e.g., student may want help in math; senior adult might want to learn about contemporary music groups).
3. Plan approvals for instances of independent, yet realistic, ideas.
4. Plan how to maintain high level of socialization during decision making.
5. Plan a closing music intervention to affirm goals established by teams and share them with group.
6. Develop evaluation procedures.

Implementation: As planned

Music Specifications: Student's choice

Recommended Time Limit: 20 minutes

Criterion for Objective:

    Competency Assessment 3: Overall Score = 75 or above

Techniques Included: Approving
                              Socialization
                              Positive Interaction
                              Mentoring
                              Evaluating

Discussion for Transfer:

1. Why would independence in goal planning be an important for persons in a senior center or nursing home?
2. What skills would a leader use to facilitate decision making without allowing the clients to become dependent upon the leader?
3. Give suggestions of other ways to use music in a mentoring relationship.

OBJECTIVE 4.10

Use music to teach decision-making skills.

Client Population: Adults with mild developmental disabilities in a group living home

    a. One will engage in stereotyped rocking
    b. One will interrupt verbally

Procedure:

Preparation:
1. Select intervention requiring several decisions.
2. Select music.
3. Review procedures for decision making: define the problem, identify options, identify pros and cons of each option, select preferred option, act upon selection, and deal with consequences.
4. Prepare form for homework assignment.
5. Plan to teach incompatible responses for the problem.
6. Develop evaluation procedures.

Implementation: As planned

Music Specifications: Student's choice

Recommended Time Limit: 20 minutes

Criterion for Objective:

       Competency Assessment 3: Overall Score = 75 or above

Techniques Included: Decision Making
                            Approving
                            Homework Assignments
                            Use of Incompatible Responses
                            Evaluating

Discussion for Transfer:

1. When persons with intellectual disabilities are taught decision-making skills, what discrimination would also be important to teach?
2. How might decision making cause a person with an intellectual challenge to be viewed as inappropriate?
3. Are there decisions people with developmental disabilities should never be allowed to make? What are the civil rights of such persons?

OBJECTIVE 4.11

Use music to stimulate positive verbal and physical responses between spouses/partners.

Client Population: Persons in couples counseling

    a. One will refuse to participate
    b. One will be verbally negative

Procedure:

Preparation:
1. Select music intervention that stimulates feedback to clients.
2. Select role-playing situations.
3. Plan to deal with uncooperative clients with approval of all positive responses in a hierarchy from music, to leader, to other clients, to spouse and verbal and physical proximity responses.
4. Develop evaluation procedure.

Implementation: As planned

Music Specifications: Student's choice

Recommended Time Limit: 20 minutes

Criterion for Objective:

    Competency Assessment 3: Overall Score = 75 or above

Techniques Included: Approving
                          Role-Playing
                          Leading Focused Group Discussion
                          Evaluating

Discussion for Transfer:

1. Do all couples in marital counseling have the goal of trying to respond positively to each other?
2. Could persons planning a divorce benefit from learning to respond positively to each other?
3. Could a positive response to an alienated spouse be learned in one session?

OBJECTIVE 4.12

Use music activities to structure positive parent visits and maintain child's developmental level.

Client Population: Children in general hospital who behave as follows and a parent or parent(s)

    a. One will cry easily
    b. One will be totally dependent
    c. One will regress to baby talk

Procedure:

Preparation:
1. Plan variety of music activities appropriate to various age levels to motivate self-feeding, self-toileting, self-dressing, etc.
2. Plan a variety of activities that can be left with child to self-structure time: coloring musical instruments, music crossword puzzles, music quizzes for interviewing families and medical staff, etc.
3. Plan ways to approve all independent, self-help skills. Ignore all whining, "sick" responses.
4. Plan ways to teach parents to positively interact with their child and use approval to help their child remain at developmental level with self-help skills.
5. Develop evaluation procedures.

Implementation: As planned

Music Specifications: Student's choice

Recommended Time Limit: 20 minutes

Criterion for Objective:

    Competency Assessment 3: Overall Score = 75 or above

Techniques Included: Approving
                           Ignoring
                           Positive Interaction
                           Parenting Techniques
                           Evaluating

Discussion for Transfer:

1. Parents may be reluctant to ignore "crying," "sick," or "feeling bad" responses from their child. How could doing the music interventions first help them get perspective on this issue?
2. What is the problem if a child regresses and loses developmental milestones due to hospitalization?

OBJECTIVE 4.13

Use music to teach role function and help each family member select a satisfactory role.

Client Population: A family in therapy who act in the following roles:

    a. The teenage daughter (age 17) is in rehab for substance abuse. She has been participating in group music therapy.

    b. The father will be a whiner/complainer

    c. The mother will be an enabler

    d. The 10 year old sibling will be attention seeking/jealous

Procedure:

Preparation:

1. Plan intervention to assess current roles in family interactions. (Possibilities would be autocrat, nurturer, irritant, whiner, nagger, victim, initiator, attention seeker, etc.).
2. Plan ways to introduce positive roles for family interaction.
3. Select music.
4. Plan situations to role-play positive roles.
5. Plan to deal with problems of individuals and problem roles.

Implementation: As planned

Music Specifications: Student's choice

Recommended Time Limit: 20 minutes

Criterion for Objective:

Competency Assessment 3: Overall Score = 75 or above

Techniques Included: Role-Playing
                        Group Decision Making
                        Cuing
                        Role Assessment
                        Relationships
                        Evaluating

Discussion for Transfer:

1. How can role clarification or selection help achieve harmony in a family grouping?

2. What type of feedback would family members need to learn in response to another's role?

3. Who is the "patient" in family therapy?

OBJECTIVE 4.14

Use music and breathing routines to teach labor management to pregnant women.

Client Population: Pregnant women and their partners in labor management class—one couple will continuously seek attention

Procedure:

Preparation:
1. Plan breathing routines, attention focusing, and muscle relaxation with music for labor stages I, II, and III.
2. Plan attention-focusing and muscle-relaxing cues.
3. Teach assistance role to partners. Plan ways to approve partners for assisting correctly.
4. Approve incompatible responses for couple with attention-seeking problem.

Implementation: As planned

Music Specifications: Student's choice

Recommended Time Limit: 20 minutes

Criterion for Objective:

Competency Assessment 3: Overall Score = 75 or above

Techniques Included: Labor Management
Focusing Attention
Relaxing Muscles
Approving
Using Incompatible Responses

Discussion for Transfer:

1. What are the cues that a woman is moving to the next stage of labor? How can the music be coordinated with changes to the next stage of labor?
2. How can breathing routines to music, focused attention, and muscle relaxation be compatible? How can the partner monitor these without interrupting?

OBJECTIVE 4.15

Use music to teach speaking in sentences and asking questions.

Client Population: Children aged 4–6 with language delay—one child will interrupt, one will be passively off task

Procedure:

Preparation:
1. Plan music intervention and cues for sentences and questions.
2. Plan approval for complete sentences and questions. Plan ways to approve responses that are incompatible with interrupting and being off task.
3. Develop evaluation procedures.

Implementation: As planned

Music Specifications: Student's choice

Recommended Time Limit: 20 minutes

Criterion for Objective:

Competency Assessment 3: Overall Score = 75 or above

Techniques Included: Cuing
Approving
Using Incompatible Responses
Evaluating

Discussion for Transfer:

1. What would indicate the child has the skills to learn to speak in sentences or ask questions?
2. What would be the next developmental language skill to teach after this?
3. What other persons in the child's environment would need to be cued to help the child maintain a language skill?

OBJECTIVE 4.16

Provide consultation on the use music to teach appropriate, positive interactions among all children in an inclusive classroom.

Client Population: Inclusive 6th grade general music classroom; some children with disabilities

    a.   One child will have behavior disorder (outbursts with frustration)
    b.   One child will have emotional disturbance (verbally negative)
    c.   One child will have attention deficit disorder with hyperactivity

Procedure:

Preparation:

Note: The music therapy leader (Consultant) will act as a consultant for a general music teacher. Two students can be used in this objective.

1.   "Teacher" will prepare a typical music lesson without modifications for students with special needs.
2.   "Consultant" will develop plan variety of activities, music, teaching techniques, use of peer tutors, means of cuing and approving positive interactions, methods of ignoring inappropriate behavior in a short handout.
3.   Consultant will be prepared to team-teach or coach teacher in re-executing lesson.
4.   Develop evaluation procedures.

Implementation: As planned

Music Specifications: Student's choice

Recommended Time Limit: 20 minutes

Criterion for Objective:

    Competency Assessment 3: Overall Score = 75 or above

Techniques Included: Consultation
    Approving
    Peer Tutoring
    Positive Interactions
    Evaluating

Discussion for Transfer:

1. Research shows that music can facilitate positive interactions in inclusive classes. What structure should the teacher add to the music to insure this?
2. What skills do consultants need? Did the leader demonstrate these skills?

OBJECTIVE 4.17

Use music to teach appropriate body image.

Client Population: Adolescents girls (aged 13–18) with eating disorders, all of who will be reluctant to participate

Procedure:

Preparation:
1. Select music intervention to overcome reluctance to participate. Plan ways to approve participation.
2. Select music and intervention to introduce the topic of body image.
3. Identify values clarification and a priori decision making with regard to the above issues.
4. Lead group discussion encouraging self-disclosure as clients indicate readiness.
5. Develop evaluation procedures.

Implementation: As planned

Music Specifications: Student's choice

Recommended Time Limit: 20 minutes

Criterion for Objective:

Competency Assessment 3: Overall Score = 75 or above

Techniques Included: Lead Group Discussion
Decision Making
Approving
Evaluating

for Transfer:

1. To what extent can adolescents deal with media pressure through personal values clarification?
2. Did the group discussion leader modify the questions or music to encourage self-disclosure by the clients? How? Was it effective?
3. Could this same intervention be used with women who have eating disorders? What modifications would be necessary?
4. What "homework" assignment could these clients be given to extend the music therapy session?

OBJECTIVE 4.18

Use music to help parents set realistic goals for their children.

Client Population: Parents of children with disabilities—all parents will have unrealistic goals (Too negative, too protective, too lofty, etc.)

Procedure:

Preparation:
1. Plan activities to help parents clarify the expectations of self vs. others, realistic goals, and appropriate parenting techniques.
2. Identify topics for focused group discussion. Help parents individually to achieve closure on each issue.
3. Plan role-playing to help parents practice their desired techniques and goal-setting skills.
4. Develop evaluation procedures.

Implementation: As planned

Music Specifications: Student's choice

Recommended Time Limit: 20 minutes

Criterion for Objective:

Competency Assessment 3: Overall Score = 75 or above

Techniques Included: Leading Focused Group Discussion
Role-Playing
Parenting Techniques
Evaluating

Discussion for Transfer:

1. How might parents' expectations for their children differ from those of others in the family? Might parents sometimes feel stress due to pressure from others without realizing it?
2. At what point should the child determine his or her future goals?

OBJECTIVE 4.19

Use music to reduce awareness of pain.

Client Population: Chronic pain patients

  a. One will complain continuously
  b. One will refuse to participate due to pain

Procedure:

  Preparation:
  1. Prepare exercise and/or movement routine to music.
  2. Plan indicators for improved endurance, participation.
  3. Plan methods to cue and approve participation, endurance/duration, and positive verbalizations during exercises and ignore complaining and lack of participation.
  4. Plan for clients to take over as leaders during routine and praise others.
  5. Plan evaluation procedures.

  Implementation: As planned

Music Specifications: Student's choice

Recommended Time Limit: 20 minutes

Criterion for Objective:

  Competency Assessment 3: Overall Score = 75 or above

Techniques Included: Cuing
                            Approving
                            Ignoring
                            Evaluating

Discussion for Transfer:

  Research shows music can reduce awareness of pain. Why would cuing and approving be important to the use of music with exercise?

OBJECTIVE 4.20

Use music to improve math skills.

Client Population: Middle school students with specific learning disability in math

    a. One will have frequent frustration responses
    b. One will be negative about personal abilities

Procedure:

Preparation:
1. Select math problems at middle school level and the methodology for their solution.
2. Select music activities to teach math solutions.
3. Approve correct answers and appropriate social behaviors: attending, positive verbalizations, etc. Ignore negative verbalizations and frustration responses.
4. Plan evaluation procedures.

Implementation: As planned

Music Specifications: Student's choice

Recommended Time Limit: 20 minutes

Criterion for Objective:

    Competency Assessment 3: Overall Score = 75 or above

Techniques Included: Approving
                             Ignoring
                             Evaluating

Discussion for Transfer:

1. Music can be an effective reinforcement for academic subject matter. Would it appeal to middle school students? What music would be most preferred? How could this be determined?
2. Females often reject math skills as being unattractive. How can this value be changed?
3. Assuming that frustration is a learned response, identify some incompatible behaviors that can be taught to offset it.

Level 5 Competencies

Spontaneous Demonstration

Level 5 is designed to allow the student to demonstrate competencies across a variety of tasks without relying on extensive prior planning.

Its purpose is to give the student experience in

a. planning quickly;
b. building and utilizing repertoire that is memorized with materials that are readily available;
c. spontaneously handling unexpected client responses.

Tasks at this level are derived from the following form, which has an array of choices for the instructor in the categories of leadership techniques, client objectives, use of music, client age, client disability, type of service site, and client characteristics.

The instructor selects a different set of specifications for each student by checking the appropriate blanks and distributes the forms at the beginning of class. The class is given 5 minutes of planning time, and then each student conducts a short, 5-minute intervention to meet the individual set of specifications. Students may utilize any instruments or materials available in the classroom.

SPONTANEOUS SKILL DEMONSTRATION FORM

_____   _____   _____
NAME   ORDER   TIME LIMIT

Objective:

____ Accepting responsibility for actions   ____ Verbal interaction
____ Social interaction   ____ Reduction of hyperactivity
____ Reduction of aggression   ____ Attending
____ Decision making   ____ Academic information
____ Memory–Reminiscence   ____ Memory–Recall
____ Motor response   ____ Self-help skill
____ Reality orientation   ____ Rule following
____ Parenting techniques   ____ Relationship development
____ Stress reduction   ____ Isoprinciple
____ Other: _____

Client Parameters:

A. Age: ____ infant   ____ child   ____ adolescent   ____ adult   ____ older adult

B. Session type: ____ Individual   ____ Group (# in group ____)   ____ Family

C. Disability area

____ Intellectual disability   ____ Mental illness
____ Delinquency   ____ Visual impairment
____ Hearing loss   ____ Physical disability
____ Emotional disturbance   ____ Medical/health problem
____ Crisis or trauma   ____ Family in distress
____ Terminal illness
____ Other: _____

Procedure:

Preparation:
1. Take 5 minutes to plan a music activity to achieve the desired objective for the identified group. Use memorized repertoire and materials available in the room.
2. Plan to deal with the following client behavior problems:

____ Withdrawn   ____ Hyperactive
____ Negative   ____ Suicidal
____ Depressed   ____ Disoriented
____ Aggressive   ____ Off-task
____ Nonparticipatory   ____ Verbally hostile
____ Other: _____

Implementation: As planned

Music Specifications:

____ Accompanying instrument: _____
____ Recorded music
____ Singing
____ Moving to music
____ Instrument playing
____ Improvisation

Recommended Time Limit: 5 minutes

Criterion for Objective: Competency Assessment 3: Overall score of 80 or above

Techniques to Be Included:

____ Approving
____ Cuing
____ Chaining
____ Approving Incompatible Response
____ Teaching Action Steps
____ Leading Focused Group Discussion
____ Use of Rules
____ Other: _____

____ Modeling
____ Ignoring
____ Scanning
____ Role-Playing
____ Signing to Music
____ Use of Relaxation Procedures
____ Use of Range-of-Motion Exercises

Therapy Orientation:

____ Person-Centered
____ Cognitive Therapy
____ Adlerian
____ Other: _____

____ Rational-Emotive Behavior Therapy
____ Behavior Therapy
____ Multimodal Therapy

Role Play Actor Cards

Level I Competencies

Follow directions	Follow directions	Follow directions
After 3 or 4 exercises, complain about being tired. Sit down or stop. If leader intervenes, rejoin exercises.	If the leader models all movements, you complete them correctly. If leader does not model, do movements incorrectly.	You will get several dance steps wrong in a row unless the leader provides 1:1 help or a peer-tutor.
Begin in the session as far away from the leader as is reasonable. Make mistakes until the leader moves closer to you (or moves you closer to him/her).	You are offbeat during the music. Once the leader cues you for rhythmic accuracy, get back on-beat.	You become off-task by talking to your neighbor. When the leader praises those who are quiet, you stop talking.
You stop participating. When the leader calls you by name, rejoin the intervention.	If the pace of the intervention is too fast, you become frustrated and refuse. If the pacing is good, stay on-task.	If the leader loses eye contact with the group, starting singing to yourself (e.g., Jingle Bells). Once eye contact is reestablished, rejoin intervention.
If the pace of the intervention is too slow, demonstrate boredom. If the pacing is good, stay on-task.	If the leader stands or sits too far from the group, act disinterested or hard of hearing. When the leader moves closer, join the intervention.	The leader's tempo for the music is too fast; show frustration and inability to perform. When the leader responds, join the intervention.

Role Play Actor Cards

Level II Competencies

Follow directions	Follow directions	Follow directions
(Objective 2.05) As leader is teaching song, mispronounce "gibbous" and "tebbad." Once corrected, rejoin intervention.	(Objective 2.08) When participants are practicing spoken greetings, you make many mistakes and are reluctant to keep trying. Leader should assist you.	(Objective 2.10) Refuse to work with your partner. When leader intervenes, you are cooperative with the plan.
(Objective 2.12) Take the stance that total abstinence (including caffeine, over the counter medicines, etc.) is the only option.	(Objective 2.14) Be resistant to joining the intervention. Make a few negative verbal comments (e.g., This is stupid.). Leader should ignore you.	(Objective 2.16) If any of the motions are too quickly sequenced or too complicated, you cannot complete the dance. When leader simplifies, rejoin.
(Objective 2.18) You really enjoy bowing for the audience. You initially refuse to leave stage.	(Objective 2.18) You do not want to go on stage. You need additional support to bow.	(Objective 2.25 or 2.26) Your attention span is very short. Whenever you lose interest, you put your head down. Leader must redirect you individually.
(Objective 2.33 or 2.34) You are the parent who initially is only always negative.	(Objective 2.38) You correct your peers when they violate rules. You are the tattle-tale.	(Objective 2.44) You can only talk about your son/daughter. Tell the same story over and over. You interrupt others.

Role Play Actor Cards

Level II Competencies, continued

Follow directions	Follow directions	Follow directions
(Objective 2.47 or 2.48) You are a shy singer.	(Objective 2.49 or 2.50) You are angry about your situation. You have a "why me" attitude.	(Objective 2.49 or 2.50) You are overly cheerful about your situation. You are in denial.
(Objective 2.56 or 2.57) You are cooperative with the intervention, but you rarely talk.	(Objective 2.56 or 2.57) You are talkative with the therapist, but need redirection to talk to other clients.	(Objective 2.59) Most of your verbal responses are "I don't know" or "I don't care."
(Objective 2.60) You complain of being sleepy from your medication. Move to back of the room and nap.	(Objective 2.60) You have a favorite musical artist that you keep mentioning during the session.	(Objective – any) Ask to go to the bathroom and leave the room. Come back in a few minutes later. Leader should "catch you up" on intervention.

Role Play Actor Cards

Level III Competencies

Follow directions	Follow directions	Follow directions
(Objective 3.01) Try to be the last person to answer questions or do role-play. Keep passing your "turn" when called upon.	(Objective 3.02) Ask how much it will cost to start a music therapy program.	(Objective 3.03) Monopolize the conversation until redirected.
(Objective 3.06) You believe that all you need to recover from depression is medication. State this belief during discussion more than once.	(Objective 3.09) You have never been married or in a serious relationship. You deny that your behavior has hurt anyone else since you are a "loner."	(Objective 3.13) You make frequent negative remarks about your singing ability.
(Objective 3.15) You have only one leisure interest (e.g., swimming, boating, hockey) that is not practical for everyone in the home. You are fixated on this.	(Objective 3.16) You are reluctant to participate. You keep referring to the leader as "the expert."	(Objective 3.16) You are eager to please the leader. You agree with everything.
(Objective 3.17) The instrument you are given is not working for you (e.g., too heavy, too soft). Be unsuccessful until you get a new instrument.	(Objective 3.22) You are unaware of your limitations and are too eager to participate. Leader must redirect you.	(Objective 3.22) It is very important that the leader and others see you as "cool" and "hip."

Role Play Actor Cards
Level IV Competencies

Follow directions	Follow directions	Follow directions
(Objective 4.07) Your hallucinations are auditory. You appear to listen to them and laugh out loud.	(Objective 4.07) Your psychosis is paranoid delusions. You believe others are reading your thoughts.	(Objective 4.07) You are experiencing side effects to your medications. You are groggy and have difficulty thinking.

Note:. The majority of objectives in Level IV have specific roles and behavioral responses assigned for participants.

Clinical Situations (Examples)
Level V Competencies

Patient in pain. Wants to celebrate some good news.	Patient in hospital. Spouse does all the talking, usually about work stress. Patient seems frustrated by spouse.	Mom and 3 year old with Down Syndrome. Mom wants MT to help with motor and speech. Mom with child in session.
Adolescent in psychiatric hospital. Refuses to participate in verbal therapy, flat affect, not eating/sleeping. Report is "s/he likes music."	Patient died suddenly and after one week of hospice care. Family wants to develop a tribute to loved one. Family includes spouse of decedent, young adult and teenage children	"Sundowners" Group. Older adults with Alzheimer's disease, agitated, pacing, unfocused in later afternoon. Need to keep them in dining hall for evening meal.

Part III

Music Resources
and References

Developing Accompanied Repertoire
for Use in Music Therapy

Introduction and Instructions

Repertoire List Assignments – Examples

Repertoire Lists
    Songs with Repeating Chord Loops
    Infants in Intensive Care
    Mothers' Songs for Infants
    PreKindergarten Songs
    Medical Music Therapy (Tallahassee Memorial)
    Hospice
    Gerontology

Evaluation Examples
    Guitar Chord Assessment
    Memorized Repertoire Evaluation
    Expanding Repertoire
    Relevance of List Check
        Semester One
        Semester Two

Introduction and Instructions

Music therapists use precomposed songs to reach client objectives. Often the music therapist performs these songs "live" by singing while playing accompanying instruments. In order for the client's objective to be successful reached, the music therapist must have selected a relevant song and recreated the song in a musically sophisticated manner (see Johnson, Ghetti, Achey, & Darrow, 2001). Music therapy students must develop a diverse repertoire of songs (see AMTA Professional Competencies, A Sections 4, 5, and 6; www.musictherapy.org/competencies.html), many of which were written, recorded, and/or popular before the students were born (see Van Weelden & Cevasco, 2007).

This section, Accompanied Repertoire, has been prepared to assist students and instructors in developing a relevant, accompanied repertoire useful for a variety of clinical populations and client objectives. Repertoire development can be concurrent with clinical training using the objectives in Part II, concurrent with practicum/fieldwork, or precede both of these training events. The lists included in the text are not intended to be inclusive of all germane songs for music therapy purposes, but serve as a guide as students begin their repertoire development. Because the field of music therapy is diverse, identifying music used in actual clinical settings may help a student and his or her instructor to be selective in the songs chosen.

Students enter music therapy training with different skills. Some are expert singers; others are novices. Many have never played the guitar, while others are quite skilled. Students, like music therapy clients, benefit from early success when playing and singing for others. A list of songs using repeating chord patterns has been included. These songs are often useful for early repertoire development, particularly for early, memorized performances.

Skillful instructors analyze students' strengths in order to prepare them for ongoing success. Competency Assessments I and II are useful for evaluating repertoire. Additionally, examples of alternative evaluation methods have been included. Any of the evaluations can be completed as self-evaluations by the students or completed by the instructor. Evaluations may be conducted in a studio with only the instructor or with the student's classmates as the "audience." Instructors are encouraged to videotape repertoire checks and allow students to self-evaluate. Students become internally motivated to develop repertoire as they see positive effects in clients. However, it is often useful to make repertoire development an assignment for credit in the beginning and middle stages of clinical training.

Requiring students to prepare 3 songs per week for 12 weeks of a semester will yield 36 songs. Thus, repertoire can be developed rather quickly if approached diligently. Instructors can assign students to develop repertoire based upon a population or age group, a musical genre, the function of the music, or a combination of these. Individualized assignments can be beneficial to students, particularly with special needs, such as beginning guitarists, timid or pitchy singers, students with performance anxiety, or students who already possess a large repertoire. Finally, as students become proficient in playing various accompanying instruments while singing, increasing emphasis upon the clinical application of the songs learned should be made. Examples of repertoire list assignments have been included.

Repertoire List Assignments
Examples by Student Level or Course-Based Assignments

Students: Lower division (freshmen or sophomores)

- Midterm Repertoire Evaluation
    - o List I – Any 15 songs sung and accompanied with a minimum of block chords. Half of the list should be memorized (words, melody, and chord changes).

- Final Repertoire Evaluation
    - o List II – List I + 8 songs for children and 8 songs for senior adults (aged 70+). All of the children's songs and at least 3 of the 8 senior adult songs are to be memorized.

Notes to instructors: Students who are new to the piano or guitar may benefit from learning accompaniment to highly familiar songs (folk, holiday, patriotic, current popular music). If the text and melody are well known, focus can be given to chord changes. The assigned populations can be varied to address student needs.

Students: Upper division (juniors, seniors, graduate)

Lists can be assigned that correspond with the clinical topics addressed in coursework. Musical requirements may include finger picking on the guitar, arpeggiated piano accompaniment, etc.

- Counseling

    - o Identify 3 songs for adolescents and 3 songs for adults that address the following:
        - – Anger and frustration
        - – Loneliness or isolation
        - – Sadness, sorrow, or depression
        - – Hope, support, or strength

- Developmental Disability or Special Education

    - o Identify 2 songs for Early Intervention (birth to age 5), 3 for school age (aged 5 to 18), and 3 for adults (over 18) to address the following concepts:
        - – Numbers, counting or math
        - – Receptive and expressive language
        - – The human body or the natural world
        - – Music education

- Medical Music Therapy
  - Identify at least 5 songs for each population. No song should be used more than once.
    - Neonatal Intensive Care Unit
    - Pediatric Burns
    - Adolescent Cancer
    - Labor and Delivery
    - Rehabilitation for adults with head injury or stroke

Repertoire List Assignments
Examples by Genre

Please list your repertoire in the following categories:

- Country (include dates)

- Folk and Patriotic (no dates)

- Children's and Nursery tunes (no dates)

- Popular (1950–1969)

- Popular (1970–1989)

- Popular Contemporary (1990–present)

- Hymns/Spirituals/Gospel/Religious (no dates)

- Older Adults (Before 1929)

- Older Adults (1930–1949)

Additionally, include:

- Original recording artists or songwriters where appropriate

- Date of composition

- Keys in which you can play the song

- First lines or cues for lyrics suggested

Note to instructors: Spreadsheets or tables work well for managing repertoire lists. Specific numbers of songs per genre can be determined for individual students.

Repertoire List: Songs With Repeating Chord Loops

Author: Jennifer D. Jones, PhD, MT-BC
Setting: Varied clinical populations
List: Songs with repeating chord "loops"

POPULAR SONGS USING 12-BAR BLUES PROGRESSION

I–I–I–I / IV–IV–I–I / V⁷–IV–I–I

Each Roman numeral represents a full measure. Slashes indicate phrase boundaries.

All Shook Up by Elvis Presley

At the Hop by Danny and The Juniors

Barbara Ann by The Beach Boys

Boogie Woogie Bugle Boy by Andrews Sisters

Blue Suede Shoes by Elvis Presley

Can't Buy Me Love (Verses are close) by the Beatles

Charlie Brown by The Coasters

Duke of Earl by Gene Chandler

Folsom Prison Blues by Johnny Cash

Hanky Panky by Tommy James and the Shondelles

Hound Dog by Elvis Presley

I Feel Good by James Brown

Jailhouse Rock (chorus) by Elvis Presley

Johnny Be Good by Chuck Berry

Kansas City by Little Richard, Chuck Berry, and others

Long Tall Sally by Little Richard

Maybellene (chorus) by Chuck Berry

Mustang Sally by Wilson Pickett

No Particular Place to Go (close) by Chuck Berry

Red House by Jimi Hendrix

Rock Around the Clock by Bill Haley and His Comets

Rockin' Robin (close, double first line) by Bobby Day, Michael Jackson

Roll Over Beethoven by Chuck Berry

School Day by Chuck Berry

Shake Rattle and Roll by Big Joe Turner; also by Bill Haley and His Comets

Sweet Home Chicago by Robert Johnson

Steamroller Blues by Elvis Presley; James Taylor

Turn Me Loose by Fabian

Tutti Frutti by Little Richard

The Twist by Hank Ballard; Chubby Checker

Wooly Bully by Sam the Sham & the Pharoahs

Worried Man's Blues by The Carter Family

Yakety Yak by The Coasters

Repeating Chord Loops, continued

SONGS USING I–IV–V–I CHORD PATTERN

Song Title and Recording Artist	Comments
Anybody Goin' to San Antone by Charley Pride	Whole song
Battle of New Orleans by Jimmy Driftwood	Verse only; chorus I–I–V–I two times
King of the Road by Roger Miller	1st, 2nd, 4th phrase; phrase 3 is I–IV–V–V
Little Brown Jug (folk song)	Whole song
Old Time Rock and Roll by Bob Seger	2 measures of each chord; all dom. 7

SONGS USING I–IV–I–V CHORD PATTERN

Song Title and Recording Artist	Comments
59th Street Bridge Song by Simon and Garfunkel	Whole song
Brown Eyed Girl by Van Morrison	Phrase 1–4 & 6; phrase 5 IV–V–I–vi
Lean on Me by Bill Withers	Verses and chorus (not bridge)
Lion Sleeps Tonight by the Weavers; Kingston Trio	Whole song

SONGS USING I–IV–V^7–V^7 CHORD PATTERN

Song Title and Recording Artist	Comments
La Bamba by Ritchie Valens	Whole song
Twist and Shout by Isley Brother; The Beatles	Whole Song (except Ah's)

SONGS USING I–IV–V^7–IV CHORD PATTERN

Song Title and Recording Artist	Comments
First Cut Is the Deepest by Cat Stevens; Sheryl Crowe	Whole song; add extra V before chorus
When You Say Nothing at All by Keith Whitley; Alison Krauss	Loop four times; IV–IV–V–V and resume loop
Wild Thing by The Troggs	Loop 4 times; VII–I–VII–I (flat 7 chord)

Repeating Chord Loops, continued

SONG USING I–V–IV–IV CHORD PATTERN

Song Title and Recording Artist	Comments
Already Gone by The Eagles	Whole song

SONGS USING I– vi–ii^7–V^7 CHORD PATTERN

Song Title and Recording Artist	Comments
All I Have to Do Is Dream by The Everly Brothers	All verses (not bridge)
Angel Baby by Rosie and the Originals	Whole song
Blue Moon (recorded by a number of artists)	All verses (not bridge)
Book of Love by The Monotones	1st two phrases
Earth Angel by The Penguins	All verses (not bridge)
Heart and Soul (recorded by a number of artists)	Verses only
In the Still of the Nite by the Five Satins	All verses; chorus IV–I–IV–V, then loop
Lollipop by The Chordettes	Chorus; Verse I–IV–I–IV; loop 2 times; V^7
Return to Sender by Elvis Presley	Verses only (chorus varies)
Sincerely by The McGuire Sisters	All but bridge

SONGS USING I–vi–IV–V^7 CHORD PATTERN

Song Title and Recording Artist	Comments
Last Kiss by J. Frank Wilson; Pearl Jam	Whole song
Teenager in Love by Dion and The Belmonts	Verses; Chorus starts IV-V-IV-V 2x; loop
Where Have All the Flowers Gone by Kingston Trio	First 4 phrases; last IV-I-V-I

SONGS USING I–I–I–V^7 / V^7–V^7–V^7–I CHORD PATTERN

Song Title and Recording Artist	Comments
Achy Breaky Heart by Billy Ray Cyrus	Whole song
Polly Wolly Doodle – Folk song	Whole Song

Repeating Chord Loops, continued

OTHER SONGS USING REPEATING CHORD PATTERN

Song Title and Recording Artist	Comments
All Shook Up by Elvis Presley	Most of verse is I chord; IV–V–I–I end
Blueberry Hill by Fats Domino	Verses are IV–I–V–I; not bridge
He's Got the Whole World in His Hands	I–I–V–V / I–I–V–I
Horse With No Name by America	2 chord loop – Em and D6/9
Hush Little Baby – Folk Song	I–V–V–I whole song
Knockin' on Heaven's Door originally by Bob Dylan	I–V–ii–ii / I–V–IV–IV
Jambalaya by Hank Williams, Sr.	I–V–V–I whole song
Leavin' on a Jet Plane by Peter, Paul, & Mary	I–IV–I–IV / I–IV–V–V whole song
Stand by Me by Ben E. King	I–I–vi–vi / I–IV–V–I
Sundown by Gordon Lightfoot	I–I–V–I / 2 loops of I–IV–VII–VII
Sweet Home Alabama by Lynyrd Skynyrd	V–IV–I–I whole song
The Way You Do the Things You Do by Temptations	Most of verse is I chord

Repertoire List: Infants in Intensive Care

Authors: Judy Nguyen, MM, MT-BC and Jennifer Jarred, MM, MT-BC
Used with the authors' permission
Setting: Neonatal Intensive Care Unit
List: Songs used for general use with infants in intensive care

LEAST ALERTING SONGS
(Three or fewer major chords, repetitious melody)

A-Hunting We Will Go

Alphabet Song

Are You Sleeping

Baby Bumble Bee

Barney Song

The Bear Went Over the Mountain

Bingo

Blowin' in the Wind

Boom Boom (Ain't it Great to Be Crazy)

Cold, Cold Heart

Down by the Bay

Down in the Valley

Farmer in the Dell

Five Green and Speckled Frogs

God Bless America

Going Over the Sea

Head, Shoulder, Knees, and Toes

He's Got the Whole World in His Hands

Hush Little Baby

I Fall to Pieces

I Know an Old Lady Who Swallowed a Fly

If All the Raindrops

If You're Happy and You Know It

I'm a Little Teapot

Itsy Bitsy Spider

London Bridge

Looby Loo

Mary Had a Little Lamb

The More We Get Together

The Muffin Man

Old MacDonald's Farm

On Top of Old Smoky

Peace Like a River

Red River Valley

Row, Row, Row Your Boat

Shake My Sillies Out

Sing a Song of Sixpence

Sing, Sing a Song

Singing in the Rain

Six Little Ducks

Skinnamarink

Skip To My Lou

The Old Man

Twinkle, Twinkle Little Star

Wheels on the Bus

Willoughby Wallaby

You Are My Sunshine

Zip-a-dee-doo-dah

Repeating Chord Loops, continued

OTHER ACCEPTABLE NICU SONGS
(Major or minor chords, Four or fewer chords per phrase)

A Dream Is a Wish Your Heart Makes	*In the Still of the Night*
Accentuate the Positive	*Kiss the Girl*
America the Beautiful	*Lean on Me*
Annie's Song	*Leaving on a Jet Plane*
Baby Mine	*Let It Be*
Beautiful Dreamer	*Let Me Call You Sweetheart*
Blue Moon	*Love Me Tender*
Blueberry Hill	*Moon River*
Brahms Lullaby	*My Heart Will Go On*
Candle on the Water	*Oh, What a Beautiful Morning*
Can't Help Falling in Love	*Old Folks at Home (Swanee River)*
Could I Have This Dance	*Over the Rainbow*
Country Roads	*Peaceful, Easy Feeling*
Dream Dream Dream	*The River*
The Dance	*The Rose*
Edelweiss	*Shenandoah*
From This Moment ON	*Simple Gifts*
Getting to Know You	*Simple Man*
Have You Ever Seen the Rain	*Stand By Me*
Hey, Jude	*Try to Remember*
Home on the Range	*Unchained Melody*
I Can See Clearly Now	*Under the Boardwalk*
I Hope You Dance	*What a Wonderful World*
I Will	*When You Wish Upon a Star*
I'm Forever Blowing Bubbles	*Wonderful Tonight*

Repertoire List: Mothers' Songs for Infants

Author: Andrea Cevasco, PhD, MT-BC
Used with the author's permission
Setting: Mothers of Hospitalized Newborns
List: Songs mothers recorded for infants

MOTHER'S SONGS FOR NEWBORNS

ABC

Amazing Grace

Are You Sleeping

Bingo

Brahm's Lullaby

Edelweiss

Favorite Things

Goodnight Sweetheart

He's Got the Whole World

Hey Diddle Diddle

Hickory Dickory Dock

Home on the Range

I'm a Little Teapot

Itsy Bitsy Spider

Jack and Jill

Jesus Loves Me

Jesus Loves the Little Children

Let Me Call You Sweetheart

Mary Had a Little Lamb

My Girl

Oh What a Beautiful Morning

Old MacDonald

Rockabye Baby

Row, Row, Row Your Boat

Skidamarink

Somewhere Over Rainbow

Swing Low, Sweet Chariot

The Wheels on the Bus

This Little Light of Mine

*Twinkle, Twinkle Little Star**

*You Are My Sunshine**

*Most frequently requested songs

Repertoire List: PreKindergarten Songs

Author: Jayne Standley, PhD, MT-BC

ACADEMIC OBJECTIVES

ABC Song

Alphabestiary

Angel Band

Calendar Song□

Dry Bones

Going to the Zoo

Green for Go, Red for Stop

Hokey Pokey

Map-Reading Song

Mary Wore Her Red Dress

Opposites

Put Your Finger in the Air

Silent E

Telephone

The Barnyard

The Clarinet

The Tactile Song

Triangle, Circle, and Square

Witch's Brew

School House Rock Songs:

   I Am a Bill

   Conjunction Junction

   A Noun

   Preamble to the Constitution

   Energy

   Inner-Planet Janet

   Lolly, Lolly, Lolly, Get Your Adverbs Here

COUNTING SONGS

Ants Are Marching One by One

Five Green-and-Speckled Frogs

Five Little Monkeys

Five Turkeys

One Little Elephant Went Out to Play

One, Two, Buckle My Shoe

Sally the Camel Has Five Humps

Six Little Ducks

Ten in the Bed

Ten Little Indians

There Were Ten in the Bed

This Old Man

PreKindergarten, continued

SOCIAL OBJECTIVES AND VALUES

Be Polite!

Best Friends

How Do You Do?

The More We Get Together

The Sharing Song

Whistle While You Work

LABELING OBJECTIVES AND CONCEPTS

A Tisket, A Tasket

Apples and Bananas

Are You Sleeping?

Baa, Baa, Black Sheep

Baby Bumblebee

Barney

Betty Martin

B-I-N-G-0

Bought Me a Cat

Did You Feed My Cow?

Down By the Station

Going to the Zoo

Happy Birthday

Hawaiian Rainbows

Hello, Everybody

Hickory Dickory Dock

It's Raining, It's Pouring

Join into the Game

Little Green Frog

Little Red Caboose

Mary Had a Little Lamb

Old Brass Wagon

Old King Cole

Old MacDonald Had a Farm

Paw Paw Patch

Pop Goes the Weasel

Rise, Sugar, Rise

Skip to My Lou (Hello, How Are You?)

Teddy Bear

The Animals Go to Sleep (Wake Up)

The Old Grey Cat

There Was an Old Lady Who Swallowed a Fly

This Is What I Can Do

What Is Your Name

PreKindergarten, continued

MOVEMENT SONGS/DANCE

Did You Ever See a Lassie?

Farmer in the Dell (Goblin in the Dark)

Hokey Pokey

In and Out the Window

London Bridge

Mulberry Bush

Ring Around the Rosy

Shake My Sillies Out

SONGS WITH MOTIONS

Clap, Clap, Clap Your Hands

Eensy Weensy Spider

Head, Shoulders, Knees, and Toes

I Wiggle

If You're Happy and You Know It

Miss Mary Mack

Now Tall, Now Small

Open Them, Shut Them

Pat-a-Cake

She'll Be Coming 'round the Mountain

The Little Teapot

The Wheels on the Bus

Where Is Thumbkin?

SONGS EASILY ADAPTED FOR SIGN LANGUAGE

Blue Bird

It's a Small World

Row, Row, Row Your Boat

Twinkle, Twinkle Little Star

Lullabies

All the Pretty Little Horses

Brahms Lullaby

Hush, Little Baby

Rock-a-Bye Baby

When You Wish upon a Star

Repertoire List: Medical Music Therapy (Tallahassee Memorial)

Author: Judy Nguyen, MM, MT-BC and Jennifer Jarred, MM, MT-BC
Used with the authors' permission
Setting: Tallahassee Memorial Hospital Internship
List: Song list given to interns for medical music therapy practice

RECOMMENDED BEGINNER REPERTOIRE FOR TMH INTERNS (*INTERMEDIATE)

Gospel
Amazing Grace
*Because He Lives
Do Lord
Down by the Riverside
*His Eye Is on the Sparrow
How Great Thou Art
Joshua Fit the Battle
Just a Closer Walk With Thee
I Have Decided to Follow Jesus
I Saw the Light
I Surrender All
*I Want Jesus to Walk With Me
I'll Fly Away
In the Garden
It is Well With My Soul
*Joyful, Joyful We Adore Thee
Leaning on the Everlasting Arms
Oh, How I Love Jesus
Oh When the Saints Go Marching In
Old Rugged Cross
Old Time Religion
Peace Like a River
Shall We Gather at the River
Soon and Very Soon
Swing Low Sweet Chariot
Steal Away
This Little Light of Mine
This Train
*Wade in the Water
What a Friend We Have in Jesus
Will the Circle be Unbroken

Praise and Worship/Contemporary Christian
As the Deer
Better is One Day
*Heart of Worship
*Here I Am to Worship
*Holiness (Take My Life)
I Could Sing of Your Love Forever
I Will Call Upon the Lord
*Jesus Lover of My Soul
Lord I Lift Your Name on High
Sanctuary
Seek Ye First
*Shout to the Lord
Thy Word is a Lamp
*Trading My Sorrows
You Alone (Are Father)
You Are My King (Amazing Love)
*Your Love, O Lord

Patriotic
America (My Country 'Tis of Thee)
America the Beautiful
God Bless America
Star Spangled Banner

Jazz
*Boogie Woogie Bugle Boy
*I Got Rhythm
*Ain't Misbehavin'
*Summertime
*It Had to Be You
*My Way
*Wonderful World
*Swing on a Star

Medical Music Therapy, continued

Old Country
Always on My Mind by Willie Nelson
Blue by LeAnn Rimes
*Blue Eyes Cryin' the Rain by Willie Nelson
Could I Have This Dance by Anne Murray
*Crazy by Patsy Cline
Hey Good Lookin' by Hank Williams
Honky Tonk Blues by Hank Williams
I Fall to Pieces by Patsy Cline
I Walk the Line by Johnny Cash
Jolene by Dolly Parton
King of the Road by Roger Miller
Lucille by Kenny Rogers
Move It On Over by Hank Williams
On the Road Again by Willie Nelson
Swingin' by John Anderson
Take These Chains by Hank Williams
Tennessee Waltz by Roy Acuff
The Gambler by Kenny Rogers
To All the Girls I've Loved Before
    by Willie Nelson
Your Cheatin' Heart by Hank Williams

New Country
Achy Breaky Heart by Billy Ray Cyrus
*Bless the Broken Road by Rascal Flatts
Breathe by Faith Hill
*Check Yes or No by George Strait
Friends in Low Places by Garth Brooks
*From This Moment On by Shania Twain
*Goodbye Earl by Dixie Chicks
I Hope You Dance by Lee Ann Womack
*I'll Take Care of You by Dixie Chicks
Let 'Er Rip by Dixie Chicks
Lovebug by George Strait
*My Best Friend by Tim McGraw
*Prayin' for Daylight by Rascal Flatts
Standing Outside the Fire by Garth Brooks
*The Dance by Garth Brooks
*The River by Garth Brooks
When You Say Nothing At All
    by Alison Krauss
*You'll Think of Me by Keith Urban
You're Still the One by Shania Twain

1950s
Blue Moon by ShaNaNas/Mel Torme
Blue Suede Shoes by Elvis
Bye Bye Love by Everly Brothers
*Can't Help Falling in Love by Elvis
Chantilly Lace by Big Bopper
Great Balls of Fire by Jerry Lee Lewis
Hound Dog by Elvis
Kansas City
Rock Around the Clock by Bill Haley and His
    Comets
Teddy Bear by Elvis

1960s
Against the Wind by Bob Seger
And I Love Her by The Beatles
*At the Hop by Danny and the Juniors
Blowin' in the Wind by Bob Dylan / Joan Baez
Brown Eyed Girl by Van Morrison
*Can't Buy Me Love by The Beatles
Eight Days a Week by The Beatles
Hey Jude by The Beatles
*House of the Rising Sun by The Animals
*I Want to Hold Your Hand by The Beatles
I Saw Her Standing There by The Beatles
Imagine by John Lennon
*Let It Be by The Beatles
*Little Help From My Friends by The Beatles
*Love Me Do by The Beatles
*Puff the Magic Dragon by Peter, Paul & Mary
Return to Sender by Elvis Presley
Twist and Shout by The Beatles
Yellow Submarine by The Beatles
*Yesterday by The Beatles

Medical Music Therapy, continued

1970s
American Pie by Don McLean
Bad Moon Rising by Creedance Clearwater Revival
Down on the Corner by CCR
Free Bird by Lynyrd Skynyrd
Gimme 3 Steps by Lynyrd Skynyrd
I Can See Clearly Now by Johnny Nash
Leaving on a Jet Plane by John Denver
Mrs. Robinson by Simon and Garfunkel
Peaceful Easy Feeling by The Eagles
Piano Man by Billy Joel
Proud Mary by CCR
Scarborough Fair by Simon and Garfunkel
Sound of Silence by Simon and Garfunkel
Sweet Home Alabama by Lynyrd Skynyrd
Take It Easy by The Eagles
Tequila Sunrise by The Eagles

1980s
All I Wanna Do Is Make Love to You by Heart
Don't Worry, Be Happy by Bobby McFerrin
Kokomo by The Beach Boys
Look Away by Chicago
Margaritaville by Jimmy Buffet
Papa Don't Preach by Madonna
Summer of '69 by Bryan Adams
The Rose by Bette Midler
Walking on Sunshine by Katrina and the Waves
Wind Beneath My Wings by Bette Midler
Wonderful Tonight by Eric Clapton
You Give Love a Bad Name by Bon Jovi

1990s
All My Life by K-Ci & Jo Jo
Angel by Sarah McLachlan
Come to My Window by Melissa Etheridge
Free Fallin' by Tom Petty
Head Over Feet by Alanis Morrissette
Heaven by Bryan Adams
I Believe I Can Fly by R. Kelly
I Will Remember You by Sarah McLachlan
Iris by Goo Goo Dolls
Love Will Keep Us Alive by The Eagles
My Heart Will Go On by Celine Dion
Strong Enough by Sheryl Crow
When a Man Loves a Woman by Michael Bolton
Without You by Mariah Carey

2000+
All For You by Sister Hazel
Fallin by Alicia Keys
God Bless the USA by Greenwood (re-release)
It's Been Awhile by Staind
Thank You by Dido
Wherever You Will Go by The Calling

Motown
Dock of the Bay by Otis Redding
I Got You by James Brown
I Heard It Through the Grapevine by Marvin Gaye
In the Still of the Night by The Five Satins
My Girl by The Temptations
Stand By Me by Ben E. King
The Way You Do /Things You Do by TheTemptations
Under the Boardwalk by The Drifters

Medical Music Therapy, continued

Oldies

*Beautiful Dreamer
By the Light of the Silvery Moon
Catch a Falling Star
Daisy Bell (Bicycle Built For Two)
*Danny Boy
Five Foot Two
Greensleeves
Home on the Range
I'm Forever Blowing Bubbles
I've Been Working on the Railroad
In the Good Old Summertime
Let Me Call You Sweetheart
My Bonnie Lies Over the Ocean
My Wild Irish Rose
Oh, Susanna
Old Folks at Home (Swanee River)
You Are My Sunshine

Showtunes

Accentuate the Positive – Here Come the Waves
Edelweiss – The Sound of Music
Getting to Know You – The King and I
Give My Regards to Broadway
My Favorite Things – The Sound of Music
Oh What a Beautiful Morning – Oklahoma
Oklahoma! – Oklahoma
*Over the Rainbow – The Wizard of Oz
Singin' in the Rain – Singin' in the Rain
*Try to Remember – The Fantasticks

Children's

3 Bears with a Beat
Alphabet Song
Are You Sleeping
BINGO
Boom Boom Ain't It Great to Be Crazy
Down by the Bay
Down on Grandpa's Farm
Five Green and Speckled Frogs
Going Over the Sea
Hagalena Magalena
Hush Little Baby
I Know an Old Lady
I Love You (Barney Theme Song)
I'm a Little Teapot
If All the Raindrops
If You're Happy and You Know It
Itsy Bitsy Spider
London Bridge
Mary Had a Little Lamb
Old Macdonald's Farm
Row Your Boat
Shake My Sillies Out
Six Little Ducks
Skip to My Lou
The Farmer and the Dell
This Old Man
Twinkle Twinkle Little Star
Wheels on the Bus
Willoughby Wallaby

Medical Music Therapy, continued

RECOMMENDED ADVANCED REPERTOIRE FOR TMH INTERNS

Gospel
Precious Lord

Praise and Worship/ Contemporary Christian
Awesome God
Breathe
Come Now Is the Time to Worship
Lord, Reign in Me
We Fall Down

Jazz
At Last
Bewitched, Bothered, and Bewildered
Chattanooga Choo Choo
Come Fly With Me
Don't Get Around Much Anymore
Fly Me to the Moon
Goody Goody
It's Only a Paper Moon
L-O-V-E ("L" is for the way you look at me)
Moon River
Sentimental Journey
Someone to Watch Over Me
Strangers in the Night
They Can't Take That Away From Me
Unforgettable
Young at Heart

Old Country
Georgia On My Mind by Willie Nelson
Hello Darlin' by Conway Twitty
I'm So Lonesome I Could Cry by Hank Williams
It's Only Make Believe by Conway Twitty
Rocky Top by Lynn Anderson
Stand By Your Man by Tammy Wynette
Through the Years by Kenny Rogers
Walkin' After Midnight by Patsy Cline
You Decorated My Life by Kenny Rogers
You Needed Me by Anne Murray

New Country
Cry by Faith Hill
Everywhere by Tim McGraw
I Cross My Heart by George Strait
This One's for the Girls by Martina McBride
Wide Open Spaces by Dixie Chicks
Young by Kenny Chesney

1950s
Dream, Dream, Dream by The Everly Brothers
Earth Angel by The Penguins
Splish Splash by Bobby Darrin
Suspicious Minds by Elvis Presley
Unchained Melody by Righteous Brothers

1960s
I'm a Believer by Neil Diamond/The Monkees
Joy to the World by Three Dog Night
Just Walk Away Renee by Left Blanke
Killing Me Softly by Robert Flack
Ob-la-di Ob-la-da by The Beatles

1970s
Annie's Song by John Denver
Bridge Over Troubled Water by Simon & Garfunkel
Close to You by The Carpenters
Desperado by The Eagles
Drift Away by Dobie Gray
Dust in the Wind by Kansas
Hotel California by The Eagles
I Will Survive by Gloria Gaynor
I'll Have to Say I Love You / Song by Jim Croce
Lonely People by America
Operator by Jim Croce
Time in a Bottle by Jim Croce
Top of the World by The Carpenters
We Are the Champions by Queen
You've Got a Friend by James Taylor/Carole King

Medical Music Therapy, continued

1980s
Alone by Heart
Always by Bon Jovi
Baby I Love Your Way by Peter Frampton
Come Monday by Jimmy Buffett
For the Longest Time by Billy Joel
Forever Young by Rod Stewart
Just the Way You Are by Billy Joel
Livin' on a Prayer by Bon Jovi
Open Arms by Journey
She's Always a Woman To Me by Billy Joel
Take My Breath Away – Top Gun theme
Uptown Girl by Billy Joel
Where Everybody Knows Your Name –
    Cheers theme
Your Song by Elton John

1990s
Because You Loved Me by Celine Dion
Don't Speak by No Doubt
Everything I Do by Bryan Adams
Give Me One Reason by Tracy Chapman
Here and Now by Luther Vandross
Hero by Mariah Carey
Running by No Doubt
Water Runs Dry by Boyz II Men

Showtunes
Climb Every Mountain – Sound of Music
I Could Have Danced All Night – My Fair
    Lady
Matchmaker – Fiddler on the Roof
Memory – Cats
Put on a Happy Face – Bye Bye Birdie
Seventy-six Trombones – Music Man
Some Enchanted Evening – South Pacific
Sunrise, Sunset – Fiddler on the Roof
Surrey with the Fringe on Top – Oklahoma!
The Impossible Dream – Man of La Mancha
Till There Was You – Music Man
Wouldn't It Be Loverly – My Fair Lady

2000+
Bad Day by Fuel
Beautiful by Christina Aguilera
Beautiful Soul by Jesse McCartney
Boulevard of Broken Dreams by Green Day
Breakaway by Kelly Clarkson
Breathe by Anna Nalick
Come Away With Me by Norah Jones
Everytime by Britney Spears
Hanging by a Moment by Lifehouse
Happy Ending by Avril Lavigne
Higher by Creed
I'll Be by Edwin McCain
Lonestar by Norah Jones
My Immortal by Evanescence
One Last Breathe by Creed
The Reason by Hoobastank
This Love by Maroon 5
Unwell by Matchbox 20
Wherever You Will Go by The Calling

Motown
Ain't No Mountain High Enough by Marvin
    Gaye
Baby Love by The Supremes
Blueberry Hill by Fats Domino
Happy Together by The Turtles
I Say a Little Prayer for You by Dionne
    Warwick
My Guy by Mary Wells
When a Man Loves a Woman by Percy Sledge

Repertoire List: Hospice

Author: Russell Hilliard, PhD, MT-BC
Used with the author's permission
Setting: Hospice Music Therapy
List: Songs used with or requested by hospice patients

AMERICANA (POPULAR PRIOR TO 1950)

America the Beautiful
After the Ball
Any Time
Battle Hymn of the Republic
Because
Bicycle Built for Two
By the Light of the Silvery Moon
Chicago
Clementine
Corrrina, Corrina
Doodle-ee-doo
Down by the Old Mill Stream
Down in the Valley
Eastside, Westside
Edelweiss
Favorite Things
Five Foot Two, Eyes of Blue
For He's a Jolly Good Fellow
Give My Regards to Broadway
Hello My Babe
Home on the Range
I'll Be With You in Apple Blossom Time
In the Good Old Summertime

I've Been Working on the Railroad
Let Me Call You Sweetheart
Moon River
My Bonnie Lies Over the Ocean
Oh, Susanna
Old Folks at Home
Peace Like a River
Polly Wolly Doodle
Ramona
Red River Valley
Shenandoah
Shine On Harvest Moon
Simple Gifts
Surrey With the Fringe on Top
Take Me Out to the Ballgame
Tell Me Why
The Glory of Love
The More We Get Together
Tumbling Tumbleweeds
When Irish Eyes Are Smiling
Wonderful World
You Are My Sunshine

COUNTRY AND WESTERN

Breathe
But I Do Love You
Buy Me a Rose
Chattahoochee
Crazy
Goodbye Earl

Please Release Me
Sixteen Tons
The Dance
The Gambler
The Way You Love Me
To All the Girls I've Loved Before

Hospice, continued

Hey, Good Lookin'
Jambalaya (On the Bayou)
King of the Road
On the Road Again

You Decorated My Life
You Look So Good in Love
Your Cheatin' Heart
Without You

POPULAR (1950+)

Annie's Song
Bad Moon Rising
Blue Suede Shoes
Brown Eyed Girl
Bye Bye Love
Candle in the Wind
Carolina on My Mind
Come Monday
Daniel
Don't Worry, Be Happy
Dust in the Wind
Everybody Hurts
Feelin' Groovy
Fire and Rain
Get Together
Happy Together
Hey Jude
Hound Dog
I Can See Clearly Now
I'd Like to Teach the World to Sing
I Saw Her Standing There
If I Had a Hammer
I'm a Believer
Joy to the World (by Three Dog Night)
Lay Lady Lay

Lean on Me
Leavin' on a Jet Plane
Let It Be
Lonely People
Love Me Tender
Margaritaville
Morning Has Broken
Morningside
My Heart Will Go On
Peaceful Easy Feeling
Proud Mary
Scarborough Fair
Stand by Me
Sweet Adeline
Take It Easy
Take Me Home Country Roads
The Rose
The Wind Beneath My Wings
Turn, Turn, Turn
Unchained Melody
Where Have All the Flowers Gone?
With a Little Help from My Friends
Yellow Submarine
Yesterday
You've Got a Friend

MUSICALS

(Clients requested "any song" from the following musicals)

Carousel
My Fair Lady
Oklahoma

Sound of Music
South Pacific

Hospice, continued

RELIGIOUS/SPIRITUAL

All Night, All Day
Alleluia
Amazing Grace
An Irish Blessing
Are Ye Able, Said the Master
As I Am
As the Deer
Blessed Assurance
Blest Be the Tie That Binds
Bringing in the Sheaves
Church in the Wildwood
Come Thou Fount of Every Blessing
Dance With Me
Do Lord
Down by the Riverside
Friends
Ev'ry Time I Feel the Spirit
Faith of Our Fathers
Great Speckled Bird
Give Me That Old Time Religion
He's Got the Whole World in His Hands
He Is Exalted
Here I Am, Lord
His Eye Is on the Sparrow
Holy, Holy, Holy
How Great Thou Art
I Could Sing of Your Love Forever
I Know Who Holds Tomorrow
I Love to Tell the Story
I Surrender All
I Wouldn't Take Nothin' for My Journey Now
In the Garden
I'll Fly Away
It Is Well with My Soul
It's Amazing
I've Been Redeemed
Jesus Loves Me
Just a Closer Walk with Thee
Just As I Am
Kum Ba Yah

Leaning on the Everlasting Arms
Light the Fire
Lonesome Valley
Lord I Lift Your Name on High
Lord, You're Beautiful
Love Lifted Me
Majesty
My All in All
My King Jesus Is All
My Stronghold – My Savior
Nearer My God to Thee
Nobody Knows the Trouble I've Seen
One Day at a Time
Onward Christian Soldiers
Peace
Precious Lord
Precious Memories
Rock-a My Soul
Rock of Ages
Sanctuary
Shall We Gather at the River
Shine, Jesus, Shine
Shout to the Lord
Softly and Tenderly
Standin' in the Need of Prayer
Step by Step
Sweet By and By
Sweet Hour of Prayer
Swing Low, Sweet Chariot
The Old Rugged Cross
The Rosary
This Is My Father's World
This Train
This Little Light of Mine
We Are One in the Spirit
What a Friend We Have in Jesus
When the Roll Is Called Up Yonder
When the Saints Go Marching In
Why Me? (Why Me, Lord?)
Will the Circle Be Unbroken

Repertoire List: Gerontology

Authors: Kimberly VanWeelden, PhD, and Andrea M. Cevasco, PhD, MT-BC
Used with the authors' permission
Setting: Gerontology
List: Songs recommended for singing interventions
by music therapists working in gerontology

For complete report see:

VanWeelden, K., & Cevasco, A. M. (2007). Repertoire recommendations by music therapists for geriatric clients during singing activities. *Music Therapy Perspectives, 25*(1), 4–12.

The following list is based upon the above authors' Table 2—top ten recommended songs by music style including dates when known. Some songs appear in more than one category. Ties are included.

POPULAR

Rank and Title	Year Composed
1. *Let Me Call You Sweetheart*	1910
2. *Five Foot Two, Eyes of Blue*	1925
3. *Take Me Out to the Ballgame*	1908
4. *In the Good Old Summertime*	1902
5. *Daisy Bell (Bicycle Built for Two)*	1892
You Are My Sunshine	1931
6. *Ain't She Sweet*	1927
Don't Sit Under the Apple Tree	1942
Shine on Harvest Moon	1903
7. *Side by Side*	1927
8. *By the Light of the Silvery Moon*	1909
Sentimental Journey	1944
9. *Bye, Bye Blackbird*	1926
10. *Bill Bailey*	1933
My Wild Irish Rose	1899

Gerontology, continued

PATRIOTIC

Rank and Title	Year Composed
1. *America the Beautiful*	1893
God Bless America	1938
2. *You're a Grand Old Flag*	1905
America	1831
3. *Battle Hymn of the Republic*	1862
Yankee Doodle Dandy	1904
4. *Star Spangled Banner*	1814
5. *This Land is Your Land*	1956
6. *Yankee Doodle*	*
Caisson Song	1907
The Marine's Hymn	1918
7. *Anchors Aweigh*	1906
8. *Over There*	1917
9. *Stars and Stripes Forever*	1896
10. *When Johnny Comes Marching Home*	1863

* Year composed is unknown

HYMNS

Rank and Title	Year Composed
1. *Amazing Grace*	1779
2. *How Great Thou Art*	1953
3. *In the Garden*	1913
4. *What a Friend We Have in Jesus*	1868
5. *Old Rugged Cross*	1913
6. *He's Got the Whole World*	*
7. *Jesus Loves Me*	1862
8. *Swing Low, Sweet Chariot*	*
9. *When the Saints Go Marching In*	*
10. *Abide With Me*	1861
Count Your Blessings	1897
Just a Closer Walk with Thee	*
Kum Ba Yah	*
Let There Be Peace on Earth	1955
Precious Lord, Take My Hand	1932

* Year composed is unknown

Gerontology, continued

FOLK

Rank and Title	Year Composed
1. *I've Been Working on the Railroad*	*
2. *Home on the Range*	*
3. *You Are My Sunshine*	1931
4. *My Bonnie Lies Over the Ocean*	*
5. *Down in the Valley*	*
Red River Valley	1896
She'll Be Comin' 'Round the Mountain	*
6. *Clementine*	*
7. *Daisy Bell (Bicycle Built for Two)*	1892
On Top of Old Smokey	*
8. *In the Good Old Summertime*	1902
9. *Dixie*	1859
My Wild Irish Rose	1899
10. *Take Me Out to the Ballgame*	1908
Swing Low, Sweet Chariot	*
School Days	1907
The More We Get Together	*
When Irish Eyes Are Smiling	1912
When the Saints Go Marching In	*

* Year composed is unknown

Gerontology, continued

MUSICALS

Rank and Title	Year Composed
1. *Edelweiss*	1965
2. *Oh, What a Beautiful Morning*	1943
3. *Hello, Dolly*	1969
4. *My Favorite Things*	1965
5. *Do Re Mi*	1965
Getting to Know You	1956
6. *Singing in the Rain*	1952
7. *Over the Rainbow*	1939
8. *Moon River*	1961
9. *Easter Parade*	1948
Summertime	1935
Try to Remember	1960
You'll Never Walk Alone	1945
10. *Climb Every Mountain*	1965
Give My Regards to Broadway	1904
I Could Have Danced All Night	1956
Oklahoma	1943

Evaluation Example: Guitar Chord Assessment
Accompanied Repertoire

Student's Name: _____ Date: _____

A chord

$$|\rule{8cm}{0.4pt}|$$
0   10

Did not remember at all   Automatic
Fingers completely lost   Highly accurate
Very poor transition to and from   Good change

A^7 chord

0   10

Did not remember at all   Automatic
Fingers completely lost   Highly accurate
Very poor transition to and from   Good change

am chord

0   10

Did not remember at all   Automatic
Fingers completely lost   Highly accurate
Very poor transition to and from   Good change

B^7 chord

0   10

Did not remember at all   Automatic
Fingers completely lost   Highly accurate
Very poor transition to and from   Good change

C chord

0   10

Did not remember at all   Automatic
Fingers completely lost   Highly accurate
Very poor transition to and from   Good change

D chord

0   10

Did not remember at all   Automatic
Fingers completely lost   Highly accurate
Very poor transition to and from   Good change

D^7 chord

0   10

Did not remember at all   Automatic
Fingers completely lost   Highly accurate
Very poor transition to and from   Good change

dm chord

0   10

Did not remember at all   Automatic
Fingers completely lost   Highly accurate
Very poor transition to and from   Good change

E chord

|————————————————————————————————————|
0   10
Did not remember at all   Automatic
Fingers completely lost   Highly accurate
Very poor transition to and from   Good change

E7 chord

|————————————————————————————————————|
0   10
Did not remember at all   Automatic
Fingers completely lost   Highly accurate
Very poor transition to and from   Good change

em chord

|————————————————————————————————————|
0   10
Did not remember at all   Automatic
Fingers completely lost   Highly accurate
Very poor transition to and from   Good change

F chord

|————————————————————————————————————|
0   10
Did not remember at all   Automatic
Fingers completely lost   Highly accurate
Very poor transition to and from   Good change

G chord

|————————————————————————————————————|
0   10
Did not remember at all   Automatic
Fingers completely lost   Highly accurate
Very poor transition to and from   Good change

G7 chord

|————————————————————————————————————|
0   10
Did not remember at all   Automatic
Fingers completely lost   Highly accurate
Very poor transition to and from   Good change

Comments:

——

——

——

Next Assignment:

——

——

——

Criterion:_____ Score:_____

Evaluation Example: Memorized Song Assessment
Accompanied Repertoire

Student's Name: _____ Date: _____

Song title _____

Circle One: Piano   Guitar   Autoharp   Omnichord   Other

- Chords – accurately performed, good tone quality, and transitions are smooth

    Above Criterion   Meets Criterion   Below Criterion

- Rhythm – steady throughout, accompanying pattern relevant to song's genre or purpose

    Above Criterion   Meets Criterion   Below Criterion

- Tempo – appropriately selected for song's genre or purpose; variations in tempo are purposeful to objective

    Above Criterion   Meets Criterion   Below Criterion

- Confident performance indicated by brief introduction of self/song, sustained eye contact with participants while playing/singing

    Above Criterion   Meets Criterion   Below Criterion

- Volume – demonstrates balance of guitar and vocal volume; expressive dynamic changes present

    Above Criterion   Meets Criterion   Below Criterion

- Minimal errors (fewer than 2) with quick recovery

    Above Criterion   Meets Criterion   Below Criterion

Instructor's Comments_____

_____

_____

_____

_____

Pass   **Try Again/Reschedule**   **Fail**

Evaluation Example: Expanding Repertoire

Group Repertoire Check – Mid-Semester One

Student's Name: _____ Date: _____

Instructors: Assign partners or small group. Complete the following using your combined
repertoire lists.

1. 4 children's songs in a row for a frightened 4-year-old in speech therapy.
    Hint: Isoprinciple.

2. Lull an 8-month-old to sleep using any 2 songs that are slow and lyrical.
    Hint: Humming.

3. A 72-year-old man with dementia who is calm when singing old songs. One each –
    folk, country, "oldies."

4. A 14-year-old female in treatment for depression. Choose a song that relates to her
    issues.

5. A 40-year-old daughter (visiting) and a 65-year-old mother (patient) in hospital. Pick
    songs they both would know. Choose 3 songs that demonstrate a variety of styles.

6. A 23-year-old male in hospital receiving dialysis. He is bored and wants to have
    something to occupy his time. Likes rap, classic rock, and 80s metal bands. Choose 2
    songs.

7. A very religious couple, both in their late 60s, are sharing a room in the assisted living
    center. He is very sick and she is distraught about his health and impending death.
    Choose 2 songs; religious songs okay.

8. Of the songs on the lists, what is your personal favorite?

9. Of the songs on the lists, what is your least favorite?

Evaluation Example: Relevance of List Check
Accompanied Repertoire – Semester One

Student's Name: _____ Date: _____

Complete the following using songs from your complete repertoire list *excluding* songs you have already performed during repertoire checks or objectives. Note that some examples require memorization and some require more than one song as a response. You may omit one question without penalty. Bring a paper copy of your repertoire list (title, key, genre, era/date on list).

1.   4 Children ages 3–4, academic objectives. 2 songs that could be used to teach colors or numbers. **Memorize** these songs.

2.   Children ages, 4 to 6, speech impairments. 2 songs that elicit a verbal or gesture response. **Memorize** these songs.

3.   A patriotic song you could use during a U.S. national holiday. **Memorize** this song.

4.   A "classic" rock or pop song that preteens would recognize and like. **Memorize** this song.

5.   A "new" song released since 2005, any genre. Memorization optional.

6.   Two folk songs that adults ages 70–85 would know and be able to sing. **Memorize** both songs.

7.   A country song that adults ages 30–60 would likely know. Memorization optional.

8.   Two gospel/spirituals/hymns – non-denominational, generic in terms of doctrine. **Memorize** at least one of them.

9.   A musical tune or oldie popular prior to 1945. Memorization optional.

10.   A holiday song – traditional or contemporary. Memorization optional.

Evaluation Example: Relevance of List Check
Accompanied Repertoire – Semester Two

Student's Name: _____ Date: _____

No songs appearing on this short list have been played before
during laboratory objectives or repertoire checks.

Spring Semester

1. 3 songs memorized this spring – any genre

2. 3 songs memorized last fall – any genre

3. 3 songs that you found particularly effective in your fieldwork (2 spring, 1 fall)

4. Best vocals – 2 songs you sound great (or really enjoy) singing (fall or spring)

5. Best guitar chops – 2 songs using your fanciest guitar skills

6. The earliest song on your list (by date – think 1900s)

7. Most recent release

8. 2 personal favorites (1 spring, 1 fall)

9. One "I hate this song, but play it for clients anyway" (fall or spring)

Discography by Counseling Topic

Michael J. Silverman, PhD, MT-BC

Please note that each song should be individually evaluated a priori for its appropriateness.

Abuse
    Abuser
    Child and Sexual
    Spousal
Active Change
Addiction/Substance Abuse
Adolescence
Aging
Anger/Violence/Mediation
Bereavement
Crisis Intervention
Decision Making
Depression/Loneliness
Disappointment
Emotional Involvement
Gay/Lesbian Support
Homeless
Marital Issues
Problem Solving/Moving On
Prostitution
Rape
Relationships
Suicide
Terminal Illness/Catastrophe
Reminiscence – 1980s
Runaway

Discography by Counseling Topic

ABUSE: ABUSER

Title	Artist
Babysitter	Morningwood
Fiddle About	The Who
Fourteen	The Vandals
Hands Clean	Alanis Morissette
The Infant Kiss	Kate Bush
Little Girls	Oingo Boingo
Mary	Supergrass
Mr. Tinkertrain	Ozzy Osbourne
A Question of Time	Depeche Mode
Prison Sex	Tool
Who Will Hold Me?	Amy Fix

ABUSE: CHILD AND SEXUAL

Title	Artist
Alyssa Lies	Jason Michael Carrol
Amelia	The Mission
Amy in the White Coat	Bright Eyes
Ask Me	Amy Grant
Bad Wisdom	Suzanne Vega
Beautiful Prize	Rick Springfield
Childcatcher	Lush
Close My Eyes	Mariah Carey
Concrete Angel	Martina McBride
Daddy's Song	Toni Childs
Disarm	Smashing Pumpkins
Down with The Sickness	Disturbed
Emotionless	Good Charlotte
Fee Fi Fo	Cranberries
Five	Machine Head
Fixxxer	Metallica
Hell Is for Children	Pat Benatar
I'm OK	Christina Aguilera
In Harm's Way	Metal Church
Janie's Got a Gun	Aerosmith
Light in the Hall	Small Fred
Long Way to Happy	Pink

Perfect	Alanis Morisette
Play Me Backwards	Joan Baez, Wally Wilson, Kenny Greenberg, Karen O'Connor
Please Don't Believe Me	Terry Sue Crawford
Precious Illusions	Alanis Morissette
Sleep	Stabbing Westward
The Story of Beauty	Destiny's Child
Twisted Ballerina	Jayne Sachs
Watch Me Bleed	Tears for Fears
What's the Matter Here?	10,000 Maniacs
Where Are You?	Wilson Phillips

ABUSE: SPOUSAL

Title	Artist
A Man's Home Is His Castle	Faith Hill
Best of You	Foo Fighters
Black Eyes, Blue Tears	Shania Twain
Blood, Sex and Booze	Green Day
Broken Wing	Martina McBride
Face Down	Red Jumpsuit Apparatus
I Would Be Stronger Than That	Faith Hill
Independence Day	Martina McBride
Island	Heather Nova
Keep Ya Head Up	Tupac Shakur
Love Is Blind	Eve
My Name Is Luka	Suzanne Vega
Never Again	Nickelback
Stay Gone	Jimmy Wayne
Sympathetic Character	Alanis Morissette
U.N.I.T.Y	Queen Latifah
Woman in Chains	Tears for Fears

ACTIVE CHANGE

Title	Artist
A Change Would Do You Good	Sheryl Crow
Am I Ever Gonna Change	Extreme
Be Somebody	TLC
Bitter Sweet Symphony	Verve
Change	Blind Melon
Change	Candlebox
Change	Deftones

Change of Habit	Elvis Presley
Change the World	The Offspring
Change Your Ways	LL Cool J
Close Range	Mystikal
Cruz	Christina Aguilera
Easier to Run	Linkin Park
Everybody's Got to Change Sometime	Taj Mahal
Face the Change	INXS
If I Could Change	Master P
In Our Small Way	Michael Jackson
Just for You	Pennywise
Lucky Man	Verve
My Own Way	Pennywise
Never Change	Puddle of Mudd
New Dress	Depeche Mode
Notgonnachange	SOS
Revolution 1993	Jamiroquai
Such a Little Thing Makes Such a Big Difference	Morrissey
Taste in Men	Placebo

ADDICTION/SUBSTANCE ABUSE

Title	**Artist**
Addicted	Kelly Clarkson
Addiction	Kanye West
Addiction	Skinny Puppy
Breaking the Habit	Linkin Park
Bright Light Fright	Aerosmith
Brown Sugar	ZZ Top
Carmelita	Counting Crows
Cigarettes and Alcohol	Oasis
Crawling	Linkin Park
Drug Ballad	Eminem
Drugs Are Good	NoFX
Elevator Up	Fountains of Wayne
Freebase	Pennywise
Geek Stink Breath	Green Day
Ghetto D	Master P
Givin' Up	The Darkness
God of Wine	Third Eye Blind
Helmet in the Bush	Korn
Heroine	Velvet Underground
How to Save a Life	The Fray
Hurt	Nine Inch Nails or Johnny Cash

Junkhead	Alice in Chains
Knock Me Down	Red Hot Chili Peppers
Life by the Drop	Stevie Ray Vaughn
Losing My Way	Justin Timberlake
Man Overboard	Blink 182
My Sundown	Jimmy Eat World
One Way Ticket	The Darkness
Powder	Yellocard
Psycho	System of a Down
Real Thing	Alice in Chains
Remedy	Seether
River of Deceit	Mad Season
Save Me	Shine Down
Slow Motion	Third Eye Blind
That's Why I'm Here	Toby Keith
This Is the Place	Red Hot Chili Peppers
Time and Time Again	Papa Roach
Uncle Johnny	The Killers
We Are All On Drugs	Weezer
Worst Hangover Ever	The Offspring
You're Not My God	Keith Urban

ADOLESCENCE

Title	Artist
Broken	Bad Religion
Disposable Teens	Marilyn Manson
Excursions	A Tribe Called Quest
Here Is No Why	Smashing Pumpkins
Let's Talk About Sex	Salt n Pepa
Pets	Porno for Pyros
Road to Acceptance	Green Day
Teenager	Better than Ezra
You Don't Belong	Bad Religion
Young Offender	Pet Shop Boys

AGING

Title	Artist
16	Green Day
83	John Mayer
Clean Up Before She Comes	Nirvanna
Good Riddance	Green Day

Growing Older but Not Up	Jimmy Buffett
In Search of Peter Pan	Kate Bush
Just Getting Older	Oasis
Just Older	Bon Jovi
Landslide	Fleetwood Mac, Dixie Chicks, Smashing Pumpkins
Life Gets Away	Clint Black
Looking Over My Shoulder	Aimee Mann
Rockin' Chair	Oasis
Songs to Aging Children Come	Joni Mitchell
This Old Man	MC Frontalot
Time	Pink Floyd
Too Old to Rock and Roll, Too Young to Die	Jethro Tull
When I Was Young	The Animals
Young	Kenny Chesney

ANGER/VIOLENCE/MEDIATION

Title	Artist
8 Blood For Blood	Machine Head
A Box	King's X
Angry	Matchbox 20
Baby Uvula Who?	Green Day
And One	Linkin Park
Black and White and Red All Over	Biohazard
Bored and Extremely Dangerous	Bad Religion
Defy You	Offspring
Don't Look Back in Anger	Oasis
I	Black Sabbath
I Am	Static-X
Inside	Toad the Wet Sprocket
Interstate 8	Modest Mouse
Love and Anger	Kate Bush
Medicate Myself	Verve Pipe
Mudshovel	Stained
New Skin	Incubus
One Angry Dwarf and 200 Solemn Faces	Ben Folds Five
Place Your Hand	Melissa Etheridge
Release the Demons	Godsmack
Romeo	Sublime
Selfless, Cold, and Composed	Ben Folds Five
Sin	Nine Inch Nails
Ticks and Leeches	Tool
Up and Gone	Hoobastank
Violence	Pet Shop Boys

Violence Fetish	Disturbed
What Angry Blue?	Seven Mary Three
You'll Never Make It	Pennywise

BEREAVEMENT

Title	Artist
All Quiet on the Western Front	Elton John
All the Love	Kate Bush
Angel	Sarah Mclachlan
Everyone I Love Is Dead	Type O Negative
In This Heart	Sinead O'Connor
Live Again	Better than Ezra
Loss	Biohazard
Made Up My Mind	David Grey
On Your Shore	Enya
One Last Love Song	Beautiful South
Redemption Day	Sheryl Crow
Requiem	Slipknot
Rise Above	Dog Eat Dog
The Brilliant Dance	Dashboard Confessional
Tiny Grief Song	Sinead O'Connor

CRISIS INTERVENTION

Title	Artist
Another Tricky Day	The Who
Better Days	Supertramp
Broken Home	Papa Roach
Can You Get Away	2pac
Crisis	Bob Marley
Crisis King	Helmet
Deafening Silence	Machine Head
For You	Staind
I Can't Remember	Alice in Chains
Get a Life	Pennywise
Leeds	Indigo Girls
Midlife Crisis	Faith No More
On Any Other Day	The Police
Take It Like a Man	The Offspring
Weird	Hanson
When the Lights Gone Out	Ziggy Marley
Why Georgia	John Mayer

DECISION MAKING

Title	Artist
A New Life	Pet Shop Boys
Black and White	INXS
Dave's Possessed Hair	Sum 41
F Train	David Usher
Follow My Heart	REO Speedwagon
Heads Carolina Tails California	Jo Dee Messina
Learn to Fly	Foo Fighters
Let Me Go	Good Charlotte
Life Is What You Make It	Outlawz
Perfectly Still	Gin Blossoms
Seal Our Fate	Gloria Estefan
Shadow Boxing	Extreme
Sign of Life	LeAnn Rimes
Solitare	Public Image Limited
Westbound Sign	Green Day

DEPRESSION/LONELINESS

Title	Artist
Another Lonely Day	Ben Harper
Anytime You Need a Friend	Mariah Carey
Black Clouds	Papa Roach
Blame	Korn
Cold and Ugly	Tool
Deeper Understanding	Kate Bush
Depression	Pennywise
Do Dad A	Green Day
Everything I Said	The Cranberries
Fade to Grey	Jars of Clay
Falling Away from Me	Korn
Four	Lit
Free	Prince
Having a Blast	Green Day
Homely Girl	UB40
I Can't Go On	Tyrese
I Love a Lonely Day	Amy Grant
I'm Sorry	Blink 182
I Want a Dog	Pet Shop Boys
Into the Night of Blue	Ace of Base
Lonely	Brian McKnight

The Lonely	Toby Keith
Lonely Days	Eagle Eye Cherry
My Own Prison	Creed
No One's Kind	Staind
Not Pretty Enough	Kasey Chambers
Occasionally	Melissa Etheridge
Ode to the Lonely Hearted	Sugar Ray
Only Lonely	Bon Jovi
Punish Me	Edwin McCain
Rage and Then Regret	Abc
Rain on Me	Ashanti
Scar Tissue	Red Hot Chili Peppers
She's Got a Problem	Fountains of Wayne
Show Me the Meaning of Being Lonely	Backstreet Boys
So Lonely	The Police
Solitaire	Sheryl Crow
Space and Time	Verve
Space Travel Is Boring	Modest Mouse
Suffer	Staind
Time and Time Again	Counting Crows
To Forgive	Smashing Pumpkins
True Dat	Outkast
Use Once and Destroy	Hole
What You Were	The Cranberries
When I'm Lonely	Hootie and the Blowfish

DISAPPOINTMENT

Title	**Artist**
3rd and Long	New Found Glory
Disappointed	Morrissey
Disappointment	The Cranberries
Exactly What You Wanted	Helmet
Fade	Stained
Father of Mine	Everclear
The Great Disappointment	A.F.I.
Hand Me Down	Wallflowers
Less	Ben Harper
Rearranged	Limp Bizkit
Sister	Creed
Sweet Surrender	Sarah McLachlan
To Think I Used to Love You	Uncle Kracker

EMOTIONAL INVOLVEMENT

Title	Artist
10 Years Later	Collective Soul
All You Wanted	Michelle Branch
Anyone	The Samples
Ball and Chain	Social Distortion
Black Again	Stone Temple Pilots
Blurry	Puddle of Mudd
By My Side	Ben Harper
Can't Take Anymore	Pennywise
Cold Nights	Social Distortion
Crazy	Gnarls Barkley
Decompression Period	Papa Roach
Do It for Love	2pac
Far Behind	Candlebox
Fix You	Coldplay
For You	Tracy Chapman
I Keep It Under My Hat	Tim McGraw
I Miss You	Blink 182
I Miss You	Incubus
I'm Not Okay	My Chemical Romance
I Won't Leave You Lonely	Shania Twain
Let Me Go	Cake
Let'er Rip	Dixie Chicks
Live Again	Better than Ezra
Look What You've Done	Jet
Memory Lane	Tim McGraw
Miserable	Lit
Only	Nine Inch Nails
Painful	Staind
Pieces	Sum 41
Send the Pain Below	Chevelle
Sister	Creed
Staring at the Sun	The Offspring
Told You for the Last Time	Eric Clapton
Turn Around	Collective Soul

GAY/LESBIAN SUPPORT

Title	Artist
101% Man	Beautiful South
Androgyny	Garbage
Coming Clean	Green Day
Controversy	Prince
In Denial	Pet Shop Boys
Faget	Korn
Girl	Tori Amos
Hey Jupiter	Tori Amos
Homophobia	Chumbawanba
My Lovely Man	Red Hot Chili Peppers
One in a Million	Pet Shop Boys
Pink Triangle	Weezer
The Secret Marriage	Sting
Silent Legacy	Melissa Etheridge
Sports and Wine	Ben Folds Five
Taxi Ride	Tori Amos
Turn It On	Flaming Lips

HOMELESS

Title	Artist
6th Avenue Heartache	The Wallflowers
Cardboard City	Roy Harper
Even Flow	Pearl Jam
God Bless the Child	Shania Twain
Homeless	Paul Simon
Homeless	Pennywise
Homeless Child	Ben Harper
On Every Corner	Ani DiFranco
Panhandlin' Prince	Ugly Kid Joe
Senator Speak	Verve Pipe
Stuck with Me	Green Day
Warchild	The Cranberries
Who Will Save Your Soul	Jewel

MARITAL ISSUES

Title	Artist
1229 Sheffield	Verve Pipe
Alice Childress	Ben Folds Five
Change	Melissa Etheridge
Evil Ways	Santana
I Had a King	Joni Mitchell
Pretty	The Cranberries
One in a Million	Pet Shop Boys
Simple Together	Alanis Morissette
Soothe Yourself	Luscious Jackson
Stay Together for The Kids	Blink 182
Tea and Sympathy	Jars of Clay
Till Death Do Us Apart	Madonna
When Love Fades	Toby Keith

PROBLEM SOLVING/MOVING ON

Title	Artist
Closure	Chevelle
Daffodil Lament	The Cranberries
Don't Cry	Faith Evans
Don't Have Time	Liz Phair
Fast Car	Tracy Chapman
Fast Car	David Usher
Fentoozler	Blink 182
Forget About Us	Tim McGraw
Gotta Move On	Verve Pipe
Hell Song	Sum 41
High Anxiety	Sugar Ray
Keep Away	Godsmack
Life Will Pass You By	Bon Jovi
Lonely Alone	Reba McEntire
London	The Smiths
Losing My Ground	Fergie
Make a Bet	Foo Fighters
Miserablism	Pet Shop Boys
Piano I	Alicia Keys
Rock and a Hard Place	Ludacris
Set Me Free	Pennywise
The Shape	Slipknot
Signs	Creed

Wake Up and Smell the Coffee	The Cranberries
Walk on By	Cake
www.memory	Alan Jackson
You Gotta Be	Desree

PROSTITUTION

Title	Artist
Brendas Got a Baby	Tupac Shakur
Build God, Then We'll Talk	Panic! At the Disco
Call Me	Blondie
Cherry Lips	Garbage
Fancy	Reba McEntire
Letters to a John	Ani Difranco
Love Her	Seether
Oh Marie	Sheryl Crow
She's Like Heroin	System of a Down
Something to Do	Depeche Mode
Wrong Way	Sublime

RAPE

Title	Artist
Baby Don't Cry	Tupac Shakur
Damaged	Plumb
Date Rape	Sublime
Flinch	Alanis Morissette
Gratitude	Ani DiFranco
Jennifer Lost the War	The Offspring
Me and a Gun	Tori Amos
No Man's Land	Tanya Tucker
Polly	Nirvanna
Pretty	Korn
Sex Type Thing	Stone Temple Pilots
Sullen Girl	Fiona Apple
Tiptoe	Ani DiFranco
Wash Those Years Away	Creed

RELATIONSHIPS

Title	Artist
All The Lovin' and the Hurtin'	LeAnn Rimes
Awake and Dreaming	Finger Eleven

Black and Blue	New Found Glory
Confusion	Alice in Chains
Crazy Amanda	Sum 41
Death and Destruction	Weezer
Don't Wanna Fall in Love	Green Day
Enid	Barenaked Ladies
Fast Changes	Seal
Here and Now	Blessed Union of Souls
If You're Gone	Matchbox 20
I'll Think of a Reason Later	Lee Ann Womack
Leaving Is the Only Way Out	Shania Twain
Loud and Clear	Cranberries
Man Overboard	Blink 182
Mindchanger	Bush
Nobody's Perfect	Madonna
No Easy Way	Seal
No Scrubs	TLC
Once Is Enough	Aerosmith
One Way Ticket	LeAnn Rimes
Play	The Cure
Show Me	Bjork
Sinking	Jars of Clay
Sticks and Stones	Alien Ant Farm
Stuart and the Ave	Green Day
There's Your Trouble	Dixie Chicks
The World Has Turned and Left Me Here	Weezer
Tomorrow	Avril Lavigne
Til the Day I Die	Garbage
Untitled	Blink 182
Violet	Bjork
Wanted It to Be	Sister Hazel
Why Do You Want Him?	Green Day
You and I & I	Matchbox 20
You Make Me Mad	Third Day

SUICIDE

Title	Artist
20 Years in the Dakota	Hole
My Friend	Phish
Chop Suey	System of a Down
Don't Go and Put a Bullet in Your Head	Lenny Kravitz
Easy Tonight	Five for Fighting
Falling Away from Me	Korn

Give and Get	Pennywise
Half Moon Café	Indigo Girls
Last Resort	Papa Roach
Loss	Biohazard
My Direction	Sum 41
No Association	Silverchair
No Hero	The Offspring
One More Suicide	Marcy Playground
Pain	Puff Daddy
Revolution	Toll
So Long Suicide	Duran Duran
Soil	System of a Down
Uptight	Green Day
When Mermaids Cry	Eagle Eye Cherry

Terminal Illness/Catastrophe

Title	Artist
Been and Son	Nirvanna
Behind the Sun	Eric Clapton
Day That I Die	Good Charlotte
Die with Your Boots On	Kenny Chesney
Dying Inside	The Cranberries
Fixin' to Die	Bob Dylan
For the Life of Me	Wallflowers
The Great Gig in the Sky	Pink Floyd
Hung the Moon	Better Than Ezra
I'm Sorry	Blink 182
In My Time of Dying	Willie Johnson
Rotting	Green Day
Tourniquet	Evanescence
Try Not to Breathe	REM
Where Angels Sing	Meat Loaf

Reminiscence: 1980s

Title	Artist
A Century Ends	David Grey
Boys of Summer	Don Henley/The Ataris
Clocks	Cold Play
Do I Know You	Toby Keith
Faded	Ben Harper
Fred Jones Pt 2	Ben Folds Five

Good Riddance (Time of Your Life)	Green Day
The Heart Never Forgets	LeAnn Rimes
Hey Now	Oasis
I Was There	Green Day
I'll Remember You, Love, in My Prayers	Alison Krauss
I Will Not Forget You	Sarah McLachlan
I Will Remember You	Amy Grant
In the End	Linkin Park
Life Fades Away	Danzig
Memorabilia	Nine Inch Nails
Scarred for Life	Biohazard
Selective Memory	Eels
Something Like That	Tim McGraw
Sweet Rain	Train
Tears Fall Down	Hootie and the Blowfish
Who Needs Pictures	Brad Paisley

RUNAWAY

Title	Artist
Anytime	Eve 6
Can't Stop	Suicidal Tendencies
Falls Apart	Sugar Ray
He's Just a Runaway	Sister Sledge
If You Leave	Destiny's Child
Island in the Sun	Weezer
Not Hollywood	The Cranberries
Runaway	Bon Jovi
Runaway	Deee-lite
Runaway	Ice T
Runaway	Linkin Park
Runaway	Wyclef Jean
Runaway Lover	Madonna
Runaway Run	Hanson
Runaway Train	Eric Clapton
Runaway Train	Soul Asylum
Running Away	Bob Marley
She's Got Her Ticket	Tracy Chapman
There's Got to Be a Way	Mariah Carey
Wherever You Will Go	The Calling

Indexes to Competency Tasks

Index by Population
Index by Technique
Index by Student Objective

Index by Population

POPULATION	TASK	STUDENT OBJECTIVE	TECHNIQUES
Adolescents			
Behavior Disorders	2.37	Teach responsibility for actions	Leading Group Discussion Role-Playing Evaluating
	2.38	Teaching rhythm and rules	Use of Rules Approving Evaluating
	4.06	Teach responsibility for actions	Decision Making Leading Focused Group Discussion Following Rules Evaluating
Cognitively Impaired	2.16	Teach circle dance	Chaining Cuing Task Analysis Evaluating data
	2.17	Teach choral performance skills	Modeling Cuing Fading Approving Incompatible Responses
Eating Disorder	4.17	Teach appropriate body image	Decision Making Leading a Group Discussion Approving Evaluating
Emotional Disturbance	2.36	Use approval/disapproval	Approving/Disapproving 4:1 Ratio Evaluating
	2.39	Teach anger control	Controlling Anger Leading a Group Discussion Overcompensation Evaluating

POPULATION	TASK	STUDENT OBJECTIVE	TECHNIQUES
Emotional Disturbance, cont.	2.40	Teach nonsexual relationship with opposite sex	Establishing Relationships Teach Action Steps Role-Playing Evaluating
	2.41	Teach resistance to peer pressure	Role-Playing Approving
Head Injury	3.22	Increase pre-mobility skills	Modeling Composing Inservicing/Coaching staff Evaluating
Hearing Loss	2.29	Teach rhythm reading	Group Leadership – Rhythm Ens. Cuing Modeling
	3.14	Increase social interaction in inclusive classroom	Approving Signing Social Interaction/Socialization Evaluating
Autism Spectrum Disorder (ASD)	3.04	Teach attending and choosing	Composing/Arranging Music Decision Making Focused Attention Transitioning Evaluating
	3.18	Extinguish mannerism, teach turn taking	Approving Ignoring Teaching Incompatible Responses Evaluating
	3.21	Teach basic preschool skills	Approving Cuing Using Visual Aids
	4.05	Teach incompatible response	Teaching Incompatible Responses

POPULATION	TASK	STUDENT OBJECTIVE	TECHNIQUES
	4.16	Consult to inclusive music class	Consultation Approving Peer Tutoring Positive Interactions Evaluating
Behavior Disorders	2.35	Reduce hyperactivity	Reducing Hyperactivity Modeling Cuing Teaching Incompatible Responses Approving Evaluating
	2.37	Teach responsibility for actions	Leading Group Discussion Role-Playing Evaluating
	2.38	Teaching rhythm and rules	Use of Rules Approving Evaluating
	2.41	Teach resistance to peer pressure	Role-Playing Approving
	4.06	Teach responsibility for actions	Decision Making Leading Focused Group Discussion Following Rules Evaluating
	4.16	Inclusive general music class	Consultation Approving Peer Tutoring Positive Interaction Evaluating

POPULATION	TASK	STUDENT OBJECTIVE	TECHNIQUES
Cerebral Palsy			
Adults	2.32	Teach group interaction	Stimulating Interaction/ Socialization Evaluating
Children	2.31	Teach range-of-motion exercise	Range-of-Motion Exercise Evaluating
	3.07	Teach academic skills/social behavior	Cuing Approving Ignoring Evaluating
	3.21	Teach basic preschool skills	Approving Cuing Using Visual Aids
Child Abuse	2.54	Teach anger control	Anger Control Role-Playing Parenting Evaluating
	3.16	Teach positive interaction	Cuing Approving Parenting Techniques Evaluating
Children			
Abused	3.16	Positive interaction with parent	Cuing Approving Parenting Techniques Evaluating
ASD	3.04	Teach attending and choosing	Composing/Arranging Music Decision Making Focused Attention Transitioning Evaluating

POPULATION	TASK	STUDENT OBJECTIVE	TECHNIQUES
	3.18	Extinguish mannerism, teach turn taking	Approving Ignoring Teaching Incompatible Responses Evaluating
Behavior Disorder	2.35	Reduce hyperactivity	Reducing Hyperactivity Modeling Cuing Teaching Incompatible Responses Approving Evaluating
	3.03	Reduce inappropriate behavior in lunchroom	Music Interruption Focused Group Discussion Approving Self-evaluating/Data
	4.16	Inclusive general music class	Consultation Approving Peer Tutoring Positive Interaction Evaluating
Cerebral Palsy	2.31	Teach range-of-motion exercise	Range-of-Motion Exercise Evaluating
	3.07	Teach academic skills/social behavior	Cuing Approving Ignoring Evaluating
	3.21	Teach basic preschool skills	Approving Cuing Using Visual Aids
Cognitively Impaired	2.19	Teach two chords on guitar (color coded)	Task Analysis Cuing Modeling Approving Correcting

Population	Task	Student Objective	Techniques
Cognitively Impaired, cont.	2.20	Teach children to follow two-part directions	Composing Chaining Cuing Guided Assistance
	2.21	Teach honesty to children	Composing Modeling Approving
	2.22	Teach one language task	Cuing Approving
	2.23	Teach one color	Cuing Approving
Early Intervention PreSchool	3.07	Teach academic skills/social behavior	Cuing Approving Ignoring Evaluating
	3.21	Teach basic preschool skills	Approving Cuing Using Visual Aids
Hearing Loss	2.28	Teach signs to music	Signing Chaining Modeling Cuing
	2.30	Teach auditory discrimination	Signing Auditory Discrimination Evaluating
Mentoring	4.09	Socialization with older adults	Approving Socialization Mentoring Evaluating

POPULATION	TASK	STUDENT OBJECTIVE	TECHNIQUES
Medical	4.12	Maintain development	Approving Ignoring Positive Interaction Parenting Techniques Evaluating
Phobia	4.08	Desensitize animal phobia	Relaxation Desensitization Imagery Evaluating
Specific Learning Disability	2.14	Teach spelling concept	Composing Song Leading Chaining Cuing Evaluating
	2.15	Teach reading	Composing Song Leading Cuing Approving Evaluating
	4.15	Teach to speak in sentences	Cuing Approving Incompatible Responses Evaluating
	4.20	Teach math skills	Approving Ignoring Evaluating
Visually Impaired	2.25	Teach body part awareness	Cuing Approving
	2.26	Teach grooming	Cuing Task Analysis Approving Incompatible Responses

POPULATION	TASK	STUDENT OBJECTIVE	TECHNIQUES
Cognitively Impaired			
Mild	2.20	Teach children to follow two-part directions	Composing Chaining Cuing Guided Assistance
	2.21	Teach honesty to children	Composing Modeling Approving
	4.10	Teach decision making	Decision Making Approving Homework Assignment Incompatible Responses Evaluating
Moderate	2.16	Teach circle dance	Chaining Cuing Task Analysis Evaluating data
	2.17	Teach choral performance skills	Modeling Cuing Fading Approving Incompatible Responses
	2.18	Teach manners appropriate for adult social occasion	Composing Teaching Social Skills Modeling Cuing Evaluating
	2.19	Teach two chords on guitar (color coded)	Task Analysis Cuing Modeling Approving Correcting

POPULATION	TASK	STUDENT OBJECTIVE	TECHNIQUES
	2.32	Teach group interaction	Stimulating Interaction Evaluating
	3.15	Teach decision making skills for leisure activity	Cuing Approving Decision Making Evaluating
Severe/Profound	2.22	Teach one language task	Cuing Approving
	2.23	Teach one color	Cuing Approving
	2.24	Teach responses to 3 types of stimulation	Infant Stimulation Evaluating
Couples Counseling	2.54	Teach anger control	Anger Control Role-Playing Evaluating
	3.10	Teach improved communication	Interpersonal Skills Evaluating
	4.11	Stimulate positive verbal and physical responses between spouse/partners	Approving Role-Playing Focused Group Discussion Evaluating
Emotionally Disturbed	2.36	Use approval/disapproval	Approving/Disapproving 4:1 Ratio Evaluating
	2.39	Teach anger control	Controlling Anger Leading a Group Discussion Overcompensation Evaluating
	2.40	Teach nonsexual relationship with opposite sex	Establishing Relationships Teach Action Steps Role-Playing Evaluating

POPULATION	TASK	STUDENT OBJECTIVE	TECHNIQUES
Emotionally Disturbed, cont.	2.41	Teach resistance to peer pressure	Role-Playing Approving
	4.16	Inclusive general music class	Consultation Approving Peer Tutoring Positive Interactions Evaluating
Families			
Distress	2.53	Identify roles of family members in group interaction	Leading Group Discussion Role Analysis Family Counseling Evaluating
	2.55	Help families have positive interaction	Rapping/Composing Approving Family Counseling Evaluating
Organ Donors	2.52	Teach how to be comfortable with decision	Empathy Role-Playing Action Steps Evaluating
Terminal Illness	2.51	Enhance relationships among family members	Establishing Relationships Role-Playing Evaluating
Substance Abuse	4.13	Teach role function and selection	Role Assessment Cuing Role-Playing Decision Making Relationships

POPULATION	TASK	STUDENT OBJECTIVE	TECHNIQUES
Geriatric Clients	2.42	Teach 3 reality orientation objectives	Composing Cuing Evaluating
	2.43	Teach exercises to music	Group Leadership – Exercise Cuing Scanning Evaluating
	2.44	Increase social interaction	Stimulating Group Interaction Evaluating Cuing
	2.45	Plan musical performance	Leading Group Discussion
	2.46	Increase interaction between staff and residents	Approving Leading Group Discussion Song Leading
	3.17	Teach creativity, social inter-action, and rhythmic skill	Approving Stimulating Creativity Evaluating
	4.09	Stimulate socialization between older adults and youth	Approving Socialization Mentoring Evaluating
Head Injury	3.22	Increase pre-mobility skills	Modeling Composing Inservicing / Coaching staff Evaluating
Hearing Loss	2.28	Teach signs to well-known song	Song Leading Chaining Modeling Cuing Signing to Music

Population	Task	Student Objective	Techniques
Hearing Loss, cont.	2.29	Teach 16 measures of rhythm	Group Leadership – Rhythm Cuing Chaining Modeling
	2.30	Teach auditory discrimination	Signing Auditory Discrimination Evaluating
	3.14	Increase social interaction in inclusive classroom	Approving Signing Social Interaction/Socialization Evaluating
	4.04	Teach music using signs; give differential feedback	Signing Approving Evaluating
Infants	2.24	Teach responses to 3 types of stimulation	Infant Stimulation Evaluating
	3.13	Teach infant directed singing	Decision Making Accompanying Infant Stimulation (Teach Parent) Evaluate
Inservice Presentation	3.02	Teach substance abuse counselors the benefits of MT in recovery	Inservice presentation Evaluate
Kidney Dialysis	4.01	Reduce discomforts of dialysis	Music Listening Relaxation Evaluating
Language Delay	3.21	Teach basic preschool skills	Approving Cuing Using Visual Aids

POPULATION	TASK	STUDENT OBJECTIVE	TECHNIQUES
	4.15	Teach to speak in sentences	Cuing Approving Incompatible Responses Evaluating
Pain	2.47	Teach focus on music to reduce pain awareness before surgery	Focused Attention Music Listening Evaluating
	4.01	Reduce discomforts of dialysis	Music Listening Relaxation Evaluating
	4.19	Reduce awareness of chronic pain during exercise	Cuing Approving Ignoring Evaluation
Parents	2.33	Teach reinforcement and positive feedback	Approving Ignoring Parenting Techniques Evaluating
	2.34	Techniques for parents with children with DD	Leading Group Discussion Role-Playing Parenting Techniques Evaluating
	2.54	Teach anger control to abusive parents	Anger Control Role-Playing Parenting Evaluating
	3.13	Teach infant directed singing	Decision Making Accompanying Infant Stimulation (Teach Parent) Evaluate

POPULATION	TASK	STUDENT OBJECTIVE	TECHNIQUES
Parents, cont.	4.12	Maintain a child's development while in hospital	Approving Ignoring Positive Interaction Parenting Techniques Evaluating
	4.18	Teach parents to set realistic goals	Leading Group Discussion Role-Playing Parenting Techniques Evaluating
Patients			
Catastrophic Illness or Injury	2.49	Demonstrate realistic life goals	Leading Group Discussion Empathetic Listening Evaluating
Chronic Pain	4.19	Reduce awareness of pain	Cuing Approving Ignoring Evaluating
Dialysis	4.01	Reduce discomforts of dialysis	Relaxation Music Listening Evaluating
General Hospital	2.48	Teach stress reduction	Relaxation Techniques Evaluating
	4.12	Structure parent visits to maintain child's developmental level	Approving Ignoring Positive Interaction Evaluating
Head Injury	3.22	Increase pre-mobility skills	Modeling Composing Inservicing/Coaching staff Evaluating

POPULATION	TASK	STUDENT OBJECTIVE	TECHNIQUES
Presurgical	2.47	Teach how to use music to relieve postoperative pain	Focusing Attention Music Listening Evaluating
Terminal Illness	2.50	Teach action step to deal with diagnosis	Teaching Action Steps Evaluating
	2.51	Enhance family relationships	Establishing Relationships Role-Playing Evaluating
	3.19	Engage reluctant patient/relax agitated patient	Isoprincipal Accompanying Repertoire Evaluate
Peers	1.01	Lead well-known, unaccompanied song	Song Leading Scanning
	1.02	Accompany with rhythm and lead well-known song	Song Leading Accompanying Scanning
	1.03	Accompany with harmony and lead well-known song	Song Leading Accompanying Scanning
	1.04	Accompany with most advanced technique and teach new song	Song Leading Accompanying Scanning Chaining Modeling
	1.05	Accompany with second-best technique and teach new song	Song Leading Accompanying Scanning Chaining Modeling

POPULATION	TASK	STUDENT OBJECTIVE	TECHNIQUES
Peers, cont.	1.06	Teach participants to accompany on the Autoharp	Song Leading Teaching from Task Analysis Chaining Modeling Approving Correcting
	1.07	Teach participants to perform melody from cues	Cuing Approving Correcting
	1.08	Compose "hello" song: teach to participants and accompany it	Composing Song Leading Accompanying Chaining Modeling Scanning
	1.09	Compose "goodbye" song: teach to participants and accompany it	Composing Song Leading Accompanying Chaining Modeling Scanning
	1.10	Teach new round	Chaining Cuing Fading Approving Correcting
	1.11	Teach 16 measure rhythm task	Group Leadership – Rhythm Cuing Chaining Modeling
	1.12	Engage participants in solo and ensemble drumming	Group Leadership – Rhythm Improvising Chaining Modeling Cuing

POPULATION	TASK	STUDENT OBJECTIVE	TECHNIQUES
	1.13	Teach signs to simple song	Song Leading Chaining Modeling Cuing Signing
	1.14	Teach eight synchronized exercises	Group Leadership – Exercise Cuing Scanning
	1.15	Teach simple dance of at least 10 sequential steps	Group Leadership – Dance Cuing Chaining Evaluating/Data
	1.16	Conduct group sing-along	Song Leading Accompanying Using Repertoire
	2.01	Use music to maintain eye contact with participants	Song Leading Maintaining Eye Contact Scanning Evaluating/Data
	2.02	Eliminate talking in group	Song Leading Scanning Approving Incompatible Responses Evaluating/Data
	2.03	Teach appropriate peer touching	Structuring Music for Response Approving Scanning Evaluating/Data
	2.04	Create 100% on task	Approving Incompatible Responses Evaluating/Data

POPULATION	TASK	STUDENT OBJECTIVE	TECHNIQUES
Peers, cont.	2.05	Teach academic task	Composing Song Leading Chaining Cuing Evaluating/Data
	2.06	Teach paired nonsense syllables	Composing Chaining Cuing Fading Evaluating/Data
	2.07	Teach vocabulary pronunciation	Composing Chaining Cuing Fading Evaluating/Data
	2.08	Teach foreign language vocabulary	Composing Chaining Cuing Fading Evaluating/Data
	2.09	Use music to teach relaxation	Structuring Music for Response Directing Relaxation Routine Evaluating/Data
	2.10	Teach participants 2 action steps to deal with disappointment	Role-Playing Teaching Action Step
	2.11	Shape unanimous decision	Shaping Group Decision Accompanying
	2.12	Introduce drug/alcohol topic and lead discussion to make guidelines	Leading Group Discussion Structuring Music for Response

POPULATION	TASK	STUDENT OBJECTIVE	TECHNIQUES
	2.13	Convey primary emotions	Music Listening Lead Group Discussion Improvisation
	4.02	Teach empathy with role of client in group therapy	Incompatible Responses Lead Group Discussion Empathy Evaluating
Phobia	3.20	Teach persons with agoraphobia to leave house	Relaxation Imagery Role-Playing Self-Evaluating Data
	4.08	Desensitize child to animal phobia	Relaxation Desensitization Imagery Evaluating
Pregnant Women	4.14	Teach labor management	Labor Management Focusing Attention Relaxing Muscles Approving Using Incompatible Responses
Psychiatric			
Acute	2.58	Facilitate reality-based verbalizations	Leading Group Discussion Ignoring Approving Rapping
	2.59	Teach action steps to resolve a problem	Role-Playing Teaching Action Steps Evaluating
	4.07	Teach to select and implement self-shaping project	Teaching Action Steps

Population	Task	Student Objective	Techniques
Chronic	2.56	Teach square dance to improve social skills	Chaining Cuing Task Analysis Peer Tutoring Approving Evaluating
	2.57	Teach social interaction in a chorus rehearsal	Stimulating Group Interaction Cuing Evaluating
	2.60	Plan facility-wide dance to increase social skills	Leading Group Discussion Teaching Social Skills Role-Playing Evaluating
	3.05	Teach reality-based, appropriate social behavior using dance	Music to Reinforce Cuing Approving Evaluating
Depressed	2.59	Teach action steps to resolve a problem	Role-Playing Teaching Action Steps Evaluating
	3.06	Teach action behavior to reduce depression	Teaching Action Steps Role-Playing Evaluating
Eating Disorder	4.17	Teach appropriate body image	Decision Making Leading a Group Discussion Approving Evaluating
Passive-Aggressive	3.01	Teach assertiveness in emotion expression	Action Steps for Assertiveness Anger Control Role-Playing Negative Modeling Evaluating/Data

POPULATION	TASK	STUDENT OBJECTIVE	TECHNIQUES
Suicidal Ideation	3.08	Establish relationship with others in group	Teaching an Interpersonal Skill Leading Group Discussion Teaching Action Steps Evaluating
Special Education Consultant	4.16	Consult to inclusive music class	Consultation Approving Peer Tutoring Positive Interactions Evaluating
Special Learning Disability	2.14	Teach spelling concept	Composing Song Leading Chaining Cuing Evaluating
	2.15	Teach reading	Composing Song Leading Song Leading Cuing Approving Evaluating
	4.15	Teach to speak in sentences	Cuing Approving Incompatible Responses Evaluating
	4.20	Teach math skills	Approving Ignoring Evaluating

POPULATION	TASK	STUDENT OBJECTIVE	TECHNIQUES
Stroke	3.11	Improve gait and ambulation	Gait Training Approving Intermittent Interruption of Music Evaluating/Data
	3.12	Conduct range-of-motion exercises while teaching communication for basic needs	Range-of-Motion Exercises Sign Language/Alternative Comm. Evaluating
Substance Abuse	3.09	Discuss negative consequences of drug abuse	Leading Group Discussion Nonverbal Approving Evaluating
	4.13	Teach role function and selection	Role Assessment Cuing Role-Playing Decision Making Relationships
Visually Impaired	2.25	Teach body parts to children	Cuing Approving
	2.26	Teach grooming skills while reducing stereotyped behaviors	Cuing Task Analysis Approving Incompatible Responses
	2.27	Extinguish inappropriate verbal behavior while teaching mobility task to adults	Mobility Training Cuing Successive Approximation Evaluating/Data

Index by Technique

CI = Cognitive Impairment
DD = Developmental Disability
SLD = Specific Learning Disability

TECHNIQUE	TASK	POPULATION	STUDENT OBJECTIVES
Accompanying	1.02	Peers	Lead well know song, rhythm
	1.03	Peers	Lead well-known song, harmony
	1.04	Peers	Teach new song
	1.05	Peers	Teach new song
	1.08	Peers	Compose "hello" song; teach
	1.09	Peers	Compose "good-bye" song; teach
	1.16	Peers	Lead group sing-along; 10 song repertoire
	2.11	Peers	Shape group decision on song
	3.13	Parents of ill newborns	Accompany infant-directed singing
	3.19	Hospice	Accompany using Isoprinciple
Action Steps	2.10	Peers	Teach to deal with disappointment
	2.40	Emotionally dis. teens	Facilitate nonsexual relationships
	2.50	Terminal illness	Teach adjustment to diagnosis
	2.52	Families of organ donors	Teach empathy, positive decision making
	2.59	Depressed persons	Teach resolution of a problem
	3.01	Passive-aggressive	Teach assertiveness
	3.06	Depression	Teach reduction of depression
	3.08	Suicidal ideation	Teach to establish relationship with others
	4.07	Acute psychiatric clients	Teach to implement self-shaping project

TECHNIQUE	TASK	POPULATION	STUDENT OBJECTIVES
Anger Control	2.39	Adolescents	Teach anger control
	2.54	Child abusers	Teach anger control
	3.01	Passive-aggressive	Teach assertiveness/anger control
Approving	1.05	Peers	Teach participants to play Autoharp
	1.07	Peers	Teach participants to perform melody
	1.08	Peers	Teach new round
	2.03	Peers	Teach appropriate touching
	2.15	SLD (reading)	Teach reading fluidity, comprehension, and pleasure
	2.19	Cognitive Impairment	Teach two guitar chords
	2.21	Cognitive Impairment	Teach honesty concept
	2.22	Severe/profound CI	Teach language development
	2.23	Severe/profound CI	Teach one color
	2.25	Visual impairment	Teach body parts
	2.33	Parents of child with DD	Teach reinforcement and feedback
	2.35	Behavior disorder	Reduce hyperactivity; increase incompatible response
	2.38	Behavior disorder	Teach rhythmic activity and rules
	2.41	Behavior disorder	Resist peer pressure
	2.46	Geriatric clients	Increase positive interactions
	2.55	Family	Teach positive interactions
	2.56	Chronic psychiatric adults	Teach square dance; improve social skills
	2.58	Acute psychiatric clients	Teach reality-based verbalizations
	3.03	Adolescents	Reduce inappropriate lunchroom behavior
	3.05	Chronic psychiatric clients	Teach reality-based, appropriate social behavior
	3.07	Cerebral palsy	Teach academic skills/social behavior
	3.11	Stroke symptoms	Improve gait and ambulation
	3.14	Adolescents with hearing loss and normal hearing	Increase social interaction

TECHNIQUE	TASK	POPULATION	STUDENT OBJECTIVES
	3.15	Adults with CI	Teach decision making
	3.16	Child abuse	Teach position interactions
	3.17	Geriatric clients	Teach creativity, interaction, and rhythmic skills
	3.18	Emotional disturbance	Extinguish stereotyped mannerisms; wait turn; identify name
	3.21	Early intervention	Teach basic skills
	4.04	Hearing loss	Teach signs and music
	4.09	Geriatric clients/youth	Teach socialization; mentoring
	4.10	Adults with DD	Teach decision-making skills
	4.11	Couples	Teach positive verbal and physical responses
	4.12	Hospitalized child	Structure parent visit; maintain developmental level
	4.14	Pregnant women	Teach labor management
	4.15	Language delay	Teach speaking in sentences and asking questions
	4.16	Inclusive music class	Teach positive interactions
	4.17	Teen girls with eating disorder	Teach appropriate body image
	4.19	Chronic pain	Reduce awareness of pain
	4.20	SLD (math)	Improve math skills
Approving/ Disapproving Ratio	2.36	Emotional disturbance	Teach on-task behavior
Approving Incompatible Response	2.02	Peers	Extinguish talking
	2.04	Peers	Teach on-task behavior
	2.17	Cognitive impairment	Teach choral performance skills
	2.26	Visual impairment	Teach 2 grooming skills; reduce stereotyped behaviors

TECHNIQUE	TASK	POPULATION	STUDENT OBJECTIVES
Approving – Nonverbal	3.09	Substance abuse	Lead discussion on harm to others
Assertiveness	3.01	Passive-aggressive	Teach assertiveness action steps
Auditory Discrimination	2.30	Hearing loss	Teach auditory discrimination task
Autoharp	1.06	Peers	Teach use of Autoharp to accompany song
Chaining	1.04	Peers	Teach new song
	1.05	Peers	Teach new song
	1.08	Peers	Teach composed "hello" song
	1.09	Peers	Teach composed "good-bye" song
	1.10	Peers	Teach new round
	1.11	Peers	Teach 16-measure rhythm
	1.12	Peers	Engage participants in drumming
	1.13	Peers	Teach signing to simple song
	1.15	Peers	Teach simple dance
	2.05	Peers	Compose and teach vocabulary song
	2.06	Peers	Teach memory of paired nonsense syllables; compose song
	2.07	Peers	Teach vocabulary pronunciation; compose song
	2.08	Peers	Teach foreign vocabulary; compose song
	2.14	SLD (spelling)	Teach spelling concept; compose song
	2.16	Cognitive impairment	Teach circle dance
	2.20	Cognitive impairment	Teach following two-part directions
	2.28	Hearing loss	Sign recorded song
	2.29	Hearing loss	Teach 16-measure rhythm
	2.56	Chronic psychiatric adults	Teach square dance and social skills

TECHNIQUE	TASK	POPULATION	STUDENT OBJECTIVES
Composing	1.08	Peers	Teach composed "hello" song
	1.09	Peers	Teach composed "good-bye" song
	2.05	Peers	Compose and teach vocabulary song
	2.06	Peers	Teach paired nonsense syllables; compose song
	2.07	Peers	Teach vocabulary pronunciation; compose song
	2.08	Peers	Teach foreign language vocabulary; compose song
	2.14	SLD (spelling)	Teach spelling concept; compose song
	2.15	SLD (reading)	Increase reading fluidity, comprehension, and pleasure
	2.18	Cognitive impairment	Teach social skills
	2.20	Cognitive impairment	Teach following two-part directions
	2.21	Cognitive impairment	Teach honesty concept
	2.42	Geriatric clients	Teach Reality-Orientation objectives
	2.55	Family	Teach positive interaction
	3.04	Autism	Teach attending and choosing
	3.22	Head injury	Arrange music for pre-mobility skills
Consultation	4.16	Inclusive music class	Teach positive interaction
Correcting	1.06	Peers	Teach use of Autoharp to accompany song
	1.07	Peers	Teach participants to perform melody
	1.10	Peers	Teach new round
	2.19	Cognitive impairment	Teach two guitar chords
Creativity	3.17	Adults with dementia	Teach creativity through rhythm playing
Cuing	1.06	Peers	Teach group to play Autoharp
	1.07	Peers	Teach participants to perform melody

TECHNIQUE	TASK	POPULATION	STUDENT OBJECTIVES
Cuing, cont.	1.10	Peers	Teach new round
	1.11	Peers	Teach 16-measure rhythm
	1.12	Peers	Engage participants in drumming
	1.13	Peers	Teach signing to simple song
	1.14	Peers	Teach exercises to music
	1.15	Peers	Teach simple dance
	2.05	Peers	Compose and teach vocabulary song
	2.06	Peers	Teach paired nonsense syllables; compose song
	2.07	Peers	Teach vocabulary pronunciation; compose song
	2.08	Peers	Teach foreign language vocabulary; compose song
	2.14	SLD (spelling)	Teach spelling concept; compose song
	2.15	SLD (reading)	Increase reading fluidity, comprehension, and pleasure
	2.16	Cognitive impairment	Teach circle dance
	2.17	Cognitive impairment	Teach choral performance skills
	2.18	Cognitive impairment	Teach social skills
	2.19	Cognitive impairment	Teach two guitar chords
	2.20	Cognitive impairment	Teach following two-part directions
	2.22	Severe/profound CI	Teach language development
	2.23	Severe/profound CI	Teach one color
	2.25	Visual impairment	Teach body parts
	2.26	Visual impairment	Teach 2 grooming skills; reduce stereotyped behaviors
	2.27	Visual impairment	Teach mobility; extinguish inappropriate verbal behavior
	2.28	Hearing loss	Sign recorded song
	2.29	Hearing loss	Teach 16-measure rhythm
	2.35	Behavior disorder	Reduce hyperactivity; increase incompatible response
	2.42	Geriatric clients	Teach Reality-Orientation objectives
	2.43	Geriatric clients	Teach exercises to music

TECHNIQUE	TASK	POPULATION	STUDENT OBJECTIVES
	2.44	Geriatric clients	Teach social interaction
	2.56	Chronic psychiatric adults	Teach square dance; improve social skills
	2.57	Chronic psychiatric adults	Teach social interaction
	3.05	Chronic psychiatric adults	Teach reality-based, appropriate social behavior
	3.07	Cerebral palsy	Teach academic skills/social behavior
	3.15	Adults with CI	Teach decision making
	3.16	Child abuse	Teach positive interactions
	3.21	Early intervention	Teach basic skills
	4.13	Families – substance abuse	Teach role function
	4.15	Language delay	Teach speaking in sentences and asking questions
	4.19	Chronic pain	Reduce awareness of pain
Data Collection	1.15	Peers	Teach simple dance
	2.01	Peers	Maintain group eye contact
	2.02	Peers	Extinguish talking
	2.03	Peers	Teach appropriate touching
	2.04	Peers	Teach on-task behavior
	2.05	Peers	Compose and teach vocabulary song
	2.06	Peers	Teach memory of paired nonsense syllables; compose song
	2.08	Peers	Teach foreign vocabulary; compose song
	2.09	Peers	Use music to teach relaxation
	2.14	SLD (spelling)	Teach spelling concept; compose song
	2.16	Cognitive impairment	Teach circle dance
	2.18	Cognitive impairment	Teach manners for social occasion
	2.27	Visual impairment	Teach mobility; extinguish inappropriate verbal behavior
	2.35	Behavior disorder	Reduce hyperactivity; increase incompatible response

TECHNIQUE	TASK	POPULATION	STUDENT OBJECTIVES
Data Collection, cont.	2.36	Emotional disturbance	Teach on-task behavior
	2.55	Family	Teach positive interactions
	3.01	Passive-aggressive	Teach assertiveness
	3.03	Adolescents	Reduce inappropriate lunchroom behavior
	3.06	Depression	Teach reduction of depression
	3.11	Stroke	Improve gait and ambulation
	3.13	Parents of ill newborns	Record parent singing
	3.15	Adults with CI	Teach decision making
	3.20	Agoraphobia	Reduce fear of leaving house
Decision Making	3.04	Autism	Teach attending and choosing
	3.13	Parents of ill newborns	Record parent singing
	3.15	Adults with CI	Teach decision making
	4.06	Behavior disorder	Teach responsibility and following rules
	4.10	Adults with DD	Teach decision-making skills
	4.13	Families – substance abuse	Teach role function
	4.17	Teen girls with eating disorder	Teach appropriate body image
Desensitization	4.08	Phobia – child	Desensitize animal phobia
Drawing to Music	4.03	Terminal illness	Teach emotional expression
Empathy	2.49	Catastrophic illness/injury	Teach identification of realistic life goals
	2.52	Families of organ donors	Teach empathy, positive decision making
	4.02	Peers	Teach empathy with clients in therapy

TECHNIQUE	TASK	POPULATION	STUDENT OBJECTIVES
Evaluating	1.15	Peers	Teach simple dance
	2.01	Peers	Maintain group eye contact
	2.02	Peers	Extinguish talking
	2.03	Peers	Teach appropriate touching
	2.04	Peers	Teach on-task behavior
	2.05	Peers	Compose and teach vocabulary song
	2.06	Peers	Teach memory of paired nonsense syllables; compose song
	2.07	Peers	Teach vocabulary pronunciation; compose song
	2.08	Peers	Teach foreign vocabulary; compose song
	2.09	Peers	Use music to teach relaxation
	2.14	SLD (spelling)	Teach spelling concept; compose song
	2.15	SLD (reading)	Increase reading fluency, comprehension, and pleasure
	2.18	Cognitive impairment	Teach social skills
	2.24	Cognitive impairment	Teach response to stimulation
	2.25	Family	Teach positive interaction
	2.27	Visual impairment	Teach mobility; extinguish inappropriate verbal behavior
	2.30 to 4.10	All	Evaluate all objectives
Eye Contact	2.01	Peers	Maintain group eye contact
	3.04	Autism	Teach joint attention
Fading	1.10	Peers	Teach new round
	2.06	Peers	Teach memory of paired nonsense syllables; compose song
	2.07	Peers	Teach vocabulary pronunciation; compose song
	2.08	Peers	Teach foreign vocabulary; compose song
	2.17	Cognitive impairment	Teach choral performance skills

TECHNIQUE	TASK	POPULATION	STUDENT OBJECTIVES
Family Counseling	2.53	Families	Teach to identify family roles
	2.55	Family	Teach positive interactions
Focused Attention	2.47	Presurgical patients	Teach to relieve postoperative pain
	4.14	Pregnant women	Teach labor management
Gait Training/ Mobility	3.11	Stroke symptoms	Improve gait and ambulation
	3.22	Head injury	Increase balance and weight shifting
Group Discussion Skill	2.11	Peers	Shape group decision on song
	2.12	Peers	Teach to formulate guidelines
	2.13	Peers	Teach to convey emotions
	2.34	Parents of a child with DD	Teach parenting techniques
	2.37	Behavior disorders	Teach to accept responsibility
	2.39	Adolescents	Teach anger control
	2.45	Geriatric clients	Plan musical performance
	2.46	Geriatric clients	Increase positive interactions
	2.49	Catastrophic illness/injury	Teach identification of realistic life goals
	2.53	Families	Teach to identify family roles
	2.55	Family	Teach positive interactions
	2.58	Acute psychiatric clients	Teach reality-based verbalizations
	2.60	Chronic psychiatric adults	Teach social skills
	3.03	Adolescents	Reduce inappropriate lunchroom behavior
	3.08	Suicidal ideation	Teach to establish relationship with others
	3.09	Substance abuse	Lead discussion on harm to others
	4.02	Peers	Teach empathy with clients in therapy
	4.03	Terminal illness	Teach emotional expression

TECHNIQUE	TASK	POPULATION	STUDENT OBJECTIVES
	4.06	Behavior Disorder	Teach responsibility and following rules
	4.11	Couples	Teach positive verbal and physical responses
	4.17	Teen girls with eating disorder	Teach appropriate body image
	4.18	Parents of child with DD	Teach realistic goal setting
Group Leadership Skills	1.11	Peers	Teach 16-measure rhythm
	1.12	Peers	Engage participants in drumming
	1.14	Peers	Teach exercises to music
	1.15	Peers	Teach simple dance
	2.29	Hearing loss	Teach 16-measure rhythm
	2.43	Geriatric clients	Teach exercises to music
Guided Assistance	2.20	Cognitive impairment	Teach following 2-part directions
Homework Assignments	4.10	Adults with DD	Teach decision making skills
Hyperactivity Reduction	2.36	Emotional disturbance	Teach on-task behavior
	4.16	Inclusive music class	Teach positive interaction
Ignoring	2.33	Parents of child with DD	Teach reinforcement and feedback
	2.58	Acute psychiatric clients	Teach reality-based verbalizations
	3.07	Cerebral palsy	Teach academic skills/social behavior
	3.18	Emotional disturbance	Extinguish stereotyped mannerisms; wait turn; identify name
	4.12	Hospitalized child	Structure parent visit; maintain developmental level
	4.19	Chronic pain	Reduce awareness of pain
	4.20	SLD (math)	Improve math skills

TECHNIQUE	TASK	POPULATION	STUDENT OBJECTIVES
Imagery	3.20	Agoraphobia	Reduce fear of leaving house
	4.08	Phobia – child	Desensitize animal phobia
Improvisation	1.12	Peers	Engage participants in drumming
Incompatible Response	2.17	Cognitive impairment	Teach choral performance skills
	2.35	Behavior disorder	Reduce hyperactivity; increase incompatible response
	3.18	Emotional disturbance	Extinguish stereotyped mannerisms; wait turn; identify name
	4.02	Peers	Teach empathy with clients in therapy
	4.05	Adults with autism	Teach music task and incompatible responses
	4.10	Adults with DD	Teach decision-making skills
	4.14	Pregnant women	Teach labor management
	4.15	Language delay	Teach speaking in sentences and asking questions
Infant Stimulation	2.24	Cognitive impairment	Teach response to stimulation
	3.13	Parents of ill newborns	Teach infant-directed singing to parents
Inservice Presentation	3.02	Alcohol/drug counselors	Teach benefits of music therapy to staff
	3.22	Assistants with head injury patients	Teach how to assist during music for pre-mobility skills
Interpersonal	3.08	Suicidal ideation	Teach to establish relationship with others
	3.10	Couples	Teach communication techniques
Isoprinciple	3.19	Hospice	Accompany using Isoprinciple

TECHNIQUE	TASK	POPULATION	STUDENT OBJECTIVES
Labor Management	4.14	Pregnant women	Teach labor management
Mentoring	4.09	Geriatric clients/ youth	Teach socialization; mentoring
Modeling	1.04	Peers	Teach new song
	1.05	Peers	Teach new song
	1.06	Peers	Teach use of Autoharp to accompany song
	1.08	Peers	Compose "hello" song; teach
	1.09	Peers	Compose "good-bye" song; teach
	1.11	Peers	Teach 16-measure rhythm
	1.12	Peers	Engage participants in drumming
	1.13	Peers	Teach signing to simple song
	2.17	Cognitive Impairment	Teach choral performance skills
	2.18	Cognitive impairment	Teach social skills
	2.19	Cognitive impairment	Teach two guitar chords
	2.28	Hearing loss	Sign recorded song
	2.29	Hearing loss	Teach 16-measure rhythm
	2.35	Behavior disorder	Reduce hyperactivity; increase incompatible response
	3.01	Passive-aggressive	Teach assertiveness
Music Interruption	3.03	Adolescents	Reduce inappropriate lunchroom behavior
	3.11	Stroke symptoms	Improve gait and ambulation
Music Listening	2.13	Peers	Teach to convey emotions
	2.47	Presurgical patients	Teach to relieve postoperative pain
	4.01	Kidney dialysis	Reduce discomforts of dialysis
Overcompensation	2.39	Adolescents	Teach anger control

TECHNIQUE	TASK	POPULATION	STUDENT OBJECTIVES
Parenting Techniques	2.33	Parents of child with DD	Teach reinforcement and feedback
	2.34	Parents of a child with DD	Teach parenting techniques
	2.54	Child abusers	Teach anger control
	3.13	Parents of ill newborns	Accompany infant-directed singing
	3.16	Child abuse	Teach position interactions
	4.12	Hospitalized child	Structure parent visit; maintain developmental level
	4.18	Parents of child with DD	Teach realistic goal setting
Peer Tutoring	2.56	Chronic psychiatric adults	Teach square dance; improve social skills
	4.16	Inclusive music class	Teach positive interactions
Positive Interactions	2.46	Geriatric clients	Increase positive interactions
	4.09	Geriatric clients/youth	Teach socialization; mentoring
	4.12	Hospitalized child	Structure parent visit; maintain developmental level
	4.16	Inclusive music class	Teach positive interactions; consultation
Range-of-Motion Exercises	2.31	Cerebral palsy	Teach range-of-motion-exercises
	3.12	Post-stroke patients	Conduct range-of-motion exercises; teach signs/alternative communication for needs
Rapping	2.55	Family	Teach positive interactions
	2.58	Acute psychiatric clients	Teach reality-based verbalizations
Reinforcement – Musical	3.05	Chronic psychiatric clients	Teach reality-based, appropriate social behavior

TECHNIQUE	TASK	POPULATION	STUDENT OBJECTIVES
Relationships	2.40	Emotionally dis. teens	Facilitate nonsexual relationships
	2.51	Terminal illness	Enhance relationships among family
	3.08	Suicidal ideation	Teach to establish relationship with others
	4.13	Families – substance abuse	Teach role function
Relaxation	2.09	Peers	Use music to teach relaxation
Techniques	2.48	General hospital patients	Teach stress reduction
	3.20	Agoraphobia	Reduce fear of leaving house
	4.01	Kidney dialysis	Reduce discomforts of dialysis
	4.08	Phobia – child	Desensitize animal phobia
	4.14	Pregnant women	Teach labor management
Repertoire	1.16	Peers	Lead group sing-along; 10 song repertoire
	3.19	Hospice	Accompany using Isoprinciple
Role Analysis	2.53	Families	Teach to identify family roles
Role Assessment	4.13	Families – substance abuse	Teach role function
Role-Playing	2.10	Peers	Teach to deal with disappointment
	2.34	Parents of a child with DD	Teach parenting techniques
	2.37	Behavior disorders	Teach to accept responsibility
	2.40	Emotionally dis. teens	Facilitate nonsexual relationships
	2.41	Behavior Disorder	Resist peer pressure
	2.51	Terminal illness	Enhance relationships among family

TECHNIQUE	TASK	POPULATION	STUDENT OBJECTIVES
Role-Playing, cont.	2.52	Families of organ donors	Teach empathy, positive decision making
	2.54	Child abusers	Teach anger control
	2.59	Depressed persons	Teach resolution of a problem
	2.60	Chronic psychiatric adults	Teach social skills
	3.01	Passive-aggressive	Teach assertiveness
	3.06	Depression	Teach reduction of depression
	3.20	Agoraphobia	Reduce fear of leaving house
	4.11	Couples	Teach positive verbal & physical responses
	4.13	Families – substance abuse	Teach role function
	4.18	Parents of child with DD	Teach realistic goal setting
Rules	2.38	Behavior disorder	Teach rhythmic activity and rules
	4.06	Behavior disorder	Teach responsibility and following rules
Scanning	1.01	Peers	Lead well-known song unaccompanied
	1.02	Peers	Lead well know song, rhythm
	1.03	Peers	Lead well-known song, harmony
	1.04	Peers	Teach new song
	1.05	Peers	Teach new song
	1.08	Peers	Compose "hello" song; teach
	1.09	Peers	Compose "good-bye" song; teach
	1.14	Peers	Teach exercises to music
	2.01	Peers	Maintain group eye contact
	2.02	Peers	Extinguish talking
	2.03	Peers	Teach appropriate touching
	2.43	Geriatric clients	Teach exercises to music

TECHNIQUE	TASK	POPULATION	STUDENT OBJECTIVES
Signing	1.13	Peers	Teach signing to simple song
	2.28	Hearing loss	Sign recorded song
	2.30	Hearing loss	Teach auditory discrimination task
	3.12	Post-stroke patients	Conduct range-of-motion exercises; teach signs/alternative communication for needs
	3.14	Adolescents with hearing loss and normal hearing	Increase social interaction
	4.04	Hearing loss	Teach signs and music
Socialization	2.32	Cerebral palsy + CI	Teach group interaction
	2.44	Geriatric clients	Teach social interaction
	2.45	Geriatric clients	Plan musical performance
	2.57	Chronic psychiatric adults	Teach social interaction
	3.14	Adolescents with hearing loss and normal hearing	Increase social interaction
	4.09	Geriatric clients/youth	Teach socialization; mentoring
Social Skills	2.18	Cognitive impairment	Teach social skills
	2.60	Chronic psychiatric adults	Teach social skills
Song Leading	1.01	Peers	Lead well-known song unaccompanied
	1.02	Peers	Lead well know song, rhythm
	1.03	Peers	Lead well-known song, harmony
	1.04	Peers	Teach new song
	1.05	Peers	Teach new song
	1.06	Peers	Teach use of Autoharp to accompany song
	1.08	Peers	Compose "hello" song; teach
	1.09	Peers	Compose "good-bye" song; teach
	1.13	Peers	Teach signing to simple song
	1.16	Peers	Lead group sing-along; 10 song repertoire

TECHNIQUE	TASK	POPULATION	STUDENT OBJECTIVES
Song Leading, cont.	2.01	Peers	Maintain group eye contact
	2.02	Peers	Extinguish talking
	2.05	Peers	Compose and teach vocabulary song
	2.14	SLD (spelling)	Teach spelling concept; compose song
	2.15	SLD (reading)	Increase reading fluidity, comprehension, and pleasure
	2.46	Geriatric clients	Increase positive interactions
Structure Music for Specific Response	2.03	Peers	Teach appropriate touching
	2.09	Peers	Use music to teach relaxation
	2.13	Peers	Teach to convey emotions
Successive Approximation	2.27	Visual impairment	Teach mobility; extinguish inappropriate verbal behavior
Task Analysis	1.06	Peers	Teach use of Autoharp to accompany song
	2.16	Cognitive impairment	Teach circle dance
	2.19	Cognitive Impairment	Teach two guitar chords
	2.26	Visual impairment	Teach 2 grooming skills; reduce stereotyped behaviors
	2.56	Chronic psychiatric adults	Teach square dance; improve social skills
Transitioning	3.04	Autism	Teach attending and choosing
Using Visual Aids	3.12	Post-stroke patients	Conduct range-of-motion exercises; teach signs/alternative communication for needs
	3.21	Early intervention	Teach basic skills

Index by Student Objective

SLD = Specific Learning Disability
DD = Developmental Disabilities

STUDENT OBJECTIVE	TASK	POPULATION	TECHNIQUES
Academic Tasks			
Teach vocabulary	2.05	Peers	Composing Song Leading Chaining Cuing Evaluating/Data
Teach paired nonsense syllables	2.06	Peers	Composing Chaining Cuing Fading Evaluating/Data
Teach vocabulary pronunciation	2.07	Peers	Composing Chaining Cuing Fading Evaluating/Data
Teach foreign language vocabulary	2.08	Peers	Composing Chaining Cuing Fading Evaluating/Data
Teach spelling concept	2.14	SLD (Spelling)	Composing Song Leading Chaining Cuing Evaluating/Data
Increase reading fluidity, comprehension, and pleasure	2.15	SLD (Reading)	Composing Song Leading Cuing Approving Evaluating/Data

STUDENT OBJECTIVE	TASK	POPULATION	TECHNIQUES
Teach circle dance	2.16	Cognitively impaired teens	Chaining Cuing Task Analysis Evaluating/Data
Teach a color	2.23	Cognitively impaired child	Cuing Approving
Teach body parts	2.25	Visually impaired 4 yr olds	Cuing Approving
Teach academic and individualized social behavior	3.07	Preschoolers with cerebral palsy	Cuing Approving Ignoring Evaluating
Teach basic preschool skills	3.21	Early intervention (ages 3–5)	Cuing Approving Using Visual Aids
Improve math skills	4.20	SLD (math)	Approving Ignoring Evaluating

Action Steps

Teach action steps	2.10	Peers	Role-Playing Teaching Action Steps
Teach responsibility acceptance	2.37	Behavior disorders	Leading Group Discussion Role-Playing Evaluating
	4.06	Behavior disorder	Decision Making Leading Group Discussion Evaluating
Teach anger control	2.39	Teens with emotional disturbance	Teaching Anger Control Leading Group Discussion Overcompensation Evaluating

STUDENT OBJECTIVE	TASK	POPULATION	TECHNIQUES
	2.54	Parents/abused child	Teaching Anger Control Role-Playing Parenting Techniques Evaluating
Facilitate nonsexual relation ships with opposite sex	2.40	Teens with emotional disturbance	Establishing Relationships Teaching Actions Steps Role-Playing Evaluating
Resist peer pressure	2.41	Teens with emotional and behavioral disorders	Role-Playing Approving Evaluating/Data
Teaching emotional adjustment	2.50	Terminal illness	Teaching Action Steps Evaluating
Teach decision acceptance	2.52	Families of organ donors	Leading Group Discussion Role-Playing Teaching Action Steps Evaluating
Teach problem solving	2.59	Acute psychiatric (adults)	Role-Playing Teaching Action Steps Evaluating
Teach assertiveness for emotions	3.01	Passive-aggressive persons	Action Steps - Assertiveness Anger Control Role-Playing Negative Modeling Evaluating/Data
Reduce depression	3.06	Depressed persons	Teaching Action Steps Role-Playing Evaluating/Data
Establish relationships	3.08	Suicidal ideation	Teaching Interpersonal Skill Teaching Action Steps Leading Group Discussion Evaluating

STUDENT OBJECTIVE	TASK	POPULATION	TECHNIQUES
Teach reduction of agoraphobia	3.20	Adult with agoraphobia	Relaxation Imagery Role-Playing Self-Evaluating/Data
Teach implementation of self-shaping project	4.07	Acute psychiatric (adults)	Teaching Action Steps Evaluating

Decision Making

Shape unanimous group decision	2.11	Peers	Shaping Group Decision Accompanying
Lead group discussion: alcohol/drugs	2.12	Peers	Leading Group Discussion Shaping Group Decision
Teach peer pressure resistance	2.41	Behavior disorder	Role-Playing Approving
Teach choice making	3.04	Autism	Composing Eye Contact Decision Making Transitioning Evaluating/Data
Discuss harm to others	3.09	Substance abuse	Leading Group Discussion Nonverbal Approving Evaluating
Teach decision making	3.15	Cognitively impaired adults	Cuing Approving Decision Making Evaluating/Data
	4.10	Adults with DD	Decision Making Approving Role-Playing Homework Assignments Incompatible Responses Evaluating

Student Objective	Task	Population	Techniques
Teach role function	4.13	Families – substance abuse	Role-Playing Group Decision Making Role Assessment Cuing Relationships
Teach appropriate body image	4.17	Adolescent girls with eating disorders	Lead Group Discussion Decision Making Approving Evaluating

Feedback

Teach reinforcement and positive feedback	2.33	Parents of children with DD	Approving Ignoring Parenting Techniques Evaluating
Demonstrate differential feedback	4.04	Hearing loss – 5 year olds	Signing Approving Evaluating

Group Discussion

Discuss primary emotions	2.13	Peers	Structuring Music Music Listening Leading Group Discussion Improvisation
Teach parenting techniques	2.34	Parents of children with DD	Leading Group Discussion Parenting Techniques Role-Playing Evaluating
Lead discussion of life goals	2.49	Patients with catastrophic illness or injury	Leading Group Discussion Empathetic Listening Evaluating
Lead discussion on organ donation	2.52	Families – organ donors	Leading Group Discussion Teaching Action Steps Role-Playing Evaluating

STUDENT OBJECTIVE	TASK	POPULATION	TECHNIQUES
Reduce inappropriate behavior	3.03	Adolescents	Music Interruption Focused Group Discussion Approving Self-Evaluating/Data
Establish relationships	3.08	Suicidal ideation	Teaching Interpersonal Skill Teaching Action Steps Leading Group Discussion Evaluating
Discuss harm to others	3.09	Substance abuse	Leading Group Discussion Nonverbal Approving Evaluating
Teach empathy with client in therapy	4.02	Peers	Incompatible Responses Leading Group Discussion Teaching Action Steps Evaluating
Language			
Teach signs	1.13	Peers	Song Leading Chaining Modeling Cuing Signing
	2.28	Students with severe/profound hearing loss	Song Leading Chaining Modeling Cuing Signing Evaluating
Teach language-development task	2.22	Cognitively impaired 8 year olds (Severe/profound)	Cuing Approving
Teach auditory discrimination	2.30	Hearing loss – 5 year olds	Signing Auditory Discrimination Evaluating

STUDENT OBJECTIVE	TASK	POPULATION	TECHNIQUES
Teach speaking in sentences and asking questions	4.15	Language delayed children	Cuing Approving Incompatible Responses Evaluating

Movement

Teach exercises	1.14	Peers	Group Leading Cuing Scanning
	2.43	Geriatric clients	Group Leading Cuing Scanning Evaluating
Teach simple dance	1.15	Peers	Group Leading Cuing Chaining Evaluating
Teach mobility	2.27	Visual impairment	Mobility Training Cuing Successive Approximation Evaluating/Data
Teach range-of-motion exercises	2.31	Cerebral palsy	Range-of-Motion Exercises Evaluating
Teach dance and social skills	2.56	Chronic psychiatric adults	Chaining Cuing Task Analysis Peer tutoring Approving Evaluating
Improve gait	3.11	Stroke symptoms	Gait Training Approving Music Interruption Evaluating/Data

STUDENT OBJECTIVE	TASK	POPULATION	TECHNIQUES
Teach range of motion exercises and communication	3.12	Stroke victims	Signing/Alternative Communication Range-of-Motion Exercises Using Visual Aids Evaluating
Increase balance, weight shifting, and crossing mid-line	3.22	Post head injury	Gait Training/Mobility Composing/Arranging Inservice – Coaching staff Evaluating
Reduce awareness of pain	4.19	Chronic pain patients	Cuing Approving Ignoring Evaluating

Music

STUDENT OBJECTIVE	TASK	POPULATION	TECHNIQUES
Lead unaccompanied, known song	1.01	Peers	Song Leading Scanning
Accompany/lead well-known song – rhythm	1.02	Peers	Song Leading Accompanying Scanning
Accompany/lead well-known song – harmony	1.03	Peers	Song Leading Accompanying Scanning
Accompany/teach new song	1.04	Peers	Song Leading Accompanying Scanning Chaining Modeling
Accompany on second-best instrument; teach new song	1.05	Peers	Song Leading Accompanying Scanning Chaining Modeling

STUDENT OBJECTIVE	TASK	POPULATION	TECHNIQUES
Teach Autoharp accompaniment	1.06	Peers	Song Leading Task Analysis Cuing Modeling Approving Correcting
Teach to perform melody	1.07	Peers	Cuing Approving Correcting
Compose "hello" song; teach/accompany	1.08	Peers	Composing Song Leading Accompanying Chaining Modeling Scanning
Compose "goodbye" song; teach/accompany	1.09	Peers	Composing Song Leading Accompanying Chaining Modeling Scanning
Teach new round	1.10	Peers	Chaining Cuing Fading Approving Correcting
Teach rhythm-reading task	1.11	Peers	Group Leading Cuing Chaining Modeling
	2.29	Hearing loss – aged 12–15	Group Leading Cuing Chaining Modeling

STUDENT OBJECTIVE	TASK	POPULATION	TECHNIQUES
Engage in drumming	1.12	Peers	Group Leading Improvising Modeling Chaining Cuing
Lead sing-along/10 song repertoire	1.16	Peers	Song Leading Accompanying Using Repertoire
Teach choral performance skills	2.17	Cognitive impairments (teens)	Modeling Cuing Fading Incompatible Responses
Teach two guitar chords	2.19	Cognitive impairments (children)	Task Analysis Cuing Modeling Approving Correcting
Plan musical performance	2.45	Geriatric clients	Lead Group Discussion Socialization
Accompany parent singing	3.13	Parents of ill newborns	Decision Making Accompanying Infant Stimulation

Reality Orientation/Awareness

Teach reality-orientation	2.42	Geriatric clients	Composing Cuing Evaluating
Facilitate reality-based verbalizations	2.58	Acute psychiatric adults	Leading Group Discussion Ignoring Approving Rapping

STUDENT OBJECTIVE	TASK	POPULATION	TECHNIQUES
Teach realistic goal setting	4.18	Parent of children with DD	Leading Group Discussion Role-Playing Parenting Techniques Evaluating

Reinforcement

Teach positive feedback	2.33	Parents of children with DD	Approving Ignoring Parenting Techniques Evaluating

Relationships/Interaction

Teach group interaction	2.32	Cerebral palsy and cognitive impairment	Stimulating Group Interaction Evaluating
	2.44	Geriatric clients	Stimulating Group Interaction Cuing Evaluating
	2.57	Chronic psychiatric adults	Stimulating Group Interaction Cuing Evaluating
Facilitate nonsexual relationship with opposite sex	2.40	Teens with emotional disturbance	Establishing Relationships Teaching Actions Steps Role-Playing Evaluating
Increase positive interactions	2.46	Geriatric clients	Approving Leading Group Discussion Song Leading
Facilitate positive family interaction	2.51	Terminal illness	Establishing Relationships Role-Playing Evaluating

STUDENT OBJECTIVE	TASK	POPULATION	TECHNIQUES
Facilitate positive family Interaction, cont.	2.53	Distressed family	Role Analysis Leading Group Discussion Family Counseling Evaluating
	2.55	Distressed family	Composing Rapping Approving Leading Group Discussion Evaluating
	3.16	Abusive parents with their children	Cuing Approving Parenting Techniques Evaluating
Teach relationships with others	3.08	Suicidal ideation	Teaching Interpersonal Skill Teaching Action Steps Leading Group Discussion Evaluating
Improve communication	3.10	Couples	Teaching Interpersonal Skill Evaluating
Increase social interaction	3.14	Adolescents with and without hearing loss	Approving Signing Teaching Interpersonal Skill Evaluating
Teaching creativity, social Interaction, rhythmic skill	3.17	Adults with emerging dementia	Approving Stimulating Creativity Evaluating
Engage reluctant patients	3.19	Hospice	Isoprinciple Accompanying Using Repertoire Evaluating
Facilitate emotional expression	4.03	Catastrophic illness	Drawing to Music Leading Group Discussion Evaluating

STUDENT OBJECTIVE	TASK	POPULATION	TECHNIQUES
Facilitate intergenerational socialization	4.09	Geriatric/youth	Mentoring Approving Socialization Evaluating
Facilitate positive verbal and physical responses	4.11	Couples in counseling	Approving Role-Playing Leading Group Discussion Evaluating
Structure positive parent visits; maintain developmental level	4.12	Hospitalized children	Approving Ignoring Self-Help Skills Teaching Interaction Parenting Techniques Evaluating
Teach positive interactions	4.16	Inclusive music class	Approving Consulting Peer Tutoring Teaching Interaction Evaluating

Relaxation

Teach relaxation	2.09	Peers	Structuring Music – Relaxing Leading Relaxation Routine Evaluating/Data
Relieve postoperative pain	2.47	Presurgical patients	Focused Attention Music Listening Evaluating
Teach stress reduction	2.48	General hospital patients	Teach Relaxation Techniques Evaluating
Reduce agitation	3.19	Hospice	Isoprinciple Accompanying Using Repertoire Evaluating

Student Objective	Task	Population	Techniques
Teach reduction of agoraphobia	3.20	Agoraphobia – adults	Teach Relaxation Techniques Imagery Role-Playing Self-Evaluating/Data
Reduce discomfort	4.01	Dialysis patients	Relaxation Music Listening Evaluating
Desensitize animal phobia	4.08	Children with animal phobia	Relaxation Desensitization Imagery Evaluating
Teach labor management	4.14	Pregnant women/partners	Labor Management Focusing Attention Relaxing Muscles Approving Using Incompatible Responses

Social Skills

Maintain group eye contact	2.01	Peers	Song Leading Maintaining Eye Contact Scanning Evaluating/Data
Extinguish talking in group	2.02	Peers	Song Leading Scanning Using Incompatible Responses Evaluating/Data
Teach appropriate peer touching	2.03	Peers	Structuring Music Approving Scanning Evaluating/Data

STUDENT OBJECTIVE	TASK	POPULATION	TECHNIQUES
Teach 100% on-task	2.04	Peers	Using Incompatible Responses Evaluating/Data
Teach manners for social event	2.18	Cognitive impairment (adults)	Modeling Cuing Social Skills Evaluating/Data
Teach following 2-part directions	2.20	Cognitive impairment (child)	Composing Chaining Cuing Guided Assistance
Teach honesty	2.21	Cognitive impairment (preteens)	Composing Modeling Approving
Teach responses to stimulation	2.24	Cognitive impairment (infants)	Infant Stimulation Evaluating
Teach grooming skills	2.26	Visually impaired 8 year olds	Cuing Task Analysis Incompatible Responses
Extinguish pity-seeking behavior	2.27	Visually impaired adults	Gait/Mobility Training Cuing Successive Approximation Evaluating/Data
Reduce hyperactivity	2.35	Behavior disorder	Reducing Hyperactivity Modeling Cuing Approving Incompatible Responses Evaluating/Data
Teach rule enforcement	2.38	Behavior disorder	Rule Following Approving Evaluating

STUDENT OBJECTIVE	TASK	POPULATION	TECHNIQUES
Increase social skills	2.60	Chronic psychiatric adults	Leading Group Discussion Teaching Social Skills Role-Playing Evaluating
Teach joint attention	3.04	Autism	Composing Focused Attention Decision Making Transitioning Evaluating
Teach appropriate social behavior	3.05	Chronic psychiatric	Music Reinforcement Cuing Approving Evaluating
Extinguish stereotyped behavior	3.18	Autism	Approving Ignoring Incompatible Response Evaluating
Teach individualized incompatible response	4.05	Autism	Incompatible Response

Music Therapy Bibliographies

General

ABR and ENG testing. Retrieved from http://www.centreforhearing.com/abr_eng.htm/

ABR versus OAE: Two similar hearing tests. Retrieved from http://deafness.about.cotnics/audiograms/a/abroae.htm/

Aigen, K. (1995). Cognitive and affective processes in music therapy with individuals with developmental delays: A preliminary model for Nordoff-Robbins practice. *Music Therapy, 13*(1), 18–46.

Alvarez, R. (2003). *Florida Legislative FTE Appropriation for 2002–2003*. Personal interview with FSU Associate Vice President Administrative Affairs, Budget Analysis. June 30, 2003.

Alvin, J. A. (1978). *Music therapy*. London: John Clare Books.

American Music Therapy Association. (1998). *Reimbursement primer: The ABC's of healthcare reimbursement for music therapy services*. Silver Spring, MD: Author.

American Music Therapy Association. (2000). *Standards for education and clinical training*. Silver Spring, MD: Author.

American Music Therapy Association. (2002). *AMTA member sourcebook 2002*. Silver Spring, MD: Author.

American Music Therapy Association. (2004). *AMTA member sourcebook 2004*. Silver Spring, MD: Author.

American Music Therapy Association Clinical Training Committee. (2001). *Frequently asked questions II*. Silver Spring, MD: Author.

Ansell, B. J., Keenan, J. E., & de la Rocha, O. (1989). *Western Neuro Sensory Stimulation Profile*. Barbara J. Ansell and Western Neuro Care Center.

Argyris, S. P. (1994). The Glasgow Coma Scale. San Antonio, TX: Communication Skill Builders.

Bernstein, P. L. (1985). *Theory and methods in dance-movement therapy: A manual for therapists, students and educators*. Dubuque, IA: Kendall-Hunt.

Beuchler, J. L. (Ed.). (1984). *Hearing impaired children*. In W. B. Lathom & C. T. Eagle (Series Eds.), *Music therapy for handicapped children, Vol. 1*. St. Louis, MO: MMB Music.

Birkenshaw, L. (1982). *Music for fun, music for learning* (3rd ed.). St. Louis, MO: MMB Music.

Bitcon, C. H. (2000). *Alike and different: The clinical and educational use of Orff-Schulwerk* (2nd ed.). Gilsum, NH: Barcelona.

Bok, D. (2001). Universities and the decline of civic responsibility. *Journal of College and Character.* Retrieved July 6, 2003, from *Journal of the Center for the Study of Values in College Student Development Featured Journal Articles,* Volume 2, http://www.collegevalues.org/articles.cfm?a=l&id=570

Bonny, H. L., & Savary, L. M. (1990). *Music and your mind: Listening with a new consciousness.* Barrytown, NY: Station Hill Press.

Bontke, C. F. (Ed.). (1992). Sensory stimulation: Accepted practice or expected practice? *The Journal of Head Trauma Rehabilitation, 7*(4), 115–120.

Boxill, E. H. (1985). *Music therapy for the developmentally disabled.* Rockville, MD: Aspen Systems.

Briggs, C. (1991). A model for understanding musical development. *Music Therapy, 10*(1), 1–21.

Bright, R. (1984). *Practical planning in music therapy for the aged.* Van Nuys, CA: Alfred.

Bringle, R. G., & Hatcher, J. A. (1996). Implementing service learning in higher education [Electronic version]. *Journal of Higher Education, 67*(2), 221–239.

Brown, F. (1977). *Come join the Geritones: Starter kit.* Lake Forest, IL: Geritones.

Bruscia, K. (Ed.) (1991). *Case studies in music therapy.* Phoenixville, PA: Barcelona.

Burlingame, J., & Skalko, T. K. (1997). *Idyll Arbor's glossary for therapists.* Ravensdale, WA: Idyll Arbor.

Burton, K., & Hughes, W. (1980). *Music play: Learning activities for young children.* Menlo Park, CA: Addison-Wesley.

Caplow-Lindner, E., Harpaz, L., & Samberg, S. (1979). *Therapeutic dance/movement: Expressive activities for older adults.* New York: Human Sciences Press.

Carter, S. A. (Ed.). (1984). *Mentally retarded children.* In W. B. Lathom & C. T. Eagle (Series Eds.), *Music therapy for handicapped children, Vol. 2.* St. Louis, MO: MMB Music.

Centers for Disease Control. (1999, April 29). *National Vital Statistics Report, 47*(18).

Chapey, R. (Ed.). (1994). *Language intervention strategies in adult aphasia.* Baltimore: Williams & Wilkins.

Clark, C., & Chadwick, D. (1980). *Clinically adapted instruments for the multiply handicapped: A sourcebook* (Rev. ed.). St. Louis, MO: MMB Music.

Codding, P. (Ed.). (1984). *Visually impaired children.* In W. B. Lathom & C. T. Eagle (Series Eds.), *Music therapy for handicapped children, Vol. 1.* St. Louis, MO: MMB Music.

Cohen, J. (1988). *Statistical power analysis for the behavioral sciences* (2nd ed.). Hillsdale, NJ: Lawrence Erlbaum Associates.

Colan, B. J. (1998, March 9). *Moving with the music.* Advance for Physical Therapists.

Coleman, J., Schoepfle, I. L., & Templeton, V. (1964). *Music for exceptional children.* Evanston, IL: Summy-Birchard.

Cormier, L. J. (Ed.). (1984). *Deaf-blind children.* In W. B. Lathom & C. T. Eagle (Series Eds.), *Music therapy for handicapped children, Vol. 1.* St. Louis, MO: MMB Music.

Costonis, M. (Ed.). (1978). *Therapy in motion.* Urbana: University of Illinois Press.

Cutietta, R. A. (1996). Language and music programs. *General Music Today, 9*(2), 26–31.

Davis, W., Gfeller, K., & Thaut, M. (1992). *An introduction to music therapy theory and practice.* Dubuque, IA: Wm. C. Brown.

Davis, W. B., Gfeller, K. E., & Thaut, M. H. (1999). *An introduction to music therapy: Theory and practice* (2nd ed.). Boston: McGraw-Hill.

DePeters, A., Gordon, L., & Wertman, J. (1981). *The magic of music.* Buffalo, NY: Potentials Development for Health & Aging Services.

Dickinson, P. I. (1985). *Music with exceptional (ESN) children.* Atlantic Highland, NJ: Humanities Press.

Dobbs, J. P. (1985). *The slow learner and music.* London: Oxford University Press.

Douglass, D. (1985). *Accent on rhythm: Music activities for the aged* (3rd ed.). St. Louis, MO: MMB Music.

Eagle, C., Jr. (1976). *Music therapy index* (Vol. 1). Lawrence, KS: National Association for Music Therapy.

Eagle, C., Jr. (1978). *Music therapy index* (Vol. 2). Lawrence, KS: National Association for Music Therapy.

Eagle, C. T., Jr. (1976). *Music psychology index* (Vol. 2). Denton, TX: Institute for Therapeutic Research.

Eagle, C., Jr., & Minter, J. J. (1984). *Music psychology index* (Vol. 3). Phoenix, AZ: Orynx Press.

Edgerton, C. D. (1990). Creative group songwriting. *Music Therapy Perspectives, 8,* 15–19.

Education Commission of the States (ECS) Notes. (2001). *Institutionalized service learning in the 50 states.* Retrieved July 6, 2003, from http://www.ecs.org/clearinghouse/23/77/2377.pdf

Edwards, E. M. (1974). *Music education for the deaf.* South Waterford, ME: Merriam-Eddy.

Edwards, J. (1999). Anxiety management in pediatric music therapy. In C. Dileo (Ed.), *Music therapy and medicine: Theoretical and clinical applications* (pp. 69–76). Silver Spring, MD: American Music Therapy Association.

Evans, D. R., & Cope, W. E. (1989). *Quality of Life Questionnaire.* North Tonawanda, NY: Multi-Health Systems.

Famsworth, P. (1958). *The social psychology of music.* New York: Holt, Rinehart, & Winston.

Florida Institute of Neurologic Rehab, Inc. *Glossary of terms.* Retrieved from http://www.finr.com/glossary.html#n/

Furco, A. (1999). *Self-assessment rubric for the institutionalization of service learning in higher education.* Retrieved July 6, 2003, from http://www.richmond.edu/vacc/Forms/rubric.pdf

Furman, C. (Ed.). (1996). *Effectiveness of music therapy procedures: Documentation of research and clinical practice* (2nd Ed.). Washington, DC: National Association for Music Therapy.

Gallina, M., & Gallina, J. (1978). *Alphabet in action.* Long Branch, NJ: Kimbo Educational.

Gallina, M., & Gallina, J. (1978). *Sing a song of sounds.* Long Branch, NJ: Kimbo Educational.

Gaston, E. T. (1968). *Music in therapy.* New York: Macmillan Press.

Gfeller, K. (Ed.). (1985). *Fiscal, regulatory-legislative issues for the music therapist.* Washington, DC: National Association for Music Therapy.

Ginglend, D. R., & Stiles, W. E. (1985). *Music activities for retarded children.* New York: Abingdon Press.

Glass, G., McGaw, B., & Smith, M. (1984). *Meta-analysis in social research.* Beverly Hills, CA: Sage.

Graham, R. M. (Ed.). (1975). *Music for the exceptional child.* Reston, VA: Music Educators National Conference.

Graham, R. M., & Beer, A. S. (1980). *Teaching music to the exceptional child.* Englewood Cliffs, NJ: Prentice-Hall.

Gregory, D. (2001). *Arts in medicine service: An elective course for university students.* Presentation at the 2001 Society for Arts in Healthcare. Retrieved July 6, 2003, from http://otto.cmr.fsu.edu/memt/sah/

Gregory, D., & Whipple, J. (2000). *Music in arts in medicine and medical music therapy: Same or different?* Retrieved July 6, 2003, from http://otto.cmr.fsu.edu/memt/tmhairn/article.htm

Hagen, C., Malkmus, D., & Durham, P. (1972). *Levels of cognitive functioning.* Downey, CA: Professional Staff Association of Ranchos Los Amigos Hospital.

Hanser, S. B. (1980). *Music therapy practicum: A manual for behavior change through music therapy.* Stockton, CA: University of the Pacific Press.

Hanser, S. B. (1999). *The new music therapist's handbook.* Boston: Berklee Press.

Hap Palmer Record Library. *Creative movement and rhythmic exploration.* Album AR 533. Freeport, NY: Educational Activities.

Hap Palmer Record Library. *Folk song carnival.* Album AR 524. Freeport, NY: Educational Activities.

Hap Palmer Record Library. *Holiday songs and rhythms: Primary–intermediate.* Album AR 538. Freeport, NY: Educational Activities.

Hap Palmer Record Library. *Learning basic skills through music, Vol. 1.* Album AR 514. Freeport, NY: Educational Activities.

Hap Palmer Record Library. *Learning basic skills through music: Building vocabulary.* Album AR 521. Freeport, NY: Educational Activities.

Hap Palmer Record Library. *Learning basic skills through music: Health and safety.* Album AR 526. Freeport, NY: Educational Activities.

Hap Palmer Record Library. *Mod marches.* Album AR 527. Freeport, NY: Educational Activities.

Hap Palmer Record Library. *Modern tunes for rhythms and instruments.* Album AR 523. Freeport, NY: Educational Activities.

Hap Palmer Record Library. *Patriotic and morning time songs: Grades 1–4.* Album AR 519. Freeport, NY: Educational Activities.

Hap Palmer Record Library. *Simplified folk songs: Special edition, Grades K–3.* Album AR 518. Freeport, NY: Educational Activities.

Hap Palmer Record Library. *Singing multiplication tables (from the 2's through the 12's).* Album AR 45. Freeport, NY: Educational Activities.

Hardesty, K. W. (1985). *Music for special education.* Morristown, NJ: Silver-Burdett.

Hedden, S. K. (1971). N = 4: A small-sample statistical technique for use in music therapy research. *Journal of Music Therapy, 8*(4), 146–151.

Henry, D. G., Knoll, C., & Reuer, B. (1999). *Music works: A handbook of job skills for music therapists* (3rd ed.). Stephenville, TX: MusicWorks.

Honnet, E. P., & Poulsen, S. J. (1989). *Principles of good practice for combining service and learning: A Wingspread special report.* Retrieved July 6, 2003, from http://www.servicelearning.org/article/archive/87

Hoshizaki, M. K. (1983). *Teaching mentally retarded children through music.* Springfield IL: Charles C. Thomas.

Hunter, L. L. (1989). Computer-assisted assessment of melodic and rhythmic discrimination skills. *Journal of Music Therapy, 26*(2), 79–87.

James, M. R. (1987). Implications of selected social psychological theories on life-long skill generalization: Considerations for the music therapist. *Music Therapy Perspectives, 4*, 29–33.

Janiak, W. (1978). Songs for music therapy. Long Branch, NJ: Kimbo Educational.

Jay, S., & Elliott, C. (1986). *Observation scale of behavioral distress-revised.* (Available from Susan M. Jay, Ph.D., Psychosocial Program, Division of Hematology-Oncology, Children's Hospital of Los Angeles, CA 90027).

Johnson, B. (1989). *DSTAT: Software for the meta-analytic review of research literature.* Hillsdale, NJ: Lawrence Erlbaum Associates.

Johnson, C. M., Ghetti, C. M., Achey, C. A., & Darrow, A. A. (2001). An analysis of music therapy student practicum behaviors and their relationship to clinical effectiveness: An exploratory investigation. *Journal of Music Therapy, 38,* 307–320.

Kotulak, R. (1993, April). Unlocking the mind, a prize-winning series from the Chicago Tribune. *Chicago Tribune.*

Kovacs, M. (1992). *Children's Depression Inventory.* North Tonawanda, NY: Multi-Health Systems.

Krout, R. (1987). Evaluating software for music therapy applications. *Journal of Music Therapy, 24*(4), 213–223.

Krout, R., Burnham, A., & Moorman, S. (1993). Computer and electronic music applications with students in special education from program proposal to progress evaluation. *Music Therapy Perspectives, 11*(1), 28–31.

Krout, R. E., & Mason, M. (1988). Using computer and electronic music resources in clinical music therapy with behaviorally disordered students, 12 to 18 years old. *Music Therapy Perspectives, 5,* 114–118.

Laker, M. (1980). *Nursing home activities for the handicapped.* Springfield, IL: Charles C. Thomas.

Lathom, W. B., & Eagle C. T. (Eds.). (1984). *Music therapy for handicapped children, Vol. 1.* St. Louis, MO: MMB Music.

Lathom, W. B., & Eagle, C. T. (Eds.). (1984). *Music therapy for handicapped children, Vol. 2.* St. Louis, MO: MMB Music.

Lathom, W. B., & Eagle C. T. (Eds.). (1985). *Music therapy for handicapped children, Vol. 3.* St. Louis, MO: MMB Music.

LeLorier, J., Gregoire, G., Benhaddad, A., Lapierre, J, & Deriderian, F. (1997). Discrepancies between meta-analyses and subsequent large randomized, controlled trials. *The New England Journal of Medicine, 337*(8), 536–542.

Lenkowsky, L. (2003). *Higher education and the making of citizens.* Retrieved July 6, 2003, from http://www.nationalservice.org/news/11032103.html

Licht, S. (1946). *Music in medicine.* Boston: New England Conservatory of Music.

Lingerman, H. A. (1995). *The healing energies of music* (2nd ed.). Wheaton, IL: Quest Books.

Luce, D. (2004). Music learning theory and audiation: Implications for music therapy clinical practice. *Music Therapy Perspectives, 22*(1), 26–33.

Madsen, C., Jr., & Madsen, C. (1981). *Teaching/discipline: A positive approach for educational development*. Boston: Allyn & Bacon.

Madsen, C. H., Jr., & Madsen, C. K. (1983). *Teaching/ discipline: A positive approach for educational development* (3rd ed.). Raleigh, NC: Contemporary.

Madsen, C. K. (1981). *Music therapy: A behavioral guide for the mentally retarded*. Lawrence, KS: National Association for Music Therapy.

Madsen, C. K., & Madsen, C. H., Jr. (1975). *Parents and children: Love and discipline: A positive guide to behavior modification*. Arlington Heights, IL: Harlan Davidson.

Madsen, C. K., & Madsen, C. H. (1997). *Experimental research in music*. Raleigh, NC: Contemporary.

Madsen, C. K., & Prickett, C. A. (Eds.). (1987). *Applications of research in music behavior*. Tuscaloosa, AL: The University of Alabama Press.

Maranto, C. D., & Bruscia, K. (Eds.). (1987). *Perspectives on music therapy education and training*. Philadelphia: Temple University.

Maranto, C. D., & Bruscia, K. (1988). *Methods of teaching and training the music therapist*. Philadelphia: Temple University.

Martin, J., Hamilton, B., Ventura, S., Menacker, F., & Park, M. (2002, February 12). Births: Final data for 2000. *National Vital Statistics Reports, 50*(5).

McCormick, J. L. (1988). Report: Status of public school music therapy. *Music Therapy Perspectives, 5*, 73–77.

Merrill, T. (1967). *Activities with the aged and infirmed: A handbook for the untrained worker*. Springfield, IL: Charles C. Thomas.

Michel, D. E. (1985). *Music therapy: An introduction, including music in special education* (2nd ed.). Springfield, IL: Charles C. Thomas.

Miller, S. G. (Ed.). (1984). *Speech impaired children*. In W. B. Lathom & C. T. Eagle (Series Eds.), *Music therapy for handicapped children, Vol. 2*. St. Louis, MO: MMB Music.

Munro, S. (1984). *Music therapy in palliative/hospice care*. St. Louis, MO: MMB Music.

National Association for Music Therapy. (1997, November). *Clinical training guidelines*. Silver Spring, MD: Author.

Nocera, S. D. (1979). *Reaching the special learner through music*. Morristown, NJ: Silver-Burdett.

Nordoff, P., & Robbins, C. (1971). *Therapy in music for handicapped children*. North Pomfret, UT: Trafalgar Square.

Nordoff, P., & Robbins, C. (1973). *Music for handicapped children*. London: Gollancz.

Nordoff, P., & Robbins, C. (1977). *Creative music therapy: Individualized treatment for the handicapped child.* New York: John Day.

Orff, G. (1980). *The Orff music therapy: Active furthering of the development of the child.* London: Schott.

Peters, J. S. (2000). *Music therapy: An introduction.* Springfield, IL: Charles C Thomas.

Paul, D. W. (Ed.). (1984). *Emotionally disturbed children.* In W. B. Lathom & C. T. Eagle (Series Eds.), *Music therapy for handicapped children, Vol. 2.* St. Louis, MO: MMB Music.

Pfeifer, M. (Ed.). (1985). *Multihandicapped children.* In W. B. Lathom & C. T. Eagle (Series Eds.), *Music therapy for handicapped children, Vol. 3.* St. Louis, MO: MMB Music.

Plach, T. (1980). *The creative use of music in group therapy.* Springfield, IL: Charles C. Thomas.

Priestley, M. (1985). *Music therapy in action.* St. Louis, MO: MMB Music.

Purvis, J., & Samet, S. (Eds.). (1976). *Music in developmental therapy.* Baltimore: University Park Press.

Ridgeway, R. (1983). Another perspective: A story—and a question. *Music Therapy Perspectives, 1*(2), 2–3.

Robbins, C., & Robbins, C. (1980). *Music for the hearing impaired.* St. Louis, MO: MMB Music.

Roeser, R. J. (1996). *Audiology desk reference.* New York: Thieme.

Roush, W. (1997). A womb with a view. *Science, 278,* 1397–1399.

Rudenberg, M. T. (Ed.). (1985). *Orthopedically handicapped children.* In W. B. Lathom & C. T. Eagle (Series Eds.), *Music therapy for handicapped children, Vol. 3.* St. Louis, MO: MMB Music.

Ruud, E. (1980). *Music therapy and its relationship to current treatment theories.* St. Louis, MO: MMB Music.

Schulberg, C. H. (1986). *The music therapy sourcebook: A collection of activities categorized and analyzed.* New York: Human Sciences Press.

Schullian, E., & Schoen, M. (Eds.). (1971). *Music and medicine.* New York: Abelard-Schuman.

Schwankowsky, L. M., & Guthrie, P. T. (Eds.). (1985). *Other health impaired children.* In W. B. Lathom & C. T. Eagle (Series Eds.), *Music therapy for handicapped children, Vol. 3.* St. Louis, MO: MMB Music.

Siegel, S. L., Cartwright, J. S., & Katz, E. (1986). Where's the research? *Journal of Music Therapy, 23*(1), 38–45.

Simpson, J., & Burns, D. (2003). *Music therapy reimbursement: Best practices and procedures.* Silver Spring, MD: American Music Therapy Association.

Slyoff, M. R. (1979). *Music for special education.* Fort Worth, TX: Harris Music.

Smith, R. B., & Flohr, J. W. (1984). *Music dramas for children with special needs.* Denton, TX: Troostwyk Press.

Soibelman, D. (1948). *Therapeutic and industrial uses of music.* New York: Columbia University Press.

Spielberger, C., Gorsuch, R., & Lushene, R. (1970). *State-trait anxiety inventory test manual.* Palo Alto, CA: Consulting Psychologists Press.

Spitzer, S. (1989). Computers and music therapy: An integrated approach. *Music Therapy Perspectives, 7,* 51–54.

Standley, J. (1996). A meta-analysis on the effects of music as reinforcement for education/therapy objectives. *Journal of Research in Music Education, 44*(2), 105–133.

Standley, J. M., & Prickett, C. (Eds.). (1994*). Research in music therapy: A tradition of excellence.* Silver Spring, MD: National Association for Music Therapy.

Steele, A. E. (Ed.). (1985). *The music therapy levels system: A manual of principles and applications.* Cleveland, OH: The Cleveland Music School Settlement.

Taylor, D. B. (1997). *Biomedical foundations of music as therapy.* St. Louis, MO: MMB Music.

Thurman, L., & Langness, A. P. (1986). *Heartsongs: A guide to active pre-birth and infant parenting through language and singing.* Englewood, CO: Music Study Services.

Tomat, J. H., & Krutzky, C. D. (1975). *Learning through music for special children and their teachers.* South Waterford, ME: Merriam-Eddy.

Tortora, G. J., & Grabowski, S. R. (1993). *Principles of anatomy and physiology* (7th ed.). New York: HarperCollins College.

Van de Wall, W. (1936). *Music in institutions.* New York: Russell Sage Foundation.

Van de Wall, W. (1946). *Music in hospitals.* New York: Russell Sage Foundation.

Venes, D. (1997). *Taber's cyclopedic medical dictionary.* Philadelphia: F. A. Davis.

Wagner, M. (1994). *Introductory musical acoustics.* Raleigh, NC: Contemporary.

Ward, D. (1976). *Hearts and hands and voices: Music in the education of slow learners.* London: Oxford University Press.

Ward, D. (1979). *Sing a rainbow: Musical activities with mentally handicapped children.* London: Oxford University Press.

Addictions/Substance Abuse

Bednarz, L., & Nikkel, R. (1992). The role of music therapy in the treatment of young adults diagnosed with mental illness and substance abuse. *Music Therapy Perspectives, 10*(1), 21–26.

Brooks, H. B. (1973). The role of music in a community drug abuse prevention program. *Journal of Music Therapy, 10*(1), 3–6.

Browne, H. E. (1961). Psychiatric treatment with drug LSD and music therapy for alcoholics. *Proceedings of the NAMT, 10,* 154–162.

Cevasco, A., Kennedy, R., & Generally, N. (2005). Comparison of movement-to-music, rhythm activities, and competitive games on depression, stress, anxiety, and anger of females in substance abuse rehabilitation. *Journal of Music Therapy, 42*(1), 64–80.

Doak, B. (2003). Relationships between adolescent psychiatric diagnoses, music preferences, and drug preferences. *Music Therapy Perspectives, 21*(2), 69–76.

Dougherty, K. (1984). Music therapy in the treatment of the alcoholic client. *Music Therapy, 4,* 47–54.

Eagle, C. T. (1972). Music and LSD: An empirical study. *Journal of Music Therapy, 9,* 23–36.

Freed, B. S. (1987). Songwriting with the chemically dependent. *Music Therapy Perspectives, 4,* 13–18.

Gaston, E. T., & Eagle, C. (1970). Function of music in LSD therapy for alcoholic patients. *Journal of Music Therapy, 7(1),* 3–19.

Ghetti, C. (2004). Incorporating music therapy into the harm reduction approach to managing substance use problems. *Music Therapy Perspectives, 22*(2), 84–90.

James, M. (1988). Music therapy and alcoholism: I. An overview of the addiction. *Music Therapy Perspectives, 5,* 60–64.

James, M. (1988). Music therapy and alcoholism: II. Treatment services. *Music Therapy Perspectives, 5,* 65–68.

James, M. (1988). Music therapy values clarification: A positive influence on perceived locus of control. *Journal of Music Therapy, 25*(4), 206–215.

Jones, J. D. (2005). A comparison of songwriting and lyric analysis techniques to evoke emotional change in a single session with people who are chemically dependent. *Journal of Music Therapy, 42*(2), 94–110.

Miller, A. S. (1970). Music therapy for alcoholics at a Salvation Army Center. *Journal of Music Therapy, 7,* 136–138.

Murphy, M. (1983). Music therapy: A self-help group experience for substance-abuse patients. *Music Therapy, 3,* 52–62.

Silverman, M. (2003). Music therapy and clients who are chemically dependent: A review of literature and pilot study. *Arts in Psychotherapy, 30*(5), 273–281.

Smith, S. M. (1975). Using music therapy with short-term alcoholic and psychiatric patients. *Hospital and Community Psychiatry, 26*(7), 420.

Soshensky, R. (2001). Music therapy and addiction. *Music Therapy Perspectives, 19*(1), 45–52.

Steele, A. L., & Gallagher, L. M. (2002). Music therapy with offenders in a substance abuse/mental illness treatment program. *Music Therapy Perspectives, 20*(2), 117–122.

Treder-Wolff, J. (1990). Affecting attitudes: Music therapy in addictions treatment. *Music Therapy Perspectives, 8*, 67–71.

Ward, K. L. (1996). *The effects of music therapy on chemically dependent offenders in a women's prison.* Unpublished master's thesis, The Florida State University, Tallahassee.

Wheeler, B. (1985). The relationship between musical and activity elements of music therapy sessions and client responses: An exploratory study. *Music Therapy, 5,* 52–60.

Winich, C., & Nyswander, M. (1961). Psychotherapy of successful musicians who are drug addicts. *American Journal of Orthopsychiatry, 31*, 622–636.

Infant, Child, and Adolescent

Aldridge, K. (1993). The use of music to relieve pre-operational anxiety in children attending day surgery. *The Australian Journal of Music Therapy, 4*, 19–35.

Allgood, N. (2005). Parents' perceptions of family–based group music therapy for children with autism spectrum disorders. *Music Therapy Perspectives, 23*(2), 92–99.

Als, H., Lester, B., Tronick, E., & Brazelton, T. (1982). Manual for the assessment of preterm infants' behavior (APIB). In H. Fitzgerald, B. Lester, & M. Yogman (Eds.), *Theory and research in behavioral pediatrics* (pp. 65–132). New York: Plenum Press.

American Academy of Pediatrics. Committee on Environmental Health. (1997). Noise: A hazard for the fetus and newborn. *Pediatrics, 100*(4), 724–727.

Ammon, K. (1968). The effects of music on children in respiratory distress. *American Nurses' Association Clinical Sessions*, 127–133.

Anderson, G., & Vidyasagar, D. (1979). Development of sucking in premature infants from 1 to 7 days post birth. *Birth Defects: Original Article Series, 15*(7), 145–171.

Ayres, B. R. (1987). The effects of a music stimulus environment versus regular cafeteria environment during therapeutic feeding. *Journal of Music Therapy, 24*(1), 14–26.

Baird, S. (1969). A technique to assess the preferences for intensity of musical stimuli in young hard-of-hearing children. *Journal of Music Therapy, 6*(1), 6–11.

Barrera, M., Kykov, M., & Doyle, S. (2002). The effects of interactive music therapy on hospitalized children with cancer: A pilot study. *Psycho-Oncology, 11*, 379–388.

Barrickman, J. (1989). A developmental music therapy approach for preschool hospitalized children. *Music Therapy Perspectives, 7*, 10–16.

Batson, A. (1994). *The effects of live music on the distress of pediatric patients receiving intravenous starts, venipunctures, injections, and heel sticks.* Unpublished master's thesis, The Florida State University, Tallahassee.

Bean, U. (1969). Music at Indiana State Prison. *Music Journal, 2Z* 31.

Behrens, G. (1982). *The use of music activities to improve the capacity, inhalation, and exhalation capabilities of handicapped children's respiration.* Unpublished master's thesis, Kent State University, Kent, OH.

Bellamy, T., & Sontag, E. (1973). Use of group contingent music to increase assembly line production rates of retarded students in a simulated shelter workshop. *Journal of Music Therapy, 10*(3), 125–136.

Benes, F. M. (1994). Development of the corticolimhic system. In G. Dawson & K. Gischer (Eds.), *Human behavior and the developing brain* (pp. 176–206). New York: Guilford Press.

Bennis, J. A. (1969). The use of music as a therapy in the special education classroom. *Journal of Music Therapy, 6*(1), 15–18.

Berlin, B. (1998). Music therapy with children during invasive procedures: Our emergency department's experience. *Journal of Emergency Nursing, 24*(6), 607–608.

Bernbaum, J., Pereira, G., Watkins, J., & Peckham, G. (1983). Nonnutritive sucking during gavage feeding enhances growth and maturation in premature infants. *Pediatrics, 71*(1), 41–45.

Berry, M. A., Conrod, H., & Usher, R. H. (1997). Growth of very premature infants fed intravenous hyperalimentation and calcium-supplemented formula. *Pediatrics, 100*(4), 647–653.

Biban, P., Baraldi, E., Pettenazzo, A., Filippone, M., & Zacchello, F. (1993). Adverse effect of chloral hydrate in two young children with obstructive sleep apnea. *Pediatrics, 92*(3), 461–463.

Bokor, C. R. (1976). A comparison of music and verbal responses of mentally retarded children. *Journal of Music Therapy, 13*(2), 101–108.

Bradt, J. (2001). *The effects of music entrainment on postoperative pain perception in pediatric patients.* Unpublished dissertation, Temple University, Philadelphia.

Braithwaite, M., & Sigafoos, J. (1998). Effects of social versus musical antecedents on communication responsiveness in five children with developmental disabilities. *Journal of Music Therapy, 35*(2), 88–104.

Brazelton, T., & Nugent, J. (1995). *Neonatal Behavioral Assessment Scale* (3rd ed.). London: Cambridge University Press.

Britt, G., & Myers, B. (1994). The effects of Brazelton intervention: A review. *Infant Mental Health, 15*(3), 278–292.

Brodsky, W. (1989). Music therapy as an intervention for children with cancer in isolation rooms. *Music Therapy, 8,* 17–34.

Brook, E. (1984). *Soothing music during the active phase of labor: Physiologic effect on mother and infant.* Unpublished master's thesis, University of Florida, Gainesville.

Broome, M. E., Lillis, P. P., & Smith, M. C. (1989). Pain interventions with children: A meta-analysis of research. *Nursing Research, 38*(3), 154–158.

Brownell, M. D. (2002). Musically adapted social stories to modify behaviors in students with autism: Four case studies. *Journal of Music Therapy, 39*(20), 117–144.

Buda, F. B., Reed, J. C., & Rabe, E. F. (1975). Skull volume in infants: Methodology, normal values, and application. *American Journal of Diseases in Children, 129*, 1117–1174.

Buday, E. M. (1995). The effects of signed and spoken words taught with music on sign and speech imitation by children with autism. *Journal of Music Therapy, 32*(3), 189–202.

Burke, M., Walsh, J., Oehler, J., & Gingras, J. (1995). Music therapy following suctioning: Four case studies. *Neonatal Network, 14*(7), 41–49.

Burleson, S. J., Center, D. B., & Reeves, H. (1989). The effect of background music on task performance in psychotic children. *Journal of Music Therapy, 26*(4), 198–205.

Burns, K., Cunningham, N., White-Traut, R., Silvestri, J., & Nelson, M. (1994). Infant stimulation: Modification of an intervention based on physiologic and behavioral cues. *Journal of Obstetric, Gynecologic, and Neonatal Nursing, 23*(7), 581–589.

Burroughs, A., Asonye, U., Anderson-Shanklin, G., & Vidyasagar, D. (1978). The effect of nonnutritive sucking on transcutaneous oxygen tension in noncrying, preterm neonates. *Research in Nursing and Health, 1*(2), 69–75.

Caine, J. (1992). The effects of music on the selected stress behaviors, weight, caloric and formula intake, and length of hospital stay of premature and low birth weight neonates in a newborn intensive care unit. *Journal of Music Therapy, 28*(4), 180–192.

Caine, J., & Erickson, S. (1986). Reducing distress in pediatric patients undergoing cardiac catheterization. *Children's Health Care, 14*(3), 146–152.

Callaham, J. E. (2004). *The effect of live music on the reduction of negative side effects experienced by pediatric patients during onset, final thirty minutes of hemodialysis treatment, and removal of needles.* Unpublished master's thesis, The Florida State University, Tallahassee.

Cartwright, J., & Huckaby, G. (1972). Intensive preschool language program. *Journal of Music Therapy, 9*(3), 137–146.

Cassidy, J., & Ditty, K. (1998). Presentation of aural stimuli to newborns and premature infants: An audiological perspective. *Journal of Music Therapy, 35*(2), 70–87.

Cassidy, J., & Ditty, K. (2001). Gender differences among newborns on a transient otoacoustic emissions test for hearing. *Journal of Music Therapy, 38*(1), 28–35.

Cassidy, J. W., & Standley, J. M. (1995). The effect of music listening on physiological responses of premature infants in the NICU. *Journal of Music Therapy, 32*(4), 208–227.

Chapman, J. S. (1975). *The relation between auditory stimulation of short gestation infants and their gross motor limb activity.* Unpublished doctoral dissertation, New York University.

Chapman, J. S. (1979). Influence of varied stimuli on development of motor patterns in the premature infant. In G. Anderson & B. Raff (Eds.), *Newborn behavioral organization: Nursing research and implications* (pp. 61–80). New York: Alan Liss.

Chase, K. (2004). Music therapy assessment for children with developmental disabilities: A survey study. *Journal of Music Therapy, 41*(1), 28–54.

Cheour-Luhtanen, M., Alho, K., Sainio, K., Rinne, T., Reinikainen, K., Pohjavuouri, M., et al. (1996). The ontogenetically earliest discriminative response of the human brain. *Psychophysiology, 33*, 478–481.

Chester, K. K., Holmberg, T. K., Lawrence, M. P., & Thurmond, L. L. (1999). A program-based consultative music therapy model for public schools. *Journal of Music Therapy, 17*(2), 82–91.

Chetta, H. D. (1980). *The effect of music therapy in reducing fear and anxiety in preoperative pediatric patients.* Unpublished master's thesis, The Florida State University, Tallahassee.

Chetta, H. D. (1981). The effect of music and desensitization on pre-operative anxiety in children. *Journal of Music Therapy, 18*, 74–87.

Chiron, C., Jambaque, I., Nabbout, R., Lounes, R., Syrota, A., & Dulac, O. (1997). The right brain hemisphere is dominant in human infants. *Brain, 120*(6), 1057–1065.

Clinton, P. K. (1984). *Music as a nursing intervention for children during painful procedures.* Unpublished master's thesis, The University of Iowa, Iowa City.

Cohen, A. (1984). *The development and implementation of a pediatric music therapy program in a short-term medical facility.* Unpublished master's thesis, New York University, New York.

Cohen, R. D. (1984). Auditory mental imagery in children. *Music Therapy, 4*(1), 73–83.

Coleman, J. M., Pratt, R. R., Stoddard, R. A., Gerstmann, D. R., & Abel, H. H. (1997). The effects of the male and female singing and speaking voices on selected physiological and behavioral measures of premature infants in the intensive care unit. *International Journal of Arts Medicine, 5*(2), 4–11.

Collins, S. K., & Kuck, K. (1991). Music therapy in the Neonatal Intensive Care Unit. *Neonatal Network, 9*(6), 23–26.

Colwell, C. (1994). Therapeutic application of music in the whole language kindergarten. *Journal of Music Therapy, 31*(4), 238–247.

Colwell, C. M. (1995). Adapting music instruction for elementary students with special needs: A pilot. *Music Therapy Perspectives, 13*(2), 97–103.

Colwell, C. M., & Murless, K. D. (2002). Music activities (singing vs. chanting) as a vehicle of reading accuracy of children with learning disabilities: A pilot study. *Music Therapy Perspectives, 20*(1), 13–19.

Cooke, R. K. (1969). The use of music in plat therapy. *Journal of Music Therapy, 6*(3), 66–75.

Cote, C. J., Alderfer, R. J., Notterman, D. A., & Fanta, K. B. (1995). Sedation disasters: adverse drug reports in pediatrics—FDA, USP, and others. *Anesthesiology, 83* (3A), 1183.

Creasey, G., Jarvis, P., Myers, B., Markowitz, P., & Kerkering, K. (1993). Mental and motor development for three groups of premature infants. *Infant Behavior and Development, 16,* 365–372.

Cripe, F. F. (1986). Rock music as therapy for children with ADD: An exploratory study. *Journal of Music Therapy, 31*(1), 30–37.

Darrow, A. A. (1979). The beat reproduction response of subjects with normal and impaired hearing: An empirical comparison. *Journal of Music Therapy, 16*(2), 91–98.

Darrow, A. A. (1984). A comparison of rhythmic responsiveness in normal and hearing impaired children and an investigation of the relationship of rhythmic responsiveness to the suprasegmental aspects of speech perception. *Journal of Music Therapy, 21*(2), 48–66.

Darrow, A. A. (1990). The effect of frequency adjustment on the vocal reproduction accuracy of hearing impaired children. *Journal of Music Therapy, 27*(1), 24–37.

Darrow, A. A. (1991). An assessment and comparison of hearing impaired children's preference for timbre and musical instruments. *Journal of Music Therapy, 28*(1), 48–59.

Darrow, A. A. (1992). The effect of vibrotactile stimuli via the SOMATRON™ on the identification of pitch change by hearing impaired children. *Journal of Music Therapy, 29*(2), 103–112.

Darrow, A. A. (1999). Music educators' perceptions regarding the inclusion of students with severe disabilities in music classrooms. *Journal of Music Therapy, 36*(4), 254–273.

Darrow, A. A., & Cohen, N. (1991). The effect of programmed pitch practice and private instruction on the vocal reproduction accuracy of children with hearing impairments: Two case studies. *Music Therapy Perspectives, 9,* 61–65.

Darrow, A. A., & Gfeller, K. (1991). A study of public school music programs mainstreaming hearing impaired students. *Journal of Music Therapy, 28*(1), 23–39.

Darrow, A. A., & Goll, H. (1989). The effect of vibrotactile stimuli via the SOMATRON™ on the identification of rhythmic concepts by hearing impaired children. *Journal of Music Therapy, 26*(3), 115–124.

Darrow, A. A., & Stammer, G. J. (1986). The effect of vocal training on the intonation and rate of hearing impaired children's speech: A pilot study. *Journal of Music Therapy, 23*(4), 194–201.

Davis, R. K. (1990). A model for the integration of music therapy within a preschool classroom for children with physical disabilities or language delays. *Music Therapy Perspectives, 8,* 82–84.

DeCasper, A. J., & Carstens, A. A. (1981). Contingencies of stimulation: Effects on learning and emotion in neonates. *Infant Behavior and Development, 4*(1), 19–35.

DeCasper, A. J., & Fifer, W. P. (1980). Of human bonding: Newborns prefer their mothers' voices. *Science, 208,* 1174–1176.

DeCasper, A. J., & Spence, M. J. (1986). Newborns prefer a familiar story over an unfamiliar one. *Infant Behavior and Development, 9,* 133–150.

Detterman, D. (1978). The effect of heartbeat sound on neonatal crying. *Infant Behavior and Development, 1,* 36–48.

DiPietro, J., Cusson, R., Caughy, M., & Fox, N. (1994). Behavioral and physiologic effects of nonnutritive sucking during gavage feeding in preterm infants. *Pediatric Research, 36*(2), 207–214.

Dureau, S. J. (2003). *The effect of gender on one day-old infants' behavior and heart rate responses to music decibel level.* Unpublished master's thesis, The Florida State University, Tallahassee.

Edenfield, T. N., & Hughes, J. E. (1991). The relationship of a choral music curriculum to the development of singing ability in secondary students with Down syndrome. *Music Therapy Perspectives, 9,* 52–55.

Edgerton, C. L. (1994). The effect of improvised music therapy on the communicative behaviors of autistic children. *Journal of Music Therapy, 31*(1), 31–62.

Eidson, C. E., Jr. (1989). The effect of behavioral music therapy on the generalization of interpersonal skills from sessions to the classroom by emotionally handicapped middle school students. *Journal of Music Therapy, 26*(4), 206–221.

Eisenstein, S. R. (1974). Effect of contingent guitar lessons on reading behavior. *Journal of Music Therapy, 11*(3), 138–146.

Fagen, T. (1982). Music therapy in the treatment of anxiety and fear in terminal pediatric patients. *Music Therapy, 2,* 13–23.

Fagen, T. S. (1982). *Music therapy as a tool for the assessment and treatment of fear and anxiety in pediatric cancer patients.* Unpublished master's thesis, New York University, New York.

Falb, M. (1982). *The use of operant procedures to condition vasoconstriction in profoundly mentally retarded (PMR) infants.* Unpublished master's thesis, The Florida State University, Tallahassee.

Field, T. (1987). Alleviating stress in intensive-care unit neonates. *Journal of American Obstetrical Association, 9,* 129–135.

Field, T., Ignatoff, E., Stringer, S., Brennan, J., Greenberg, R., Widmayer, S., et al. (1982). Nonnutritive sucking during tube feedings: Effects on preterm neonates in an intensive care unit. *Pediatrics, 70*(3), 381–384.

Flowers, A. L., McCain, A. P., & Hilker, K. A. (1999, April). *The effects of music listening on premature infants.* Paper presented at the biennial meeting of the Society for Research in Child Development, Albuquerque, NM.

Flowers, E. (1984). Musical sound perception in normal children and children with Down syndrome. *Journal of Music Therapy, 21*(3), 146–154.

Ford, S. C. (1984). Music therapy for cerebral palsied children. *Music Therapy Perspectives, 1*(3), 8–13.

Ford, T. A. (1988). The effect of musical experiences and age on the ability of deaf children to discriminate pitch. *Journal of Music Therapy, 25*(1), 2–16.

Forslund, M., & Bjerre, I. (1990). Follow-up of preterm children: II. Growth and development at four years of age. *Early Human Development, 24*(2), 107–118.

Fowler-Kerry, S., & Lander, J. (1987). Management of injection pain in children. *Pain, 30,* 169–175.

Froelich, M. (1984). A comparison of the effect of music therapy and medical play therapy on the verbalization behavior of pediatric patients. *Journal of Music Therapy, 21,* 2–15.

Froehlich, M. (Ed.). (1996). *Music therapy with hospitalized children.* Cherry Hill, NJ: Jeffery Books.

Furman, C., & Steele, A. (1982). Teaching the special student: A survey of independent music teachers with implications for music therapists. *Journal of Music Therapy, 19*(2), 66–73.

Galloway, H. F., & Bean, M. F. (1974). The effects of action songs on the development of body-image and body-part identification in hearing-impaired preschool children. *Journal of Music Therapy, 11*(3), 125–134.

Garcia-Prats, J. A., & Hornfischer, S. S. (2000). *What to do when your baby is premature.* New York: Three Rivers Press.

Gardner, S. L., Garland, K. R., Merenstein, S. L., & Lubchenco, L. O. (1997). The neonate and the environment: Impact on development. In G. B. Merenstein & S. L. Gardner (Eds.), *Handbook of neonatal intensive care* (4th ed., pp. 564–608). St. Louis: Mosby.

Gardstrom, S. C. (1987). Positive peer culture: A working definition for the music therapist. *Music Therapy Perspectives, 4,* 19–23.

Getsie, R., Langer, P., & Glass, G. (1985). Meta-analysis of the effects of type and combination of feedback on children's discrimination learning. *Review of Educational Research, 55*(1), 9–22.

Gettel, M. K. (1985). *The effect of music on anxiety in children undergoing cardiac catheterization.* Unpublished master's thesis, Hahnemann University, Philadelphia.

Gfeller, K. E. (1983). Musical mnemonics as an aid to retention with normal and learning disabled students. *Journal of Music Therapy, 20*(4), 179–189.

Gfeller, K. E. (1990). A cognitive-linguistic approach to language development for the preschool child with hearing impairments for music therapy practice. *Music Therapy Perspectives, 8,* 47–51.

Gfeller, K. E. (2000). Accommodating children who use cochlear implants in music therapy or educational setting. *Music Therapy Perspectives, 18*(2), 122–130.

Gfeller, K., & Baumann, A. A. (1988). Assessment procedures for music therapy with hearing impaired children: Language development. *Journal of Music Therapy, 25*(4), 192–205.

Gfeller, K., Logan, H., & Walker, J. (1988). The effect of auditory distraction and suggestion on tolerance for dental restorations in adolescents and young adults. *Journal of Music Therapy, 27*(1), 13–23.

Ghetti, C. M. (2002). Comparison of the effectiveness of three music therapy conditions to modulate behavior states in students with profound disabilities: A pilot study. *Music Therapy Perspectives, 20*(1), 20–30.

Giacobbe, G. A., & Graham, R. M. (1978). The response of aggressive emotionally disturbed and normal boys to selected musical stimuli. *Journal of Music Therapy, 15*(3), 118–135.

Gibbons, A. C. (1983). Rhythm responses in emotionally disturbed children with differing needs for external structure. *Music Therapy, 3*(1), 94–102.

Gill, N., Behnke, M., Conlon, M., McNeely, J., & Anderson, G. (1988). Effect of nonnutritive sucking on behavioral state in preterm infants before feeding. *Nursing Research, 37*(6), 347–350.

Glass, P. (1994). The vulnerable neonate and the neonatal intensive care environment. In G. B. Avery, M. A. Fletcher, & M.G. MacDonald (Eds.), *Neonatology: Pathophysiology and management of the newborn* (4th ed., pp. 77–94). Philadelphia: J.B. Lippincott.

Goff, D. M. (1985). The effects of nonnutritive sucking on state regulation in preterm infants. *Dissertation Abstracts International, 46*(8-B), 2835.

Goldstein, C. (1964). Music and creative arts therapy for an autistic child. *Journal of Music Therapy, 1*(4), 135–138.

Gomes-Pedro, J., Patricio, M., Carvalho, A., Goldschmidt, T, Torgal-Garcia, F., & Monteiro, M. (1995). Early intervention with Portuguese mothers: A 2-year follow-up. *Journal of Developmental and Behavioral Pediatrics, 16*(1), 21–28.

Goolsby, T. M., Jr., Frary, R. B., & Rodgers, M. M. (1974). Observational techniques in determination of the effects of background music upon verbalizations of disadvantaged kindergarten children. *Journal of Music Therapy, 11*(1), 21–32.

Gordin, P.C. (1990). Assessing and managing agitation in a critically ill infant. *MCN, 15*, 26–32.

Gordon, E. (1968). The use of the musical aptitude profile with exceptional children. *Journal of Music Therapy, 5*(2), 37–40.

Gorski, P., Davison, M., & Brazelton, T. (1979). Stages of behavioral organization in the high-risk neonate theoretical and clinical considerations. *Seminars in Perinatology, 3*(1), 61–72.

Grant, R. E. (1989). Music therapy guidelines for developmentally disabled children. *Music Therapy Perspectives, 6*, 18–22.

Grasso, M. C., Button, B. M., Allison, D. J., & Sawyer, S. M. (2000). Benefits of music therapy as an adjunct to chest physiotherapy in infants and toddlers with cystic fibrosis. *Pediatric Pulmonology, 29*, 371–381.

Greenberg, S. B., Faerber, E. N., & Aspinall, C. L., & Adams, R. C. (1993). High-dose chloral hydrate sedation for children undergoing MR imaging: Safety and efficacy in relation to age. *American Journal of Roentgenology, 161*, 639–641.

Griggs-Drane, E. R., & Wheeler, J. J. (1997). The use of functional assessment procedures and individualized schedule in the treatment of autism: Recommendations for music therapists. *Music Therapy Perspectives, 15*(2), 87–93.

Gromko, J. E., & Poorman, A. S. (1998, July). *The effect of music training on preschoolers' spatial-temporal task performance.* Paper presented at International Society for Music Education, Johannesburg, South Africa.

Grossman, S. (1978). An investigation of Crocker's music projective techniques for emotionally disturbed children. *Journal of Music Therapy, 15*(4), 179–184.

Gunsberg, A. (1988). Improvised musical play: A strategy for fostering social play between developmentally delayed and nondelayed preschool children. *Journal of Music Therapy, 25*(4), 178–191.

Gunsberg, A. S. (1991). A method for conducting improvised musical play with children both with and without developmental delays in preschool classrooms. *Music Therapy Perspectives, 9*, 46–51.

Guo, S. S., Roche, A. F., Chumlea, W. C., Casey, P. H., & Moore, W. M. (1997). Growth in weight, recumbent length, and head circumference for preterm low-birthweight infants during the first three years of life using gestation-adjusted ages. *Early Human Development, 47*, 305–325.

Hack, M., Klein, N., & Taylor, H. (1995). Long-term developmental outcomes of low birth weight infants. *The Future of Children* [Online serial], *5*(1). Retrieved from http://www. futureofchildren.org/LBW/12LBWHAC.htm

Haines, J. H. (1989). The effects of music therapy on the self esteem of emotionally disturbed adolescents. *Music Therapy, 8*(1), 78–91.

Hair, H. I., & Graham, R. M. (1983). A comparison of verbal descriptions used by TMR students and music therapists. *Journal of Music Therapy, 20*(2), 59–68.

Hairston, M. J. (1990). Analyses of responses of mentally retarded autistic and mentally retarded nonautistic children to art and music therapy. *Journal of Music Therapy, 27*(3), 137–150.

Hanamoto, J., & Kajiyama, T. (1974). Some experiences in use of environmental music in pediatric roentgenography. *Radiologia Diagnostica, 15*(6), 787–794.

Hanser, S. B. (1974). Group-contingent music listening with emotionally disturbed boys. *Journal of Music Therapy, 11*(4), 220–225.

Harding, C., & Ballard, K. D. (1982). The effectiveness of music as a stimulus and as a contingent reward in promoting the spontaneous speech of three physically handicapped preschoolers. *Journal of Music Therapy, 19*(2), 86–101.

Harrison, L. (1987). Effects of early supplemental stimulation programs for premature infants: Review of the literature. *Maternal-Child Nursing Journal, 14*(2), 69–90.

Herman, F. (1985). Music therapy for the young child with cerebral palsy who uses blissymbols. *Journal of Music Therapy, 5*(1), 28–36.

Herron, C. J. (1970). Some effects of instrumental music training on cerebral palsied children. *Journal of Music Therapy, 7*(2), 55–58.

Hill, A. (1992). Preliminary findings: A maximum oral feeding time for premature infants, the relationship to physiological indicators. *Maternal-Child Nursing Journal, 20*(2), 81–92.

Hilliard, R. (2001). The effects of music therapy-based bereavement groups on mood and behavior of grieving children: A pilot study. *Journal of Music Therapy, 38*(4), 291–306.

Hoelzley, P. D. (1991). Reciprocal inhibition in music therapy: A case study involving wind instrument usage to attenuate fear, anxiety, and avoidance reactivity in a child with pervasive developmental disorders. *Music Therapy, 10*(1), 58–76.

Hoffman, P. (1975). The use of guitar and singing in a child life program. *Journal of the Association for the Care of Children in Hospitals, 4*(1), 45–47.

Hollander, F. M., & Juhrs, P. D. (1974). Orff-Schulwerk, an effective treatment tool with autistic children. *Journal of Music Therapy, 11*(1), 1–12.

Holloway, M. S. (1980). A comparison of passive and active music reinforcement to increase preacademic and motor skills in severely retarded children and adolescents. *Journal of Music Therapy, 17*(2), 58–69.

Horbar, J., & Lucey, J. (1995). Evaluation of neonatal intensive care technologies. *The Future of Children* [Online serial], *5*(1). Retrieved from http://www.futureofchildren.org/LBW/12LBWHAC.htm

Hoskins, C. (1988). Use of music to increase verbal response and improve expressive language abilities of preschool language delayed children. *Journal of Music Therapy, 25*(2), 73–84.

Howell, R. D., Flowers, P. J., & Wheeler, J. E. (1995). The effects of keyboard experiences on rhythmic responses of elementary school children with physical disabilities. *Journal of Music Therapy, 32*(2), 91–112.

Hughes, J. E., Robbins, B. J., McKenzie, B. A., & Robb, S. S. (1990). Integrating exceptional and nonexceptional young children through music play: A pilot program. *Music Therapy Perspectives, 8*, 52–56.

Humpal, M. (1990). Early intervention: The implications for music therapy. *Music Therapy Perspectives, 8*, 30–35.

Humpal, M. (1991). The effects of an integrated early childhood music program on social interaction among children with handicaps and their typical peers. *Journal of Music Therapy, 28(3)*, 161–177.

Humpal, M. (2001). Annotated bibliography of music therapy articles related to young children: From music therapy journals (1990–2000). *Early Childhood Connections, 7(2)*, 16–17.

Humpal, M. (2001). Music therapy and the young child. *Early Childhood Connections, 7(2)*, 9–15.

Humphrey, T. (1980). The effects of music ear training upon the auditory discrimination abilities of trainable mentally retarded adolescents. *Journal of Music Therapy, 17(2)*, 70–74.

Inder, T, Huppi, P., Zientara, G., Maier, S., Jolesz, F., di Slavo, D., Robertson, et al. (1999). Early detection of peri leukomalacia by diffusion-weighted magnetic resonance imaging techniques. *Journal of Pediatrics, 134(5)*, 631–634.

Jackson, N. (2003). A survey of music therapy methods and their role in the treatment of early elementary school children with ADHD. *Journal of Music Therapy, 40(4)*, 302–323.

Jarred, J. (2003). Music assisted surgery: Preoperative and postoperative interventions. In S. L. Robb (Ed.), *Music therapy in pediatric healthcare: Research and evidence-based practice* (pp. 147–162). Silver Spring, MD: American Music Therapy Association.

Jellison, J. A. (1979). The music therapist in the educational setting: Developing and implementing curriculum for the handicapped. *Journal of Music Therapy, 16(3)*, 128–137.

Jellison, J. A., & Duke, R. A. (1994). The mental retardation label: Music teachers' and perspective teachers' expectations of children's social and music behaviors. *Journal of Music Therapy, 31(3)*, 166–185.

Jellison, J. A., & Gainer, E. W. (1995). Into the mainstream: A case-study of a child's participation in music education and music therapy. *Journal of Music Therapy, 32(4)*, 228–247.

Johnson, E. R. (1981). The role of objective and concrete feedback in self-concept treatment of juvenile delinquents in music therapy. *Journal of Music Therapy, 18*, 137–147.

Johnston, C., Sherrard, A., Stevens, B., Franck, L., Stemler, R., & Jack, A. (1999). Do cry features reflect pain intensity in preterm neonates? A preliminary study. *Biology of the Neonate, 76(2)*, 120–124.

Jones, R. E. (1986). Assessing developmental levels of mentally retarded students with the musical-perception assessment of cognitive development. *Journal of Music Therapy, 23(3)*, 166–173.

Jorgenson, H., & Parnell, M. K. (1970). Modifying social behaviors of mentally retarded children in music activities. *Journal of Music Therapy, 7(3)*, 83–87.

Josepha, M. (1964). Therapeutic values of instrumental performance for severely handicapped children. *Journal of Music Therapy, 1(3)*, 73–79.

Joyce, B., Keck, J., & Gerkensmeyer, J. (2001). Evaluation of pain management interventions for neonatal circumcision pain. *Journal of Pediatric Healthcare, 15*(3), 105–114.

Kagan, J., & Lewis, M. (1965). Studies of attention in the human infant. *Merrill-Palmer Quarterly, 11*, 95–127.

Kaminski, J., & Hall, W. (1996). The effect of soothing music on neonatal behavioral states in the hospital newborn nursery. *Neonatal Network, 15*(1), 45–54.

Kanarek, K., & Shulman, D. (1992). Non-nutritive sucking does not increase blood levels of gastrin, motilin, insulin and insulin-like growth factor 1 in premature infants receiving enteral feedings. *Acta Paediatrica Scandinavica, 81*(12), 974–977.

Kaplan, R. S., & Steele, A. L. (2005). An analysis of music therapy program goals and outcomes for clients with diagnoses on the autism spectrum. *Journal of Music Therapy, 42*(1), 2–19.

Karmel, B., Gardner, J., & Magnano, C. (1991). Attention and arousal in early infancy. In M. Weiss & P. Zelazo (Eds.), *Newborn attention: Biological constraints and the influence of experience* (pp. 339–376). Norwood, NJ: Ablex.

Katz, V. (1971). Auditory stimulation and developmental behavior of the premature infant. *Nursing Research, 20*, 196–201.

Keller, V. (1995). Management of nausea and vomiting in children. *Journal of Pediatric Nursing, 10*(5), 280–286.

Kemper, K., Martin, K., Block, S., Shoaf, R., & Woods, C. (2004). Attitudes and expectations about music therapy for premature infants among staff in a neonatal intensive care unit. *Alternative Therapies, 10*(2), 50–54.

Kennedy, R. (2005). A pilot study: The effects of music therapy interventions on middle school students' ESL skills. *Journal of Music Therapy, 42*(4), 244–261.

Kenner, C., & McGrath, J. (2004). *Developmental care of newborns and infants: A guide for health professionals.* St. Louis, MO: Mosby.

Kern, P., & Wolery, M. (2001). Participation of a preschooler with visual impairments on the playground: Effects of music adaptations and staff development. *Journal of Music Therapy, 38*(2), 149–164.

Kessler, J. (1967). Therapeutic methods for exceptional children. *Journal of Music Therapy, 4*(1), 1–2.

King, J. (1982). *Music therapy results with pediatric patients.* Unpublished research manuscript, The Florida State University, Tallahassee.

King, J. (1984). *Five case studies: The integrative use of music therapy with hospitalized children on a pediatric ward.* Unpublished research study, The Florida State University, Tallahassee.

Kivland, M. J. (1986). The use of music to increase self-esteem in a conduct-disordered adolescent. *Journal of Music Therapy, 23*(1), 25–29.

Klaus, M. H., & Fanaroff, A. A. (1993). *Care of the high risk infant.* Philadelphia: W. B. Saunders.

Kleiber, C., & Harper, D. (1999). Effects of distraction on children's pain and distress during medical procedures: A meta-analysis. *Nursing Research, 48*(1), 44–49.

Kolata, G. (1984). Studying learning in the womb. *Science, 225*(4659), 302–303.

Korduba, O. M. (1975). Duplicated rhythmic patterns between deaf and normal hearing children. *Journal of Music Therapy, 12*(3), 136–146.

Kostka, M. J. (1993). A comparison of selected behaviors of a student with autism in a special education and regular music classes. *Music Therapy Perspectives, 11*(6), 57–60.

Kovacs, M. (1992). *Children's depression inventory.* North Tonawanda, NY: Multi-Health Systems.

Kozak, Y. (1968). Music therapy for orthopedic patients in a rehabilitative setting. In E. T. Gaston (Ed.), *Music in therapy* (pp. 166–168). New York: Macmillan.

Kramer, S. A. (1978). The effects of music as a cue in maintaining handwriting in preschool children. *Journal of Music Therapy, 15*(3), 138–144.

Krout, R. (1986). Use of a group token contingency with school-aged special education students to improve a music listening skill. *Music Therapy Perspectives, 3*, 13–16.

Krout, R. (1987). Music therapy with multi-handicapped students: Individualizing treatment within two group settings. *Journal of Music Therapy, 24*(1), 2–13.

Krout, R., Burnham, A., & Moorman, S. (1993). Computer and electronic music applications with students in special education from program proposal to progress evaluation. *Music Therapy Perspectives, 11*(1), 28–31.

Krout, R. E., & Mason, M. (1988). Using computer and electronic music resources in clinical music therapy with behaviorally disordered students, 12 to 18 years old. *Music Therapy Perspectives, 5*, 114–118.

Kuhn, D. (2002). The effects of active and passive participation in musical activity on the immune system as measured by salivary immunoglobulin A (SIgA). *Journal of Music Therapy, 39*(1), 30–39.

Lane, D. (1991). *The effect of a single music therapy session on hospitalized children as measured by salivary Immunoglobulin A, speech pause time, and a patient opinion Likert scale.* Unpublished doctoral dissertation, Case Western Reserve University, Cleveland, OH. (UMI No. 9137062)

Lane, D. (1991). The effect of a single music therapy session on hospitalized children as measured by salivary Immunoglobulin A, speech pause time, and a patient opinion Likert scale. *Pediatric Research, 29*(4, part 2), 11A.

Larson, B. A. (1977). A comparison of singing ranges of mentally retarded and normal children with published songbooks used in singing activities. *Journal of Music Therapy, 14*(3), 139–143.

Larson, B. A. (1981). Auditory and visual rhythmic pattern recognition by emotionally disturbed and normal adolescents. *Journal of Music Therapy, 18*(3), 128–136.

Larson, K., & Ayllon, T. (1990). The effects of contingent music and differential reinforcement on infantile colic. *Behavior Research Therapy, 28*(2), 119–125.

Lathom, W. (1964). Music therapy as a means of changing the adaptive behavior level of retarded children. *Journal of Music Therapy, 1*(4), 132–134.

Lathom, W. (1982). Report on the Office of Special Education Grant, Special Project: A national in-service training model for educational personnel providing music education/therapy for severely/profoundly handicapped children. *Music Therapy Perspectives, 1*(1), 27–29.

Layman, D. L. (1998). *A descriptive analysis of the music therapy assessment technique for hospitalized children ages birth to three years.* Unpublished master's thesis, The Florida State University, Tallahassee.

Layman, D. L., Hussey, D. L., & Laing, S. J. (2002). Music therapy assessment for severely emotionally disturbed children: A pilot study. *Journal of Music Therapy, 40*(3), 164–187.

Lecanuet, J., Graniere-Deferre, C., & Busnel, M. (1995). Human fetal auditory perception. In J. P. Lecanuet, W. P. Fifer, N. A. Krasnegor, & W. P. Smotherman (Eds.), *Fetal development: A psychobiological perspective* (pp. 239–262). Hillsdale, NJ: Lawrence Erlbaum.

Lecanuet, J., Graniere-Deferre, C., Jacquet, A., & DeCasper, A. (2000). Fetal discrimination of low-pitched musical notes. *Developmental Psychobiology, 36,* 29–39.

Leonard, J. E. (1983). Music therapy: Fertile ground for application of research in practice. *Neonatal Network, 12*(2), 47–48.

Lewit, E., Baker, L., Corman, H., & Shiono, P. (1995). The direct cost of low birth weight. *The Future of Children* [Online serial], *5*(1). Retrieved from http://www.futureofchildren.org/LBW/12LBWHAC.htm

Liebman, S., & MacLaren, A. (1991). The effects of music and relaxation on third trimester anxiety in adolescent pregnancy. *Journal of Music Therapy, 28*(2), 89–100.

Liebman, S., & MacLaren, A. (1993). The effects of music and relaxation on third trimester anxiety in adolescent pregnancy. In F. J. Bejjani (Ed.), *Current research in arts medicine* (pp. 427–430). Chicago: A Cappella Books.

Lienhard, M. E. (1976). Factors relevant to the rhythmic perception of a group of mentally retarded children. *Journal of Music Therapy, 13*(2), 58–65.

Lindecker, J. M. (1953). Music therapy in a juvenile detention home. *Music Therapy* 108–114.

Lindsay, K. (1981). The value of music for hospitalized infants. *Journal of the Association for the Care of Children in Hospitals, 9*(4), 104–107.

Lininger, L. (1987). *The effects of instrumental and vocal lullabies on the crying behavior of newborn infants.* Unpublished master's thesis, Southern Methodist University, Dallas, TX.

Loewy, J. (1995). The musical stages of speech: A developmental model of pre-verbal sound making. *Music Therapy, 13*(1), 47–73.

Loewy, J. (Ed.). (1997). *Music therapy and pediatric pain.* Cherry Hill, NJ: Jeffrey Books.

Loewy, J. (1999). The use of music psychotherapy in the treatment of pediatric pain. In C. Dileo (Ed.), *Music therapy and medicine: Theoretical and clinical applications* (pp. 189–206). Silver Spring, MD: American Music Therapy Association.

Long, L., & Johnson, J. (1978). Dental practice using music to aid relaxation and relieve pain. *Dental Survey, 54,* 35–38.

Lorch, C. A., Lorch, V., Diefendorf, A. O., & Earl, P. W. (1994). Effect of stimulative and sedative music on systolic blood pressure, heart rate, and respiratory rate in premature infants. *Journal of Music Therapy, 31*(2), 105–118.

Lutz, W. (1997). *The effect of music distraction on children's pain, fear, and behavior during laceration repairs.* Unpublished master's thesis, The University of Texas at Arlington.

Maalouf, E., Duggan, P., Rutherford, M., Counsell, S., Fletcher, A., Baffin, M., et al. (1999). Magnetic resonance imaging of the brain in a cohort of extremely preterm infants. *Journal of Pediatrics, 135*(3), 351–357.

Madsen, C. K., & Madsen, C. H., Jr. (1968). Music as a behavior modification technique with a juvenile delinquent. *Journal of Music Therapy, 5*(3), 72–76.

Madsen, C. K., Smith, D. S., & Feeman, C. C., Jr. (1988). The use of music in cross-age tutoring within special education settings. *Journal of Music Therapy, 25*(3), 135–144.

Mahlberg, M. (1973). Music therapy in the treatment of an autistic child. *Journal of Music Therapy, 10*(4), 189–193.

Malloy, G. (1979). The relationship between maternal and musical auditory stimulation and the developmental behavior of premature infants. *Birth Defects: Original Article Series, 15*(7), 81–98.

Malone, A. B. (1996). The effects of live music on the distress of pediatric patients receiving intravenous starts, venipunctures, injections, and heel sticks. *Journal of Music Therapy, 33*(1), 19–33.

Marchette, L., Main, R., Redick, E., Bagg, A., & Leatherland, J. (1991). Pain reduction interventions during neonatal circumcision. *Nursing Research, 40*(4), 241–244.

Marchette, L., Main, R., Redick, E., & Shapiro, A. (1989). Pain reduction during neonatal circumcision. In R. Spintge & R. Droh (Eds.), *MusicMedicine* (pp. 131–136). Ann Arbor, MI: Malloy Lithographing.

Marley, L. (1984). The use of music with hospitalized infants and toddlers: A descriptive study. *Journal of Music Therapy, 21*(3), 126–132.

Marrero, D., Fremion, A., & Golden, M. (1988). Improving compliance with exercise in adolescents with insulin-dependent diabetes mellitus: Results of a self-motivated home exercise program. *Pediatrics, 81*(4), 519–525.

Martin, J., Hamilton, B., Ventura, S., Menacker, F., & Park, M. (2002, February 12). Births: Final data for 2000. *National Vital Statistics Reports, 50*(5).

Marwick, C. (2000, January 26). Music hath charms for care of preemies. *Journal of the American Medical Association, 283*(4), 468–469.

McCain, G. (1992). Facilitating inactive awake states in preterm infants: A study of three interventions. *Nursing Research, 41*(3), 157–160.

McCain, G. (1995). Promotion of preterm infant nipple feeding with nonnutritive sucking. *Journal of Pediatric Nursing, 10*(1), 3–8.

McCormick, J. L. (1988). Report: Status of public school music therapy. *Music Therapy Perspectives, 5,* 73–77.

McDonnell, L. (1984). Music therapy with trauma patients and their families on a pediatric service. *Music Therapy, 4,* 55–66.

Medoff-Cooper, B., & Gennaro, S. (1996). The correlation of sucking behaviors and Bayley Scales of Infant Development at six months of age in VLBW infants. *Nursing Research, 45*(5), 291–296.

Megel, M., Houser, C., & Gleaves, L. (1998). Children's responses to immunizations: Lullabies as a distraction. *Issues in Comprehensive Pediatric Nursing, 21*(3), 129–145.

Merle-Fishman, C. R., & Marcus, M. L. (1982). Musical behaviors and preferences in emotionally disturbed and normal children: An exploratory study. *Music Therapy, 2*(1), 1–11.

Metzler, R. K. (1973). Music therapy at the Behavioral Learning Center, St. Paul Public School. *Journal of Music Therapy, 10*(4), 177–183.

Micci, N. (1984). The use of music therapy with pediatric patients undergoing cardiac catheterization. *The Arts in Psychotherapy, 11,* 261–266.

Michel, D. E., & Martin, D. (1970). Music and self-esteem research with disadvantaged problem boys in an elementary school. *Journal of Music Therapy, 7*(4), 124–127.

Michel, P. (1973). The optimum development of musical abilities in the infant years of life. *Psychology of Music, 1*(2), 14–20.

Miller, D. M., Dorow, L., & Greer, R. D. (1974). The contingent use of music and art for improving arithmetic scores. *Journal of Music Therapy, 11*(2), 57–64.

Miller, L. (1984). *Spontaneous music therapy sessions for hospitalized children.* Unpublished research paper, The Florida State University, Tallahassee.

Miller, L. L., & Orsmond, G. (1994). Assessing structure in the musical explorations of children with disabilities. *Journal of Music Therapy, 31*(4), 248–265.

Montello, L., & Coons, E. E. (1998). Effects of active versus passive group music therapy on preadolescents with emotional, learning, and behavioral disorders. *Journal of Music Therapy, 35*(1), 49–67.

Monti, R. (1985). Music therapy in a therapeutic nursery. *Music Therapy, 5*(1), 22–27.

Moog, H. (1976). *The musical experience of the preschool child.* London: Schott.

Moon, C., Cooper, R. P., & Fifer, W. P. (1993). Two-day-olds prefer their native language. *Infant Behavior and Development, 16*, 495–500.

Moore, R., Gladstone, I., & Standley, J. (1994). *Effects of music, maternal voice, intrauterine sounds and white noise on the oxygen saturation levels of premature infants.* Paper presented at the National Association for Music Therapy National Conference, Orlando, FL.

Moore, R., & Mathenius, L. (1989). The effects of modeling, reinforcement, and tempo on imitative rhythmic responses of moderately retarded adolescents. *Journal of Music Therapy, 24*(3), 160–169.

Muir, D. W. (1985). The development of infants' auditory spatial sensitivity. In S. E. Trehub & B. A. Schneider (Eds.), *Auditory development in infancy* (pp. 55–83). New York: Plenum.

Munoz, M., Gomez, A., Soult, J. A., Marquez, C., Lopez-Castilla, J. D., Cervera, A., et al. (1997). Seizures caused by chloral hydrate sedative doses (letter). *Journal of Pediatrics, 131*(5), 787–788.

Myers, E. G. (1979). The effect of music on retention in a paired-associate task with EMR children. *Journal of Music Therapy, 16*(4), 190–198.

Nelson, D. L., Anderson, V. G., Gonzales, A. D. (1984). Music activities as therapy for children with autism and other pervasive developmental disorders. *Journal of Music Therapy, 21*(3), 100–116.

North, E. F. (1966). Music therapy as an important treatment modality with psychotic children. *Journal of Music Therapy, 3*(1), 22–24.

Oehler, J. (1993). Developmental care of low birth weight infants. *Advances in Clinical Nursing Research, 28*(2), 289–301.

Ogenfuss, J. (2001). *Pediatric surgery and patient anxiety: Can music therapy effectively reduce stress and anxiety levels while waiting to go to surgery?* Unpublished master's thesis, The Florida State University, Tallahassee.

Orsmond, G. I., & Miller, L. K. (1995). Correlates of musical improvisation in children with disabilities. *Journal of Music Therapy, 32*(3), 152–166.

Owens, L. (1979). The effects of music on the weight loss, crying, and physical movement of newborns. *Journal of Music Therapy, 16*, 83–90.

Palmer, M. M. (1993). Identification and management of the transitional suck pattern in premature infants. *Journal of Perinatal and Neonatal Nursing, 7*(1), 66–75.

Patterson, W. (1972). Our own thing. *Journal of Music Therapy, 9*, 119.

Perlman, J. (2001). Neurobehavioral deficits in premature graduates of intensive care: Potential medical and neonatal environmental risk factors. *Pediatrics, 108*(6), 1339–1348.

Perry, M. (2003). Relating improvisational music therapy with severely and multiply disabled children to communication development. *Journal of Music Therapy, 40*(3), 217–246.

Peters, M. L. (1970). A comparison of the musical sensitivity of mongoloid and normal children. *Journal of Music Therapy, 7*(4), 113–123.

Peterson, B., Vohr, B., Staib, L., Cannistraci, C., Dolber, A., Schneider, K., et al. (2000). Regional brain volume abnormalities and long-term cognitive outcome in preterm infants. *Journal of the American Medical Association, 284*(15), 1939–1947.

Pfaff, V., Smith, K., & Gowan, D. (1989). The effects of music-assisted relaxation on the distress of pediatric cancer patients undergoing bone marrow aspirations. *Children's Health Care, 18*(4), 232–236.

Pfeifer, M. (1989). A step in the right direction: Suggested strategies for implementing music therapy with the multihandicapped child. *Music Therapy Perspectives, 6*, 57–60.

Polverini-Rey, R. (1992). Intrauterine musical learning: The soothing effect on newborns of a lullaby learned prenatally. *Dissertation Abstracts International, 53*, 10A–3481.

Ragland, Z., & Apprey, M. (1974). Community music therapy with adolescents. *Journal of Music Therapy, 11*, 147–155.

Rath, V., Nurcombe, B., Achenbach, T., & Howell, C. (1987). The mother-infant transaction program: An intervention for the mothers of low-birthweight infants. In N. Gunzenhauser (Ed.), *Infant stimulation: For whom, what kind, when, and how much?* (Pediatric Round Table Series: 13). Skillman, NJ: Johnson & Johnson Baby Products.

Rauscher, F., Shaw, G., Levine, L., Wright, E., Dennis, W., & Newcomb, R. (1997). Music training causes long-term enhancement of preschool children's spatial-temporal reasoning. *Neurological Research, 19*(1), 2–8.

Register, D. (2001). The effects of an early intervention music curriculum on prereading/writing. *Journal of Music Therapy, 38*(3), 239–248.

Register, D. (2004). The effects of live music groups versus an educational children's television program on the emergent literacy of young children. *Journal of Music Therapy, 41*(1), 2–27.

Register, D. (2004). Teaching child-care personnel to use music in the classroom: A comparison of workshop training versus on-site modeling. *Music Therapy Perspectives, 22*(2), 109–115.

Reid, D. H., Hill, B. K., Rawers, R. J., & Montegar, C. A. (1975). The use of contingent music in teaching social skills to a nonverbal, hyperactive boy. *Journal of Music Therapy, 12*(1), 2–18.

Rickert, V., Kozlowski, K., Warren, A., Hendron, A., & Davis, P. (1994). Adolescents and colposcopy: The use of different procedures to reduce anxiety. *American Journal of Obstetrics and Gynecology, 170*(2), 504–508.

Rickson, D. J., & Watkins, W. G. (2003). Music therapy to promote prosocial behaviors in aggressive adolescent boys—A pilot study. *Journal of Music Therapy, 40*(4), 283–301.

Ries, N. L. (1982). An analysis of the characteristics of infant-child singing expressions. *Dissertation Abstracts International, 43,* 06A-1871.

Ritholz, M. S., & Turry, A. (1994). The journey by train: Creative music therapy with a 17-year-old boy. *Music Therapy, 12*(2), 58–87.

Robb, S. (1996). Techniques in song writing: Restoring emotional and physical well being in adolescents who have been traumatically injured. *Music Therapy Perspectives, 14*(1), 30–37.

Robb, S. (2000). The effect of therapeutic music interventions on the behavior of hospitalized children in isolation: Developing a contextual support model of music therapy. *Journal of Music Therapy, 37*(2), 118–146.

Robb, S. L. (2003). Music interventions and group participation skills of preschools with visual impairment: Raising questions about music, arousal, and attention. *Journal of Music Therapy, 40*(4), 266–282.

Robb, S. (2003). *Music therapy in pediatric healthcare.* Silver Spring, MD: American Music Therapy Association.

Robb, S., & Ebberts, A. (2003). Songwriting and digital video production interventions for pediatric patients undergoing bone marrow transplantation. Part I: An analysis of depression and anxiety levels according to phase of treatment. *Journal of Pediatric Oncology Nursing, 20,* 2–15.

Roberts, P. (2002). *The effect of contingent music with physical therapy in children who toe-walk.* Unpublished master's thesis, The Florida State University, Tallahassee.

Rogers, P. J. (1995). Childhood sexual abuse: Dilemmas in therapeutic practice. *Music Therapy Perspectives, 13*(1), 24–30.

Rudenberg, M. T., & Royka, A. M. (1989). Promoting psychosocial adjustment in pediatric burn patients through music therapy and child life therapy. *Music Therapy Perspectives, 7,* 40–43.

Rybski, D., Almli, C., Gisel, E., Powers, J., & Maurer, M. (1984). Sucking behaviors of normal 3-day-old female neonates during a 24-hr period. *Developmental Psychobiology, 17*(1), 79–86.

Saperston, B. (1973). The use of music in establishing communication with an autistic retarded child. *Journal of Music Therapy, 10*(4), 184–188.

Schaefer, M., Hatcher, P., & Barglow, P. (1980). Prematurity and infant stimulation: Review of research. *Child Psychiatry and Human Development, 10*(4), 199–212.

Scheve, A. (2002). *The effect of music therapy intervention on preoperative anxiety of pediatric patients as measured by self-report.* Unpublished master's thesis, The Florida State University, Tallahassee.

Schneider, F. (1982). *Assessment and evaluation of audio-analgesic effects on the pain experience of acutely burned children during dressing changes.* Unpublished doctoral dissertation, University of Cincinnati.

Schunk, H. A. (1993). *The relationship between background music during feeding time and weight gain of low-birthweight infants: A pilot study.* Unpublished study presented at the national conference of the National Association for Music Therapy, Toronto, Canada.

Schur, J. (1986). *Alleviating behavioral distress with music or Lamaze pant-blow breathing in children undergoing bone marrow aspirations and lumbar punctures.* Unpublished doctoral dissertation, The University of Texas Health Science Center at Dallas.

Schwankovsky, L., & Guthrie, P. (1982). *Music therapy for handicapped children: Other health impaired. NAMT Monograph Series.* Washington, DC: National Association for Music Therapy.

Schwartz, R., Moody, L., Yarndi, H., & Anderson, G. (1987). A meta-analysis of critical outcome variables in nonnutritive sucking in preterm infants. *Nursing Research, 36*(5), 292–295.

Seybold, C. D. (1971). The value and use of music activities in the treatment of speech delayed children. *Journal of Music Therapy, 8*(3), 102–110.

Shehan, P. K. (1981). A comparison of mediation strategies in paired-associate learning for children with learning disabilities. *Journal of Music Therapy, 18*(3), 120–127.

Sheth, R. D., Mullett, M. D., Bodensteiner, J. B., & Hobbs, G. R. (1995). Longitudinal head growth in developmentally normal preterm infants. *Archives of Pediatric and Adolescent Medicine, 149*(12), 1358–1361.

Shetler, D. (1989). The inquiry into prenatal musical experience: A report of the Eastman Project 1980–1987. *Pre- and Peri-Natal Psychology, 3*(3), 171–189.

Siegel, S. L. (1983). *The use of music as treatment in pain perception with post surgical patients in a pediatric hospital.* Unpublished master's thesis, The University of Miami.

Slivka, H., & Magill, L. (1986). The conjoint use of social work and music therapy in working with children of cancer patients. *Music Therapy, 6A*(1), 30–40.

Smith, D. S., & Hairston, M. J. (1999). Music therapy in school settings: Current practice. *Journal of Music Therapy, 36*(4), 274–292.

Snow, W., & Fields, B. (1950). Music as an adjunct in the training of children with cerebral palsy. *Occupational Therapy, 29,* 147–156.

Sommerfelt, K., Ellertsen, B., & Markestad, T. (1996). Low birthweight and neuromotor development: A population based, controlled study. *Acta Paediatrica, 85*(5), 604–610.

Soraci, S., Jr., Deckner, C. W., McDaniel, C., & Blanton, R. L. (1982). The relationship between rate of rhythmicity and the stereotypic behaviors of abnormal children. *Journal of Music Therapy, 19*(1), 46–54.

Spencer, S. L. (1988). The efficiency of instrumental and movement activities in developing mentally retarded adolescents' ability to follow directions. *Journal of Music Therapy, 25*(1), 44–50.

Spitzer, A. R. (1996). *Intensive care of the fetus and neonate.* Baltimore: Mosby-Year Book.

Standley, J. (1991). Long-term benefits of music intervention in the newborn intensive care unit: A pilot study. *Journal of the International Association of Music for the Handicapped, 6*(1), 12–23.

Standley, J. (1991). The role of music in pacification/stimulation of premature infants with low birthweights. *Music Therapy Perspectives, 9*(1), 19–25.

Standley, J. (1998). The effect of music and multimodal stimulation on physiologic and developmental responses of premature infants in neonatal intensive care. *Pediatric Nursing, 21*(6), 532–539.

Standley, J. (1998). Pre- and perinatal growth and development: Implications of music benefits for premature infants. *International Journal of Music Education, 31,* 1–13.

Standley, J. (1999). Music therapy in the NICU: Pacifier-Activated Lullabies (PAL) for reinforcement of non-nutritive sucking. *International Journal of Arts Medicine, 6*(2), 17–21.

Standley, J. (1999). Music therapy research with premature infants: Clinical implications. In R. R. Pratt & D. E. Grocke (Eds.), *MusicMedicine 3. MusicMedicine and Music Therapy: Expanding Horizons* (pp. 131–139). Parkville, Victoria, Australia: University of Melbourne Press.

Standley, J. (2000). The effect of contingent music to increase non-nutritive sucking of premature infants. *Pediatric Nursing, 26*(5), 493–499.

Standley, J. (2001). Music therapy for premature infants in neonatal intensive care: Physiological and developmental benefits. *Early Childhood Connections, 7*(2), 18–25.

Standley, J. (2001). Music therapy for the neonate. *Newborn and Infant Nursing Reviews, 1*(4), 211–216.

Standley, J. (2001). Musicoterapia para recien prematuros en cuidados intensivos neonatales (Music therapy for premature infants in neonatal intensive care) (C. Clancy, Trans.). *Acta Pediatrica Espanola, 59*(11), 623–629.

Standley, J. (2001, Spring). The power of contingent music for infant learning. *Bulletin of the Council for Research in Music Education, 149,* 65–71.

Standley, J. (2002). A meta-analysis of the efficacy of music therapy for premature infants. *Journal of Pediatric Nursing, 17*(2), 107–113.

Standley, J. (2002). Music therapy in the NICU: Promoting the growth and development of premature infants. *Zero to Three, 25*(1), 23–30.

Standley, J. (2003). The effect of music-reinforced non-nutritive sucking on feeding rate of premature infants. *Journal of Pediatric Nursing, 17*(2), 107–113.

Standley, J. (2003). *Music therapy with premature infants: Research and developmental interventions*. Silver Spring, MD: American Music Therapy Association.

Standley, J. M., & Hanser, S. B. (1995). Music therapy research and applications in pediatric oncology treatment. *Journal of Pediatric Oncology Nursing, 12*(1), 3–8.

Standley, J. M., & Hughes, J. E. (1996). Documenting developmentally appropriate objectives and benefits of a music therapy program for early intervention: A behavioral analysis. *Music Therapy Perspectives, 14*(2), 87–94.

Standley, J. M., & Hughes, J. E. (1997). Evaluation of an early intervention music curriculum for enhancing prereading/writing skills. *Music Therapy Perspectives, 15*(2), 79–86.

Standley, J., & Madsen, C. (1990). Comparison of infant preferences and responses to auditory stimuli: Music, mother, and other female voice. *Journal of Music Therapy, 27*(2), 54–97.

Standley, J., & Madsen, C. (1994). Comparison of infant preferences and responses to auditory stimuli: Music, mother, and other female voice. Reprinted in J. M. Standley & C. A. Prickett (Eds.), *Research in music therapy: A tradition in excellence* (pp. 680–713). Silver Spring, MD: National Association for Music Therapy.

Standley, J., & Moore, R. (1995). Therapeutic effects of music and mother's voice on premature infants. *Pediatric Nursing, 21*(6), 509–512.

Standley, J., & Moore, R. (1996). Therapeutic effects of music and mother's voice on premature infants. Abstracted in M. Broome (Ed.), *Capsules and comments in pediatric nursing*. Chicago: Mosby-Year Book.

Standley, J., & Prickett, C. (Eds.). (1994). *Research in music therapy: A tradition of excellence*. Silver Spring, MD: National Association for Music Therapy.

Standley, J., & Whipple, J. (2003). Music therapy for premature infants in the Neonatal Intensive Care Unit: Health and developmental benefits. In S. Robb (Ed.), *Music therapy in pediatric healthcare: Research and best practice* (pp. 19–30). Silver Spring, MD: American Music Therapy Association.

Standley, J., & Whipple, J. (2003). Pediatric music therapy: A meta-analysis. In S. Robb (Ed.), *Music therapy in pediatric healthcare: Research and best practice* (pp. 1–18). Silver Spring, MD: American Music Therapy Association.

Staum, M. J. (1987). Music notation to improve the speech prosody of hearing impaired children. *Journal of Music Therapy, 24*(3), 146–159.

Staum, M. J., & Flowers, P. J. (1984). The use of simulated training and music lessons in teaching appropriate shopping skills to an autistic child. *Music Therapy Perspectives, 1*(3), 14–17.

Steele, A. L. (1967). Effects of social reinforcement on the musical preference of mentally retarded children. *Journal of Music Therapy, 4*(2), 57–62.

Steele, A. L., Vaughan, M., & Dolan, C. (1976). The school support program: Music therapy for adjustment problems in elementary schools. *Journal of Music Therapy, 13*(2), 87–100.

Steele, L. (1975). Three-year study of a music-therapy program in a residential-treatment center. *Journal of Music Therapy, 12,* 67–83.

Stelmachowicz, P. G. (2000). Amplification for infants. *Seminars in Hearing, 12*(4), 409–422.

Stevens, E., & Clark, F. (1969). Music therapy in the treatment of autistic children. *Journal of Music Therapy, 6*(4), 98–104.

Stordahl, J. (2002). Song recognition and appraisal: A comparison of children who use cochlear implants and normally hearing children. *Journal of Music Therapy, 39*(1), 2–19.

Summers, E. K. (1984). Categorization and conservation of melody in infants. *Dissertation Abstracts International, 45,* 11B-3643-3644.

Sutter, K., Engstrom, J. L., Johnson, T. S., Kavanaugh, K., & Ifft, D. L. (1997). Reliability of head circumference measurements in preterm infants. *Pediatric Nursing, 23*(5), 485–490.

Thaut, M. H. (1984). A music therapy treatment model for autistic children. *Music Therapy Perspectives, 1*(4), 7–13.

Thaut, M. H. (1985). The use of auditory rhythm and rhythmic speech to aid temporal muscular control in children with gross motor dysfunction. *Journal of Music Therapy, 22*(3), 108–128.

Tideman, E., Ley, D., Bjerre, I., & Forslund, M. (2001). Longitudinal follow-up of children born preterm: Somatic and mental health, self-esteem and quality of life at age 19. *Early Human Development, 61,* 97–110.

Tracy, A. E., & Maroney, D. I. (1999). *Your premature baby and child.* New York: Berkley.

Trehub, S. E., Unyk, A., & Trainor, L. (1993). Adults identify infant-directed music across cultures. *Infant Behavior and Development, 16*(2), 193–211.

Tuns, F. (1978). Contrasting music conditions, visual attending behavior and state in eight-week-old infants. *Dissertation Abstracts International, 39,* 07A-4111.

Underhill, K. K., & Harris, C. M. (1974). The effect of contingent music on establishing imitation in behaviorally disturbed retarded children. *Journal of Music Therapy, 11*(3), 156–166.

VanWeelden, K., & Whipple, J. (2005). Preservice teachers' predictions, perceptions, and actual assessment of students with special needs in secondary general music. *Journal of Music Therapy, 42*(3), 200–215.

Velásquez, V. (1991). Beginning experiences in piano performance for a girl with Down syndrome: A case study. *Music Therapy Perspectives, 9,* 82–85.

Wade, L. (2002). A comparison of the effects of vocal exercises/singing versus music-assisted relaxation on peak expiratory flow rates of children with asthma. *Music Therapy Perspectives, 20*(1), 31–37.

Walworth, D. (2003). Procedural support: Music therapy assisted CT, EKG, EEG, X-ray, IV, ventilator, and emergency services. In S. L. Robb (Ed.), *Music therapy in pediatric healthcare: Research and evidence-based practice* (pp. 137–146). Silver Spring, MD: American Music Therapy Association.

Watt, T. J. (1994). Intraventricular hemorrhage in the premature infant. *Nebraska Medical Journal, 79*, 322–325.

Wendrich, K. A. (1981). Pitch imitation in infancy and early childhood: Observations and implications. *Dissertation Abstracts International, 41*, 12A–5019.

Werbner, N. (1966). The practice of music therapy with psychotic children. *Journal of Music Therapy, 3*(1), 25–31.

Wharrad, H., & Davis, A. (1997). Behavioural and autonomic responses to sound in pre-term and full-term babies. *British Journal of Audiology, 31*(5), 315–329.

Wheeler, B. L. (1999). Experiencing pleasure in working with severely disabled children. *Journal of Music Therapy, 32*(4), 265–285.

Whipple, J. (2000). The effect of parent training in music and multimodal stimulation on parent-neonate interactions in the neonatal intensive care unit. *Journal of Music Therapy, 37*(4), 250–268.

Whipple, J. (2003). Surgery Buddies: A music therapy program for pediatric surgical patients. *Music Therapy Perspectives, 21*(2), 77–83.

Whipple, J. (2004). *The effect of music-reinforced nonnutritive sucking on state of preterm, low birthweight infants experiencing heelstick.* Unpublished doctoral dissertation, The Florida State University.

Whipple, J. (2004). Music in intervention for children and adolescents with autism: A meta-analysis. *Journal of Music Therapy, 41*(2), 90–106.

Whipple, J. (2005). Music and multimodal stimulation as developmental intervention in neonatal intensive care. *Music Therapy Perspectives, 23*(2), 100–105.

White-Traut, R. C., & Tubeszewski, K. A. (1986). Multimodal stimulation of the premature infant. *Journal of Pediatric Nursing, 1*(2), 90–95.

Wigram, T. (2000). A method of music therapy assessment for the diagnosis of autism and communication disorders in children. *Music Therapy Perspectives, 18*(1), 13–22.

Wilson, A. (1964). Special education for the emotionally disturbed child. *Journal of Music Therapy, 1*(1), 16–18.

Wilson, B. L., & Smith, D. S. (2000). Music therapy assessment in school settings: A preliminary investigation. *Journal of Music Therapy, 37*(2), 97–117.

Wilson, C. V. (1976). The use of rock music as a reward in behavior therapy with children. *Journal of Music Therapy, 13*(1), 39–48.

Wolfe, D. E. (1982). The effects of interrupted and continuous music on bodily movement and task performance of third grade students. *Journal of Music Therapy, 19*(2), 74–85.

Wolfe, D. E., & Hom, C. (1993). Use of melodies as structural prompts for learning and retention of sequential information by preschool students. *Journal of Music Therapy, 30*(2), 100–118.

Wolfe, D., & Jellison, J. (1995). Interviews with preschool children about music videos. *Journal of Music Therapy, 32*(4), 265–285.

Wolfe, D., & Stambaugh, S. (1993). Musical analysis of Sesame Street: Implication for music therapy practice and research. *Journal of Music Therapy, 30*(4), 224–235.

Woodson, R., & Hamilton, C. (1988). The effect of nonnutritive sucking on heart rate in preterm infants. *Developmental Psychobiology, 21*(3), 207–213.

Woodward, S., Guidozzi, F., Hofmeyr, G., De Jong, P., Anthony, J., & Woods, D. (1992). Discoveries in the fetal and neonatal worlds of music. In H. Lees (Ed.), *Music education: Sharing musics of the world* (pp. 58–66). Proceedings of the 20th World Conference of the International Society for Music Education, Seoul, Korea.

Wylie, M. E. (1996). A case study to promote hand use in children with Rett syndrome. *Music Therapy Perspectives, 14*(2), 83–86.

Yeh, T. F., Voora, S., & Lilien, D. (1980). Oxygen consumption and insensible water loss in premature infants in single- versus double-walled incubators. *Journal of Pediatrics, 97,* 967–971.

Zahr, L. K., & Balian, S. (1995). Responses of premature infants to routine nursing interventions and noise in the NICU. *Nursing Research, 44,* 179–185.

Gerontology/Geriatric

Allen, D. M. (1977). Music therapy with geriatric patients. *British Journal of Music Therapy, 8,* 2–6.

Altman, K. P. (1977). The effect of a music-participation program on self-concept and extraversion of senior citizens in a day treatment facility (Doctoral dissertation, California School of Professional Psychology, 1977). *Dissertation Abstracts International, 38,* 3863A.

Altschuler, I. M. (1960). The value of music in geriatrics. In E. H. Schneider (Ed.), *Music therapy 1959* (pp. 109–115). Lawrence, KS: Allen Press.

Anderson, M. (1965). Music therapy. *Professional Nursing Home, 7,* 14–18.

Armstrong, M. (1974). *Music therapy and physical exercises for frail, elderly residents of a therapeutic community.* Ann Arbor: University of Michigan–Wayne State University.

Bartlett, J. C., & Snelus, P. (1980). Lifespan memory for popular songs. *American Journal of Psychology, 93,* 551–560.

Boxberger, R. (1960). Music for the geriatric wards. *Bulletin for NAMT, 9,* 7–10.

Boxberger, R., & Cotter, V. W. (1968). Music therapy for geriatric patients. In E. T. Gaston (Ed.), *Music in therapy* (pp. 271–281). New York: Macmillan.

Bright, R. (1981). Music and the management of grief reactions. In I. M. Burnside (Ed.), *Nursing and the aged* (pp. 137–142). New York: McGraw-Hill.

Bright, R. (1984). *Practical planning in music therapy for the aged.* Van Nuys, CA: Alfred.

Bright, R. (1991). *Music in geriatric care: A second look.* Wahroonga, NSW, Australia: Music Therapy Enterprises.

Brotons, M., & Koger, S. M. (2000). The impact of music therapy on language functioning in dementia. *Journal of Music Therapy, 37,* 183–195.

Brotons, M., Koger, S. M., & Pickett-Cooper, P. (1997). Music and dementias: A review of literature. *Journal of Music Therapy, 34*(4), 204–245.

Brotons, M., & Marti, P. (2003). Music therapy with Alzheimer's patients and their family caregivers: A pilot project. *Journal of Music Therapy, 40*(2), 138–150.

Brown, T. D. (1981, February). Elderhostel. *Music Educators Journal, 67*(6), 57.

Browne, H. E., & Winkelmayer, R. A. (1968). Structured music-therapy program in geriatrics. In E. T. Gaston (Ed.), *Music in therapy* (pp. 285–190). New York: Macmillan.

Burnside, I. M. (Ed.). (1981). *Nursing and the aged.* New York: McGraw-Hill.

Caplow-Lindner, E., Harpaz, L., & Samberg, S. (1979). *Therapeutic dance/movement, expressive activities for older adults* (pp. 156–160). New York: Human Sciences Press.

Carle, I. L. (1982). Music therapy in a different key. *Music Therapy, 2*(1), 63–71.

Catron, B. S. (1977). Class piano for senior citizens. *Clavier, 16,* 23.

Cevasco, A. M., & Grant, R. E. (2006). Value of musical instruments used by the therapist to elicit responses from individuals in various stages of Alzheimer's disease. *Journal of Music Therapy, 43*(3), 226–246.

Christie, M. E. (1995). The influence of a highly participatory peer on motivating group behaviors of lower functioning persons who have probable Alzheimer's type dementia: A feasibility study. *Music Therapy Perspectives, 13*(2), 87–90.

Clair, A. A. (1996). The effect of singing on alert responses in persons with late stage dementia. *Journal of Music Therapy, 33*(4), 234–247.

Clair, A. A. (1996). *Therapeutic uses of music with older adults.* Baltimore: Health Professions Press.

Clair, A. A., & Ebberts, A. G. (1997). The effects of music therapy on interactions between family caregivers and their care receivers with late stage dementia. *Journal of Music Therapy, 34*(3), 148–164.

Clair, A. A., Johnson, G., & Bernstein, B. (1995). Rhythm playing characteristics in persons with severe dementia including those with probable Alzheimer's type. *Journal of Music Therapy, 32*(2), 113–131.

Coates, P. (1984). Sixty and still growing. *Music Educators Journal, 70,* 34–35.

Cotter, V. W. (1959). *Effects of the use of music on the behavior of geriatric patients.* Unpublished master's thesis, University of Kansas, Lawrence, KS.

Curran, J. M. (1982). A design for the development of a beginning group piano curriculum for leisure-age adults (Doctoral dissertation, The University of Oklahoma, 1982). *Dissertation Abstracts International, 43,* 319A.

Davidson, J. B. (1978). The status of music programs for residents of sheltered housing, nursing and domiciliary care in Maryland (Doctoral dissertation, the University of Maryland, 1978). *Dissertation Abstracts International, 40,* 145A.

Davidson, J. B. (1980). Music and gerontology: A young endeavor. *Music Educators Journal, 66,* 26–31.

Davidson, J. B. (1982). Music for the young at heart. *Music Educators Journal, 68,* 33–35.

Donahue, W. (1954). The challenge of growing older. In M. Bing (Ed.), *Music therapy 1953.* Lawrence, KS: Allen Press.

Douglass, D. (1985). *Accent on rhythm: Music activities for the aged* (3rd ed.). St. Louis, MO: MMB Music.

Eberly, J. W. (1952). *The aptitude of elderly people for learning the piano.* Unpublished doctoral dissertation, University of Nebraska, Lincoln.

Eberly, J. W. (1954). The aptitude of elderly people for learning to play the piano. In M. Bing (Ed.), *Music therapy 1953.* Lawrence, KS: Allen Press.

Ebersole, P., & Hess, P. (1985). *Toward healthy aging, Human needs and nursing responses.* St. Louis, MO: C. V. Mosby.

Eckerle, M. J. (1982). Expanding our pedagogy programs. *American Music Teacher, 31,* 33–34.

Fisher, R. G. (1984). Beginning keyboard instruction as a nonverbal intervention for elderly persons to stimulate reminiscence, to structure life review, and to improve psychological well-being and adjustment (Doctoral dissertation, University of Georgia, 1984). *Dissertation Abstracts International, 44,* 2399A.

Flynn, P. T., & Rich, A. J. (1982). Photographic enlargement of printed music: Technique, application and implications. *The Gerontologist, 22,* 540–543.

Gaston, E. T. (Ed.). (1968). *Music in therapy.* New York: Macmillan.

Gibbons, A. C. (1977). Popular music preferences of older people. *Journal of Music Therapy, 14,* 180–189.

Gibbons, A. C. (1979). Music aptitude profile scores in the elderly and their relationships to morale and selected other variables (Doctoral dissertation, University of Kansas, 1979). *Dissertation Abstracts International, 41*, 150A.

Gibbons, A. C. (1982). Music aptitude profile scores in a non-institutionalized, elderly population. *Journal of Research in Music Education, 30*, 23–29.

Gibbons, A. C. (1982). Musical skill level self-evaluation in non-institutionalized elderly. *Activities, Adaptation and Aging, 3*, 61–67.

Gibbons, A. C. (1983). Primary measures of music audiation scores in an institutionalized elderly population. *Journal of Music Therapy, 20*, 21–29.

Gibbons, A. C. (1985). Stop babying the elderly. *Music Educators Journal, 71*(7), 48–51.

Gilbert, J. (1977). Music therapy perspectives on death and dying. *Journal of Music Therapy, 14*, 165–171.

Gilbert, J., & Beal, M. (1982). Preferences of elderly individuals for selected music activities. *Journal of Research in Music Education, 30*, 247–253.

Gilliland, E. G. (1954). Music in geriatrics. In M. Bing (Ed.), *Music therapy 1953*. Lawrence, KS: Allen Press.

Glassman, L. R. (1966). *The use of music with a geriatric population: Its effects on self-esteem.* Unpublished master's thesis, Hahnemann Medical College.

Glassman, L. R. (1983). The talent show: Meeting the needs of the healthy elderly. *Music Therapy, 3*, 82–93.

Glynn, N. J. (1985). The therapy of music. *Journal of Gerontological Nursing, 12*, 7–10.

Grant, R. E. (1977). *Sing-along senior citizens.* Springfield, IL: Charles C. Thomas.

Greenwald, M. A., & Salzberg, R. S. (1979). Vocal range assessment of geriatric clients. *Journal of Music Therapy, 16*, 172–179.

Griffin, J. (1959). *The effects of a planned music program on habits of incontinency and interest in music activities of geriatric patients.* Unpublished master's thesis, University of Kansas, Lawrence.

Griffin, J., Kurz, C., & Cotter, C. (1957). The influence of music in geriatric patients. In E. T. Gaston (Ed.), *Music therapy 1957* (pp. 159, 168, 174). Lawrence, KS: Allen Press.

Groene, R. (2001). The effect of presentation and accompaniment styles on attentional and responsive behaviors of participants with dementia diagnoses. *Journal of Music Therapy, 38*(1), 36–50.

Groene, R., Zapchenk, S., Marble, G., & Kantar, S. (1998). The effect of therapist and activity characteristics on the purposeful responses of probable Alzheimer's disease participants. *Journal of Music Therapy, 35*(2), 119–136.

Guerin, M. E. (1982). Come sing along with me. *Geriatric Nursing, 3*, 70–71.

Hall, D. (1957). Music activity for the older patient. In E. T. Gaston (Ed.), *Music therapy 1956* (pp. 115–118). Lawrence, KS: Allen Press.

Hart, A. (1960). The development of a music-therapy program in a convalescent home. In E. H. Schneider (Ed.), *Music therapy 1959*. Lawrence, KS: Allen Press.

Hauck, L. P., & Martin, P. L. (1970). Music as a reinforcement in patient-controlled duration of time out. *Journal of Music Therapy, 7*(2), 43–53.

Hennessey, M. J. (1976). Music and music therapy group work with the aged. In I. M. Burnside (Ed.), *Nursing and the aged* (pp. 255–269). New York: McGraw-Hill.

Hennessey, M. J. (1978). Music and music therapy groups. In I. M. Burnside (Ed.), *Working with the elderly: Group processes and techniques* (pp. 255–274). North Scituate, MA: Duxbury Press.

Hintz, M. R. (2000). Geriatric music therapy clinical assessment: Assessment of music skills and related behaviors. *Music Therapy Perspectives, 18*(1), 31–40.

Hoffman, D. H. (1980). *Pursuit of arts activities with older adults: An administration and programmatic handbook*. Washington, DC: National Center on Arts and the Aging/National Council on the Aging, Inc., and the Center for Professional Development, University of Kentucky.

Holt, J. (1978). *Never too late: My musical life story*. New York: Delacorte Press/Seymour Lawrence.

James, M. R. (1987). Implications of selected social psychological theories on life-long skill generalization: Considerations for the music therapist. *Music Therapy Perspectives, 4*, 29–33.

Jason, B., & Arrau, C. (1983). New horizons in class piano. *Clavier, 22*, 46–47.

Jeanette, M. J. (1966). Music for the aging. *Professional Nursing Home, 8*, 12.

Johnson, G., Otto, D., & Clair, A. (2001). The effects of instrumental and vocal music on adherence to a physical rehabilitation exercise program with persons who are elderly. *Journal of Music Therapy, 38*(2), 82.

Jones, J. D., & Cevasco, A. M. (2007). A comparison of music therapy students' and professional music therapists' nonverbal behavior: A pilot study. *Music Therapy Perspectives, 25*(1), 19–24.

Kaplan, M. (1980). Retirement is more than parties and gold watches. *Music Educators Journal, 67*(4), 31 & 64.

Kartman, L. (1977). The use of music as a program tool with regressed patients. *Journal of Gerontological Nursing, 3*, 38–42.

Kartman, L. L. (1980). The power of music with patients in a nursing home. *Activities, Adaptations, and Aging, 1*(1), 9–17.

Kartman, L. L. (1984). Music hath charms. *Journal of Gerontological Nursing, 10*(6), 20–24.

Kellman, R. H. (1984). The development of a music education program for older adults suitable for use in senior citizens centers, retirement homes, or other sites. *Dissertation Abstracts International, 46*, 95A. (University Microfilms No. 85-05-458)

Koger, S. M., Chapin, K., & Brotons, M. (1999). Is music therapy an effective intervention for dementia? A meta-analytic review of literature. *Journal of Music Therapy, 36*(1), 2–15.

Kurz, C. E. (1957). The effects of a planned music program on the day, hall, sound level, and personal appearance of geriatric patients. *Music therapy*. Lawrence, KS: Allen Press.

Lancaster, E. L. (1979). The beginner, the retread, the retiree. *Clavier, 18*, 27.

Landon, E. A. (1981). Piano workshop for senior citizens. *Clavier, 20*, 40.

Larson, P. S. (1983). An exploratory study of lifelong musical interest and activity: Case studies of twelve retired adults (Doctoral dissertation, Temple University, 1983). *Dissertation Abstracts International, 44*, 100A.

Lathom, W. B., Peterson, M., & Havlicek, L. (1982). Music preferences of older people attending nutrition sites. *Educational Gerontology: An International Bimonthly Journal, 8*, 155–165.

Leitner, M. J. (1981). The effects of intergenerational music activities on senior day-care participants and elementary school children (Doctoral dissertation, University of Maryland, 1981). *Dissertation Abstracts International, 42*, 3752A.

Leonhard, C. (1981). Expand your classroom. *Music Educators Journal, 68*(54), 61–62.

Liederman, P. C. (1967). Music and rhythm group therapy for geriatric patients. *Journal of Music Therapy, 4*, 11–27.

Linoff, M., & West, C. (1982). Relaxation training systematically combined with music: Treatment of tension headaches in a geriatric patient. *International Journal of Behavioral Geriatrics, 1*, 11–16.

Lipe, A. (1995). The use of music performance tasks in the assessment of cognitive functioning among older adults with dementia. *Journal of Music Therapy, 32*(3), 137–151.

Mason, C. (1978). Musical activities with elderly patients. *Physiotherapy, 64*(3), 80–82.

McCullough, E. C. (1982). An assessment of the musical needs and preferences of individuals 65 and over (Doctoral dissertation, University of Arizona, 1981). *Dissertation Abstracts International, 42*, 909A.

Miller, T. C., & Crosby T. W. (1979). Musical hallucinations in a deaf elderly patient. *Annals of Neurology, 5*, 301–302.

Moore, E. C. (1978). Using music with the elderly: Group processes and techniques. In I. M. Burnside (Ed.), *Working with the elderly: Group processes and techniques*. North Scituate, MA: Duxbury Press.

Munro, S., & Mount, B. (1978). Music therapy in palliative care. *Canadian Medical Association Journal, 119,* 1029–1034.

Needler, W., & Baer, M. (1982). Movement, music, and remotivation with the regressed elderly. *Journal of Gerontological Nursing, 8,* 497–503.

Norman, J. S. (1978). Arts programming for senior citizens (Doctoral dissertation, University of Northern Colorado, 1978). *Dissertation Abstracts International, 39,* 2611A.

Olson, B. K. (1984). Player piano music as therapy for the elderly. *Journal of Music Therapy, 21,* 35–45.

Palmer, M. D. (1977). Music therapy in a comprehensive program of treatment and rehabilitation for the geriatric resident. *Journal of Music Therapy, 14,* 190–197.

Palmer, M. D. (1980). Music therapy and gerontology. *Activities, Adaptations, and Aging, 1*(1), 37–40.

Palmer, M. D. (1983). Music therapy in a comprehensive program of treatment and rehabilitation for the geriatric patient. *Activities, Adaptations, and Aging, 3*(3), 53–59.

Palmore, E. B. (1968). The effects of aging on activities and attitudes. *The Gerontologist, 8,* 259–263.

Paulman, L. (1982). Reaching the confused and withdrawn through music. *Aging, 333–334,* 7–11.

Phillips, J. R. (1980). Music in the nursing of elderly persons in nursing homes. *Journal of Gerontological Nursing, 6,* 209–220.

Prickett, C. (1988). Music therapy for the aged. In C. E. Furman (Ed.), *Effectiveness of music therapy procedures: Documentation of research and clinical practice* (pp. 107–134). Washington, DC: National Association for Music Therapy.

Prickett. C. A. (2000). Music therapy for older people: Research comes of age across two decades. In American Music Therapy Association (Ed.), *Effectiveness of music therapy procedures: Documentation of research and clinical practice* (3rd ed.) (pp. 297–322). Silver Spring, MD: American Music Therapy Association.

Prickett, C. A., & Bridges, M. S. (2000). Song repertoire across the generations: A comparison of music therapy majors' and senior citizens' recognitions. *Journal of Music Therapy, 37*(3), 196–204.

Ramsay, D. (1982). *Music therapy and depression in the elderly.* Unpublished master's thesis, University of Kansas, Lawrence, KS.

Riegler, J. (1980). Comparison of a reality-orientation program for geriatric patients with and without music. *Journal of Music Therapy, 17,* 26–33.

Riegler, J. (1980). Most comfortable loudness level of geriatric patients as a function of seashore loudness discrimination scores, detection threshold, age, sex, setting, and musical background. *Journal of Music Therapy, 17,* 214–222.

Shapiro, A. (1969). A pilot program in music therapy with residents of a home for the aged. *Gerontologist, 9*, 128–133.

Silber, F. (1999). The influence of background music on the performance of the Mini Mental State Examination with patients diagnosed with Alzheimer's disease. *Journal of Music Therapy, 36*(3), 196–206.

Smith, D. S. (1987). *Preferences for differentiated frequency loudness levels in older adult music listening.* Unpublished doctoral dissertation, The Florida State University, Tallahassee.

Smith, J. J. (1973). A survey of avocational music activities for adults (Doctoral dissertation, University of Michigan, 1973). *Dissertation Abstracts International, 33*, 1910A.

Steele, A. L. (1982). New audiences for young musicians (children perform for retirement and nursing homes). *American Music Teacher, 31*, 34–35.

Stern, J. (1968). A plan for developing an adult music education program in Charlotte, North Carolina (Doctoral dissertation, Columbia University, 1968). *Dissertation Abstracts International, 29*, 460A.

Sterrett, D. E. (1957). Music in the recreation program for the senior citizens in the state of Florida (Doctoral dissertation, George Peabody College for Teachers, 1957). *Dissertation Abstracts International, 18*(03), 1063.

Strang, C. D. (1970). Music at night: An experiment in a geriatric ward. *Royal College of General Practitioners Journal, 20*, 246–247.

Takahashi, T., & Matsushita, H. (2006). Long-term effects of music therapy on elderly with moderate/severe dementia. *Journal of Music Therapy, 43*(4), 317–333.

Tanaka, T. (1980). Music therapy for psychiatric rehabilitation of the aged. *Kangogaku Zasshi, 44*, 500–502.

Tanner, D. R., & O'Briant, R. M. (1980). Music can color a graying America. *Music Educators Journal, 67*(4), 28–30.

Toombs, M. R. (1958). Musical activities for geriatric patients, music as a means toward revitalization. In E. T. Gaston (Ed.), *Music therapy 1958.* Lawrence KS: The Allen Press.

Vanderark, S., Newman, I., & Bell, S. (1983). The effects of music participation on quality of life of the elderly. *Music Therapy, 3*, 71–81.

VanWeelden, K. D., & Whipple, J. (2004). Effect of field experiences on music therapy students' perceptions of choral music for geriatric wellness programs. *Journal of Music Therapy, 41*, 340–352.

Walker, D. L. (1980). A study of music education in community development, continuing education, and correctional programming as reported by state arts agency directors in the United States (Doctoral dissertation, George Peabody College for Teachers of Vanderbilt University, 1980). *Dissertation Abstracts International, 40*, 3293A.

Watts, T. D. (1980). Theories of aging: The difference in orientations. *Journal of Music Therapy, 17*, 84–89.

Weissman, J. A. (1981). Meeting selected needs and treatment goals of aged individuals in long-term care facilities through the therapeutic use of music activities (Doctoral dissertation, New York University, 1981). *Dissertation Abstracts International, 42*, 12B.

Weissman, J. A. (1983). Planning music activities to meet the needs and treatment goals of aged individuals in long-term care facilities. *Music Therapy, 3*, 63–70.

Wells, A. (1954). Rhythmic activities on wards of senile patients. In. M. Bing (Ed.), *Music therapy 1953* (pp. 127–132). Lawrence, KS: Allen Press.

Wilson, A. V. (1983). Recharging retirement life. *Music Educators Journal, 69*, 27–28.

Wolfe, J. R. (1983). The use of music in a group sensory training program for regressed geriatric patients. *Activities, Adaptations, and Aging, 4*, 49–62.

Medical/Dental

Abdul-Baqi, K. J. (1991). Chloral hydrate and middle ear pressure. *Journal of Laryngol Otolaryngology, 105*, 421–423.

ABR and ENG testing. Retrieved from http://www.centreforhearing.com/abr_eng.htm/

ABR versus OAE: Two similar hearing tests. Retrieved from http://deafness.about.cotnics/audiograms/a/abroae.htm/

Adams, K. S. (2005). *The effects of music therapy and deep breathing on pain in patients recovering from gynecologic surgery in the PACU.* Unpublished master's thesis, The Florida State University, Tallahassee.

Ainlay, G. W. (1948). The place of music in military hospitals. In D. M. Schullian & M. Schoen (Eds.), *Music in medicine.* New York: Books for Libraries Press.

Aldridge, K. (1993). The use of music to relieve pre-operational anxiety in children attending day surgery. *The Australian Journal of Music Therapy, 4*, 19–35.

Alpha Mu Alpha. (2002). *The effects of amplitude and rhythmic strength on heart rate entrainment and perceived relaxation.* Study presented at the national conference poster session of the American Music Therapy Association, Atlanta, GA.

Alpha Mu Alpha (2003). *The effects of music on relaxation as measured by heart rate and self-evaluation.* Study presented at the conference poster session of the Southeastern Region of the American Music Therapy Association, Chattanooga, TN.

American Academy of Pediatrics. Committee on Environmental Health. (1997). Noise: A hazard for the fetus and newborn. *Pediatrics, 100*(4), 724–727.

Ammon, K. (1968). The effects of music on children in respiratory distress. *American Nurses' Association Clinical Sessions*, 127–133.

Anderson, W. (1981). The effectiveness of audio-nitrous oxide-oxygen psychosedation on dental behavior of a child. *Journal of Pedodontics, 5*(10), 963–971.

Ansell, B. J., Keenan, J. E., & de la Rocha, O. (1989). *Western Neuro Sensory Stimulation Profile*. Barbara J. Ansell and Western Neuro Care Center.

Argyris, S. P. (1994). *The Glasgow Coma Scale*. San Antonio, TX: Communication Skill Builders.

Armatas, C. (1964). *A study of the effect of music on postoperative patients in the recovery room*. Unpublished master's thesis, The University of Kansas, Lawrence.

Arts, S., Abu-Saad, H., Champion, G., Crawford, M., Fisher, R., Juniper, K., et al. (1994). Age-related response to Lidocaine-Prilocaine (EMLA) emulsion and effect of music distraction on the pain of intravenous cannulation. *Pediatrics, 93*(5), 797–801.

Atterbury, R. A. (1974). Auditory pre-sedation for oral surgery patients. *Audioanalgesia, 38*(6), 12–14.

Augustin, P., & Hains, A. (1996). Effect of music on ambulatory surgery patients' preoperative anxiety. *AORN Journal, 63*(4), 750–758.

Ayers, S. E. (2000). *The effect of preferred music on the amount of pain medication administered by patient controlled analgesia pump in patients recovering from abdominal hysterectomies*. Unpublished master's thesis, The Florida State University, Tallahassee.

Bailey, L. M. (1983). The effects of live music versus tape-recorded music on hospitalized cancer patients. *Music Therapy, 3*(1), 17–28.

Bailey, L. M. (1984). The use of songs in music therapy with cancer patients and their families. *Music Therapy, 4*(1), 5–17.

Bailey, L. M. (1986). Music therapy in pain management. *Journal of Pain and Symptom Management, 1*(1), 25–28.

Bampton, P., & Draper, B. (1997). Effect of relaxation music on patient tolerance of gastrointestinal endoscopic procedures. *Journal of Clinical Gastroenterology, 25*(1), 343–345.

Barker, L. (1991). The use of music and relaxation techniques to reduce pain of burn patients during daily debridement. In C. D. Maranto (Ed.), *Applications of music in medicine* (pp. 163–178). Washington, DC: National Association for Music Therapy.

Barnason, S., Zimmerman, L., & Nieveen, J. (1995). The effects of music interventions on anxiety in the patient after coronary artery bypass grafting. *Heart and Lung, 24*(2), 124–132.

Barrera, M., Kykov, M., & Doyle, S. (2002). The effects of interactive music therapy on hospitalized children with cancer: A pilot study. *Psycho-Oncology, 11*, 379–388.

Barrickman, J. (1989). A developmental music therapy approach for preschool hospitalized children. *Music Therapy Perspectives, 7,* 10–16.

Bartlett, K. (1967). Audio-analgesia evaluated as hypnosis. *The American Journal of Clinical Hypnosis, 9*(4), 275–284.

Bason, P. (1972). Control of the heart rate by external stimuli. *Nature, 4,* 279–280.

Bason, P., & Celler, B. (1972). Control of the heart rate by external stimuli. *Nature, 238,* 279–280.

Batson, A. (1994). *The effects of live music on the distress of pediatric patients receiving intravenous starts, venipunctures, injections, and heel sticks.* Unpublished master's thesis, The Florida State University, Tallahassee.

Beck, S. (1991). The therapeutic use of music for cancer-related pain. *Oncology Nursing Forum, 18*(8), 1327–1336.

Behrens, G. A. (1982). *The use of music activities to improve the capacity, inhalation, and exhalation capabilities of handicapped children's respiration.* Unpublished master's thesis, Kent State University, Kent, OH.

Benes, F. M. (1994). Development of the corticolimhic system. In G. Dawson & K. Gischer (Eds.), *Human behavior and the developing brain* (pp. 176–206). New York: Guilford Press.

Berkow, R. (Ed.). (1997). *The Merck manual of medical information.* New York: Pocket Books.

Berlin, B. (1998). Music therapy with children during invasive procedures: Our emergency department's experience. *Journal of Emergency Nursing, 24*(6), 607–608.

Bernbaum, J., Pereira, G., Watkins, J., & Peckham, G. (1983). Nonnutritive sucking during gavage feeding enhances growth and maturation in premature infants. *Pediatrics, 71*(1), 41–45.

Berry, M. A., Conrod, H., & Usher, R. H. (1997). Growth of very premature infants fed intravenous hyperalimentation and calcium-supplemented formula. *Pediatrics, 100*(4), 647–653.

Beyer, J., Villarruel, A. M., & Denyes, M. (1993). *The Oucher: The new user's manual and technical report.* Denver, CO: Health Sciences Center, School of Nursing, University of Colorado.

Biban, P., Baraldi, E., Pettenazzo, A., Filippone, M., & Zacchello, F. (1993). Adverse effect of chloral hydrate in two young children with obstructive sleep apnea. *Pediatrics, 92*(3), 461–463.

Blackstone, R. J. (1998). *Is music therapeutic or distracting when life hangs in the balance: Surgeons' perception.* Unpublished master's thesis, The Florida State University, Tallahassee.

Blankfield, R., Zyzanski, S., Flocke, S., Alemagno, S., & Scheurman, K. (1995). Taped patients. *American Journal of Clinical Hypnosis, 37*(3), 32–37.

Blass, B. (1975). Sound analgesia. *Journal of the American Podiatry Association, 65*(10), 963–971.

Bob, S. R. (1962). Audioanalgesia in podiatric practice, a preliminary study. *Journal of the American Podiatry Association, 52*, 503–504.

Boldt, S. (1996). The effects of music therapy on motivation, psychological well-being, physical comfort, and exercise endurance of bone marrow transplant patients. *Journal of Music Therapy, 33*(3), 164–188.

Bolwerk, C. (1990). Effects of relaxing music on state anxiety in myocardial infarction patients. *Critical Care Nursing, 13*(2), 63–72.

Bonny, H. L. (1983). Music listening for intensive coronary care units: A pilot project. *Music Therapy, 3*(1), 4–16.

Bonny, H. L., & Savary, L. M. (1990). *Music and your mind: Listening with a new consciousness.* Barrytown, NY: Station Hill Press.

Bontke, C. F. (Ed.). (1992). Sensory stimulation: Accepted practice or expected practice? *The Journal of Head Trauma Rehabilitation, 7*(4), 115–120.

Borzecki, M., & Zakrzewski, K. (1978). Music autohypnorelaxation in pain: Some objective correlates. *World Journal of Psychosynthesis, 10*(4), 22–25.

Boyle, M. E. (1981). *Operant procedures and the comatose patient.* Unpublished doctoral dissertation, Teachers College, Columbia University.

Boyle, M. E., & Greer, R. (1983). Operant procedures and the comatose patient. *Journal of Applied Behavioral Analysis, 16*(1), 3–12.

Bradt, J. (2001). *The effects of music entrainment on postoperative pain perception in pediatric patients.* Unpublished doctoral dissertation, Temple University, Philadelphia, PA.

Brazelton, T., & Nugent, J. (1995). *Neonatal Behavioral Assessment Scale* (3rd ed.). London: Cambridge University Press.

Britt, G., & Myers, B. (1994). The effects of Brazelton intervention: A review. *Infant Mental Health, 15*(3), 278–292.

Brodsky, W. (1989). Music therapy as an intervention for children with cancer in isolation rooms. *Music Therapy, 8*, 17–34.

Brook, E. (1984). *Soothing music during the active phase of labor: Physiologic effect on mother and infant.* Unpublished master's thesis, University of Florida, Gainesville.

Broome, M. E., Lillis, P. P., & Smith, M. C. (1989). Pain interventions with children: A meta-analysis of research. *Nursing Research, 38*(3), 154–158.

Brown, J. (1992). Music dying. *American Journal of Hospice and Palliative Care, 9*(4), 17–20.

Brown, J. (1992). When words fail, music speaks. *American Journal of Hospice and Palliative Care, 9*(2), 13–16.

Buda, F. B., Reed, J. C., & Rabe, E. F. (1975). Skull volume in infants: Methodology, normal values, and application. *American Journal of Diseases in Children, 129*, 1117–1174.

Budzynski, T., Stoyva, J., & Adler, C. (1970). Feedback-induced muscle relaxation: Application to tension headache. *Journal of Behavior Therapy and Experimental Psychiatry, 1*, 205–211.

Burke, M., Walsh, J., Oehler, J., & Gingras, J. (1995). Music therapy following suctioning: Four case studies. *Neonatal Network, 14*(7), 41–49.

Burns, D. (2001). The effect of the Bonny Method of Guided Imagery and Music on the mood and life quality of cancer patients. *Journal of Music Therapy, 38*(1), 51.

Burns, J. L., Labbe, E., Arke, B., Capeless, K., Cooksey, B., Steadman, A., et al. (2002). The effects of different types of music on perceived and physiological measures of stress. *Journal of Music Therapy, 39*(2), 101–116.

Burns, K., Cunningham, N., White-Traut, R., Silvestri, J., & Nelson, M. (1994). Infant stimulation: Modification of an intervention based on physiologic and behavioral cues. *Journal of Obstetric, Gynecologic, and Neonatal Nursing, 23*(7), 581–589.

Burroughs, A., Asonye, U., Anderson-Shanklin, G., & Vidyasagar, D. (1978). The effect of nonnutritive sucking on transcutaneous oxygen tension in noncrying, preterm neonates. *Research in Nursing and Health, 1*(2), 69–75.

Burt, R. K., & Korn, G. W. (1964). Audio-analgesia in obstetrics. White noise analgesia during labor. *American Journal of Obstetrics and Gynecology, 88*, 361–366.

Byers, J., & Smyth, K. (1997). Effect of a music intervention on noise annoyance, heart rate, and blood pressure in cardiac surgery patients. *American Journal of Critical Care, 6*(3), 183–191.

Caine, J. (1992). The effects of music on the selected stress behaviors, weight, caloric and formula intake, and length of hospital stay of premature and low birth weight neonates in a newborn intensive care unit. *Journal of Music Therapy, 28*(4), 180–192.

Caire, J., & Erickson, S. (1986). Reducing distress in pediatric patients undergoing cardiac catheterization. *Children's Health Care, 14*(3), 146–152.

Callaham, J. E. (2004). *The effect of live music on the reduction of negative side effects experienced by pediatric patients during onset, final thirty minutes of hemodialysis treatment, and removal of needles.* Unpublished master's thesis, The Florida State University, Tallahassee.

Camp, W., Martin, R., & Chapman, L. F. (1962). Pain threshold and discrimination of pain intensity during brief exposure to intense noise. *Science, 135*, 788–789.

Carlin, S., Ward, W. D., Gershon, A., & Ingraham, R. (1962). Sound stimulation and its effect on dental sensation threshold. *Science, 138*, 1258–1259.

Carothers, R. W., Gregory, S. W., & Gallagher, T. J. (2000). Measuring emotional intelligence of medical school applicants. *Academic Medicine, 75*(5), 456–463.

Cassidy, J. W., & Ditty, K. M. (1998). Presentation of aural stimuli to newborns and premature infants: An audiological perspective. *Journal of Music Therapy, 35*(2), 70–87.

Cassidy, J. W., & Ditty, K. M. (2001). Gender differences among newborns on a transient otoacoustic emissions test for hearing. *Journal of Music Therapy, 38*(1), 28–35.

Cassidy, J. W., & Standley, J. M. (1995). The effect of music listening on physiological responses of premature infants in the NICU. *Journal of Music Therapy, 32*(4), 208–227.

Centers for Disease Control. (1999, April 29). *National Vital Statistics Report, 47*(18).

Cepeda, M., Diaz, J., Hernandez, V., Daza, E., & Carr, D. (1998). Music does not reduce alfentanil requirement during patient-controlled analgesia (PCA) use in extracorporeal shock wave lithotripsy for renal stones. *Journal of Pain and Symptom Management, 16*(6), 382–387.

Chalmers, I., Enkin, M., & Keirse, M. (1989). *Effective care in pregnancy and childbirth.* Oxford: Oxford Medical Publications.

Chapey, R. (Ed.). (1994). *Language intervention strategies in adult aphasia.* Baltimore: Williams & Wilkins.

Chapman, J. S. (1975). *The relation between auditory stimulation of short-gestation infants and their gross motor limb activity.* Unpublished doctoral dissertation, New York University, New York.

Chapman, J. S. (1979). Influence of varied stimuli on development of motor patterns in the premature infant. In G. Anderson & B. Raff (Eds.), Newborn behavioral organization: *Nursing research and implications* (pp. 61–80). New York: Alan Liss.

Cheour-Luhtanen, M., Alho, K., Sainio, K., Rinne, T., Reinikainen, K., Pohjavuouri, M., et al. (1996). The ontogenetically earliest discriminative response of the human brain. *Psychophysiology, 33*, 478–481.

Cherry, H., & Pallin, I. (1948). Music as a supplement in nitrous oxide-oxygen anesthesia. *Anesthesiology, 9*, 391–399.

Chesky, K. (1992). The effects of music and music vibration using the MVT™ on the relief of rheumatoid arthritis pain. *Dissertation Abstracts International, 53*(08), 2725.

Chetta, H. D. (1980). *The effect of music therapy in reducing fear and anxiety in preoperative pediatric patients.* Unpublished master's thesis, The Florida State University, Tallahassee.

Chetta, H. D. (1981). The effect of music and desensitization on pre-operative anxiety in children. *Journal of Music Therapy, 18*, 74–87.

Chian, L. (1998). Effectiveness of a music therapy intervention on relaxation and anxiety for patients receiving ventilatory assistance. *Heart and Lung, 27*(3), 169–176.

Chiron, C., Jambaque, I., Nabbout, R., Lounes, R., Syrota, A., & Dulac, O. (1997). The right brain hemisphere is dominant in human infants. *Brain, 120*(6), 1057–1065.

Christenberry, E. (1979). The use of music therapy with burn patients. *Journal of Music Therapy, 16*, 138–148.

Clark, M. (1986). Music therapy-assisted childbirth: A practical guide. *Music Therapy Perspectives, 3,* 34–41.

Clark, M., McCorkle, R., & Williams, S. (1981). Music therapy-assisted labor and delivery. *Journal of Music Therapy, 18,* 88–109.

Clinton, P. K. (1984). *Music as a nursing intervention for children during painful procedures.* Unpublished master's thesis, The University of Iowa, Iowa City.

Cockrell, B. A. (1953). Music therapy for T.B. patients. *Bulletin of the NAMT, 2,* 9.

Codding, P. A. (1982). *An exploration of the uses of music in the birthing process.* Unpublished master's thesis, The Florida State University.

Cofrancesco, E. (1985). The effect of music therapy on hand grasp strength and functional task performance in stroke patients. *Journal of Music Therapy, 22,* 129–145.

Cohen, A. (1984). *The development and implementation of a pediatric music therapy program in a short-term medical facility.* Unpublished master's thesis, New York University, New York.

Cohen, N. S. (1992). The effect of singing instruction on the speech production of neurologically impaired persons. *Journal of Music Therapy, 29,* 87–102.

Cohen, N. S. (1993). The application of singing and rhythmic instruction as a therapeutic intervention for persons with neurogenic communication disorders. *Journal of Music Therapy, 30,* 81–99

Cohen, N. S., & Ford, J. (1991). The effect of musical cues on nonpurposeful speech in people with aphasia. *Journal of Music Therapy, 22,* 46–57.

Coleman, J. M., Pratt, R. R., Stoddard, R. A., Gerstmann, D. R., & Abel, H. H. (1997). The effects of the male and female singing and speaking voices on selected physiological and behavioral measures of premature infants in the intensive care unit. *International Journal of Arts Medicine, 5*(2), 4–11.

Colgrove, T. (1991). *The effects of music versus guided imagery and progressive muscle relaxation versus guided imagery and progressive muscle relaxation with music on the pulse rate and peripheral finger temperature of hemodialysis patients undergoing treatment.* Unpublished master's thesis, The Florida State University, Tallahassee.

Collins, S. K., & Kuck, K. (1991). Music therapy in the Neonatal Intensive Care Unit. *Neonatal Network, 9*(6), 23–26.

Cook, J. (1982). *The use of music to reduce anxiety in oncology patients exposed to the altered sensory environment of betaron radiation.* Unpublished master's thesis, The University of Texas, Austin.

Corah, N. L., Gale, E., Pace, L., & Seyrek, S. (1981). Relaxation and musical programming as means of reducing psychological stress during dental procedures. *Journal of the American Dental Association, 103*(2), 232–234.

Cordobes, T. (1997). Group songwriting as a method for developing group cohesion for HIV-Seropositive adult patients with depression. *Journal of Music Therapy, 34*(1), 46–67.

Cote, C. J., Alderfer, R. J., Notterman, D. A., & Fanta, K. B. (1995). Sedation disasters: adverse drug reports in pediatrics-FDA, USP, and others. *Anesthesiology, 83*(3A), 1183.

Crago, B. R. (1981). Reducing the stress of hospitalization for open heart surgery. *Dissertation Abstracts International, 41*(7B), 2752.

Crowe B. J. (1985). Music therapy and physical medicine: Expanding opportunities for employment. *Music Therapy, 5*(1), 44–51.

Curtis, S. (1986). The effect of music on pain relief and relaxation of the terminally ill. *Journal of Music Therapy, 23*(1), 10–24.

Davila, J., & Menendez, J. (1986). Relaxing effects of music in dentistry for mentally handicapped patients. *Special Care in Dentistry, 6*(1), 18–21.

Davis, C. (1992). The effects of music and basic relaxation instruction on pain and anxiety of women undergoing in-office gynecological procedures. *Journal of Music Therapy, 29*(4), 202–216.

Davis-Rollans, C., & Cunningham, S. (1987). Physiologic responses of coronary care patients to selected music. *Heart and Lung, 16*(4), 370–378.

Detterman, D. (1978). The effect of heartbeat sound on neonatal crying. *Infant Behavior and Development, 1*, 36–48.

DiPietro, J., Cusson, R., Caughy, M., & Fox, N. (1994). Behavioral and physiologic effects of nonnutritive sucking during gavage feeding in preterm infants. *Pediatric Research, 36*(2), 207–214.

Domec, C. M. (2000). *Stroke patient responses to a variety of stimuli during music and non-music conditions.* Unpublished master's thesis, The Florida State University, Tallahassee.

Dureau, S. J. (2003). *The effect of gender on one day-old infants' behavior and heart rate responses to music decibel level.* Unpublished master's thesis, The Florida State University, Tallahassee.

Durham, L., & Collins, M. (1986). The effect of music as a conditioning aid in prepared childbirth education. *Journal of Obstetrical, Gynecological, and Neonatal Nursing, 15*(3), 268–270.

Echternach, J. L. (1966). Audioanalgesia as an adjunct to mobilization of the chronic frozen shoulder. *Journal of the American Physical Therapy Association, 46*, 839–846.

Eiseman, A., & Cohen, B. (1995). Music therapy for patients undergoing regional anesthesia. *AORN Journal, 62*(6), 947–950.

Elliott, D. (1994). The effects of music and muscle relaxation on patient anxiety in a coronary care unit. *Heart and Lung, 23*(1), 27–35.

Ellis, D. S., & Brighthouse, G. (1952). Effects of music on respiration and heart rate. *American Journal of Psychology, 65*, 39–47.

Epstein, L., Hersen, M., & Hemphill, D. (1974). Music feedback in the treatment of tension headache: An experimental case study. *Journal of Behavior Therapy and Experimental Psychiatry, 5*(9), 59–63.

Evans, D. (2002). The effectiveness of music as an intervention for hospital patients: A systematic review. *Journal of Advanced Nursing, 37*(1), 8–18.

Ezzone, S., Baker, C., Rosselet, R., & Terepka, E. (1998). Music as an adjunct to antiemetic therapy. *Oncology Nursing Forum, 25*(9), 1551–1556.

Fagen, T. S. (1982). *Music therapy as a tool for the assessment and treatment of fear and anxiety in pediatric cancer patients.* Unpublished master's thesis, New York University, New York.

Fagen, T. S. (1982). Music therapy in the treatment of anxiety and fear in terminal pediatric patients. *Music Therapy, 2*(1), 13–23.

Falb, M. (1982). *The use of operant procedures to condition vasoconstriction in profoundly mentally retarded PMR infants.* Unpublished master's thesis, The Florida State University, Tallahassee.

Ferrell, D. (1984). *Music therapy case studies of patients in a regional medical center.* Unpublished research manuscript, The Florida State University, Tallahassee.

Field, T. (1987). Alleviating stress in intensive-care unit neonates. *Journal of American Obstetrical Association, 9,* 129–135.

Field, T., Dempsey, J., Hatch, J., Ting, G., & Clifton, R. (1979). Cardiac and behavioral responses to repeated tactile and auditory stimulation by pre-term and term neonates. *Developmental Psychology, 15*(4), 406–416.

Field, T., Ignatoff, E., Stringer, S., Brennan, J., Greenberg, R., Widmayer, S., et al. (1982). Nonnutritive sucking during tube feedings: Effects on preterm neonates in an intensive care unit. *Pediatrics, 70*(3), 381–384.

Fischer, K. W., & Rose, S. T. (1994). Dynamic development of coordination of components in brain and behavior: A framework for theory and research. In G. Dawson & K. W. Fischer (Eds.), *Human behavior and the developing brain* (pp. 3–66). New York: Guilford Press.

Fisher, S., & Greenberg, R. (1972). Selective effects upon women of exciting and calm music. *Perceptual and Motor Skills, 34,* 987–990.

Florida Institute of Neurologic Rehab, Inc. *Glossary of terms.* Retrieved from http://www.finr.com/glossary.html#n/

Flowers, A., McCain, A., & Hilker, K. (1999). *The effects of music listening on premature infants.* Paper presented at the biennial meeting of the Society for Research in Child Development, Albuquerque, NM.

Forslund, M., & Bjerre, I. (1990). Follow-up of preterm children: II. Growth and development at four years of age. *Early Human Development, 24*(2), 107–118.

Foutz, C. D. (1970). Routine audio-nitrous oxide analgesia simplified. *Arizona Dental Journal, 16,* 15–16.

Fowler-Kerry, S., & Lander, J. (1987). Management of injection pain in children. *Pain, 30,* 169–175.

Frank, J. (1985). The effects of music therapy and guided visual imagery on chemotherapy induced nausea and vomiting. *Oncology Nursing Forum, 12*(5), 47–52.

Fratianne, R., Presner, J., Huston, M., Super, D., Yowler, C., & Standley, J. (2001). The effect of music based imagery and musical alternate engagement on the burn debridement process. *Journal of Burn Care and Rehabilitation, 22*(1), 47–53.

Froelich, M. (1984). A comparison of the effect of music therapy and medical play therapy on the verbalization behavior of pediatric patients. *Journal of Music Therapy, 21,* 2–15.

Froehlich, M. (Ed.). (1996). *Music therapy with hospitalized children.* Cherry Hill, NJ: Jeffery Books.

Gaberson, K. (1995). The effect of humorous and musical distraction on preoperative anxiety. *AORN Journal, 62*(5), 784–791.

Gardner, S. L., Garland, K. R., Merenstein, S. L., & Lubchenco, L. O. (1997). The neonate and the environment: Impact on development. In G. B. Merenstein & S. L. Gardner (Eds.), *Handbook of neonatal intensive care* (4th ed., pp. 564–608). St. Louis: Mosby.

Gardner, W. J., & Licklider, J. C. R. (1959). Auditory analgesia in dental operation. *Journal of the American Dental Association, 59,* 1144–1150.

Gardner, W. J., Licklider, J. C. R., & Weisz, A. Z. (1960). Suppression of pain by sound. *Science, 132,* 32–33.

Gaston, E. T. (1951). Dynamic music factors in mood change. *Music Educators Journal, 20,* 50–58.

Gatewood, E. L. (1921). The psychology of music in relation to anesthesia. *American Journal of Surgery, Anesthesia Supplement, 35,* 47–50.

Gervin, A. P. (1991). Music therapy compensatory technique utilizing song lyrics during dressing to promote independence in the patient with a brain injury. *Music Therapy Perspectives, 9,* 87–90.

Gettel, M. K. (1985). *The effect of music on anxiety in children undergoing cardiac catheterization.* Unpublished master's thesis, Hahnemann University, Philadelphia.

Gfeller, K., Logan, H., & Walker, J. (1988). The effect of auditory distraction and suggestion on tolerance for dental restorations in adolescents and young adults. *Journal of Music Therapy, 27*(1), 13–23.

Gilbert, J. (1977). Music therapy perspectives on death and dying. *Journal of Music Therapy, 14,* 165–171.

Gill, N., Behnke, M., Conlon, M., McNeely, J., & Anderson, G. (1988). Effect of nonnutritive sucking on behavioral state in preterm infants before feeding. *Nursing Research, 37*(6), 347–350.

Glass, P. (1994). The vulnerable neonate and the neonatal intensive care environment. In G. B. Avery, M. A. Fletcher, & M. G. MacDonald (Eds.), *Neonatology: Pathophysiology and management of the newborn* (4th ed., pp. 77–94). Philadelphia: J. B. Lippincott.

Godley, C. (1987). The use of music therapy in pain clinics. *Music Therapy Perspectives, 4*, 24–28.

Goff, D. M. (1985). The effects of nonnutritive sucking on state regulation in preterm infants. *Dissertation Abstracts International, 46*(08B)2835.

Goloff, M. S. (1981). The responses of hospitalized medical patients to music therapy. *Music Therapy, 1*(1), 51–56.

Good, M. (1995). A comparison of the effects of jaw relaxation and music on postoperative pain. *Nursing Research, 44*(1), 52–57.

Gordin, P. C. (1990). Assessing and managing agitation in a critically ill infant. *MCN, 15*, 26–32.

Goroszeniuk, T., & Morgan, B. (1984). Music during epidural caesarean section. *The Practitioner, 228*, 441–443.

Gorski, P., Davison, M., & Brazelton, T. (1979). Stages of behavioral organization in the high-risk neonate theoretical and clinical considerations. *Seminars in Perinatology, 3*(1), 61–72.

Grasso, M. C., Button, B. M., Allison, D. J., & Sawyer, S. M. (2000). Benefits of music therapy as an adjunct to chest physiotherapy in infants and toddlers with cystic fibrosis. *Pediatric Pulmonology, 29*, 371–381.

Greenberg, S. B., Faerber, E. N., & Aspinall, C. L., & Adams, R. C. (1993). High-dose chloral hydrate sedation for children undergoing MR imaging: Safety and efficacy in relation to age. *American Journal of Roentgenology, 161*, 639–641.

Grundy, A. (1989). *The effects of music and the Somatron™ on the physiological and speech responses of head injured and comatose subjects.* Unpublished master's thesis, The Florida State University, Tallahassee.

Guo, S. S., Roche, A. F., Chumlea, W. C., Casey, P. H., & Moore, W. M. (1997). Growth in weight, recumbent length, and head circumference for preterm low-birthweight infants during the first three years of life using gestation-adjusted ages. *Early Human Development, 47*, 305–325.

Gutheil, E. (Ed.). (1952). *Music and your emotions.* New York: Liveright.

Guzzetta, C. (1989). Effects of relaxation and music therapy on patients in a coronary care unit with presumptive acute myocardial infarction. *Heart and Lung, 18*, 609–616.

Hack, M., Klein, N., & Taylor, H. (1995). Long-term developmental outcomes of low birth weight infants. *The Future of Children* [Online serial], *5*(1). Retrieved from http://www.futureofchildren.org /LBW/12LBWHAC.htm

Hagen, C., Malkmus, D., & Durham, P. (1972). *Levels of cognitive functioning.* Downey, CA: Professional Staff Association of Ranchos Los Amigos Hospital.

Hall, G. D., & Reiss, B. S. (1997). *Appleton and Lange's review of pharmacy* (7th ed.). New York: McGraw-Hill Medical Publishing Division.

Hanamoto, J., & Kajiyama, T. (1974). Some experiences in use of environmental music in pediatric roentgenography. *Radiologia Diagnostica, 15*(6), 787–794.

Haneishi, E. (2001). Effects of a music therapy voice protocol on speech intelligibility, vocal acoustic measures, and mood of individuals with Parkinson's disease. *Journal of Music Therapy, 38*(4), 273.

Hanser, S. (1985). Music therapy and stress reduction research. *Journal of Music Therapy, 22*, 193–206.

Hanser, S., Larson, S., & O'Connell, A. (1983). The effect of music on relaxation of expectant mothers during labor. *Journal of Music Therapy, 20*, 50–58.

Harrison, L. (1987). Effects of early supplemental stimulation programs for premature infants: Review of the literature. *Maternal-Child Nursing Journal, 14*(2), 69–90.

Heiser, R., Chiles, K., Fudge, M., & Gray, S. (1997). The use of music during the immediate postoperative recovery period. *AORN Journal, 65*(4), 777–785.

Heitz, L., Symreng, T., & Scamman, F. (1992). Effect of music therapy in the postanesthesia care unit: A nursing intervention. *Journal of Post Anesthesia Nursing, 7*(1), 22–31.

Henry, L. (1995). Music therapy: A nursing intervention for the control of pain and anxiety in the ICU: A review of the research literature. *Dimensions of Critical Care Nursing, 14*(6), 295–304.

Hill, A. (1992). Preliminary findings: A maximum oral feeding time for premature infants, the relationship to physiological indicators. *Maternal-Child Nursing Journal, 20*(2), 81–92.

Hilliard, R. (2001). The effects of music therapy-based bereavement groups on mood and behavior of grieving children: A pilot study. *Journal of Music Therapy, 38*(4), 291–306.

Hilliard, R. (2003). The effects of music therapy on the quality and length of life of people diagnosed with terminal cancer. *Journal of Music Therapy, 40*(2), 113–137.

Hirokawa, E., & Ohira, H. (2003). The effects of music listening after a stressful task on immune functions, neuroendocrine responses, and emotional states in college students. *Journal of Music Therapy, 40*(3), 189–211.

Hoffman, J. (1980). *Management of essential hypertension through relaxation training with sound.* Unpublished master's thesis, University of Kansas, Lawrence.

Hoffman, P. (1975). The use of guitar and singing in a child life program. *Journal of the Association for the Care of Children in Hospitals, 4*(1), 45–47.

Horbar, J., & Lucey, J. (1995). Evaluation of neonatal intensive care technologies. *The Future of Children* [Online serial], *5*(1). Retrieved from http://www.futureofchildren.org/LBW/12LBWHAC.htm

Howitt, J. W. (1967). An evaluation of audio-analgesia effects. *Journal of Dentistry for Children, 34*, 406–411.

Howitt, J. W. (1972). In this intensive care unit, the downbeat helps the heartbeats. *Modern Hospital, 118*, 91.

Howitt, J. W., & Stricklerk, G. (1966). Objective evaluation of audio-analgesia effects. *Journal of the ADA, 73*, 874–877.

Humpal, M. (2001). Annotated bibliography of music therapy articles related to young children: From music therapy journals (1990–2000). *Early Childhood Connections, 7*(2), 16–17.

Hurt, C. P., Rice, R. R., McIntosh, G. C., & Thaut, M. H. (1998). Rhythmic auditory stimulation in gait training for patients with traumatic brain injury. *Journal of Music Therapy, 35*, 228–241.

Hyde, I. (1924). Effects of music upon electrocardiograms and blood pressure. *Journal of Experimental Psychology, 7*, 213–224.

In this intensive care unit, the downbeat helps the heartbeats. *Modern Hospital, 118*, 91.

Inder, T., Huppi, P., Zientara, G., Maier, S., Jolesz, F., di Slavo, D., et al. (1999). Early detection of peri leukomalacia by diffusion-weighted magnetic resonance imaging techniques. *Journal of Pediatrics, 134*(5), 631–634.

Iwaki, T., Tanaka, H., & Hori, T. (2003). The effects of preferred familiar music on falling asleep. *Journal of Music Therapy, 40*(1), 15–26.

Jacobs, I. H. (1983). Use of stereo headphones for patient relaxation and surgical drape support during local anesthesia. *Ophthalmic Surgery, 14*(4), 356–357.

Jacobson, A. (1999). Intradermal normal saline solution, self-selected music, and insertion difficulty effects on intravenous insertion pain. *Heart and Lung, 28*(2), 114–122.

Jacobson, E. (1983). *Progressive relaxation* (2nd ed.). Chicago: University of Chicago Press.

Jacobson, H. L. (1957). The effect of sedative music on the tensions, anxiety and pain experienced by mental patients during dental procedures. In E. T. Gaston (Ed.), *Music therapy 1956*: Book of proceedings of the National Association for Music Therapy, Inc. (pp. 231–234). Lawrence, KS: National Association for Music Therapy.

Jarred, J. (2003). *The effect of live music on anxiety levels of persons waiting in a surgical waiting room as measured by self-report.* Unpublished master's thesis, The Florida State University, Tallahassee.

Jarred, J. (2003). Music assisted surgery: Preoperative and postoperative interventions. In S. L. Robb (Ed.), *Music therapy in pediatric healthcare: Research and evidence-based practice* (pp. 147–162). Silver Spring, MD: American Music Therapy Association.

Jay, S., & Elliott, C. (1986). *Observation scale of behavioral distress-revised.* (Available from Susan M. Jay, Ph.D., Psychosocial Program, Division of Hematology-Oncology, Children's Hospital of Los Angeles, California, 90027).

Jellison, J. (1975). The effect of music on autonomic stress responses and verbal reports. In C. K. Madsen, R. D. Greer, & C. H. Madsen, Jr. (Eds.), *Research in music behavior* (pp. 206–219). Teachers College Press, Columbia University, New York.

Johnston, C., Sherrard, A., Stevens, B., Franck, L., Stemler, R., & Jack, A. (1999). Do cry features reflect pain intensity in preterm neonates? A preliminary study. *Biology of the Neonate, 76*(2), 120–124.

Jones, R., Hux, K., Morton-Anderson, K., & Knepper, L. (1994). Auditory stimulation effect on a comatose survivor. *Archives of Physical Medicine and Rehabilitation, 75*(2), 164–171.

Joyce, B., Keck, J., & Gerkensmeyer, J. (2001). Evaluation of pain management interventions for neonatal circumcision pain. *Journal of Pediatric Healthcare, 15*(3), 105–114.

Judd, E. (1982). *Music therapy on a kidney dialysis unit: A pilot study.* Unpublished master's thesis, Hahnemann University, Philadelphia, PA.

Kaempf, G., & Amodei, G. (1989). The effect of music on anxiety. *AORN Journal, 50*(1), 112–118.

Kamin, A., Kamin, H., Spintge, R., & Droh, R. (1982). Endocrine effect of anxiolytic music and psychological counseling before surgery. In R. Droh & R. Spintge (Ed.), *Angst, schmerz, musik in der anasthesie* (pp. 163–166). Basel: Editiones Roche.

Kaminski, J., & Hall, W. (1996). The effect of soothing music on neonatal behavioral states in the hospital newborn nursery. *Neonatal Network, 15*(1), 45–54.

Kamps, M. (1992). *The effects of singing on the respiratory abilities of cystic fibrosis patients.* Unpublished research paper, The Florida State University, Tallahassee.

Kanarek, K., & Shulman, D. (1992). Non-nutritive sucking does not increase blood levels of gastrin, motilin, insulin and insulin-like growth factor 1 in premature infants receiving enteral feedings. *Acta Paediatrica Scandinavica, 81*(12), 974–977.

Katz, V. (1971). Auditory stimulation and developmental behavior of the premature infant. *Nursing Research, 20*, 196–201.

Kazandijan, M., & Dikeman, K. (1998, September 17). *Managing communication and swallowing impairments in tracheostomized and ventilator-dependent adults* ASHA/RTN Self-Study Satellite Broadcast.

Keller, V. (1995). Management of nausea and vomiting in children. *Journal of Pediatric Nursing, 10*(5), 280–286.

Kemp, A. M. (2002). *The effect of music therapy on the duration, frequency, and perceived importance of social interactions among patients in a physical rehabilitation setting.* Unpublished master's thesis, The Florida State University, Tallahassee.

Kemper, K., Martin, K., Block, S., Shoaf, R., & Woods, C. (2004). Attitudes and expectations about music therapy for premature infants among staff in a neonatal intensive care unit. *Alternative Therapies, 10*(2), 50–54.

Kendall, P. C. (1981). *Medical psychology: Contributions to medical psychology.* New York: Academic Press.

Kendall, P. C. (1983). Stressful medical procedures: Cognitive behavioral strategies for stress management prevention. In D. H. Meichenbaum & M. J. Jaremko (Eds.), *Stress management and prevention: A cognitive behavioral analysis.* New York: Plenum Press.

Kendelhardt, A. (2003). *The effect of live music on exercise duration, negative verbalizations, and self-perception of pain, anxiety and rehabilitation levels of physical therapy patients.* Unpublished master's thesis, The Florida State University, Tallahassee.

Kenner, C., & McGrath, J. (2004). *Developmental care of newborns and infants: A guide for health professionals.* St. Louis, MO: Mosby.

Kerr, S. E. (2004). *The effect of music on non-responsive patients in a hospice setting.* Unpublished master's thesis, The Florida State University, Tallahassee.

Kibler, V. E., & Rider, M. S. (1983). The effect of progressive muscle relaxation and music on stress as measured by finger temperature response. *Journal of Clinical Psychology, 39*(2), 213–215.

King, J. (1982). *Music therapy results with pediatric patients.* Unpublished research manuscript, The Florida State University, Tallahassee.

King, J. (1984). *Five case studies: The integrative use of music therapy with hospitalized children on a pediatric ward.* Unpublished research study, The Florida State University, Tallahassee.

Kleiber, C., & Harper, D. (1999). Effects of distraction on children's pain and distress during medical procedures: A meta-analysis. *Nursing Research, 48*(1), 44–49.

Knight, W., & Rickard, N. (2001). Relaxing music prevents stress-induced increases in subjective anxiety, systolic blood pressure and heart rate in healthy males and females. *Journal of Music Therapy, 38*(4), 254-272.

Kopp, M. (1991). Music's effect on stress-related responses during surgery. *The Kansas Nurse, 66*(7), 4–5.

Kozak, Y. A. (1968). Music therapy for orthopedic patients in a rehabilitative setting. In E. T. Gaston (Ed.), *Music in therapy* (pp. 166–168). New York: Macmillan.

Kuhn, D. (2002). The effects of active and passive participation in musical activity on the immune system as measured by salivary immunoglobulin A (SIgA). *Journal of Music Therapy, 39*(1), 30–39.

Kumar, A., Bajaj, A., Sarkar, P., & Grover, V. (1992). The effect of music on ketamine induced emergence phenomena. *Anesthesia, 47*, 438–439.

Landreth, J., & Landreth, M. R. (1974). Effects of music on physiological response. *Journal of Research in Music Education, 22*(1), 4–12.

Lane, D. (1991). *The effect of a single music therapy session on hospitalized children as measured by salivary Immunoglobulin A, speech pause time, and a patient opinion Likert scale.* Unpublished doctoral dissertation, Case Western Reserve University, Cleveland, OH. (UMI No. 9137062)

Lane, D. (1991). The effect of a single music therapy session on hospitalized children as measured by salivary Immunoglobulin A, speech pause time, and a patient opinion Likert scale. *Pediatric Research, 29*(4, part 2), 11A.

Larson, K., & Ayllon, T. (1990). The effects of contingent music and differential reinforcement on infantile colic. *Behavior Research Therapy, 28*(2), 119–125.

Lasswell, A. (2001). *The effects of music assisted relaxation on the relaxation, sleep quality, and daytime sleepiness of sheltered, abused women.* Unpublished master's thesis, The Florida State University, Tallahassee.

Lavine, R., Buchsbaum, M., & Poncy, M. (1976). Auditory analgesia: Somatosensory evoked response and subjective pain rating. *Psychophysiology, 13*(2), 140–148.

Layman, D. L. (1998). *A descriptive analysis of the music therapy assessment technique for hospitalized children ages birth to three years.* Unpublished master's thesis, The Florida State University, Tallahassee.

Lecanuet, J., Graniere-Deferre, C., & Busnel, M. (1995). Human fetal auditory perception. In J. P. Lecanuet, W. P. Fifer, N. A. Krasnegor, & W. P. Smotherman, (Eds.), *Fetal development: A psychobiological perspective* (pp. 239–262). Hillsdale, NJ: Lawrence Erlbaum.

Lehrer, P., Hochron, S., Mayne, T., Isenberg, S., Carlson, V., Lasoski, A., Gilchrist, J., Morales, D., & Rausch, L. (1994). Relaxation and music therapies for asthma among patients prestabilized on asthma medication. *Journal of Behavioral Medicine, 17*(1), 1–24.

LeLorier, J., Gregoire, G., Benhaddad, A., Lapierre, J, & Deriderian, F. (1997). Discrepancies between meta-analyses and subsequent large randomized, controlled trials. *The New England Journal of Medicine, 337*(8), 536–542.

Levine-Gross, J., & Swartz, R. (1982). The effects of music therapy on anxiety in chronically ill patients. *Music Therapy, 2*(1), 43–52.

Liebman, S., & MacLaren, A. (1991). The effects of music and relaxation on third trimester anxiety in adolescent pregnancy. *Journal of Music Therapy, 28*(2), 89–100.

Liebman, S., & MacLaren, A. (1993). The effects of music and relaxation on third trimester anxiety in adolescent pregnancy. In F. J. Bejjani (Ed.), *Current research in arts medicine* (pp. 427–430). Chicago: A Cappella Books.

Light, G., Love, D., Benson, D., & Morch, E. (1954). Music in surgery. *Current Researches in Anesthesia and Analgesia, 33,* 258–264.

Lindsay, K. (1981). The value of music for hospitalized infants. *Journal of the Association for the Care of Children in Hospitals, 9*(4), 104–107.

Lininger, L. (1987). *The effects of instrumental and vocal lullabies on the crying behavior of newborn infants.* Unpublished master's thesis, Southern Methodist University, Dallas, TX.

Linoff, M. G., & West, C. M. (1982). Relaxation training systematically combined with music treatment of tension headaches in a geriatric patient. *Journal of Behavioral Geriatrics, 1*(3), 11–16.

Livingood, A., Kiser, K., & Paige, N. (1984). *A study of families to determine the effect of sedate music on their state anxiety level while they await the out-come of surgery.* Unpublished study, Eastern Kentucky University, Richmond, KY.

Livingston, J. (1979). Music for the childbearing family. *JOGN Nursing, 8,* 363–367.

Lochner, C., & Stevenson, R. (1988). Music as a bridge to wholeness. *Death Studies, 12*(2), 173–180.

Locsin, R. (1981). The effect of music on the pain of selected post-operative patients. *Journal of Advanced Nursing, 6,* 19–25.

Loewy, J. (Ed.). (1997). Music therapy and pediatric pain. Cherry Hill, NJ: Jeffrey Books.

Loewy, J. (1999). The use of music psychotherapy in the treatment of pediatric pain. In C. Dileo (Ed.), *Music therapy and medicine: Theoretical and clinical applications* (pp. 189–206). Silver Spring, MD: American Music Therapy Association.

Logan, T. G., & Roberts, A. R. (1984). The effects of different types of relaxation music on tension level. *Journal of Music Therapy, 21,* 177–183.

Long, L., & Johnson, J. (1978). Dental practice using music to aid relaxation and relieve pain. *Dental Survey, 54,* 35–38.

Lorch, C. A., Lorch, V., Diefendorf, A. O., & Earl, P. W. (1994). Effect of stimulative and sedative music on systolic blood pressure, heart rate, and respiratory rate in premature infants. *Journal of Music Therapy, 31*(2), 105–118.

Lucia, C. M. (1987). Toward developing a model of music therapy intervention in the rehabilitation of head trauma patients. *Music Therapy Perspectives, 4,* 34–39.

Lutz, W. (1997). *The effect of music distraction on children's pain, fear, and behavior during laceration repairs.* Unpublished master's thesis, The University of Texas at Arlington.

Maalouf, E., Duggan, P., Rutherford, M., Counsell, S., Fletcher, A., Baffin, M., et al. (1999). Magnetic resonance imaging of the brain in a cohort of extremely preterm infants. *Journal of Pediatrics, 135*(3), 351–357.

MacClelland, D. (1979). Music in the operating room. *AORN Journal, 29*(2), 252–260.

Madsen, C., Standley, J., & Gregory, D. (1991). The effect of a vibrotactile device, Somatron™, on physiological and psychological responses: Musicians versus non-musicians. *Journal of Music Therapy, 28*(1), 14–22.

Magee, W., & Davidson, J. (2002). The effect of music therapy on mood states in neurological patients: A pilot study. *Journal of Music Therapy, 39*(1), 20–29.

Malloy, G. (1979). The relationship between maternal and musical auditory stimulation and the developmental behavior of premature infants. *Birth Defects: Original Article Series, 15*(7), 81–98.

Malone, A. B. (1996). The effects of live music on the distress of pediatric patients receiving intravenous starts, venipunctures, injections, and heel sticks. *Journal of Music Therapy, 33*(1), 19–33.

Mandle, C., Domar, A., Harrington, D., Leserman, J., Bozadjian, E., Friedman, R., et al. (1990). Relaxation response in femoral angiography. *Radiology, 174*(3), 737–739.

Mann, C. (1990). Meta-analysis in the breech. *Science, 249*, 476–480.

Marchette, L., Main, R., Redick, E., Bagg, A., & Leatherland, J. (1991). Pain reduction interventions during neonatal circumcision. *Nursing Research, 40*(4), 241–244.

Marchette, L., Main, R., Redick, E., & Shapiro, A. (1989). Pain reduction during neonatal circumcision. In R. Spintge & R. Droh (Eds.), *MusicMedicine* (pp. 131–136). Ann Arbor, MI: Malloy Lithographing.

Marley, L. (1984). The use of music with hospitalized infants and toddlers: A descriptive study. *Journal of Music Therapy, 21*(3), 126–132.

Marrero, D., Fremion, A., & Golden, M. (1988). Improving compliance with exercise in adolescents with insulin-dependent diabetes mellitus: Results of a self-motivated home exercise program. *Pediatrics, 81*(4), 519–525.

Martin, M. (1987). *The influence of combining preferred music with progressive relaxation and biofeedback techniques on frontalis muscle.* Unpublished master's thesis, Southern Methodist University, Dallas, TX.

Maslar, P. (1986). The effect of music on the reduction of pain: A review of the literature. *The Arts in Psychotherapy, 13*, 215–219.

McCain, G. (1992). Facilitating inactive awake states in preterm infants: A study of three interventions. *Nursing Research, 41*(3), 157–160.

McCain, G. (1995). Promotion of preterm infant nipple feeding with nonnutritive sucking. *Journal of Pediatric Nursing, 10*(1), 3–8.

McDonnell, L. (1984). Music therapy with trauma patients and their families on a pediatric service. *Music Therapy, 4*(1), 55–56.

McDowell, C. R. (1966). Obstetrical applications of audio-analgesia. *Hospital Topics, 44*, 102–104.

McElwain, J. (1993). The effect of Somatron™ and music on headache. In F. J. Bejjani (Ed.), *Current research in arts medicine* (pp. 437–439). Chicago: A Cappella Books.

Medoff-Cooper, B., & Gennaro, S. (1996). The correlation of sucking behaviors and Bayley Scales of Infant Development at six months of age in VLBW infants. *Nursing Research, 45*(5), 291–296.

Megel, M., Houser, C., & Gleaves, L. (1998). Children's responses to immunizations: Lullabies as a distraction. *Issues in Comprehensive Pediatric Nursing, 21*(3), 129–145.

Melzack, R., Weisz, A. Z., & Sprague, L. T. (1963). Stratagems for controlling pain: Contributions of auditory stimulation and suggestion. *Experimental Neurology, 8*(3), 239–247.

Menegazzi, J., Paris, P., Kersteen, C., Flynn, B., & Trautman, D. (1991). A randomized, controlled trial of the use of music during laceration repair. *Annals of Emergency Medicine, 20*(4), 348–350.

Merriam-Webster's medical dictionary. (1995). Springfield, MA: Merriam-Webster.

Metera, A., & Metera, A. (1975, July–September). Influence of music on the minute oxygen consumption and basal metabolism rate. *Anesthesia, Resuscitation, and Intensive Therapy, 3*, 259–269.

Metzger, L. K. (1986). The selection of music for therapeutic use with adolescents and young adults in a psychiatric facility. *Music Therapy Perspectives, 3*, 20–24.

Metzler, R., & Berman, T. (1991). The effect of sedative music on the anxiety of bronchoscopy patients. In C. D. Maranto (Ed.), *Applications of music in medicine* (pp. 163–178). Washington, DC: National Association for Music Therapy.

Micci, N. (1984). The use of music therapy with pediatric patients undergoing cardiac catheterization. *The Arts in Psychotherapy, 11*, 261–266.

Miller, A., Hickman, L., & Lemasters, G. (1992). A distraction technique for control of burn pain. *The Journal of Burn Care and Rehabilitation, 13*(5), 576–580.

Miller, L. (1984). *Spontaneous music therapy sessions for hospitalized children.* Unpublished research paper, The Florida State University, Tallahassee.

Miller, R. A., & Bornstein, P. H. (1977). Thirty-minute relaxation: A comparison of some methods. *Journal of Behavior Therapy and Experimental Psychiatry, 8*(3), 291–294.

Miluk-Kolasa, B., Matejek, M., & Stupnicki, R. (1996). The effects of music listening on changes in selected physiological parameters in adult pre-surgical patients. *Journal of Music Therapy, 33*(3), 208–218.

Miluk-Kolasa, B., Obminski, Z., Stupnicki, R., & Golec, L. (1994). Effects of music treatment on salivary cortisol in patients exposed to pre-surgical stress. *Experimental and Clinical Endocrinology, 102*(2), 118–120.

Monsey, H. L. (1960). Preliminary report of the clinical efficacy of audioanalgesia. *Journal of California State Dental Association, 36*, 432–437.

Moore, R., Gladstone, I., & Standley, J. (1994). *Effects of music, maternal voice, intrauterine sounds and white noise on the oxygen saturation levels of premature infants.* Paper presented at the national conference of the National Association for Music Therapy, Orlando, FL.

Moore, W. M., McClure, J. C., & Hill, I. D. (1964). Effect of white sound on pain threshold. *British Journal of Anaesthesia, 36*, 268–271.

Morosko, T. E., & Simmons, F. F. (1966). The effect of audio-analgesia on pain threshold and pain tolerance. *Journal of Dental Research, 45,* 1608–1617.

Moss, V. (1987). The effect of music on anxiety in the surgical patient. *Perioperative Nursing Quarterly, 3*(1), 9–16.

Mowatt, K. S. (1967). Background music during radiotherapy. *Medical Journal, Australia, 1,* 185–186.

Muir, D. W. (1985). The development of infants' auditory spatial sensitivity. In S. E. Trehub & B. A. Schneider (Eds.), *Auditory development in infancy* (pp. 55–83). New York: Plenum.

Mullooly, V., Levin, R., & Feldman, H. (1988). Music for postoperative pain and anxiety. *The Journal of the New York State Nurses Association, 19*(2), 4–7.

Munoz, M., Gomez, A., Soult, J. A., Marquez, C., Lopez-Castilla, J. D., Cervera, A., et al. (1997). Seizures caused by chloral hydrate sedative doses (letter). *Journal of Pediatrics, 131*(5), 787–788.

Munro, S. (1984). *Music therapy in palliative/hospice care.* St. Louis, MO: MMB Music.

Munro, S., & Mount, B. (1980). Music therapy in palliative care. In I. Ajemain & B. Mount (Eds.), *R.V.H. manual on palliative/ hospice care.* New York: Arno Press.

Nguyen, J. (2003). *The effect of music therapy on end-of-life patients' quality of life, emotional state, and family satisfaction as measured by self-report.* Unpublished master's thesis, The Florida State University, Tallahassee.

Oehler, J. (1993). Developmental care of low birth weight infants. *Advances in Clinical Nursing Research, 28*(2), 289–301.

Ogenfuss, J. (2001). *Pediatric surgery and patient anxiety: Can music therapy effectively reduce stress and anxiety levels while waiting to go to surgery?* Unpublished master's thesis, The Florida State University, Tallahassee.

Ohlsen, J. L. (1987). Audio-analgesia in podiatry. *Journal of the American Podiatry Association, 57,* 153–156.

O'Moore, A. M. (1983). Psychosomatic aspects in biopathic infertility: Effects of treatment with autogenic training. *Journal of Psychosomatic Research, 27,* 145–151.

Owens, L. (1979). The effects of music on the weight loss, crying, and physical movement of newborns. *Journal of Music Therapy, 16,* 83–90.

Oyama, T., Hatano, K., Sato, Y., Kudo, M., Spintge, R., & Droh, R. (1983). Endocrine effect of anxiolytic music in dental patients. In R. Droh & R. Spintge (Eds.), *Angst, schmerz, musik in der anasthesie* (pp. 143–146). Basel: Editiones Roche.

Oyama, T., Sato, Y., Kudo, M., Spintge, R., & Droh, R. (1983). Effect of anxiolytic music in endocrine function in surgical patients. In R. Droh & R. Spintge (Eds.), *Angst, schmerz, musik in der anasthesie* (pp. 147–152). Basel: Editiones Roche.

Pacchetti, C., Aglieri, R., Mancini, F., Martignoni, E., & Nappi, G. (1998). Active music therapy and Parkinson's disease: Methods. *Functional Neurology, 13*(1), 57–67.

Padfield, A. (1976). Letter: Music as sedation for local analgesia. *Anaesthesia, 31*(2), 300–301.

Palmer, M. M. (1993). Identification and management of the transitional suck pattern in premature infants. *Journal of Perinatal and Neonatal Nursing, 7*(1), 66–75.

Parker, D. (2004). *The effect of music therapy for pain and anxiety versus literature on immediate and future perception of cardiac patients.* Unpublished master's thesis, The Florida State University, Tallahassee.

Peach, S. C. (1984). Some implications for the clinical use of music-facilitated imagery. *Journal of Music Therapy, 21*, 27–34.

Pelletier, C. L. (2004). The effect of music on decreasing arousal due to stress: A meta-analysis. *Journal of Music Therapy, 41*(3), 192–214.

Peretti, P. O. (1975). Changes in galvanic skin response as affected by musical selection, sex, and academic discipline. *Journal of Psychology, 89*, 183–187.

Peretti, P. O., & Swenson, K. (1974). Effects of music on anxiety as determined by physiological skin responses. *Journal of Research in Music Education, 22*, 278–283.

Perlman, J. (2001). Neurobehavioral deficits in premature graduates of intensive care: Potential medical and neonatal environmental risk factors. *Pediatrics, 108*(6), 1339–1348.

Peterson, B., Vohr, B., Staib, L., Cannistraci, C., Dolber, A., Schneider, K., et al. (2000). Regional brain volume abnormalities and long-term cognitive outcome in preterm infants. *Journal of the American Medical Association, 284*(15), 1939–1947.

Pfaff, V. K., Smith, K., & Gowan, D. (1989). The effects of music-assisted relaxation on the distress of pediatric cancer patients undergoing bone marrow aspirations. *Children's Health Care, 18*(4), 232–236.

Pfister, T., Berrol, C., & Caplan, C. (1998). Effects of music on exercise and perceived symptoms in patients with chronic obstructive pulmonary disease. *Journal of Cardiopulmonary Rehabilitation, 18*(3), 228–232.

Phillips, J. R. (1980). Music in the nursing of elderly persons in nursing homes. *Journal of Gerontological Nursing, 6*(1), 37–39.

Pickerall, K. L., Metzger, J. T., Wilde, J. N., Broadbent, R. R., & Edwards, B. F. (1950). The use and therapeutic value of music in the hospital and operating room. *Plastic and Reconstructive Surgery, 6*, 142–152.

Piekos, M., & Gaertner, H. (1968). Own observations of the analgesia effects of music during dental treatment (English Summary). *Czas. Stomat., 21*, 1181–1187.

Polaner, D. M., Houck, C. S., Rockoff, M. A., Mancuso, T. J., Finley, G. A., Maxwell, L. G., et al. (2001). Sedation, risk, and safety: Do we really have data at last? *Pediatrics, 108*(4), 1006–1008.

Pratt, R. R., & Grocke, D. E. (Eds.). (1999). *MusicMedicine 3—MusicMedicine and music therapy: Expanding horizons.* Parkville, Victoria, Australia: University of Melbourne Press.

Prensner, J., Fratianne, R., Yowler, C., Standley, J., Steele, A., & Smith, L. (2000, March). *The effect of music based imagery and musical alternate engagement on the burn debridement process.* Paper presented at the national conference of the American Burn Association, Las Vegas, NV.

Prokop, C. K., & Bradley, L. A. (Eds.). (1981). *Medical psychology: Contributions to behavioral medicine.* New York: Academic Press.

Rasco, C. (1992). Using music therapy as distraction during lumbar punctures. *Journal of Pediatric Oncology Nursing, 9*(1), 33–34.

Rauscher, F., Shaw, G., Levine, L., Wright, E., Dennis, W., & Newcomb, R. (1997). Music training causes long-term enhancement of preschool children's spatial-temporal reasoning. *Neurological Research, 19*(1), 2–8.

Reynolds, S. B. (1984). Biofeedback, relaxation training, and music: Homeostasis for coping with stress. *Biofeedback and Self-Regulation, 9*(2), 169–179.

Richards, K. (1998). Effect of a back massage and relaxation intervention on sleep in critically ill patients. *American Journal of Critical Care, 7*(4), 288–299.

Rickert, V., Kozlowski, K., Warren, A., Hendron, A., & Davis, P. (1994). Adolescents and colposcopy: The use of different procedures to reduce anxiety. *American Journal of Obstetrics and Gynecology, 170*(2), 504–508.

Rider, M. (1985). Entrainment mechanisms are involved in pain reduction, muscle relaxation, and music-mediated imagery. *Journal of Music Therapy, 22*(4), 183–192.

Rider, M. S. (1987). Music therapy: Therapy for debilitated musicians. *Music Therapy Perspectives, 4*, 40–43.

Rider, M. S., Floyd, J. W., & Kirkpatrick, J. (1985). The effect of music, imagery, and relaxation on adrenal corticosteroids and the re-entrainment of circadian rhythms. *Journal of Music Therapy, 22*, 46–58.

Rider, M. S., & Kibler, V. (1990). Treating arthritis and lupus patients with music-mediated imagery and group psychotherapy. *The Arts in Psychotherapy, 17*, 29–33.

Robb, S. (1996). Techniques in song writing: Restoring emotional and physical well being in adolescents who have been traumatically injured. *Music Therapy Perspectives, 14*(1), 30–37.

Robb, S. (2000). The effect of therapeutic music interventions on the behavior of hospitalized children in isolation: Developing a contextual support model of music therapy. *Journal of Music Therapy, 37*(2), 118–146.

Robb, S. (2000). Music assisted progressive muscle relaxation, progressive muscle relaxation, music listening, and silence. *Journal of Music Therapy, 37*(1), 2.

Robb, S. (2003). *Music therapy in pediatric healthcare.* Silver Spring, MD: American Music Therapy Association.

Robb, S., & Ebberts, A. (2003). Songwriting and digital video production interventions for pediatric patients undergoing bone marrow transplantation part I: An analysis of depression and anxiety levels according to phase of treatment. *Journal of Pediatric Oncology Nursing, 20,* 2–15.

Robb, S. L., Nichols, R. J., Rutan, R. L., Bishop, B. L., & Parker, J. C. (1995). The effects of music assisted relaxation on preoperative anxiety. *Journal of Music Therapy, 32*(1), 2–21.

Roberts, C. (1986). *Music: A nursing intervention for increased intracranial pressure.* Unpublished master's thesis, Grand Valley State College, Allendale, MI.

Roberts, P. (2002). *The effect of contingent music with physical therapy in children who toe-walk.* Unpublished master's thesis, The Florida State University, Tallahassee.

Robinson, D. (1962). Music therapy in a general hospital. *Bulletin of the National Association for Music Therapy, 11*(3), 13–18.

Robson, J. G., & Davenport, H. T. (1962). The effects of white sound and music upon the superficial pain threshold. *Canadian Anaesthetists' Society Journal, 9,* 105–108.

Roeser, R. J. (1996). Audiology desk reference. New York: Thieme.

Roter, M. (1957). *The use of music in medical reception rooms.* Unpublished master's thesis, University of Kansas, Lawrence.

Roush, W. (1997). A womb with a view. *Science, 278,* 1397–1399.

Rudenberg, M. T., & Royka, A. M. (1989). Promoting psychosocial adjustment in pediatric burn patients through music therapy and child life therapy. *Music Therapy Perspectives, 7,* 40–43.

Sabo, C., & Michael, S. (1996). The influence of personal message with music on anxiety and side effects associated with chemotherapy. *Cancer Nursing, 19*(4), 283–289.

Sammons, L. (1984). The use of music by women in childbirth. *Journal of Nurse-Midwifery, 29*(4), 266–270.

Sanderson, S. (1984). *Music therapy with a terminally ill cancer patient.* Unpublished research manuscript, The Florida State University, Tallahassee.

Sanderson, S. K. (1986). *The effect of music on reducing preoperative anxiety and postoperative anxiety and pain in the recovery room.* Unpublished master's thesis, The Florida State University, Tallahassee.

Scartelli, J. (1982). The effect of sedative music on electromyographic biofeedback assisted relaxation training of spastic cerebral palsied adults. *Journal of Music Therapy, 19,* 210–218.

Scartelli, J. (1984). The effect of EMG biofeedback and sedative music, EMG biofeedback only, and sedative music only on frontalis muscle relaxation ability. *Journal of Music Therapy, 21*(2), 67–78.

Schermer, R. (1960). Distraction analgesia using the stereogesic portable. *Military Medicine, 125,* 843–848.

Scheve, A. (2002). *The effect of music therapy intervention on preoperative anxiety of pediatric patients as measured by self-report.* Unpublished master's thesis, The Florida State University, Tallahassee.

Schieffelin, C. (1988, April). *A case study: Stevens–Johnson Syndrome.* Paper presented at the annual conference of the Southeastern Conference of the National Association for Music Therapy, Tallahassee, FL.

Schirmer, K., Chisholm, A., Grap, M., Siva, P., Hallinan, M., & LaVoice-Hawkins, A. (1995). Effects of auditory stimuli on intracranial pressure and cerebral perfusion pressure in traumatic brain injury. *Journal of Neuroscience Nursing, 27*(6), 348–354.

Schneider, F. A. (1983). Assessment and evaluation of audio-analgesic effects on the pain experience of acutely burned children during dressing changes. *Dissertation Abstracts International, 43*(8-B), 2716.

Schorr, J. (1993). Music and pattern change in chronic pain. *Advances in Nursing Science, 15*(4), 27–36.

Schultz, J., & Luthe, W. (1959). *Autogenic training: A psychophysiologic approach in psychotherapy.* New York: Grune & Stratton.

Schunk, H. A. (1993, November). *The relationship between background music during feeding time and weight gain of low-birthweight infants: A pilot study.* Unpublished study presented at national conference of the National Association for Music Therapy, Toronto, Canada.

Schur, J. (1986). *Alleviating behavioral distress with music or Lamaze pant-blow breathing in children undergoing bone marrow aspirations and lumbar punctures.* Unpublished doctoral dissertation, The University of Texas Health Science Center at Dallas.

Schuster, B. (1985). The effect of music listening on blood pressure fluctuations in adult hemodialysis patients. *Journal of Music Therapy, 22,* 146–153.

Schwankovsky, L. M., & Guthrie, P. T. (1985). Music therapy for other health impaired children. In W. Lathom & C. Eagle (Eds.), *Music therapy for handicapped children* (Vol. 3). St. Louis, MO: MMB Music.

Schwartz, R., Moody, L., Yarndi, H., & Anderson, G. (1987). A meta-analysis of critical outcome variables in nonnutritive sucking in preterm infants. *Nursing Research, 36*(5), 292–295.

Sears, W. W. (1958). The effect of music on muscle tonus. In E. T. Gaston (Ed.), *Music therapy* (pp. 199–205). Lawrence, KS: Allen Press.

Sedei, C. (1980). *The effectiveness of music therapy on specific statements verbalized by cancer patients.* Unpublished manuscript, Colorado State University, Fort Collins.

Segall, M. (1970). *The relationship between auditory stimulation and heart rate response of the premature infant.* Unpublished doctoral dissertation, New York University, New York.

Seigel, S. L. (1983). *The use of music as treatment in pain perception with post-surgical patients in a pediatric hospital.* Unpublished master's thesis, University of Miami, FL.

Seki, H. (1983). Influence of music on memory and education, and the application of its underlying principles to acupuncture. *International Journal of Acupuncture and Electro-Therapeutic Research, 8,* 1–16.

Senelick, R. C., & Ryan, C. E., (1998). *Living with brain injury: A guide for families.* Birmingham, AL: HealthSouth Press.

Shapiro, A. G., & Cohen, H. (1983). Auxiliary pain relief during suction cutterrage. In R. Droh & R. Spintge (Eds.), *Angst, schmerz, musik in der anasthesie* (pp. 89–95). Basel: Editiones Roche.

Sheth, R. D., Mullett, M. D., Bodensteiner, J. B., & Hobbs, G. R. (1995). Longitudinal head growth in developmentally normal preterm infants. *Archives of Pediatric and Adolescent Medicine, 149*(12), 1358–1361.

Sifton, D. W. (Ed.). (1998). *PDR® Generics^{TM}.* Montvale, NJ: Medical Economics.

Sing, K., Erickson, T., Amitai, Y., & Hryhorczuk, D. (1996). Chloral hydrate toxicity from oral and intravenous administration. *Clinical Toxicology, 34*(1), 101–106.

Skille, O., Wigram, T., & Weeks, L. (1989). Vibroacoustic therapy: The therapeutic effect of low frequency sound on specific physical disorders and disabilities. *Journal of British Music Therapy, 3*(2), 6–10.

Slesnick, J. (1983). *Music in medicine: A critical review.* Unpublished master's thesis, Hahnemann University, Philadelphia, PA.

Slivka, H., & Magill, L. (1986). The conjoint use of social work and music therapy in working with children of cancer patients. *Music Therapy, 6A*(1), 30–40.

Smith, C. A., & Morris, L. W. (1976). Effects of stimulative and sedative music on cognitive and emotional components of anxiety. *Psychological Reports, 38,* 1187–1193.

Smith, C. A., & Morris, L. W. (1977). Differential effects of stimulative and sedative music on anxiety, concentration, and performance. *Psychological Reports, 41,* 1047–1053.

Snow, W., & Fields, B. (1950). Music as an adjunct in the training of children with cerebral palsy. *Occupational Therapy, 29,* 147–156.

Sommerfelt, K., Ellertsen, B., & Markestad, T. (1996). Low birthweight and neuromotor development: A population based, controlled study. *Acta Paediatrica, 85*(5), 604–610.

Spintge, R. (1982). Psychophysiological surgery preparation with and without anxiolytic music. In R. Droh & R. Spintge (Eds.), *Angst, schmerz, musik in der anasthesie* (pp. 77–88). Basel: Editiones Roche.

Spintge, R., & Droh, R. (1982). The preoperative condition of 1910 patients exposed to anxiolytic music and Rohypnol (Flurazepam) before receiving an epidural anesthetic. In R. Droh & R. Spintge (Eds.), *Angst, scherz, musik in der anasthesie* (pp. 193–196). Basel: Editiones Roche.

Spitzer, A. R. (1996). *Intensive care of the fetus and neonate.* Baltimore: Mosby-Year Book.

Stach, B. A. (2002). Introduction. In J. Katz (Eds.), *Handbook of clinical audiology.* Philadelphia: Lippincott Williams & Wilkins.

Standley, J. (1986). Music research in medical/dental treatment: Meta-analysis and clinical applications. *Journal of Music Therapy, 23*(2), 56–122.

Standley, J. (1991). Long-term benefits of music intervention in the newborn intensive care unit: A pilot study. *Journal of the International Association of Music for the Handicapped, 6*(1), 12–23.

Standley, J. (1991). The role of music in pacification/stimulation of premature infants with low birthweights. *Music Therapy Perspectives, 9*(1), 19–25.

Standley, J. (1992). Clinical applications of music and chemotherapy: The effects on nausea and emesis. *Music Therapy Perspectives, 10*(1), 27–35.

Standley, J. (1996). Music research in medical/dental treatment: An update of a prior meta-analysis. In C. Furman (Ed.), *Effectiveness of music therapy procedures: Documentation of research and clinical practice* (2nd ed., pp. 1–60). Silver Spring, MD: National Association for Music Therapy.

Standley, J. (1998). The effect of music and multimodal stimulation on physiologic and developmental responses of premature infants in neonatal intensive care. *Pediatric Nursing, 21*(6), 532–539.

Standley, J. (1998). Pre- and perinatal growth and development: Implications of music benefits for premature infants. International *Journal of Music Education, 31*, 1–13.

Standley, J. (1999). Music therapy in the NICU: Pacifier-Activated Lullabies (PAL) for reinforcement of non-nutritive sucking. *International Journal of Arts Medicine, 6*(2), 17–21.

Standley, J. (1999). Music therapy research with premature infants: Clinical implications. In R. R. Pratt & D. E. Grocke (Eds.), *MusicMedicine 3, MusicMedicine and Music Therapy: Expanding Horizons* (pp. 131–139). Parkville, Victoria, Australia: University of Melbourne Press.

Standley, J. (2000). The effect of contingent music to increase non-nutritive sucking of premature infants. *Pediatric Nursing, 26*(5), 493–495, 498–499.

Standley, J. (2000). Music research in medical/dental treatment: An update of a prior meta-analysis. In American Music Therapy Association (Ed.), *Effectiveness of music therapy procedures: Documentation of research and clinical practice* (3rd ed., pp. 1–60). Silver Spring, MD: American Music Therapy Association.

Standley, J. (2001). Music therapy for premature infants in neonatal intensive care: Physiological and developmental benefits. *Early Childhood Connections, 7*(2), 18–25.

Standley, J. (2001). Music therapy for the neonate. *Newborn and Infant Nursing Reviews, 1*(4), 211–216.

Standley, J. (2001). Musicoterapia para recien prematuros en cuidados intensivos neonatales (Music therapy for premature infants in neonatal intensive care) (C. Clancy, Trans.). *Acta Pediatrica Espanola, 59*(11), 623–629.

Standley, J. (2001, Spring). The power of contingent music for infant learning. *Bulletin of the Council for Research in Music Education, 149,* 65–71.

Standley, J. (2002). A meta-analysis of the efficacy of music therapy for premature infants. *Journal of Pediatric Nursing, 17*(2), 107–113.

Standley, J. (2002). *Music techniques in therapy, counseling and special education* (2nd ed.). St. Louis: MMB.

Standley, J. (2002). Music therapy in the NICU: Promoting the growth and development of premature infants. *Zero to Three, 25*(1), 23–30.

Standley, J. (2003). The effect of music-reinforced non-nutritive sucking on feeding rate of premature infants. *Journal of Pediatric Nursing, 17*(2), 107–113.

Standley, J. (2003). *Music therapy with premature infants: Research and developmental interventions.* Silver Spring, MD: American Music Therapy Association.

Standley, J., & Hanser, S. B. (1995). Music therapy research and applications in pediatric oncology treatment. *Journal of Pediatric Oncology Nursing, 12*(1), 3–8.

Standley, J., & Hughes, J. E. (1996). Documenting developmentally appropriate objectives and benefits of a music therapy program for early intervention: A behavioral analysis. *Music Therapy Perspectives, 14*(2), 87–94.

Standley, J., & Madsen, C. (1990). Comparison of infant preferences and responses to auditory stimuli: Music, mother, and other female voice. *Journal of Music Therapy, 27*(2), 54–97.

Standley, J., & Madsen, C. (1994). Comparison of infant preferences and responses to auditory stimuli: Music, mother, and other female voice. Reprinted in J. M. Standley and C. A. Prickett (Eds.), *Research in music therapy: A tradition in excellence* (pp. 680–713). Silver Spring, MD: National Association for Music Therapy.

Standley, J., & Moore, R. (1995). Therapeutic effects of music and mother's voice on premature infants. *Pediatric Nursing, 21*(6), 509–512.

Standley, J., & Moore, R. (1996). Therapeutic effects of music and mother's voice on premature infants. Abstracted in M. Broome (Ed.), *Capsules and comments in pediatric nursing.* Chicago: Mosby-Year Book.

Standley, J., & Whipple, J. (2003). Music therapy for premature infants in the Neonatal Intensive Care Unit: Health and developmental benefits. In S. Robb (Ed.), *Music therapy in pediatric healthcare: Research and best practice* (pp. 19–30). Silver Spring, MD: American Music Therapy Association.

Standley, J., & Whipple, J. (2003). Pediatric music therapy: A meta-analysis. In S. Robb (Ed.), *Music therapy in pediatric healthcare: Research and best practice* (pp. 1–18). Silver Spring, MD: American Music Therapy Association.

Staples, S. E. (1991). The effect of music listening on blood pressure, pulse rate, respiration rate, and anxiety state of patients in the preoperative room. *Music Therapy Perspectives, 9*, 19–25.

Staum, M. (1983). Music and rhythmic stimuli in the rehabilitation of gait disorders. *Journal of Music Therapy, 20*, 69–87.

Staum, M. J. (1988). Music for physical rehabilitation: An analysis of literature from 1950–1986 and applications for rehabilitation settings. In C. E. Furman (Ed.), *Effectiveness of music therapy procedures: Documentation of research and clinical practice* (pp. 65–104). Washington, DC: National Association for Music Therapy.

Steelman, V. (1990). Intraoperative music therapy. *AORN Journal, 52*(5), 1026–1034.

Stein, A. (1991). Music to reduce anxiety during Caesarean births. In C. D. Maranto (Ed.), *Applications of music in medicine* (pp. 179–190). Washington, DC: National Association for Music Therapy.

Steinke, W. (1991). The use of music, relaxation, and imagery in the management of postsurgical pain for scoliosis. In C. D. Maranto (Ed.), *Applications of music in medicine* (pp. 141–162). Washington, DC: National Association for Music Therapy.

Stelmachowicz, P. G. (2000). Amplification for infants. *Seminars in Hearing, 12*(4), 409–422.

Stevens, K. (1990). Patients' perceptions of music during surgery. *Journal of Advanced Nursing, 15*, 1045–1051.

Stice, K., & Mornhinweg, G. (1995). Effect of imagery with music on anxiety and dyspnea in patients with chronic obstructive pulmonary disease. *Kentucky Nurse, 43*(3), 37.

Stoudenmire, J. (1975). A comparison of muscle-relaxation training and music in the reduction of state and trait anxiety. *Journal of Clinical Psychology, 31*, 490–492.

Stratton, V. N., & Zalanowski, A. H. (1984). The relationship between music, degree of liking, and self-reported relaxation. *Journal of Music Therapy, 21*, 184–191.

Strauser, J. (1997). The effects of music versus silence on measures of state anxiety, perceived relaxation, and physiological responses of patients receiving chiropractic interventions. *Journal of Music Therapy, 34*(2), 88–105.

Sunderman, F. W. (1969). Medicine, music, and academia. *Transactions of the College of Physicians of Philadelphia, 37*, 140–148.

Sutter, K., Engstrom, J. L., Johnson, T. S., Kavanaugh, K., & Ifft, D. L. (1997). Reliability of head circumference measurements in preterm infants. *Pediatric Nursing, 23*(5), 485–490.

Tanioka, F., Takazawa, T., Kamata, S., Kudo, M., Matsuki, A., & Oyama, T. (1983). Hormonal effect of anxiolytic music in patients during surgical operations under epidural anesthesia. In R. Droh & R. Spintge (Eds.), *Angst, schmerz, musik in der aneisthesie* (pp. 285–290). Basel: Editiones Roche.

Taylor, D. (1981). Music in general hospital treatment from 1900 to 1950. *Journal of Music Therapy, 18*, 62–73.

Taylor, D. B. (1997). *Biomedical foundations of music as therapy.* St. Louis, MO: MMB Music.

Taylor, L., Kuttler, K., Parks, T., & Milton, D. (1998). The effect of music in the postanesthesia care unit on pain levels in women who have had abdominal hysterectomies. *Journal of PeriAnesthesia Nursing, 13*(2), 88–94.

Thaut, M. H., McIntosh, G. C., Prassa, S. G., & Rice, R. R. (1993). Effect of rhythmic auditory cueing on temporal stride parameters and EMG patterns in hemiparetic gait of stroke patients. *Journal of Neuro Rehabilitation, 7*, 7–16.

Thaut, M. H., Rice, R. R., & McIntosh, G. C. (1994). *Rhythmic sensorimotor music therapy for gait training with Parkinson's disease patients* [Video]. St. Louis, MO: MMB Music.

Thaut, M. H., Schleiffers, S., & Davis, W. (1991). The analysis of EMG activity in biceps and triceps muscle in an upper extremity gross motor task under the influence of auditory rhythm. *Journal of Music Therapy, 28*, 64–88.

Thomby, M., Haas, F., & Axen, K. (1995). Effect of distractive auditory stimuli on exercise tolerance in patients with COPD. *Chest, 107*(5), 1213–1217.

Tortora, G. J., & Grabowski, S. R. (1993). *Principles of anatomy and physiology* (7th ed.). New York: HarperCollins College Publishers.

Tsao, C., Gordon, T., Maranto, C., Lerman, C., & Murasko, D. (1991). The effects of music and directed biological imagery on immune response (S-IgA). In C. D. Maranto (Ed.), *Applications of music in medicine* (pp. 85–121). Washington, DC: National Association for Music Therapy.

Turk, D. C., & Genest, M. (1979). Regulation of pain: the application of cognitive and behavioral techniques for prevention and remediation. In P. C. Kendall & S. D. Hollon (Eds.), *Cognitive behavioral interventions: Theory, research, and procedures* (pp. 287–289). New York: Academic Press.

Tusek, D., Church, J., & Fazio, V. (1997). Guided imagery as a coping strategy for perioperative patients. *AORN Journal, 66*(4), 644–649.

Updike, P. (1990). Music therapy results for ICU patients. *Dimensions of Critical Care Nursing, 9*(1), 39–45.

Updike, P., & Charles, D. (1987). Music Rx: Physiological and emotional responses to taped music programs of preoperative patients awaiting plastic surgery. *Annals of Plastic Surgery, 19*(1), 29–33.

Venes, D. (1997). *Taber's cycolpedic medical dictionary.* Philadelphia: F. A. Davis.

Vincent, S., & Thompson, J. H. (1929). The effects of music upon the human blood pressure. *The Lancet, 1*, 534–537.

Wade, L. (2002). A comparison of the effects of vocal exercises/singing versus music-assisted relaxation on peak expiratory flow rates of children with asthma. *Music Therapy Perspectives, 20*(1), 31–37.

Wagner, M. (1975). Brainwaves and biofeedback: A brief history. *Journal of Music Therapy, 12*, 46–58.

Wagner, M. (1975). Effect of music and biofeedback on alpha brain wave rhythms and attentiveness. *Journal of Research in Music Education, 23*(1), 3–13.

Waldon, E. (2001). The effects of group music therapy on mood states and cohesiveness in adult oncology patients. *Journal of Music Therapy, 38*(3), 212.

Wallace, L. M. (1984). Psychological preparation as a method of reducing the stress of surgery. *Journal of Human Stress: Research and Management, 10*(2), 62–76.

Walters, C. (1996). The psychological and physiological effects of vibrotactile stimulation, via a Somatron™, on patients awaiting scheduled gynecological surgery. *Journal of Music Therapy, 33*(4), 261–287.

Walther-Larsen, S., Diemar, V., & Valentin, N. (1988, April–June). Music during regional anesthesia: A reduced need of sedatives. *Regional Anesthesia, 13*, 69–71.

Walworth, D. (2002, November). *Music therapy as procedural support: Benefits for patients and staff.* Research paper presented at the national conference of the American Music Therapy Association, Atlanta, GA.

Walworth, D. (2003). Procedural support: Music therapy assisted CT, EKG, EEG, X-ray, IV, ventilator, and emergency services. In S. L. Robb (Ed.), *Music therapy in pediatric healthcare: Research and evidence-based practice* (pp. 137–146). Silver Spring, MD: American Music Therapy Association.

Walworth, D. D., Nguyen, J., & Jarred, J. (2004, November). *The effects of live music on quality of life indicators for brain tumor surgical patients.* Poster session presented at the annual meeting of the American Music Therapy Association, Austin, TX

Watanabe, K. (2001). *The effects of music with abbreviated progressive relaxation techniques on occupational stress in female nurses in a hospital.* Unpublished master's thesis, The Florida State University, Tallahassee.

Watt, T. J. (1994). Intraventricular hemorrhage in the premature infant. *Nebraska Medical Journal, 79*, 322–325

Webster, C. (1973). Relaxation, music, and cardiology: The physiological and psychological consequences of their interrelation. *Australian Occupational Therapy Journal, 20*, 9–20.

Weisbrod, R. L. (1969, January). Audio-analgesia revisited. *Anesthesia Progress*, 8–15.

What is auditory brainstem response? Retrieved from http://www.vmmc.org/

Whipple, J. (2000). The effect of parent training in music and multimodal stimulation on parent-neonate interactions in the neonatal intensive care unit. *Journal of Music Therapy, 37*(4), 250–268.

Whipple, J. (2003). Surgery Buddies: A music therapy program for pediatric surgical patients. *Music Therapy Perspectives, 21*(2), 77–83.

Whipple, J. (2004). *The effect of music-reinforced nonnutritive sucking on state of preterm, low birthweight infants experiencing heelstick.* Unpublished doctoral dissertation, The Florida State University.

Whipple, J. (2005). Music and multimodal stimulation as developmental intervention in neonatal intensive care. *Music Therapy Perspectives, 23*(2), 100–105.

White-Traut, R. C., & Tubeszewski, K. A. (1986). Multimodal stimulation of the premature infant. *Journal of Pediatric Nursing, 1*(2), 90–95.

Wiand, N. (1997). Relaxation levels achieved by Lamaze-trained pregnant women listening to music and ocean sound tapes. *The Journal of Perinatal Education, 6*(4), 1–8.

Wilson, C. U., & Aiken, L. S. (1977). The effect of intensity levels upon physiological and subjective affective response to rock music. *Journal of Music Therapy, 14*, 60–76.

Wilson, V. M. (1957). Variations in gastric motility due to musical stimuli. *Music Therapy, 6*, 243–249.

Winokur, M. A. (1984). *The use of music as an audio-analgesia during childbirth.* Unpublished master's thesis, The Florida State University, Tallahassee.

Winslow, G. A. (1986). Music therapy in the treatment of anxiety in hospitalized high-risk mothers. *Music Therapy Perspectives, 3*, 29–33.

Wlodarczyk, N. (2003). *The effect of music therapy on the spirituality of persons in an in-patient hospice unit as measured by self-report.* Unpublished master's thesis, The Florida State University, Tallahassee.

Wolfe, D. (1978). Pain rehabilitation and music therapy. *Journal of Music Therapy, 15*(4), 184–206.

Wolfe, D. (1980). The effect of automated interrupted music on head posturing of cerebral palsied individuals. *Journal of Music Therapy, 17*, 184–206.

Wolinsky, G. F., & Koehler, N. (1973). A cooperative program in materials development for very young hospitalized children. *Rehabilitation Literature, 34*(2), 34–41.

Wong, E. (2003). *Clinical guide to music therapy in physical rehabilitation settings.* Silver Spring, MD: American Music Therapy Association.

Woodson, R., & Hamilton, C. (1988). The effect of nonnutritive sucking on heart rate in preterm infants. *Developmental Psychobiology, 21*(3), 207–213.

Wylie, M. E., & Blom, R. C. (1986). Guided imagery and music with hospice patients. *Music Therapy Perspectives, 3*, 25–28.

Yeh, T. F., Voora, S., & Lilien, D. (1980). Oxygen consumption and insensible water loss in premature infants in single- versus double-walled incubators. *Journal of Pediatrics, 97,* 967–971.

Zahr, L. K., & Balian, S. (1995). Responses of premature infants to routine nursing interventions and noise in the NICU. *Nursing Research, 44,* 179–185.

Zelazny, C. (2001). Therapeutic instrumental playing in hand rehabilitation for older adults with osteoarthritis: Four case studies. *Journal of Music Therapy, 38*(2), 97.

Zimmerman, L., Pierson, M., & Marker, J. (1988). Effects of music on patient anxiety in coronary care units. *Heart and Lung, 17*(5), 560–566.

Zimmerman, L., Pozehl, B., Duncan, K., & Schmitz, R. (1989). Effects of music in patients who had chronic cancer pain. *Western Journal of Nursing Research, 11*(3), 298–309.

Zimny, G. H., & Weidenfeller, E. W. (1963). Effects of music upon GSR and heart rate. *American Journal of Psychology, 76,* 311–314.

Mental Health/Psychiatric

Adelman, E. J. (1985). Multimodal therapy and music therapy: Assessing and treating the whole person. *Music Therapy, 5,* 12–21.

Ain, E. (1978). *The relationship of musical structure and verbal interaction process during adult music therapy.* Unpublished master's thesis, Hahnemann Medical College and Hospital, Philadelphia.

Allen, W. R., & White, W. F. (1966). Psychodramatic effects of music as a psychotherapeutic agent. *Journal of Music Therapy, 3,* 69–71.

Alvin, J. (1981). Regressional techniques in music therapy. *Music Therapy, 1,* 3–8.

Applebaum, E., Egel, A., Koegel, R., & Imhoff, B. (1979). Measuring musical abilities of autistic children. *Journal of Autism and Developmental Disorders, 9,* 279–287.

Arnold, M. (1975). Music therapy in a transactional analysis setting. *Journal of Music Therapy, 12,* 104–120.

Baker, F., & Wigram, T. (2005). *Songwriting: Methods, techniques and clinical applications for music therapy clinicians, educators and students.* Philadelphia: Jessica Kingsley.

Baumel, L. N. (1973). Psychiatrist as music therapist. *Journal of Music Therapy, 2,* 83–85.

Boenheim, C. (1967). The importance of creativity in contemporary psychotherapy. *Journal of Music Therapy, 4,* 3–6.

Boenheim, C. (1968). The position of music and art therapy in contemporary psychotherapy. *Journal of Music Therapy, 5,* 85–87.

Bolduc, T. E. (1962). A psychologist looks at music therapy. *Proceedings of the NAMT, 11,* 40–42.

Bonny, H. L. (1968). Preferred loudness of recorded music of hospitalized psychiatric patients and hospital employees. *Journal of Music Therapy, 2,* 44–52.

Bonny, H. L. (1975). Music and consciousness. *Journal of Music Therapy, 13,* 121–135.

Bonny, H. L. (1978). *Facilitating GIM sessions: GIM monograph #1.* Baltimore: ICM Books.

Bonny, H. L., & Pahnke, W. (1972). The use of music in psychedelic (LSD) psychotherapy. *Journal of Music Therapy, 9,* 64–87

Bonny, H. L., & Savary, L. M. (1990). *Music and your mind: Listening with a new consciousness.* Barrytown, NY: Station Hill Press.

Braswell, C. (1962). The future of psychiatric music therapy. *Proceedings of the NAMT, 11,* 65–76.

Braswell, C. (1962). Psychiatric music therapy: A review of the profession. *Proceedings of the NAMT, 11,* 53–64.

Braswell, C., Brooks, D., Decuir, A., Humphrey, T., Jacobs, K., & Sutton, K. (1986). Development and implementation of a music-activity therapy intake assessment for psychiatric patients. Part II: Standardization procedures on data from psychiatric patients. *Journal of Music Therapy, 23*(3), 126–141.

Brooke, S. L. (Ed.). (2006). *The use of the creative therapies with sexual abuse survivors.* Springfield, IL: Charles C. Thomas.

Brooking, M. (1959). Music therapy in British mental hospitals. *Music Therapy,* 38–46.

Brown, M. E., & Selinger, M. (1969). A nontherapeutic device for approaching therapy in an institutional setting. *International Journal of Group Psychotherapy, 19,* 88–95.

Brunner-Orne, M., & Flinn, S. S. (1960). Music therapy at Westwood Lodge. *Music Therapy,* 44–46.

Bryant, D. R. (1987). A cognitive approach to therapy through music. *Journal of Music Therapy, 24*(1), 27–34.

Burleson, S. J., Center, D. B., & Reeves, H. (1989). The effect of background music on task performance in psychotic children. *Journal of Music Therapy, 26*(4), 198–205.

Cassity, M. D. (1976). Influence of a music therapy activity upon peer acceptance, group cohesiveness, and interpersonal relationships of adult psychiatric patients. *Journal of Music Therapy, 13*(2), 66–76.

Cassity, M. D., & Cassity, J. E. (1994). Psychiatric music therapy assessment and treatment in clinical training facilities with adults, adolescents, and children. *Journal of Music Therapy, 31*(1), 2–30.

Cassity, M. D., & Cassity, J. E. (2006). *Multimodal psychiatric music therapy for adults, adolescents, and children: A clinical manual* (3rd ed.). Philadelphia: Jessica Kingsley.

Chace, M. (1954). Report of a group project. St. Elizabeth Hospital. *Music Therapy*, 187–190.

Choi, B. (1997). Professional and patient attitudes about the relevance of music therapy as a treatment modality in NAMT approved psychiatric hospitals. *Journal of Music Therapy, 34*(4), 277–292.

Clark, M., & Ficken, C. (1988). Music therapy in the new health care environment. *Music Therapy Perspectives, 5*, 23–27.

Clemetson, B. C., & Chen, R. (1968). Music therapy in a day-treatment program. In E. T. Gaston (Ed.), *Music in therapy* (pp. 394–400). New York: Macmillan.

Conrad, J. (1962). A music therapy program for short-term psychiatric patients. *Bulletin of the NAMT, 3*, 7–12.

Cooke, R. M. (1969). The use of music in play therapy. *Journal of Music Therapy, 6*, 66–75.

Cordobes, T. (1997). Group songwriting as a method for developing group cohesion for HIV-Seropositive adult patients with depression. *Journal of Music Therapy, 34*(1), 46–67.

Corsini, R. J., & Wedding, D. (Eds.). (2007). *Current psychotherapies* (8th ed.). Stamford, CT: Thompson Learning.

Crocker, D. B. (1955). Music as a projective technique. *Music Therapy*, 86–97.

Daveson, B., & Edwards, J. (2001). A descriptive study exploring the role of music therapy in prisons. *Arts in Psychotherapy, 28*(2), 137–141.

de l'Etoile, S. (2002). The effectiveness of music therapy in group psychotherapy for adults with mental illness. *Arts in Psychotherapy, 29*(2), 69–78.

DeWolfe, A. S., & Konieczny, J. A. (1973). Responsiveness in schizophrenia. *Journal of Personality Assessment, 37*, 568–573.

DeWolfe, A. S., Youkilis, H. D., & Konieczny, J. A. (1975). Psychophysiological correlates of responsiveness in schizophrenia. *Journal of Consulting and Clinical Psychology, 43*, 192–197.

Díaz de Chumaceiro, C. (1992). Transference–countertransference in psychology integrations for music therapy in the 1970s and 1980s. *Journal of Music Therapy, 29*(4), 217–235.

Dickens, G., & Sharpe, M. (1970). Music therapy in the setting of a psychotherapeutic centre. *British Journal of Medical Psychology, 43*, 83–94.

Dickenson, M. (1957). Music as a tool in psychotherapy for children. *Music Therapy*, 97–104.

Diephouse, J. W. (1986). Music therapy: A valuable adjunct to psychotherapy with children. *Psychiatric Quarterly Supplement, 42*, 75–85.

Doak, B. (2003). Relationships between adolescent psychiatric diagnoses, music preferences, and drug preferences. *Music Therapy Perspectives, 21*(2), 69–76.

Douglass, D. R., & Wagner, M. K. (1965). A program for the activity therapist in group psychotherapy. *Journal of Music Therapy, 2,* 56–60.

Dreikurs, R. (1961). The psychological and philosophical significance of rhythm. *Bulletin of the NAMT, 10,* 8–17.

Dreikurs, R., & Crocker, E. B. (1955). Music therapy with psychotic children. *Music Therapy,* 62–73.

Dvorkin, J. (1982). Piano improvisation: A therapeutic tool in acceptance and resolution of emotions in a schizoafffective personality. *Music Therapy, 2,* 53–62.

Egan, W. H. (1977). Teaching medical student psychiatry through contemporary music. *Journal of Medical Education, 52,* 851–853.

Euper, J. A. (1970). Contemporary trends in mental health work. *Journal of Music Therapy, 1,* 20–27.

Farmer, R. (1963). A musical activities program with young psychotic girls. *American Journal of Occupational Therapy, 17,* 116–119.

Farnan, L. A. (1987). Composing music for use in therapy. *Music Therapy Perspectives, 4,* 8–12.

Ficken, T. (1976). The use of song-writing in a psychiatric setting. *Journal of Music Therapy, 13,* 163–172.

Ford, S. (1999). The effect of music on the self-injurious behavior of an adult female with severe developmental disabilities. *Journal of Music Therapy, 36*(4), 293–313.

Forrest, C. (1968). Music in psychiatry. *Nursing Mirror Midwives Journal, 127*(24), 22–23.

Forrest, C. (1972). Music and the psychiatric nurse. *Nursing Times, 68,* 410–411.

Friedlander, L. (1994). Group music psychotherapy in an inpatient psychiatric setting for children: A developmental approach. *Music Therapy Perspectives, 12*(2), 92–97.

Friedman, E. R. (1968). Psychological aspects of folk music. *American Psychological Proceedings of the Annual Convention, 3,* 449–450.

Friedrich, D., Beno, F., & Graham, H. (1976). A second testing of paranoid schizophrenia on a dichotic listening task. *Journal of Abnormal Psychology, 85,* 622–644.

Frisch, A. (1990). Symbol and structure: Music therapy for the adolescent psychiatric inpatient. *Music Therapy, 9*(1), 16–34.

Froelich, M. (1985). An annotated bibliography for the creative arts therapies. *Journal of Music Therapy, 22*(4), 218–226.

Fulford, M. (2002). Overview of a music therapy program at a maximum security unit of a state psychiatric facility. *Music Therapy Perspectives, 20*(2), 112–116.

Gibbons, A. (1986). The development of square dancing activity in a music therapy program and Rockland State Hospital. *Music Therapy, 6,* 140–147.

Giles, M., Cogan, D., & Cox, C. (1991). A music and art program to promote emotional health in elementary school children. *Journal of Music Therapy, 28*(3), 135–148.

Glover, R. (1962). New concepts in psychiatric treatment. *Proceedings of the NAMT, 11,* 48–49.

Goldstein, C. (1964). Music and creative arts therapy for an autistic child. *Journal of Music Therapy, 1*(4), 135–138.

Goldstein, C., Lingas, C., & Sheafer, D. (1965). Interpretive or creative movement as a sublimation tool in music therapy. *Journal of Music Therapy, 2,* 11–15.

Greenburg, R. P., & Fisher, S. (1971). Some differential effects of music on projective and structured psychological tests. *Psychological Reports, 28,* 817–818.

Greven, G. M. (1957). Music as a tool in psychotherapy for children. *Music Therapy,* 105–108.

Grossman, S. (1978). An investigation of Crocker's music-projective techniques for emotionally disturbed children. *Journal of Music Therapy, 15*(4), 179–184.

Hadsell, N. (1974). A sociological theory and approach to music therapy with adult psychiatric patients. *Journal of Music Therapy, 3,* 113–124.

Hanser, S. (1986). Music therapy and stress reduction research. *Journal of Music Therapy, 22*(4), 193–207.

Harris, C., Bradley, R., & Titus, S. (1992). A comparison of the effects of hard rock and easy listening on the frequency of observed inappropriate behaviors: Control of environmental antecedents in a large public area. *Journal of Music Therapy, 29*(1), 6–17.

Hauck, L. P., & Martin, P. L. (1970). Music as a reinforcer in patient-controlled duration of time out. *Journal of Music Therapy, 7,* 43–53.

Heaney, C. (1992). Evaluation of music therapy and other treatment modalities by adult psychiatric inpatients. *Journal of Music Therapy, 29*(2), 70–86.

Hilliard, R. (2001). The use of cognitive-behavioral music therapy in the treatment of women with eating disorders. *Music Therapy Perspectives, 19*(2), 109–113.

Hollander, F. M., & Juhrs, P. D. (1974). Orff-Schulwerk, an effective tool with autistic children. *Journal of Music Therapy, 11,* 1–12.

Howe, A. W. (1960). Music therapy in the psychiatric treatment program. *Journal of the South Carolina Medical Association, 56,* 59–65.

Ishiyama, T. (1963). Music as a psychotherapeutic tool in the treatment of a catatonic. *Psychiatric Quarterly, 37,* 473–461.

Justice, R. (1994). Music therapy interventions for people with eating disorders in an inpatient setting. *Music Therapy Perspectives, 12*(2), 104–110.

Kahans, D., & Calfora, M. B. (1982). The influence of music on psychiatric patients' immediate attitude change toward therapists. *Journal of Music Therapy, 19*(3), 179–187.

Kantor, M., & Pinsker, H. (1973). Musical repression of psychopathology. *Perspective in Biology and Medicine, 16,* 263–269.

Kerr, T., Walsh, J., & Marshall, A. (2001). Emotional change processes in music-assisted reframing. *Journal of Music Therapy, 38*(3), 193–211.

King, H. E. (1976). Incidental serial reaction time: Normal and schizophrenic response to the onset and cessation of auditory signals. *Journal of Psychology, 93*(part 2), 299–311.

Koh, S. D., & Shears, G. (1970). Psychophysical scaling by schizophrenics and normals: Line lengths and music preferences. *Archives of General Psychiatry, 23,* 249–259.

Korboot, P., & Damiani, N. (1976). Auditory processing speed and signal detection in schizophrenia. *Journal of Abnormal Psychology, 85,* 287–295.

Lerner, J., Nachson, I., & Carmon, A. (1977). Responses of paranoid and non-paranoid schizophrenics in a dichotic listening task. *Journal of Nervous and Mental Disease, 164,* 247–252.

Lewis, D. (1964). Chamber music: Proposed as a therapeutic medium. *Journal of Music Therapy, 4,* 126–127.

Lord, W. (1971). Communication of activity therapy rationale. *Journal of Music Therapy, 2,* 68–71.

Luce, D. (2001). Cognitive therapy and music therapy. *Music Therapy Perspectives, 19*(2), 96–103.

Matteson, C. A. (1972, April). Finding the self in space. *Music Educators Journal,* 47–49.

Maultsby, M. C. (1977). Combining music therapy and rational-behavior therapy. *Journal of Music Therapy, 14,* 89–97.

McClean, M. (1974). One therapist; one patient: A success story. *Hospital and Community Psychiatry, 25,* 153–156.

Mercado, C., & Mercado, E. (2006). A program using environmental manipulation, music therapy activities, and the Somatron™ vibroacoustic chair to reduce agitation behaviors of nursing home residents with psychiatric disorders. *Music Therapy Perspectives, 24*(1), 30–38.

Metzger, L. K. (1986). The selection of music for therapeutic use with adolescents and young adults in a psychiatric facility. *Music Therapy Perspectives, 3,* 20–24.

Mitchell, G. C. (1966). Bedtime music for psychotic children. *Nursing Mirror Midwives Journal, 122,* 452.

Moreno, I. (1980). Music psychodrama: A new direction in music therapy. *Journal of Music Therapy, 17,* 34–42.

Morgenstern, A. M. (1982). Group therapy: A timely strategy for music therapists. *Music Therapy Perspectives, 1,* 16–20.

Murphy, M. (1992). Coping in the short term: The impact of acute care on music therapy practice. *Music Therapy, 11*(1), 99–119.

Myers, K. F. (1985). The relationship between degree of disability and vocal range, vocal range midpoint, and pitch-matching ability of mentally retarded and psychiatric clients. *Journal of Music Therapy, 22*(1), 35–45.

Nass, M. L. (1971). Some considerations of a psychoanalytic interpretation of music. *Psychoanalytic Quarterly, 40,* 303–316.

Nelson, D. L., Anderson, V., & Gonzales, A. (1984). Music activities as therapy for children with autism and other pervasive developmental disorders. *Journal of Music Therapy, 21*(3), 100–116.

Nolan, P. (1981). *The use of guided imagery and music in the clinical assessment of depression.* Unpublished master's thesis. Hahnemann University, Philadelphia.

Nolan, P. (1983). Insight therapy: Guided imagery and music in a forensic psychiatric setting. *Music Therapy, 1,* 43–51.

Nolan, P. (1989). Music as a transitional object in the treatment of bulimia. *Music Therapy Perspectives, 6,* 49–51.

North, E. F. (1966). Music therapy as an important treatment modality with psychotic children. *Journal of Music Therapy, 3,* 22–24.

Noy, P. (1966). The psychodynamic meaning of music, Part I. *Journal of Music Therapy, 3*(4), 126–134.

Noy, P. (1967). The psychodynamic meaning of music, Part II. *Journal of Music Therapy, 4*(1), 7–23.

Noy, P. (1967). The psychodynamic meaning of music, Part III. *Journal of Music Therapy, 4*(2), 45–51.

Noy, P. (1967). The psychodynamic meaning of music, Part IV. *Journal of Music Therapy, 4*(3), 81–94.

Noy, P. (1967). The psychodynamic meaning of music, Part V. *Journal of Music Therapy, 4*(4), 117–125.

Odell, H. (1988). A music therapy approach in mental health. *Psychology of Music, 16*(1), 52–61.

Odell-Miller, H. (1995). Approaches to music therapy in psychiatry with specific emphasis upon a research project with the elderly mentally ill. In T. Wigram, B. Saperston, & R. West (Eds.), *The art and science of music therapy: A handbook* (pp. 83–111). Langhorne, PA: Harwood Academic.

Parente, A. (1989). Feeding the hungry soul: Music as a therapeutic modality in the treatment of anorexia nervosa. *Music Therapy Perspectives, 6,* 44–48.

Peach, S. C. (1984). Some implications for the clinical use of music-facilitated imagery. *Journal of Music Therapy, 21*(1), 27–34.

Pickler, A. G. (1962). Music as an aid in psychotherapy. *Proceedings of the NAMT, 11*, 23–29.

Pishkin, V., & Hershiser, D. (1964). White sound and schizophrenic's reaction to stress. *Journal of Oklahoma State Medical Association, 57*, 215–217.

Plach, T. (1980). *The creative use of music in group therapy.* Springfield, IL: Charles C. Thomas.

Racker, H. (1965). Psychoanalytic considerations on music and the musician. *Psychoanalytic Review, 52*, 75–94.

Reed, K. (2002). Music therapy treatment groups for mentally disordered offenders (MDO) in a state hospital setting. *Music Therapy Perspectives, 20*(2), 98–104.

Robbins, A. (1980). *Expressive therapy.* New York: Human Sciences Press.

Robbins, L. (1966). Role of music therapy in a psychiatric treatment. *Journal of Music Therapy, 3*, 1–7.

Rollin, H. R. (1962). Therapeutic use of music in a mental hospital. *Transactions of the College of Physicians of Philadelphia, 29*, 130–136.

Rollin, H. R. (1964). Music therapy in a mental hospital. *Nursing Times, 60*, 1219–1222.

Rosenfeld, A. H. (1985, December). Music, the beautiful disturber. *Psychology Today*, 48–56.

Rubin, B. (1975). Music therapy in a community mental health program. *Journal of Music Therapy, 7*, 59–66.

Ruppenthal, W. (1965). "Scribbling" in music therapy. *Journal of Music Therapy, 2*, 8–10.

Schmidt, J. A. (1983). Songwriting as a therapeutic procedure. *Music Therapy Perspectives, 2*, 4–7.

Schneider, S. J. (1976). Selective attention in schizophrenia. *Journal of Abnormal Psychology, 85*, 167–173.

Sears, W. (1968). Processes in music therapy. In E. T. Gaston (Ed.), *Music in therapy* (pp. 30–40). New York: Macmillan.

Seeley, M. C. (1960). Problems and techniques of a public radio broadcast from a mental hospital. *Bulletin of the NAMT, 2*, 7–8, 11.

Shashan, D. H. (1972). Group psychotherapy: Present trends in management of the more severe emotional problems. *Psychiatric Annals, 2*, 4–10.

Shatin, L., Kotter, W. L., & Douglas-Longmore, G. (1961). Music therapy for schizophrenia. *Journal of Rehabilitation, 27*, 30–31.

Shatin, L., Kotter, W. L., & Douglas-Longmore, G. (1961). Music therapy for schizophrenics. *Proceedings of the NAMT, 11*, 99–104.

Shatin, L., Kotter, W. L., & Douglas-Longmore, G. (1964). A psychological study of the music therapist in rehabilitation. *Journal of General Psychology, 71*, 193–205.

Shatin, L., Kotter, W. L., & Longmore, G. (1967). Psycho-social prescription for music therapy in hospital. *Diseases of the Nervous System, 4*, 231–233.

Shrodes, C. (1960). Bibliotherapy. An application of psychoanalytic therapy. *American Image, 17*, 311–317.

Silverman, M. (2003). The influence of music on the symptoms of psychosis: A meta-analysis. *Journal of Music Therapy, 40*(1), 27–40.

Silverman, M. (2005). Using music therapy games with adult psychiatric patients. *Arts in Psychotherapy, 32*(2), 121–129.

Silverman, M. (in press). Evaluating current trends in psychiatric music therapy: A descriptive analysis. *Journal of Music Therapy, 44*(4).

Silverman, M. (2006). Psychiatric patients' perception of music therapy and other psychoeducational programming. *Journal of Music Therapy, 43*(2), 111–122.

Silverman, M., & Marcionetti, M. (2004). Immediate effects of a single music therapy intervention with persons who are severely mentally ill. *Arts in Psychotherapy, 31*(5), 291–301.

Slaughter, F. (1960). Some concepts concerning the therapeutic use of music in a psychiatric setting. *Bulletin of the NAMT, 1*, 11.

Slaughter, F. (1968). Approaches to the use of music therapy. In E. T. Gaston (Ed.), *Music in therapy* (pp. 238–244). New York: Macmillan.

Slotoroff, C. (1994). Drumming technique for assertiveness and anger management in the short-term psychiatric setting for adult and adolescent survivors of trauma. *Music Therapy Perspectives, 12*(2), 111–116.

Smeijsters, H. (1993). Music therapy and psychotherapy. *Arts in Psychotherapy, 20*(3), 223–229.

Smeijsters, H., Wijzenbeek, G., & van Nieuwenhuijzen, N. (1995). The effect of musical excerpts on the evocation of values for depressed patients. *Journal of Music Therapy, 32*(3), 167–188.

Smith, S. M. (1975). Using music therapy with short-term alcoholic and psychiatric patients. *Hospital and Community Psychiatry, 7*, 420–421.

Sommers, D. T. (1961). Music in the autobiographies of mental patients. *Mental Hygiene, 45*, 402–407.

Stanford, G. A. (1964). Orchestration of the new mental hospital theme. *Journal of Music Therapy, 4*, 124–428.

Staum, M. J. (1981). An analysis of movement in therapy. *Journal of Music Therapy, 18*(1), 7–24.

Steele, P. H. (1984). Aspects of resistance in music therapy: Theory and technique. *Music Therapy, 4*, 64–72.

Stein, J., & Euper, J. A. (1974). Advances in music therapy. In J. H. Masserman (Ed.), *Current psychiatric therapies* (Vol. 14, pp. 107–113). New York: Grune and Stratton.

Stein, J., & Thompson, S. V. (1971). Crazy music: Theory. *Psychotherapy: Theory, Research, and Practice, 8*, 137–145.

Stephens, G. (1981). Adele: A study in silence. *Music Therapy, 1*, 25–31.

Stephens, G. (1983). The use of improvisation for developing relatedness in the adult client. *Music Therapy, 3*, 29–42.

Stephens, G. (1984). Group supervision in music therapy. *Music Therapy, 4*, 29–38.

Sterba, R. F. (1965). Psychoanalysis and music. *American Image, 22*, 96–111.

Sylwester, K., Barg, M., Frueh, B., Baker, K., Patrick, F., & Shaffer, S. (1971). Music therapy in a decentralized hospital. *Journal of Music Therapy, 8*(2), 53–67.

Thaut, M. (1989). The influence of music therapy interventions on self-rated changes in relaxation, affect, and thought in psychiatric prisoner-patients. *Journal of Music Therapy, 26*(3), 155–166.

Thomas, M. W. (1976). Implications for music therapy as a treatment modality for the mentally ill deaf. *Voice of the Lakes, 76*, 19–22.

Toedter, A. D. (1954). Music therapy for the criminally insane and the psychopath. *Music Therapy*, 95–103.

Tunks, J. L. (1983). The ward music therapy group and the integral involvement of nursing aides. *Music Therapy Perspectives, 2*, 23–24.

Tyson, F. (1965, April). Therapeutic elements in out-patient music therapy. *The Psychiatric Quarterly*, 315–327. Tyson, F. (1966). Music therapy in private practices: Three case histories. *Journal of Music Therapy, 3*, 8–18.

Tyson, F. (1979). Child at the gate: Individual music therapy with a schizophrenic woman. *Art Psychotherapy, 6*, 77–83.

Tyson, F. (1981). *Psychiatric music therapy: Origins and development.* New York: Creative Arts Rehabilitation Center.

Tyson, F. (1982). Individual singing instruction: An evolutionary framework for psychiatric music therapists. *Music Therapy Perspectives, 1*, 5–15.

Tyson, F. (1984). Music therapy as a choice for psychotherapeutic intervention: A preliminary study of motivational factors among adult psychiatric patients. *Music Therapy Perspectives, 1*, 2–8.

Tyson, F. (1987). Analytically oriented music therapy in a case of generalized anxiety disorder. *Music Therapy Perspectives, 4*, 51–55.

Unkefer, R. F., & Thaut, M. H. (Eds.). (2002). *Music therapy in the treatment of adults with mental disorders: Theoretical bases and clinical interventions* (2nd ed.). Gilsum, NH: Barcelona.

Wang, R. P. (1968). Psychoanalytic theories and music therapy practice. *Journal of Music Therapy, 5,* 114–116.

Warren, J. (1980). Paired-associate learning in chronic institutionalized subjects using synthesized sounds, nonsense syllables, rhythmic sounds. *Journal of Music Therapy, 17*(1), 16–25.

Wasserman, N. (1972). Music therapy for the emotionally disturbed in a private hospital. *Journal of Music Therapy, 9,* 99–104.

Wasserman, N., Plutchik, R., Deutsch, R., & Taketomo, Y. (1973). The musical background of a group of mentally retarded psychotic patients: Implications for music therapy. *Journal of Music Therapy, 10,* 78–82.

Weidenfeller, E. W., & Zimny, G. H. (1962). Effects of music upon GSR of depressives and schizophrenics. *Journal of Abnormal Psychology, 64,* 307–312.

Weintraub, I. G. (1961). Emotional responses of schizophrenics to selected musical compositions. *Delaware Medical Journal, 33,* 186–187.

Weisbrod, J. A. (1971, April). Shaping a body image through movement therapy. *Music Educators Journal,* 50–53.

Wells, A. M. (1953). Rhythm activities on wards of senile patients. *Music Therapy,* 127–132.

Werbner, N. (1966). The practice of music therapy with psychotic children. *Journal of Music Therapy, 3,* 25–31.

Wheeler, B. (1981). The relationship between music therapy and theories of psychotherapy. *Music Therapy, 1,* 9–16.

Wheeler, B. L. (1983). A psychotherapeutic classification of music therapy practices: A continuum of procedures. *Music Therapy Perspectives, 2,* 8–12.

Wilke, M. (1960). Music therapy at work in the short-term psychiatric setting at Charity Hospital of New Orleans. *Bulletin of the NAMT, 2,* 5–10.

Williams, G., & Dorow, L. G. (1983). Changes in complaints and non-complaints of a chronically depressed psychiatric patient as a function of an interrupted music/verbal feedback package. *Journal of Music Therapy, 20*(3), 143–155.

Wolfe, D. E. (1988). Group music therapy in short-term psychiatric care. In C. E. Furman (Ed.), *Effectiveness of music therapy procedures: Documentation of research and clinical practice* (pp. 175–205). Washington, DC: National Association for Music Therapy.

Wolfe, D. E. (2000). Group music therapy in acute mental health care: Meeting the demands of effectiveness and efficiency. In American Music Therapy Association (Ed.), *Effectiveness of music therapy procedures: Documentation of research and clinical practice* (3rd ed.; pp. 265–296). Silver Spring, MD: American Music Therapy Association.

Wolfe, D. E., Burns, S., Stoll, M., & Wichmann, K. (1975). *Analysis of music therapy group procedures.* Minneapolis, MN: Golden Valley Health Center.

Wolfgram, B. J. (1978). Music therapy for retarded adults with psychotic overlay: A day treatment approach. *Journal of Music Therapy, 15*(4), 199–207.

Wooten, M. (1992). The effects of heavy metal music on affects shifts of adolescents in an inpatient psychiatric setting. *Music Therapy Perspectives, 10*(2), 93–98.

Wortis, R. P. (1960). Music therapy for the mentally ill: The effect of music on emotional activity and the value of music as a resocializing agent. *Journal of General Psychology, 62,* 311–318.

Wright, B. (1976). A study in the use of music therapy techniques for behavior modification at St. Thomas Psychiatric Hospital, Ontario. *Journal of the Canadian Association for Music Therapy, 4,* 2–4.

Zwerling, I. (1979). The creative arts therapies as "real therapies." *Hospital and Community Psychiatry, 30,* 841–844.

Special Education

Adamek, A. S., & Darrow, A. A. (2005). *Music in special education.* Silver Spring, MD: American Music Therapy Association.

Aebischer, D., & Sheridan, W. (1982). For John, music makes a difference. *Music Educators Journal, 68*(8), 29.

Aigen, K. (1995). Cognitive and affective processes in music therapy with individuals with developmental delays: A preliminary model for contemporary Nordoff-Robbins practice. *Music Therapy, 13*(1), 18–46.

Albert, M., Sparks, R., & Helm, N. (1973). Melodic intonation therapy for aphasia. *Archives of Neurology, 29*(2), 130–131.

Alford, R. L. (1974). Music and the mentally retarded ethnic minority child. *The Pointer, 19*(2), 138–139.

Alley, J. M. (1977). Education for the severely handicapped: The role of music therapy. *Journal of Music Therapy, 14*(2), 50–59.

Alley, J. M. (1979). Music in the IEP: Therapy/education. *Journal of Music Therapy, 16*(3), 111–127.

Alley, J. M. (1982). Music therapy. In C. R. Reynolds & T. B. Gutkin (Eds.), *The handbook of school psychology* (pp. 667–678). New York: John Wiley & Sons.

Allgood, N. (2005). Parents' perceptions of family-based group music therapy for children with autism spectrum disorders. *Music Therapy Perspectives, 23*(2), 92–99.

Alvin, J. A. (1965). *Music for the handicapped child.* London: Oxford University Press.

Alvin, J. A. (1969). *Music therapy for severely subnormal boys.* London: British Society for Music Therapy.

Alvin, J. A. (1978). *Music therapy.* London: John Clare Books.

Alvin, J. A., & Warwick, A. (1991). *Music therapy for the autistic child* (2nd ed.). London: Oxford University Press.

Amir, D., & Schuchman, G. (1985, December). Auditory training through music with hearing-impaired preschool children. *The Volta Review, 87*(7), 333–343.

Anderson, V. G., Gonzales, A. D., & Nelson, D. L. (1984). Music activities as therapy for children with autism and other pervasive developmental disorders. *Journal of Music Therapy, 21*(3), 100–116.

Appell, M. J. (1980). Arts for the handicapped: A researchable item. *Journal of Music Therapy, 17*(2), 75–83.

Atterbury, B. W. (1984). Music teachers need your help. *Journal of Learning Disabilities, 17*(2), 75–77.

Atterbury, B. W. (1985). Musical differences in learning-disabled and normal-achieving readers, aged seven, eight, and nine. *Psychology of Music, 13*(2), 114–123.

Austen, M. P. (1977). The effects of music on the learning of random shapes and syllables with institutionalized severely mentally retarded adolescents. *Contributions to Music Education, 5,* 54–69.

Ayres, B. R. (1987). The effects of a music stimulus environment versus regular cafeteria environment during therapeutic feeding. *Journal of Music Therapy, 24*(1), 14–26.

Bailey, J. Z. (1976). *The relationships between the Colwell Music Achievement Tests I and II, the SRA Achievement Series, intelligence quotient, and success in instrumental music in the sixth grade of the public school of Prince William County, Virginia.* Unpublished doctoral dissertation, University of Illinois at Urbana-Champaign.

Baird, S. (1969). A technique to assess the preferences for intensity of musical stimuli in young hard-of-hearing children. *Journal of Music Therapy, 6*(1), 6–11.

Banik, S. N., & Mendelson, M. A. (1974). A comprehensive program for multiply handicapped, mentally retarded children. *Journal of Special Educators of the Mentally Retarded, 11*(1), 44–49.

Barber, E. (1973). Music therapy with retarded children. *Australian Journal of Mental Retardation, 2*(7), 210–213.

Beal, M. R., & Gilbert, J. P. (1982). Music curriculum for the handicapped. *Music Educators Journal, 68*(8), 52–55.

Beall, L. (1985). The making of a special Oliver! *Music Educators Journal, 71*(6), 30–32.

Beer, A. S., Bellows, N. L., & Frederick, A. M. D. (1982). Providing for different rates of music learning. *Music Educators Journal, 68*(8), 40–43.

Bellamy, T., & Sontag, E. (1973). Use of group contingent music to increase assembly line production rates of retarded students in a simulated sheltered workshop. *Journal of Music Therapy, 10*(3), 125–136.

Benigno, J. (1985). Settlement music school advances music for the handicapped. *Music Educators Journal, 71*(6), 22–25.

Bennis, J. (1969). The use of music as a therapy in the special education classroom. *Journal of Music Therapy, 6*, 15–18.

Berel, M., Diller, L., & Orgel, M. (1971). Music as a facilitator for visual motor sequencing tasks in children with cerebral palsy. *Developmental Medicine and Child Neurology, 13*, 335–342.

Bevans, J. (1969). The exceptional child and Orff. *Music Educators Journal, 55*(7), 41–43.

Bibliography of mainstreaming materials. (1982). *Music Educators Journal, 68*(8), 56–57.

Birkenshaw, L. (1965). Teaching music to deaf children. *The Volta Review, 67*(5), 352–358, 387.

Birkenshaw, L. (1975). Consider the lowly kazoo. *The Volta Review, 77*(7), 440–444.

Birkenshaw, L. (1982). *Music for fun, music for learning* (3rd ed.). St. Louis, MO: MMB Music.

Bitcon, C. (2000). *Alike and different: The clinical and educational use of Orff-Schulwerk* (2nd ed.). Gilsum, NH: Barcelona.

Bitcon, C., & Ball, T. (1974). Generalized imitation and Orff-Schulwerk. *Mental Retardation, 12*(34), 36–39.

Bixler, J. (1960). Operetta production with physically handicapped children. *Music therapy* (p. 101). Lawrence, KS: Allen Press.

Bixler, J. (1968). Musical aptitude in the educable mentally retarded child. *Journal of Music Therapy, 5*(2), 41–43.

Bios, L. (1974). Traditional nursery rhymes and games: Language learning for preschool blind children. *New Outlook for the Blind, 68*, 268–274.

Bokor, C. R. (1976). A comparison of musical and verbal responses of mentally retarded children. *Journal of Music Therapy, 13*(2), 101–108.

Bove, C. F., & Flugrath, J. M. (1973). Frequency components of noisemakers for use in pediatric audiological evaluations. *The Volta Review, 75*(9), 551–556.

Boxill, E. H. (1981). A continuum of awareness: Music therapy with the developmentally handicapped. *Music Therapy, 1*(1), 17–23.

Boxill, E. H. (1985). *Music therapy for the developmentally disabled*. Rockville, MD: Aspen Systems.

Braitwaite, M., & Sigafoos, J. (1998). Effects of social versus musical antecedents on communication responsiveness in five children with developmental disabilities. *Journal of Music Therapy, 35*(2), 88–104.

Breen, J., & Cratty, B. (1982). *Educational games for physically handicapped children*. Denver, CO: Love.

Brick, R. M. (1973). Eurythmics: One aspect of audition. *The Volta Review, 75*, 155–160.

Briller, S., & Morrison, B. (1971). Teaching rock and roll dancing to totally blind teenagers. *The New Outlook for the Blind, 65*(4), 129–131.

Brooks, B. H., Huck, A. M., & Jellison, J. A. (1984). Structuring small groups and music reinforcement to facilitate positive interactions and acceptance of severely handicapped students in the regular music classroom. *Journal of Research in Music Education, 32*(4), 243–264.

Brownell, M. D. (2002). Musically adapted social stories to modify behaviors in students with autism: Four case studies. *Journal of Music Therapy, 39*(20), 117–144.

Bruner, O. (1951). Music to aid the handicapped child. *Music Therapy*, 1–46.

Brunk, B. K., & Coleman, K. A. (2000). Development of a special education music therapy assessment process. *Music Therapy Perspectives, 18*(1), 59–68.

Buday, E. M. (1995). The effects of signed and spoken words taught with music on sign and speech imitation by children with autism. *Journal of Music Therapy, 32*(3), 189–202.

Cameron, R. (1970). The uses of music to enhance the education of the mentally retarded. *Mental Retardation, 8*, 32–34.

Campbell, D. (1972). One out of twenty: The LD. *Music Educators Journal, 58*(4), 38–39.

Campbell, D. (1992). *Introduction to the Musical Brain* (2nd ed.). St. Louis, MO: MMB Music.

Careers in Music. (1982). *Music Educators Journal, 69*(2). (Entire issue gives overview and information about possible careers in music, including music education and music therapy)

Cartwright, J., & Huckaby, G. (1972). Intensive preschool language program. *Journal of Music Therapy, 9*, 137.

Case, M. (1966). *Recreation for blind adults*. Springfield, IL: Charles C. Thomas.

Cassity, M. D. (1977). Nontraditional guitar techniques for the educable and trainable mentally retarded residents in music therapy activities. *Journal of Music Therapy, 14*(1), 39–42.

Cassity, M. D. (1978). Social development of TMRs involved in performing and nonperforming groups. *Journal of Music Therapy, 15*(2), 100–105.

Cassity, M. D. (1981). The influence of a socially valued skill on peer acceptance in a music therapy group. *Journal of Music Therapy, 18*(3), 148–154.

Chadwick, D. R. (1976). Speech disorders and music. *Instrumentalist, 31*(1), 28–30.

Chadwick, D. R., & Clark, C. A. (1980). Adapting music instruments for the physically handicapped. *Music Educators Journal, 67*(3), 56–59.

Chase, K. (2004). Music therapy assessment for children with developmental disabilities: A survey study. *Journal of Music Therapy, 41*(1), 28–54.

Clark, C., & Chadwick, D. (1980). *Clinically adapted instruments for the multiply handicapped: A sourcebook* (Rev. ed.). St. Louis, MO: MMB Music.

Clegg, J. O. (1982). *The effect of non-contingent and contingent music on work production rate of mentally retarded adults in a work activity center.* Unpublished master's thesis, The Florida State University, Tallahassee.

Cleland, C. C., & Swartz, J. D. (1970). The blind retardate-three program suggestions. *Training School Bulletin, 67*(3), 172–177.

Coates, P. (1987). "Is it functional?" A question for music therapists who work with the institutionalized mentally retarded. *Journal of Music Therapy, 24*(3), 170–175.

Codding, P. (1988). Music in the education/rehabilitation of visually disabled and multi-handicapped persons: A review of literature from 1946–1987. In C. E. Furman (Ed.), *Effectiveness of music therapy procedures: Documentation of research and clinical practice* (pp. 107–134). Washington, DC: National Association for Music Therapy.

Codding, P. A. (2000). Music therapy literature and clinical applications for blind and severely visually impaired persons: 1940–2000. In American Music Therapy Association (Ed.), *Effectiveness of music therapy procedures: Documentation of research and clinical practice* (3rd ed., pp. 159–198). Silver Spring, MD: American Music Therapy Association.

Cohen, G., Averbach, J., & Katz, E. (1978). Music therapy assessment of the developmentally disabled client. *Journal of Music Therapy, 15*(2), 88–99.

Cohen, G., & Gericke, L. (1972). Music therapy assessment: Requisite for determining patient objectives. *Journal of Music Therapy, 9*, 161–189.

Cohen, N. A. (1994). Speech and song: Implications for therapy. *Music Therapy Perspectives, 12*(1), 8–14.

Cole, F. (1965). *Music for children with special needs.* North Hollywood, CA: Bowar Records.

Coleman, J. L., et al. (1964). *Music for exceptional children.* Evanston, IL: Summy-Birchard.

Colwell, C. M. (1995). Adapting music instruction for elementary students with special needs: A pilot. *Music Therapy Perspectives, 13*(2), 97–103.

Colwell, C. M., & Murlless, K. D. (2002). Music activities (singing vs. chanting) as a vehicle of reading accuracy of children with learning disabilities: A pilot study. *Music Therapy Perspectives, 20*(1), 13–19.

Cook, M., & Freethy, M. (1973). The use of music as a positive reinforcer to eliminate complaining behavior. *Journal of Music Therapy, 10*(4), 213–216.

Cooke, R. M. (1969). The use of music in play therapy. *Journal of Music Therapy, 6*(3), 66–75.

Cortazzi, D. (1969). The bottom of the barrel. *Journal of Mental Subnormality, 15*(1), 3–10.

Cotter, V. W. (1971). Effects of music on performance of manual tasks with retarded adolescent females. *American Journal of Mental Deficiency, 78*(2), 242–248.

Cotter V. W., & Toombs, S. (1966). A procedure for determining the music preferences of mental retardates. *Journal of Music Therapy, 3*(2), 57–64.

Couch, K. (1984). *The effect of the art + reading, writing, arithmetic + music + science project (AR3-MS) on the acquisition of reading skills.* Unpublished master's thesis, The Florida State University, Tallahassee.

County School Board of Fairfax County. (1978). *Project Beacon: Perceptual motor activities handbook music supplement.* Fairfax, VA: County School Board.

Cratty, B. (1969). *Developmental games for physically handicapped children.* Palo Alto, CA: Peer Publications.

Cripe, F. F. (1986). Rock music as therapy for children with attention deficit disorder: An exploratory study. *Journal of Music Therapy, 23*(1), 30–37.

Crocker, D. B. (1956). Music therapy for the blind. *Music Therapy,* 175–196.

Danhauer, J. L., Johnson, C., & Asp, C. W. (1984). Hearing-impaired children's performance on the Edgerton and Danhauer nonsense syllable test. *The Journal of Auditory Research, 24,* 231–238.

Darrow, A. A. (1979). The beat reproduction response of subjects with normal and impaired hearing: An empirical comparison. *Journal of Music Therapy, 16*(2), 91–98.

Darrow, A. A. (1984). A comparison of rhythmic responsiveness in normal and hearing-impaired children and an investigation of the relationship of rhythmic responsiveness to the suprasegmental aspects of speech perception. *Journal of Music Therapy, 21*(2), 48–66.

Darrow, A. A. (1985). Music for the deaf. *Music Educators Journal, 71*(6), 33–35.

Darrow, A. A. (1987). An investigative study: The effect of hearing-impairment on musical aptitude. *Journal of Music Therapy, 24*(2), 88–96.

Darrow, A. A. (1989). Music therapy in the treatment of the hearing-impaired. *Music Therapy Perspectives, 6,* 61–70.

Darrow, A. A. (1990). The effect of frequency adjustment on the vocal reproduction accuracy of hearing impaired children. *Journal of Music Therapy, 27*(1), 24–37.

Darrow, A. A. (1991). An assessment and comparison of hearing impaired children's preference for timbre and musical instruments. *Journal of Music Therapy, 28*(l), 48–59.

Darrow, A. A. (1992). The effect of vibrotactile stimuli via the SOMATRON™ on the identification of pitch change by hearing impaired children. *Journal of Music Therapy, 29*(2), 103–112.

Darrow, A. A. (1999). Music educators' perceptions regarding the inclusion of students with severe disabilities in music classrooms. Jo*urnal of Music Therapy, 36*(4), 254–273.

Darrow, A. A., & Cohen, N. (1991). The effect of programmed pitch practice and private instruction on the vocal reproduction accuracy of children with hearing impairments: Two case studies. *Music Therapy Perspectives, 9*, 61–65.

Darrow, A. A., & Gfeller, K. (1988). Music therapy with hearing-impaired children. In C. E. Furman (Ed.), *Effectiveness of music therapy procedures: Documentation of research and clinical practice* (pp. 137–172). Washington, DC: National Association for Music Therapy.

Darrow, A. A., & Gfeller, K. (1991). A study of public school music programs mainstreaming hearing impaired students. *Journal of Music Therapy, 28*(1), 23–39.

Darrow, A. A., Gfeller, K. E., Gorsuch, A., & Thomas, T. (2000). Muisc therapy with children who are deaf and hard of hearing. In American Music Therapy Association (Ed.), *Effectiveness of music therapy procedures: Documentation of research and clinical practice* (3rd ed., pp. 135–158). Silver Spring, MD: American Music Therapy Association.

Darrow, A. A., & Goll, H. (1989). The effect of vibrotactile stimuli via the SOMATRON™ on the identification of rhythmic concepts by hearing impaired children. *Journal of Music Therapy, 26*(3), 115–124.

Darrow, A. A., & Stammer, G. J. (1986). The effect of vocal training on the intonation and rate of hearing impaired children's speech: A pilot study. *Journal of Music Therapy, 23*(4), 194–201.

Davis, R. K. (1990). A model for the integration of music therapy within a preschool classroom for children with physical disabilities or language delays. *Music Therapy Perspectives, 8*, 82–84.

Decuir, A. A. (1975). Vocal responses of mentally retarded subjects of four musical instruments. *Journal of Music Therapy, 12*(1), 40–43.

Denenholz, B. (1953). The use of music with mentally retarded children. In M. Bing (Ed.), *Annual book of proceedings NAMT, Inc., 1953* (p. 55). Lawrence, KS: Allen Press.

DePeters, J., Gordon, L., & Wertman, A. (1981). *The magic of music.* Buffalo, NY: Potentials Development.

Dervan, N. (1982). Building Orff ensemble skills with mentally handicapped adolescents. *Music Educators Journal, 68*(8), 35–36.

Deutsch, M., & Parks, A. (1978). The use of contingent music to increase appropriate conversational speech. *Mental Retardation, 16*(1), 33–36.

Diephouse, D. A. (1968). Music therapy in a child psychiatry clinic school. *American Music Teacher, 17*(3), 27–28, 39–40.

Dileo, C. L. (1975). The use of a token economy program with mentally retarded persons in a music therapy setting. *Journal of Music Therapy, 12*(3), 155–160.

Dileo, C. L. (1976). The relationship of diagnostic and social factors to the singing ranges of institutionalized mentally retarded persons. *Journal of Music Therapy, 13*(1), 16–28.

Dobbs, J. P. B. (1966). *The slow learner and music.* New York: Oxford University Press.

Dorow, L. G. (1975). Conditioning music and approval as new reinforcers for imitative behavior with the severely retarded. *Journal of Music Therapy, 12*(1), 30–39.

Dorow, L. G. (1976). Televised music lessons as educational reinforcement for correct mathematical responses with the educable mentally retarded. *Journal of Music Therapy, 13*(2), 77–86.

Dorow, L. G., & Horton, J. (1982). Effect of the proximity of auditory stimuli and sung versus spoken stimuli on activity levels of severely/profoundly mentally retarded females. *Journal of Music Therapy, 19*(2), 114–124.

Douglass, D. (1985). *Accent on rhythm: Music activities for the aged* (3rd ed.). St. Louis, MO: MMB Music.

Dryer, J., & Dix, J. (1968). Reaching the blind child through music therapy. *Journal of Emotional Education, 8*(4), 202–211.

Dunton, M. J. (1969). Handicapped children respond to music therapy. *International Musician, 8*(4), 2.

Dykman, R. A. (1979). In step with PL 94-142. *Music Educators Journal, 65*(5), 58–63.

Eagle, C. T., & Lathom, W. (1982). Music for the severely handicapped. *Music Educators Journal, 68*(8), 30–31.

Eddy, G. (1972). No fingers to play a horn. *Music Educators Journal, 58*(4), 61–62.

Edenfield, T. N., & Hughes, J. E. (1991). The relationship of a choral music curriculum to the development of singing ability in secondary students with Down syndrome. *Music Therapy Perspectives, 9,* 52–55.

Edgerton, C. L. (1994). The effect of improvised music therapy on the communicative behaviors of autistic children. *Journal of Music Therapy, 31*(1), 31–62.

Edwards, E. M. (1974). *Music education for the deaf.* South Waterford, ME: Merriam-Eddy.

Eidson, C. E., Jr. (1989). The effect of behavioral music therapy on the generalization of interpersonal skills from sessions to the classroom by emotionally handicapped middle school students. *Journal of Music Therapy, 26*(4), 206–221.

Eisenstein, S. R. (1974). Effect of contingent guitar lessons on reading behavior. *Journal of Music Therapy, 11,* 138–146.

Eisenstein, S. R. (1976). A successive approximation procedure for learning music symbol names. *Journal of Music Therapy, 13*(4), 173–179.

Fahey, J., & Birkenshaw, L. (1972). Bypassing the ear: The perception of music by feeling and touch. *Music Educators Journal, 58*(4), 44–49, 127–128.

Falb, M. E. (1982). *The use of operant procedures to condition vasoconstriction in profoundly mentally retarded (PMR) infants.* Unpublished master's thesis, The Florida State University, Tallahassee.

Feierabend, J., Saunders, T., Holahan, J., & Getnick, P. (1998). Song recognition among preschool-age children: An investigation of words and music. *Journal of Research in Music Education, 46*(3), 351–359.

Feil, N. (1982). *Validation/fantasy/therapy.* Cleveland, OH: Edward Feil.

Fellendorf, G. (1969). The verbotonal method. *The Volta Review, 71,* 213–224.

Fisher, G. L. (1980). *The effect of instrumental music instruction on fine motor coordination and other variables of mentally retarded adolescents.* Unpublished master's thesis, The Florida State University, Tallahassee.

Flodmark, A. (1986). Augmented auditory feedback as an aid in gait training of the cerebral-palsied child. *Developmental Medicine & Child Neurology, 28,* 147–155.

Flowers, S. E. (1984). Musical sound perception in normal children and children with Down's syndrome. *Journal of Music Therapy, 21*(3), 146–154.

Folio, M. R. (1986). *Physical education programming for exceptional learners.* Gaithersburg, MD: Aspen Systems.

Force, B. (1983). The effects of mainstreaming on the learning of nonretarded children in an elementary music classroom. *Journal of Music Therapy, 20*(1), 2–13.

Ford, S. C. (1984). Music therapy for cerebral palsied children. *Music Therapy Perspectives, 1*(3), 8–13.

Ford, T. A. (1988). The effect of musical experiences and age on the ability of deaf children to discriminate pitch. *Journal of Music Therapy, 25*(1), 2–16.

Forsythe, J. L., & Jellison, J. A. (1977). It's the law. *Music Educators Journal, 65*(3), 30–35.

Foster, B. (1979). *Training songs for special people.* Boulder, CO: Myklas Music Press.

Frances, R., Thermitte, F. S., & Verdy, M. F. (1973). Music deficiency among aphasics. *International Review of Applied Psychology, 22*(2), 117–136.

Furman, C., & Furman, A. (1988). Music therapy research with mental retardation. In C. E. Furman (Ed.), *Effectiveness of music therapy procedures: Documentation of research and clinical practice* (pp. 285–299). Washington, DC: National Association for Music Therapy.

Furman, C., & Steele, A. (1982). Teaching the special student: A survey of independent music teachers with implications for music therapists. *Journal of Music Therapy, 19*(2), 66–73.

Gallagher, P. (1982). *Educational games for visually handicapped children.* Denver, CO: Love.

Galloway, H. F. (1974). Stuttering and the myth of therapeutic singing. *Journal of Music Therapy, 11*(4), 202.

Galloway, H. F. (1975). A comprehensive bibliography of music referential to communicative development, processing, disorders, and remediation. *Journal of Music Therapy, 12,* 164–196.

Galloway, H. F., & Bean, M. F. (1974). Effects of action songs on the development of body image and body part identification in hearing-impaired preschool children. *Journal of Music Therapy, 11*(3), 125–134.

Galloway, H. F., & Berry, A. (1981). A survey of communicative disorders in college vocal performance and pedagogy majors. *Journal of Music Therapy, 18*(1), 25–40.

Gardiner, B. L. (1984). *Improving the peer acceptance of educable mentally handicapped students in a mainstreamed setting: Aerobics music therapy program in a physical education class.* Unpublished master's thesis, The Florida State University, Tallassee.

Gardiner, E. C. (1978). *The effect of music on retention in a paired-associate task with EMR children.* Unpublished master's thesis, The Florida State University, Tallahassee.

Gaston, E. T. (Ed.). (1968). *Music in therapy.* New York: Macmillan.

Gfeller, K. (1983). Music mnemonics as an aid to retention with normal and learning-disabled students. *Journal of Music Therapy, 20*(4), 179–189.

Gfeller, K. (1984). Prominent theories in learning disabilities and implications for music therapy methodology. *Music Therapy Perspectives, 2*(1), 9–13.

Gfeller, K. (1987). Songwriting as a tool for reading and language remediation. *Music Therapy, 6*(2), 28–38.

Gfeller, K. (1990). A cognitive-linguistic approach to language development for the preschool child with hearing impairments for music therapy practice. *Music Therapy Perspectives, 8,* 47–51.

Gfeller, K. (2000). Accommodating children who use cochlear implants in music therapy or educational setting. *Music Therapy Perspectives, 18*(2), 122–130.

Gfeller, K, & Baumann, A. A. (1988). Assessment procedures for music therapy with hearing impaired children: Language development. *Journal of Music Therapy, 25*(4), 192–205.

Ghetti, C. M. (2002). Comparison of the effectiveness of three music therapy conditions to modulate behavior states in students with profound disabilities: A pilot study. *Music Therapy Perspectives, 20*(1), 20–30.

Giacobbe, G. A. (1972). Rhythm builds order in brain-damaged children. *Music Educators Journal, 58*(4), 40–43.

Giacobbe, G. A., & Graham, R. M. (1978). The response of aggressive emotionally disturbed and normal boys to selected musical stimuli. *Journal of Music Therapy, 15*(3), 118–135.

Gibbons, A. C. (1983). Rhythm responses in emotionally disturbed children with differing needs for external structure. *Music Therapy, 3*(1), 94–102.

Gilbert, J., Gampel, D., & Budoff, M. (1975). Classroom behavior of retarded children before and after integration into regular classes. *Journal of Special Education, 9*, 307–315.

Gilbert, J. P. (1977). Mainstreaming in your classroom: What to expect. *Music Educators Journal, 63*(6), 64–68.

Gilbert, J. P. (1983). A comparison of the motor music skills of nonhandicapped and learning-disabled children. *Journal of Research in Music Education, 31*(2), 147–155.

Gilliland, E. (1957). Prescriptions set to music: Musical instruments in orthopedic therapy. *Exceptional Children, 18*, 68.

Giovanni, S. (1959). Music as an aid in teaching the deaf. *Music Therapy Proceedings, NAMT*, 88–90.

Goldstein, C. (1964). Music and creative arts therapy for an autistic child. *Journal of Music Therapy, 1*(4), 135–138.

Gollnitz, G. (1975). Fundamentals of rhythmic-psychomotor music therapy. *Acta Paedopsychiatrica, 41*(4–5), 130–134.

Goodenough, F., & Goodenough, D. (1970). The importance of music in the life of a visually handicapped child. *Education of Visually Handicapped, 2*(1), 28–32.

Goodnow, C. C. (1968). The use of dance in therapy with retarded children. *Journal of Music Therapy, 5*(4), 98–102.

Goolsby, T. M., Frary, R. B., & Rogers, M. M. (1974). Observational techniques in determination of the effects of background music upon verbalizations of disadvantaged kindergarten children. *Journal of Music Therapy, 11*(1), 21–32.

Gordon, E. (1965). *Music aptitude profile.* Boston: Houghton Mifflin.

Gordon, E. (1968). The use of the musical aptitude profile with exceptional children. *Journal of Music Therapy, 5*(2), 38–40.

Graham, R. M. (1972). Seven million plus need special attention. Who are they? *Music Educators Journal, 58*(4), 22–25, 134.

Graham, R. M. (Ed.). (1975). *Music for the exceptional child.* Reston, VA: Music Educators National Conference.

Graham, R. M., & Beer, A. (1980). *Teaching music to the exceptional child.* Englewood Cliffs, NJ: Prentice-Hall.

Grant, R. E. (1989). Music therapy guidelines for developmentally disabled children. *Music Therapy Perspectives, 6*, 18–22.

Grant, R. E., & LeCroy, S. (1986). Effects of sensory mode input on the performance of rhythmic perception tasks by mentally retarded subjects. *Journal of Music Therapy, 23*(1), 2–9.

Grant, R. E., & Share, M. R. (1985). Relationship of pitch discrimination skills and vocal ranges of mentally retarded subjects. *Journal of Music Therapy, 22*(2), 99–103.

Grayson, J. (1972). A playground of musical sculpture. *Music Educators Journal, 58*(4), 51–54.

Greaves, E. R., & Anderson, L. P. (1981). *101 activities for exceptional children.* Palo Alto, CA: Peek.

Greene, B. (1974). Opening locked doors with music. *Children's House, 7*(4), 6–10.

Greenwald, M. A. (1978). The effectiveness of distorted music versus interrupted music to decrease self-stimulatory behaviors in profoundly retarded adolescents. *Journal of Music Therapy, 15*(2), 58–66.

Greer, R. D., Randall, A., & Timberlake, C. (1971). The discriminate use of music listening as a contingency for improvement in vocal pitch acuity and attending behavior. *Council for Research in Music Education Bulletin, 26*, 10–18.

Gregoire, M. A. (1984). Music as a prior condition to task performance. *Journal of Music Therapy, 21*(3), 133–145.

Griffin, J. E. (1966). Administration of a music therapy department in an institution for the mentally retarded with suggested activities. *Journal of Music Therapy, 3*(3), 99–105.

Griggs-Drane, E. R., & Wheeler, J. J. (1997). The use of functional assessment procedures and individualized schedule in the treatment of autism: Recommendations for music therapists. *Music Therapy Perspectives, 15*(2), 87–93.

Grossman, S. (1978). An investigation of Crocker's music projective techniques for emotionally disturbed children. *Journal of Music Therapy, 15*(4), 179–184.

Guenzler, S. L. (1980). *Observation of interpersonal relationships between handicapped and normal children and their teacher in music.* Unpublished master's thesis, The Florida State University, Tallahassee.

Gunsberg, A. (1988). Improvised musical play: A strategy for fostering social play between developmentally delayed and nondelayed preschool children. *Journal of Music Therapy, 25*(4), 178–191.

Gunsberg, A. (1991). A method for conducting improvised musical play with children both with and without developmental delays in preschool classrooms. *Music Therapy Perspectives, 9*, 46–51.

Hadsell, N. A., & Coleman, K. A. (1988). Rett syndrome: A challenge for music therapists. *Music Therapy Perspectives, 5*, 52–56.

Haines, J. H. (1989). The effects of music therapy on the self esteem of emotionally disturbed adolescents. *Music Therapy, 8*(1), 78–91.

Hair, H. I. (1983). A comparison of verbal descriptions used by TMR students and music therapists. *Journal of Music Therapy, 20*(2), 59–68.

Hairston, M. J. (1990). Analyses of responses of mentally retarded autistic and mentally retarded nonautistic children to art and music therapy. *Journal of Music Therapy, 27*(3), 137–150.

Hall, J. C. (1952). The effect of background music on the reading comprehension of 278 eighth and ninth grade students. *Journal of Educational Research, 45,* 451–458.

Halliday, G. W., & Evans, J. H. (1974). Somatosensory enrichment of a deaf, blind, retarded adolescent through vibration. *Perceptual and Motor Skills, 38,* 880.

Hanser, S. B. (1974). Group-contingent music listening with emotionally disturbed boys. *Journal of Music Therapy, 11*(4), 220–225.

Harbert, W. (1974). *Opening doors through music.* Springfield, IL: Charles C. Thomas.

Hardesty, K. W. (1979). *Music for special education.* Morristown, NJ: Silver Burdett.

Harding, C., & Ballard, K. (1982). The effectiveness of music as a stimulus and as a contingent reward in promoting the spontaneous speech of three physically handicapped preschoolers. *Journal of Music Therapy, 19*(2), 88–101.

Haring, N., & Bricker, D. (1978). *Teaching the severely handicapped.* Seattle, WA: American Association for the Education of the Severely/Profoundly Handicapped.

Harris, P. (1982). *Learning, poco-a-poco.* Hanford, CA: Learning, Poco-a-Poco.

Harrison, W., Lacrone, H., Temerlin, M. K., & Trousdale, W. W. (1966). The effect of music and exercise upon the self-help skills of non-verbal retardates. *American Journal of Mental Deficiencies, 71,* 279–282.

Hastings, P., & Hayes, B. (1981). *Encouraging language development.* London, UK: Groom Helm.

Hauck, L. P., & Martin, P. L. (1970). Music as a reinforcer in patient-controlled duration of time-out. *Journal of Music Therapy, 7*(2), 43–53.

Henderson, L. M. (1977). *A music therapy assessment for the mentally retarded: Field testing the instrument.* Unpublished master's thesis, The Florida State University, Tallahassee.

Henderson, S. M. (1983). Effects of a music therapy program upon awareness of mood in music, group cohesion, and self-esteem among hospitalized adolescent patients. *Journal of Music Therapy, 20*(1), 14–20.

Henson, F. O., Parks, A. L., & Cotter, V. (1977). A technique for analyzing rhythmic drum responses. *Behavioral Engineering, 4,* 29–32.

Herlein, D. (1975). Music reading of the sightless-Braille notation. *Music Educators Journal, 62*(1), 42–45.

Herman, F. (1985). Music therapy for the young child with cerebral palsy who uses blissymbols. *Journal of Music Therapy, 5*(1), 28–36.

Herron, C. J. (1970). Some effects of instrumental music training on cerebral-palsied children. *Journal of Music Therapy, 7,* 55–58.

Hoelzley, P. D. (1991). Reciprocal inhibition in music therapy: A case study involving wind instrument usage to attenuate fear, anxiety, and avoidance reactivity in a child with pervasive developmental disorders. *Music Therapy, 10*(1), 58–76.

Hoem, J. C. (1972). Don't dump the students who "can't do." *Music Educators Journal, 58*(4), 29–30.

Hollander, F. M., & Juhrs, P. D. (1974). Orff-Schulwerk, an effective treatment tool with autistic children. *Journal of Music Therapy, 11*(1), 1–12.

Holloway, M. S. (1980). A comparison of passive and active music reinforcement to increase preacademic and motor skills in severely retarded children and adolescents. *Journal of Music Therapy, 17*(2), 58–69.

Hoper, C. J., Kutzleb, U., Stobbe, A., & Weber, B. (1975). *Awareness games: Personal growth through group interaction.* New York: St. Martin's Press.

Hoshizaki, M. K. (1983). *Teaching mentally retarded children through music.* Springfield, IL: Charles, C. Thomas.

Hoskins, C. (1988). Use of music to increase verbal response and improve expressive language abilities of preschool language delayed children. *Journal of Music Therapy, 25*(2), 73–84.

Houchins, R. (1971). Pitch discrimination in learning-impaired children. *The Volta Review, 64*, 424.

Howell, R. D., Flowers, P. J., & Wheeler, J. E. (1995). The effects of keyboard experiences on rhythmic responses of elementary school children with physical disabilities. *Journal of Music Therapy, 32*(2), 91–112.

Hughes, J. E., Robbins, B. J., & King, R. J. (1988). A survey of perception and attitudes of exceptional student educators toward music therapy services in a county-wide school district. *Journal of Music Therapy, 25*(4), 216–222.

Hughes, J. E., Robbins, B. J., McKenzie, B. A., & Robb, S. S. (1990). Integrating exceptional and nonexceptional young children through music play: A pilot program. *Music Therapy Perspectives, 8*, 52–56.

Hummel, C. J. M. (1971). The value of music in teaching deaf students. *The Volta Review, 73*(4), 224–228.

Humpal, M. (1991). The effects of an integrated early childhood music program on social interaction among children with handicaps and their typical peers. *Journal of Music Therapy, 28*(3), 161–177.

Humpal, M. (1998). Song repertoire of young children. *Music Therapy Perspectives, 16*(1), 37–39.

Humpal, M., & Colwell, C. (Eds.). (2006). *Effective clinical practice in music therapy early childhood and school age educational settings* (AMTA Monograph Series). Silver Spring, MD: American Music Therapy Association.

Humphrey, T. (1980). The effect of music ear training upon the auditory-discrimination abilities of trainable mentally retarded adolescents. *Journal of Music Therapy, 17*(2), 70–74.

Hurwitz, I., Wolff, P., Bortnick, B., & Kokas, K. (1975). Nonmusical effects of the Kodaly music curriculum in primary grade children. *Journal of Learning Disabilities, 8*(3), 167–174.

Implementation of Part B of the Education of the Handicapped Act. (1977, August 23). *Federal Register*, 42474–42518.

Irwin, C. E. (1971). *The use of music in a speech and language development program with mentally retarded children with emphasis on the Down's syndrome child.* Unpublished master's thesis, The Florida State University, Tallahassee.

Isern, B. (1961). Summary, conclusion, and implications: The influence of music upon the memory of mentally retarded children. In E. H. Schneider (Ed.), *Annual book of proceedings NAMT, 1960.* Lawrence, KS: The Allen Press.

Isern, B. (1964). Music in special education. *Journal of Music Therapy, 1*(4), 139–142.

Jackson, N. (2003). A survey of music therapy methods and their role in the treatment of early elementary school children with ADHD. *Journal of Music Therapy, 40*(4), 302–323.

James, M., Weaver, A., Clemens, P., & Plaster, G. (1985). Influence of paired auditory and vestibular stimulation on levels of motor skill development in a mentally retarded population. *Journal of Music Therapy, 22*(1), 22–34.

James, M. R. (1986). Neurophysical treatment of cerebral palsy: A case study. *Music Therapy Perspectives, 3*, 5–8.

Janiak, W. (1978). *Songs for music therapy.* Long Branch, NJ: Kimbo Educational.

Jellison, J. A. (1977). Music instructional programs for the severely handicapped. In E. Sontag (Ed.), *Educational programming for the severely/profoundly handicapped.* Reston, VA: The Council for Exceptional Children.

Jellison, J. A. (1979). The music therapist in the educational setting: Developing and implementing curriculum for the handicapped. *Journal of Music Therapy, 16*(3), 128–137.

Jellison, J. A. (1984). Structuring small groups and music reinforcement to facilitate positive interactions and acceptance of severely handicapped students in the regular music classroom. *Journal of Research in Music Education, 32*(4), 243–364.

Jellison, J. A. (1988). A content analysis of music research with handicapped children (1975–1986): Application in special education. In C. E. Furman (Ed.), *Effectiveness of music therapy procedures: Documentation of research and clinical practice* (pp. 223–281). Washington, DC: National Association for Music Therapy.

Jellison, J. A. (2000). A content analysis of music research with disabled children and youth (1975–1999): Applications in special education. In American Music Therapy Association (Ed.), *Effectiveness of music therapy procedures: Documentation of research and clinical practice* (3rd ed., pp. 199–264). Silver Spring, MD: American Music Therapy Association.

Jellison, J. A., & Duke, R. A. (1994). The mental retardation label: Music teachers' and perspective teachers' expectations of children's social and music behaviors. *Journal of Music Therapy, 31*(3), 166–185.

Jellison, J. A., & Gainer, E. W. (1995). Into the mainstream: A case-study of a child's participation in music education and music therapy. *Journal of Music Therapy, 32*(4), 228–247.

Johnson, J. M., & Zinner, C. C. (1974). Stimulus fading and schedule learning in generalizing and maintaining behaviors. *Journal of Music Therapy, 11*(2), 84–96.

Jones, L. L., & Cardinal, D. N. (1998). A descriptive analysis of music therapists' perceptions of delivering of services in inclusive settings: A challenge to the field. *Journal of Music Therapy, 35*(1), 34–48.

Jones, M. E. (1982). *A comparison of play therapy versus play/music therapy with three emotionally disturbed children.* Unpublished master's thesis, The Florida State University, Tallahassee.

Jones, R. E. (1986). Assessing developmental levels of mentally retarded students with the musical-perception assessment of cognitive development. *Journal of Music Therapy, 23*(3), 166–173.

Jorgenson, H. (1971). Effects of contingent preferred music in reducing two stereotyped behaviors of a profoundly retarded child. *Journal of Music Therapy, 8*(4), 139–145.

Jorgenson, H. (1974). The use of a contingent music activity to modify behaviors which interfere with learning. *Journal of Music Therapy, 11*(1), 41–46.

Jorgenson, H., & Parnell, M. K. (1970). Modifying social behaviors of mentally retarded children in music activities. *Journal of Music Therapy, 7*(3), 83–87.

Josepha, M. (1964). Therapeutic values of instrumental performance for severely handicapped children. *Journal of Music Therapy, 1*(3), 73–79.

Josepha, M. (1969). Music therapy with certain physically handicapped children. In E. H. Schneider (Ed.), *Music therapy* (p. 90). Lawrence, KS: Allen Press.

Kaplan, M. (1955). Music therapy in the speech program. *Exceptional Children, 20*, 112.

Kaplan, R. S., & Steele, A. L. (2005). An analysis of music therapy program goals and outcomes for clients with diagnoses on the autism spectrum. *Journal of Music Therapy, 42*(1), 2–19.

Kaslow, F. W. (1974). Movement, music, and art therapy techniques adapted for special education. In R. Hyatt & N. Rolnick (Eds.), *Teaching the mentally handicapped child.* New York: Behavior.

Kaufman, F. M., & Sheckart, G. R. (1985). The effects of tempo variation and white noise on the general activity level of profoundly retarded adults. *Journal of Music Therapy, 22*(4), 207–217.

Keith, R. W. (1981). *Central auditory and language disorders in children*. San Diego, CA: College-Hill Press.

Kennedy, R. (2000). *Bach to rock* (13th ed.). New Orleans, LA: Rosemary Corp.

Kennedy, R. (2005). A pilot study: The effects of music therapy interventions on middle school students' ESL skills. *Journal of Music Therapy, 42*(4), 244–261.

Kern, P., & Aldridge, D. (2006). Using embedded music therapy interventions to support outdoor play of young children with autism in an inclusive community-based child care program. *Journal of Music Therapy, 43*(4), 270–294.

Kern, P., & Wolery, M. (2001). Participation of a preschooler with visual impairments in the playground: Effects of music adaptations and staff development. *Journal of Music Therapy, 38*(2), 149–164.

Kerr, N., Myerson, L., & Michael, J. (1965). A procedure for shaping vocalizations in a mute child. In L. P. Ullman & L. Krasner (Eds.), *Case studies in behavior modification* (pp. 366–370). New York: Holt, Rinehard, & Winston.

Kessler, J. (1967). Therapeutic methods for exceptional children. *Journal of Music Therapy, 4*(1), 1–2.

Kivland, M. J. (1986). The use of music to increase self-esteem in a conduct-disordered adolescent. *Journal of Music Therapy, 23*(1), 25–29.

Klinger, H., & Peter, D. (1963). Techniques in group singing for aphasics. In E. H. Schneider (Ed.), *Music therapy* (pp. 108–112). Lawrence, KS: Allen Press.

Knolle, L. (1973). Sioux City's special brass band: An instrumental program for the mentally retarded. *Music Educators Journal, 60*(2), 47–48.

Korduba, O. (1975). Duplicated rhythmic patterns between deaf and normal-hearing children. *Journal of Music Therapy, 12(*3), 136–146.

Kostka, M. J. (1993). A comparison of selected behaviors of a student with autism in a special education and regular music classes. *Music Therapy Perspectives, 11*(6), 57–60.

Kral, C. (1972). Musical instruments for upper-limb amputees. *Inter-Clinic Information Bulletin, 12*(3), 13–26.

Kramer, S. A. (1978). The effects of music as a cue in maintaining handwashing in preschool children. *Journal of Music Therapy, 15*(3), 136–144.

Kratz, L. E. (1973). *Movement without sight*. Palo Alto, CA: Peek.

Krauss, T., & Galloway, H. (1982). Melodic intonation therapy with language delayed apraxic children. *Journal of Music Therapy, 19*(2), 102–113.

Krout, R. E. (1983). *Teaching basic guitar skills to special learners*. St. Louis, MO: MMB Music.

Krout, R. E. (1986). Use of a group token contingency with school-aged special education students to improve a music listening skill. *Music Therapy Perspectives, 3*, 13–16.

Krout, R. (1987). Evaluating software for music therapy applications. *Journal of Music Therapy, 24*(4), 213–223.

Krout, R. (1987). Music therapy with multi-handicapped students: Individualizing treatment within two group settings. *Journal of Music Therapy, 24*(1), 2–13.

Krout, R., Burnham, A., & Moorman, S. (1993). Computer and electronic music applications with students in special education: From program proposal to progress evaluation. *Music Therapy Perspectives, 11*(1), 28–31.

Krout, R. E., & Mason, M. (1988). Using computer and electronic music resources in clinical music therapy with behaviorally disordered students, 12 to 18 years old. *Music Therapy Perspectives, 5*, 114–118.

Kuper, E. C. (1972). Speech training through musical ear-training for pitch deficient children having articulatory defects. *Journal of Auditory Research, 12*(2), 168–172.

Laffley, N. A. (1984). *Music therapy intervention in the deinstitutionalization and community integration of the mentally retarded.* Unpublished master's thesis, The Florida State University, Tallahassee.

LaFon, D. (1989). Music therapy with developmentally disabled: Will we continue to be unique? *Music Therapy Perspectives, 6*, 23–25.

Lam, R. C., & Wang, C. (1982). Integrating blind and sighted through music. *Music Educators Journal, 68*(8), 44–45.

Larson, B. A. (1977). A comparison of singing ranges of mentally retarded and normal children with published songbooks used in singing activities. *Journal of Music Therapy, 14*(3), 139–143.

Larson, B. A. (1978). Use of the motorvator in improving gross-motor coordination, visual perception and IQ scores: A pilot study. *Journal of Music Therapy, 15*(3), 145–149.

Larson, B. A. (1981). Auditory and visual rhythmic pattern recognition by emotionally disturbed and normal adolescents. *Journal of Music Therapy, 18*(3), 128–136.

Lathom, W. (1963). The effect of certain action songs on body concept. In E. H. Schneider (Ed.), *Annual book of proceedings NAMT, 1962* (pp. 115–121). Lawrence, KS: The Allen Press.

Lathom, W. (1964). Music therapy as a means of changing the adaptive behavior level of retarded children. *Journal of Music Therapy, 1*(4), 132.

Lathom, W. (1974). Application of Kodaly concepts in music therapy. *Journal of Music Therapy, 11*, 13–20.

Lathom, W. (1982). Report on the Office of Special Education Grant, Special Project: A national in-service training model for educational personnel providing music education/therapy for severely/profoundly handicapped children. *Music Therapy Perspectives, 1*(1), 27–29.

Lathom, W. B., & Eagle C. T. (Eds.). (1984–1985). *Music therapy for handicapped children* (Vols. 1–3). St. Louis, MO: MMB Music.

Lathom, W. B., Edson, S., & Toombs, M. R. (1965). A coordinated speech therapy and music therapy program. *Journal of Music Therapy, 2*(4), 118–120.

Layman, D. L., Hussey, D. L., & Laing, S. J. (2002). Music therapy assessment for severely emotionally disturbed children: A pilot study. *Journal of Music Therapy, 40*(3), 164–187.

Lehr, J. K. (1982). Teaching training programs for exceptional classes. *Music Educators Journal, 68*(8), 46–48.

Lehr, J. K. (1983). Investigation of music in the education of mentally and physically handicapped children in the United Kingdom with particular reference to the course of Music for Slow Learners at Dartington College of Arts. *Contributions to Music Education, 9,* 60–69.

Leland, H. (1964). Adaptive behavior as related to the treatment of the mentally retarded. *Journal of Music Therapy, 1*(4), 129–131.

Levin, H. D., & Levin, G. M. (1972). Instrumental music: A great ally in promoting self image. *Music Educators Journal, 58*(4), 31–34.

Levin, H. D., & Levin, G. M. (1977). *Garden of bellflowers.* Bryn Mawr, PA: Theodore Presser.

Levin, H. D., & Levin, G. M. (1981). *Learning songs.* Bryn Mawr, PA: Theodore Presser.

Levin, H. D., & Levin, G. M. (1998). *Learning through music* (2nd ed.). Gilsum, NH: Barcelona.

Levine, S. J. (1968). *A recorded aid for Braille music. Paper No. 3, The Prospectus Series.* Michigan State University, East Lansing. Regional Instructional Materials Center for Handicapped Children and Youth. Washington, DC: Bureau of Education for the Handicapped.

Levine, S. J. (1968). The recorded aid for Braille music. *Journal of Music Therapy, 5*(1), 1–2.

Levinson, S., & Bruscia, K. (1985, October). Putting blind students in touch with music. *Music Educators Journal,* 49.

Lewis, M. F. (1974). A handbell choir for blind students. *The New Outlook for the Blind, 68*(7), 297–299.

Liebman, J., & Liebman, A. (1973). On stage, everybody. *Music Educators Journal, 60*(2), 45–46.

Liehmohn, W. (1976). Rhythm and motor ability in developmentally disabled boys. *American Corrective Therapy Journal, 30,* 12–14.

Lienhard, M. E. (1976). Factors relevant to the rhythmic perception of a group of mentally retarded children. *Journal of Music Therapy, 13*(2), 58–65.

Lipman, M. H. (1972). Blinded at 63, I can still learn. *Music Educators Journal, 58*(8), 60.

Loeb, R., & Sarigiani, P. (1986, February–March). The impact of hearing impairment on self-perceptions of children. *The Volta Review,* 89–99.

Luce, D. (2004). Music learning theory and audiation: Implications for music therapy clinical practice. *Music Therapy Perspectives, 22*(1), 26–33.

Lunt, I. (1973). Rhythm and the slow learner. *Special Education, 62*(4), 21–23.

Madsen, C. K. (1981). *Music therapy: A behavioral guide for the mentally retarded.* Lawrence, KS: National Association for Music Therapy.

Madsen, C. K., & Alley, J. M. (1979). The effect of reinforcement on attentiveness: A comparison of behaviorally trained music therapists and other professionals with implications for competency-based academic preparation. *Journal of Music Therapy, 16*(2), 70–82.

Madsen, C. K., Cotter, V. W., & Madsen, C. H., Jr. (1968). A behavioral approach to music therapy. *Journal of Music Therapy, 5*(3), 69–71.

Madsen, C. K., & Darrow, A. A. (1989). The relationship between music aptitude and sound conceptualization of the visually impaired. *Journal of Music Therapy, 26*(2), 71–78.

Madsen, C. K., Dorow, L. G., Moore, R. S., & Womble, J. U. (1976). The effect of music via television as reinforcement for correct mathematics. *Journal of Research in Music Education, 24*(2), 51–59.

Madsen, C. K., & Forsythe, J. L. (1975). Effect of contingent music listening on increases of mathematical responses. In C. K. Madsen, R. D. Greer, & C. H. Madsen, Jr. (Eds.), *Research in music behavior in the classroom.* New York: Columbia University, Teachers College Press.

Madsen, C. K., & Geringer, J. M. (1976). Choice of televised music lessons versus free play in relationship to academic improvement. *Journal of Music Therapy, 13*(4), 154–162.

Madsen, C. K., & Kuhn, T. L. (1978). *Contemporary music education.* Arlington Heights, IL: AHM.

Madsen, C. K., & Madsen, C. H., Jr. (1968). Music as a behavior modification technique with a juvenile delinquent. *Journal of Music Therapy, 5,* 72–76.

Madsen, C. K., & Madsen, C. H., Jr. (1980). *Teaching/discipline: A positive approach for educational development* (3rd ed.). Boston: Allyn & Bacon.

Madsen, C. K., Madsen, C. H., Jr., & Greer, R. D. (Eds.). (1975). *Research in music behavior in the classroom.* New York: Columbia University, Teachers College Press.

Madsen, C. K., Madsen, C. H., Jr., & Michel, D. (1975)..The use of music stimuli in teaching language discrimination. In C. K. Madsen, R. D. Greer, & C. H. Madsen, Jr. (Eds.), *Research in music behavior in the classroom.* New York: Columbia University, Teachers College Press.

Madsen, C. K., Moore, R. S., Wagner, M. J., & Yarbrough, C. A. (1975). Comparison of music as reinforcement for correct mathematical responses versus music as reinforcement for attentiveness. *Journal of Music Therapy, 12,* 84–95.

Madsen, C. K., Smith, D. S., & Feeman, C. C., Jr. (1988). The use of music in cross-age tutoring within special education settings. *Journal of Music Therapy, 25*(3), 135–144.

Mahlberg, M. (1973). Music therapy in the treatment of an autistic child. *Journal of Music Therapy, 10*(4), 189–193.

Maranto, C. D., Decuir, A., & Humphrey, T. (1984). A comparison of digit span scores, rhythm span scores, and diagnostic factors or mentally retarded persons. *Music Therapy, 4*(1), 84–90.

Marsh, J., & Fitch, J. (1970). The effect of singing on the speech articulation of Negro disadvantaged children. *Journal of Music Therapy, 7*(3), 88–94.

Matteson, C. A. (1972). Finding the self in space: More than one handicap doesn't make less than one child. *Music Educators Journal, 58*(4), 63–65, 135.

McCann, B. J. (1985). Assume every child will succeed. *Music Educators Journal,, 71*(6), 18–21.

McCarthy, H. (1973). Use of the Draw-a-Person test to evaluate a dance therapy program. *Journal of Music Therapy, 10*(3), 141–155.

McCarty, B. C., McElfresh, C. T., Rice, S. V., & Wilson, S. J. (1978). The effect of contingent background music on inappropriate bus behavior. *Journal of Music Therapy, 15*(3), 150–156.

McClelland, E. (1970). Music for the trainable mentally retarded. *Deficiente Mentale: Mental Retardation, 20*(1), 18–20.

McCollom, M. A. (1969). Piano-tuning: A new look at an old skill. *The New Outlook for the Blind, 63*(8), 152.

McCoy, M. (1982). In the mainstream: Selected music activities. *Music Educators Journal, 68*(8), 51.

McRae, S. W. (1982). The Orff connection . . . Reaching the special child. *Music Educators Journal, 68*(8), 32–34.

Merle-Fishman, C. R., & Marcus, M. L. (1982). Musical behaviors and preferences in emotionally disturbed and normal children: An exploratory study. *Music Therapy, 2*(1), 1–11.

Merrill, T. (1976). *Activities with the aged and infirmed: A handbook for the untrained worker.* Springfield, IL: Charles C. Thomas.

Metzler, R. K. (1973). Music therapy at the Behavioral Learning Center, St. Paul Public School. *Journal of Music Therapy, 10*(4), 177–183.

Metzler, R. K. (1974). The use of music as a reinforcer to increase imitative behavior in severely and profoundly retarded female residents. *Journal of Music Therapy, 11*(2), 97–110.

Michel, D. E. (1971). Self-esteem and academic achievement in black junior high school students: Effects of automated guitar instruction. *Council for Research in Music Education Bulletin, 24*, 15–23.

Michel, D. E. (1985). *Music therapy: An introduction, including music in special education* (2nd ed.). Springfield, IL: Charles C. Thomas.

Michel, D. E., & Martin, D. (1970). Music and self-esteem research with disadvantaged problem boys in an elementary school. *Journal of Music Therapy, 7*(4), 124–127.

Michel, D. E., & May, N. H. (1974). The development of music therapy procedures with speech and language disorders. *Journal of Music Therapy, 11*(2), 74–80.

Michel, D. E., Parker, P., Giokas, D., & Werner, J. (1982). Music therapy and remedial reading: Six studies testing specialized hemispheric processing. *Journal of Music Therapy, 19*(4), 219–229.

Miller, D. M. (1977). Effects of music listening contingencies on arithmetic performance and music preference of EMR children. *American Journal of Mental Deficiency, 8*, 371–378.

Miller, D. M., Dorow, L. G., & Greer, R. D. (1974). The contingent use of music and art in improving arithmetic scores. *Journal of Music Therapy, 11*, 57–64.

Miller, L. L., & Orsmond, G. (1994). Assessing structure in the musical explorations of children with disabilities. *Journal of Music Therapy, 31*(4), 248–265.

Mills, S. R. (1975). Band for the trainable child. *Education and Training of the Mentally Retarded, 10*(4), 268–270.

Montello, L., & Coons, E. E. (1998). Effects of active versus passive group music therapy on preadolescents with emotional, learning, and behavioral disorders. *Journal of Music Therapy, 35*(1), 49–67.

Moog, H. (1979). On the perception of rhythmic forms by physically handicapped children and those of low intelligence in comparison with non-handicapped children. *Council for Research in Music Education Bulletin, 59*, 73–78.

Mooney, M. K. (1972). Blind children need training, not sympathy. *Music Educators Journal, 58*(4), 56–60.

Moore, R., & Mathenius, L. (1989). The effects of modeling, reinforcement, and tempo on imitative rhythmic responses of moderately retarded adolescents. *Journal of Music Therapy, 24*(3), 160–169.

Munro, S. (1986). *Music therapy in palliative/hospice care.* St. Louis, MO: MMB Music.

Murphy, J., & Slorach, N. (1983). The language development of pre-preschool hearing children of deaf parents. *British Journal of Disorders of Communication, 18*(2), 118–126.

Music and the physically handicapped: Report of the Joint Study Conference, London, England. (1970). London England: National Council of Special Service, Disabled Living Foundation.

Music in Special Education. (1972). Reston, VA: Music Educators National Conference. [Originally *Music Educators Journal, 59*(8)]

Music in Special Education. (1972). *Music Educators Journal, 68*(8). [Entire issue].

Musselwhite, C. R., & St. Louis, K. W. (1982). *Communication programming for the severely handicapped.* San Diego, CA: College Hill Press.

Myers, E. G. (1979). The effect of music on retention in a paired-associate task with EMR children. *Journal of Music Therapy, 16*(4), 190–198.

Myers, K. F. (1985). The relationship between degree of disability and vocal range, vocal range midpoint, and pitch-matching ability of mentally retarded and psychiatric clients. *Journal of Music Therapy, 22*(1), 35–45.

Nash, G. C. (1974). *Creative approaches to child development with music, language, and movement.* Port Washington, NY: Alfred.

Nelson, D., Anderson, V., & Gonzales, A. (1984). Music activities as therapy for children with autism and other pervasive developmental disorders. *Journal of Music Therapy, 21*(3), 100–116.

Nocera, S. (1972). Special education teachers need a special education. *Journal of Music Therapy, 58*(4), 73–74.

Nocera, S. D. (1979). *Reaching the special learner through music.* Morristown, NJ: Silver Burdett.

Nordoff, P. (1979). *Fanfares and dances.* Bryn Mawr, PA: Theodore Presser.

Nordoff, P. (1981). *My mother goose, I.* Bryn Mawr, PA: Theodore Presser.

Nordoff, P. (1981). *My mother goose, II.* Bryn Mawr, PA: Theodore Presser.

Nordoff, P. (1982). *Folk songs for children to sing and play on resonator bells.* Bryn Mawr, PA: Theodore Presser.

Nordoff, P., & Robbins, C. (1962). *Children's play songs.* Bryn Mawr, PA: Theodore Presser.

Nordoff, P., & Robbins, C. (1968). *Fun for four drums.* Bryn Mawr, PA: Theodore Presser.

Nordoff, P., & Robbins, C. (1969). *Pif-paf-poltrie.* Bryn Mawr, PA: Theodore Presser.

Nordoff, P., & Robbins, C. (1971). *Spirituals for children to sing and play.* Bryn Mawr, PA: Theodore Presser.

Nordoff, P., & Robbins, C. (1973). *Songs for children.* Bryn Mawr, PA: Theodore Presser.

Nordoff, P., & Robbins, C. (1986). *Music therapy in special education.* St. Louis, MO: MMB Music.

North, E. F. (1966). Music therapy as an important treatment modality with psychotic children. *Journal of Music Therapy, 3*(1), 22–24.

Obrecht, D. (1968). The wheeling motor facilitation program. *Journal of the Association for the Study of Perception, 3*(2), 11–17.

Orff, G. (1974). *The Orff music therapy.* London: Schott.

Orsmond, G. I., & Miller, L. K. (1995). Correlates of musical improvisation in children with disabilities. *Journal of Music Therapy, 32*(3), 152–166.

Palmer, H. (1971). *Songbook: Learning basic skills through music, I.* Activity Records, Inc.

Palmer, H. (1972). *Songbook: Learning basic skills through music, II.* Activity Records, Inc.

Palmer, H. (1974). *Songbook: Getting to know myself.* Activity Records, Inc.

Pasiali, V. (2004). The use of prescriptive therapeutic songs in a home-based environment to promote social skills acquisition by children with autism: Three case studies. *Music Therapy Perspectives, 22*(1), 11–20.

Perry, M. (2003). Relating improvisational music therapy with severely and multiply disabled children to communication development. *Journal of Music Therapy, 40*(3), 217–246.

Peters, M. L. (1970). A comparison of the musical sensitivity of mongoloid and normal children. *Journal of Music Therapy, 7*(4), 113–123.

Peterson, C. A. (1969). Sharing your knowledge of folk guitar with a blind friend. *The New Outlook for the Blind, 63*(4), 142–146.

Pfeifer, M. (1989). A step in the right direction: Suggested strategies for implementing music therapy with the multihandicapped child. *Music Therapy Perspectives, 6*, 57–60.

Pirtle, M., & Seaton, K. P. (1973). Use of music training to actuate conceptual growth in neurologically handicapped children. *Journal of Research in Music Education, 21*(4), 292–301.

Plach, T. (1996). *Creative use of music in group therapy* (2nd ed.). Springfield, IL: Charles C. Thomas.

Podvin, M. G. (1967). The influence of music on the performance of a work task. *Journal of Music Therapy, 4*(2), 52–56.

Poffenberger, N. (1982). *Poffenberger keyboard method: For normal, exceptional and the handicapped population.* Cincinnati, OH: Fun.

Ponath, L. H., & Bitcon, C. H. (1972). A behavioral analysis of Orff-Schulwerk. *Journal of Music Therapy, 9*(2), 56–63.

Presti, G. M. (1984). A levels system approach to music therapy with severely handicapped children in the public school. *Journal of Music Therapy, 21*(3), 117–125.

Price, R., Rast, L., & Winterfeldt, C. (1972). Out of pandemonium-music! *Music Educators Journal, 58*(4), 35–36.

Purvis, J., & Samet, S. (Eds.). (1976). *Music in developmental therapy: A curriculum guide.* Baltimore: University Park Press.

Ramsey, J. (1982). For Peggy, a chance to excel. *Music Educators Journal, 68*(8), 28–29.

Reardon, D. M., & Bell, G. (1970). Effects of sedative and stimulative music on activity levels of severely retarded boys. *American Journal of Mental Deficiency, 75*(2), 156–159.

Reeves, H. (1985). *Song and dance activities for elementary children.* West Nyack, NY: Parker.

Register, D. (2001). The effects of an early intervention music curriculum on prereading/writing. *Journal of Music Therapy, 38*(3), 239–248.

Register, D. (2004). The effects of live music groups versus an educational children's television program on the emergent literacy of young children. *Journal of Music Therapy, 41*(1), 2–27.

Reid, D. H., Hill, B. K., Rawers, R. J., & Montegar, C. A. (1975). The use of contingent music in teaching social skills to a nonverbal hyperactive boy. *Journal of Music Therapy, 12*(1), 2–18.

Rejto, A. (1973). Music as an aid to the remediation of learning disabilities. *Journal of Learning Disabilities, 6*, 286–295.

Resnick, R. (1973). Creative movement classes for visually handicapped children in a public school setting. *The New Outlook for the Blind, 67*(10), 442–447.

Rice, T. A. (1978). *Music as auditory stimuli to facilitate visual memory in learning-disabled children.* Unpublished master's thesis, The Florida State University, Tallahassee.

Richman, J. S. (1976). Background music for repetitive task performance of severely retarded individuals. *American Journal of Mental Deficiency, 81*(3), 251–255.

Rickson, D. J. (2006). Instructional and improvisational models of music therapy with adolescent who have attention deficit hyperactivity disorder (ADHD): A comparison of the effects on motor impulsivity. *Journal of Music Therapy, 43*(1), 39–62.

Rieber, M. (1965). The effect of music on the activity level of children. *Psychonomic Science, 3*, 325–326.

Rigrodsky, S., Hanley, T. D., & Steer, M. D. (1959). *Application of Mowrers autistic theory to the speech habilitation of the mentally retarded pupils.* Lafayette, IN: Purdue University.

Ritholz, M. S., & Turry, A. (1994). The journey by train: Creative music therapy with a 17-year-old boy. *Music Therapy, 12*(2), 58–87.

Ritschl, C., Mongrella, J., & Presbie, R. (1972). Group time out from rock-and-roll music and out-of-seat behavior of handicapped children while riding a school bus. *Psychological Reports, 31*, 967–973.

Robb, S. L. (2003). Music interventions and group participation skills of preschools with visual impairment: Raising questions about music, arousal, and attention. *Journal of Music Therapy, 40*(4), 266–282.

Robbins, C., & Robbins, C. (1980). *Music for the hearing impaired: A resource manual and curriculum guide.* St. Louis, MO: MMB Music.

Robins, F., & Robins, J. (1968). *Educational rhythmics for mentally and physically handicapped children.* New York: Association Press.

Robinson, D. (1970). Is there a correlation between rhythmic response and emotional disturbance? *Journal of Music Therapy, 7*(2), 54.

Rosene, P. E. (1982). Instrumental music . . . A success opportunity. *Music Educators Journal, 68*(8), 37–39.

Roskam, K. (1976). Music as a remediation tool for learning disabled children. *Journal of Music Therapy, 16*, 31–42.

Roskam, K. (1976, May). Music as a remediation tool for learning disabled children. *Sounding Board, 20.*

Roskam, K. (1979). Music therapy as an aid for increasing auditory awareness and improving reading skill. *Journal of Music Therapy, 16*(1), 31–42.

Ross, D. M., Ross, S. A., & Kuchenbecker, S. L. (1973). Rhythmic training for educable mentally retarded children. *Mental Retardation, 11*, 20–23.

Ruud, E. (1980). *Music therapy and its relationship to current treatment theories.* St. Louis, MO: MMB Music.

Salsburg, R. S., & Greenwald, M. A. (1977). Effects of a token system on attentiveness and punctuality in two string instrument classes. *Journal of Music Therapy, 14*(1), 27–38.

Saperston, B. (1973). The use of music in establishing communication with an autistic mentally retarded child. *Journal of Music Therapy, 10*(4), 184–188.

Saperston, B., Chan, R., Morphew, C., & Carsrud, K. (1980). Music listening versus juice as a reinforcement for learning in profoundly mentally retarded individuals. *Journal of Music Therapy, 17*(4), 174–183.

Scartelli, J. (1982). The effect of sedative music on electromyographic biofeedback assisted relaxation of spastic cerebral palsied adults. *Journal of Music Therapy, 19*(4), 210–218.

Schlanger, B. (1953). Speech measurement of handicapped children. *American Journal of Mental Deficiency, 58*, 114–120.

Schloss, P. J., Smith, M. A., Goldsmith, L., & Selinger, J. (1984, September). Identifying current and relevant curricular sequences for multiply involved hearing-impaired learners. *American Annals of the Deaf*, 370–374.

Schulberg, C. H. (1981). *The music therapy sourcebook.* New York: Human Sciences Press.

Schwankovsky, L., & Guthrie, P. (1982). *Music therapy for handicapped children: Other health impaired. NAMT Monograph Series.* Washington, DC: National Association for Music Therapy.

Seybold, C. D. (1971). The value and use of music activities in the treatment of speech-delayed children. *Journal of Music Therapy, 8*(3), 102–110.

Shames, G. H., & Rubin, H. (Eds.). (1985). *Stuttering: Then and now.* Columbus, OH: Charles E. Merrill.

Shames, G. H., Wiig, E. H., & Secord, W. A. (Eds.). (1985). *Human communication disorders: An introduction* (5th ed.). Boston: Allyn and Bacon.

Shehan, P. K. (1981). A comparison of mediation strategies in paired-associate learning for children with learning disabilities. *Journal of Music Therapy, 18*(3), 120–127.

Shepherd, L. T., Jr., & Simons, G. M. (1970). Music training for the visually handicapped. *Music Educators Journal, 57*(6), 80–81.

Sheridan, W. (1977). *The Oregon plan for mainstreaming in music.* Salem, OR: State Department of Education.

Sherwin, A. C. (1953). Reactions to music of autistic (schizophrenic) children. *American Journal of Psychiatry, 109*, 823–831.

Slyoff, M. R. (1979). *Music for special education.* Fort Worth, TX: Harris Music.

Smith, R. B., & Flohr, J. W. (1984). *Music dramas for children with special needs.* Denton, TX: Troostwyk Press.

Snow, W., & Fields, B. (1950). Music as an adjunct in the training of children with cerebral palsy. *Occupational Therapy, 29*, 147–156.

Sontag, E., Smith, S., & Certo, N. (Eds.). (1977). *Educational programming for the severely and profoundly handicapped.* Reston, VA: Council for Exceptional Children.

Soraci, S., Deckner, C., McDaniel, C., & Blanton, R. (1982). The relationship between rate of rhythmicity and the stereotypic behaviors of abnormal children. *Journal of Music Therapy, 19*(1), 46–54.

Sparks, R. W., & Holland, A. (1976). Melodic intonation therapy for aphasia. *Journal of Music Therapy, 4*(41), 287–297.

Spencer, S. L. (1988). The efficiency of instrumental and movement activities in developing mentally retarded adolescents' ability to follow directions. *Journal of Music Therapy, 25*(1), 44–50.

Spitzer, M. (1984, December). A survey of the use of music in schools for the hearing impaired. *The Volta Review,* 362–363.

Stainback, S. B., Stainback, W. C., & Hallahan, D. P. (1973). Effect of background music on learning. *Exceptional Children, 40*(2), 109–110.

Standley, J. M. (2002). *Music techniques in therapy, counseling, and special education* (2nd ed.). St. Louis, MO: MMB.

Standley, J. M., & Hughes, J. E. (1996). Documenting developmentally appropriate objectives and benefits of a music therapy program for early intervention: A behavioral analysis. *Music Therapy Perspectives, 14*(2), 87–94.

Standley, J. M., & Hughes, J. E. (1997). Evaluation of an early-intervention music curriculum for prereading/writing skills. *Music Therapy Perspectives, 15*(2), 79–86.

Staples, S. M. (1968). A paired-associates learning task utilizing music as the mediator: An exploratory study. *Journal of Music Therapy, 5*(2), 53–57.

Staum, M. J. (1983). Music and rhythmic stimuli in the rehabilitation of gait disorders. *Journal of Music Therapy, 20*(2), 69–87.

Staum, M. J. (1987). Music notation to improve the speech prosody of hearing-impaired children. *Journal of Music Therapy, 24*(3), 146–159.

Staum, M. J., & Flowers, P. J. (1984). The use of simulated training and music lessons in teaching appropriate shopping skills to an autistic child. *Music Therapy Perspectives, 1*(3), 14–17.

Steele, A. L. (1967). Effects of social reinforcement on the musical preference of mentally retarded children. *Journal of Music Therapy, 4*(2), 57–62.

Steele, A. L. (1968). Programmed use of music to alter uncooperative problem behavior. *Journal of Music Therapy, 5*(4), 103–107.

Steele, A. L. (1975). In R. Zolinger & N. Klein (Eds.), *Learning disabilities: An interdisciplinary perspective.* Case Western Reserve, Department of Education.

Steele, A. L. (1979). A report on the First World Congress on Future Special Education. *Journal of Music Therapy, 16*(1), 43–47.

Steele, A. L. (1984). Music therapy for the learning disabled: Intervention and instruction. *Music Therapy Perspectives, 1*(3), 2–7.

Steele, A. L., & Jorgenson, H. A. (1971). Music therapy: An effective solution to problems in related disciplines. *Journal of Music Therapy, 8*(4), 131–145.

Steele, A. L., Vaughan, M., & Dolan, C. (1976). The school support program: Music therapy for adjustment problems in elementary schools. *Journal of Music Therapy, 13*, 87–100.

Sterlicht, M., Deutsch, M. R., & Siegel, I. (1967). Influence of musical stimulation upon the functioning of institutionalized retardates. *Psychiatric Quarterly Supplement, 41*(2), 323.

Stern, V. (1975). They shall have music. *The Volta Review, 77*(8), 495–500.

Stevens, E. (1969). Music therapy in the treatment of autistic children. *Journal of Music Therapy, 6*(4), 98.

Stevens, E. (1971). Some effects of tempo changes on stereotyped rocking movement of low-level mentally retarded subjects. *American Journal of Mental Deficiency, 76*(1), 76–81.

Stevens, E., & Clark, F. (1969). Music therapy in the treatment of autistic children. *Journal of Music Therapy, 6*(4), 98–104.

Stoesz, G. (1966). *A suggested guide to piano literature for the partially seeing.* New York: National Society for the Prevention of Blindness.

Stordahl, J. (2002). Song recognition and appraisal: A comparison of children who use cochlear implants and normally hearing children. *Journal of Music Therapy, 39*(1), 2–19.

Stubbs, B. (1970). A study of the effectiveness of an integrated, personified approach to learning with trainable mental retardates. *Journal of Music Therapy, 7*(3), 77–82.

Swaiko, N. (1974). The role and value of an eurhythmics program in a curriculum for deaf children. *American Annals of the Deaf, 119*(3), 321–324.

Talkington, L. W., & Hall, S. M. (1970). A musical application of Premack's hypothesis to low verbal retardates. *Journal of Music Therapy, 7*(3), 95–99.

Thaut, M. H. (1984). A music therapy treatment model for autistic children. *Music Therapy Perspectives, 1*(4), 7–13.

Thaut, M. H. (1985). The use of auditory rhythm and rhythmic speech to aid temporal muscular control in children with gross motor dysfunction. *Journal of Music Therapy, 22*(3), 108–128.

Thompson, K. (1982). Music for every child: Education of handicapped learners. *Music Educators Journal, 68*(8), 25–28.

Thresher, J. M. (1972). A music workshop for special class teachers. *Journal of Music Therapy, 9*(1), 40–43.

Tomat, J. H., & Krutzky, C. D. (1975). *Learning through music for special children and their teachers.* South Waterford, MA: Merriam-Eddy.

Tomatis, A. (1986). *Education and dyslexia.* Dallas, TX: Sound of Light.

Topics in Language Disorders. (1983). *Case studies of phonological disorders, 3*(2). Gaithersberg, MD: Aspen Systems.

Topics in Language Disorders. (1983). *Nonbiased assessment of language difference, 3*(3). Gaithersberg, MD: Aspen Systems.

Topics in Language Disorders. (1983). *Pragmatics in language-disordered children, 4*(1). Gaithersberg, MD: Aspen Systems.

Topics in Language Disorders. (1984). *Adolescent language-learning disorders, 4*(2). Gaithersberg, MD: Aspen Systems.

Topics in Language Disorders. (1984). *Language development and disorders in the social context, 4*(4). Gaithersberg, MD: Aspen Systems.

Topics in Language Disorders. (1984). *Language intervention with the mentally retarded child, 5*(1). Gaithersberg, MD: Aspen Systems.

Topics in Language Disorders. (1984). *Neurolinguistic approaches to language disorders, 4*(3). Gaithersberg, MD: Aspen Systems.

Topics in Language Disorders. (1985). *Discourse and language-impaired children: Clinical issues, 5*(2). Gaithersberg, MD: Aspen Systems.

Topics in Language Disorders. (1985). *High technology and language disorders. , 6*(1). Gaithersberg, MD: Aspen Systems.

Topics in Language Disorders. (1985). *Implications for Ll and L2 learning*, 5(4). Gaithersberg, MD: Aspen Systems.

Topics in Language Disorders. (1985). *The years between 10 and 18, 5*(3). Gaithersberg, MD: Aspen Systems.

Topics in Language Disorders. (1986). *Discourse disorders*, 6(2). Gaithersberg, MD: Aspen Systems.

Traub, C. (1969). The relation of music to speech of low-verbalizing subjects in a music-listening activity. *Journal of Music Therapy, 6*(4), 105–107.

Underhill, K. K., & Harris, C. M. (1974). The effect of contingent music on establishing imitation in behaviorally disturbed retarded children. *Journal of Music Therapy, 11*(3), 156–166.

VanWeelden, K., & Whipple, J. (2005). Preservice teachers' predictions, perceptions, and actual assessment of students with special needs in secondary general music. *Journal of Music Therapy, 42*(3), 200–215.

Vaughn, M. M. (1972). Music for our gifted children: A bridge to consciousness. *Music Educators Journal, 58*(4), 70–72; 131–132.

Velásquez, V. (1991). Beginning experiences in piano performance for a girl with Down syndrome: A case study. *Music Therapy Perspectives, 9*, 82–85.

Vernazza, M. (1967). What are we doing about music in special education? *Music Educators Journal, 68*(8), 49–50.

Vettese, J. (1974). Instrumental lessons for deaf children. *The Volta Review, 76*(4), 219–222.

Walker, D. (1974). When it comes to music, they see the light. *The Pointer, 19*(2), 127.

Walker, J. B. (1972). The use of music as an aid in developing functional speech in the institutionalized mentally retarded. *Journal of Music Therapy, 9*(1), 1–12.

Walworth, D. (2007). The use of music therapy within the SCERTS model for children with autism spectrum disorder. *Journal of Music Therapy, 44*(1), 2–22.

Ward, D. (1976). *Hearts and hands and voices: Music in the education of slow learners.* London: Oxford University Press.

Ward, D. (1979). *Sing a rainbow: Musical activities with mentally handicapped children.* London: Oxford University Press.

Wasserman, N., Plutchik, R., Deutsch, R., & Taketomo, Y. (1973). A music therapy evaluation scale and its clinical application to mentally retarded adult patients. *Journal of Music Therapy, 10*, 64–77.

Wasserman, N., Plutchik, R., Deutsch, R., & Taketomo, Y. (1973). The musical background of a group of mentally retarded psychotic patients: Implications for music therapy. *Journal of Music Therapy, 10*(2), 78–82.

Weber, R. D. (1971). The use of musical instruments in the education of TMRs. *Council for Research in Music Education, 25,* 79–88.

Weigl, V. (1959). Functional music, a therapeutic tool in working with the mentally retarded. *American Journal of Mental Deficiency, 63,* 672–678.

Weigl, V. (1969). Music for the retarded. *Music Journal, 27,* 56–57.

Weiner, P. S. (1967). Auditory discrimination and articulation. *Journal of Speech and Hearing Disorders, 32,* 19–28.

Weisbrod, J. (1972). Shaping a body image through movement therapy. *Music Educators Journal, 58*(4), 66–69.

Welsbacher, B. T. (1972). The neurologically handicapped child: More than a package of bizarre behaviors. *Music Educators Journal, 58*(4), 26–28.

Werbner, N. (1966). The practice of music therapy with psychotic children. *Journal of Music Therapy, 3*(1), 25–31.

Wheeler, B. L. (1999). Experiencing pleasure in working with severely disabled children. *Journal of Music Therapy, 32*(4), 265–285.

Whipple, J. (2004). Music in intervention for children and adolescents with autism: A meta-analysis. *Journal of Music Therapy, 41*(2), 90–106.

White, L. D. (1982). How to adapt for special students. *Music Educators Journal, 68*(8), 49–50.

Wigram, T. (2000). A method of music therapy assessment for the diagnosis of autism and communication disorders in children. *Music Therapy Perspectives, 18*(1), 13–22.

Williams, L. D. (1985). A band that exceeds all expectations. *Music Educators Journal, 71*(6), 26–29.

Wilson, A. (1964). Special education for the emotionally disturbed child. *Journal of Music Therapy, 1*(1), 16–18.

Wilson, B. L. (1971). *The effects of music and verbal mediation on the learning of paired-associates by institutionalized retardates.* Unpublished master's thesis, The Florida State University, Tallahassee.

Wilson, B. L. (Ed.). (1996). *Models of music therapy interventions in school settings: From institution to inclusion.* Silver Spring, MD: National Association for Music Therapy.

Wilson, B. L. (Ed.). (2002). *Models of music therapy intervention in school settings* (2nd ed.). Silver Spring, MD: American Music Therapy Association.

Wilson, B. L., & Smith, D. S. (2000). Music therapy assessment in school settings: A preliminary investigation. *Journal of Music Therapy, 37*(2), 97–117.

Wilson, C. V. (1976). The use of rock music as a reward in behavior therapy with children. *Journal of Music Therapy, 13*(1), 39–48.

Wingert, M. L. (1972). Effects of a music-enrichment program in the education of the mentally retarded. *Journal of Music Therapy, 9*(1), 13–22.

Winsor, M. T. (1972). *Arts and crafts for special education*. Belmont, CA: Fearon Teacher-Aids.

Wolfe, D. E. (1980). The effect of automated interrupted music on head posturing of cerebral-palsied individuals. *Journal of Music Therapy, 17*(4), 184–206.

Wolfe, D. E., & Hom, C. (1993). Use of melodies as structural prompts for learning and retention of sequential verbal information by preschool students. *Journal of Music Therapy, 30*(2), 100–118.

Wolfgram, B. J. (1978). Music therapy for retarded adults with psychotic overlay: A day treatment approach. *Journal of Music Therapy, 15*(4), 199–207.

Wolpow, R. L. (1976). The independent effects of contingent social and academic approval upon the musical on-task performance behaviors of profoundly retarded adults. *Journal of Music Therapy, 13*(1), 29–38.

Wylie, M. E. (1983). Eliciting vocal responses in severely and profoundly mentally retarded handicapped subjects. *Journal of Music Therapy, 20*(4), 190–200.

Wylie, M. E. (1996). A cast study to promote hand use in children with Rett syndrome. *Music Therapy Perspectives, 14*(2), 83–86.

Yarbrough, C., Charboneau, M., & Wapnick, J. (1977). Music as reinforcement for correct math and attending in ability-assigned math classes. *Journal of Music Therapy, 14*(2), 77–78.

Zimmer, U. (1976). *Music handbook for the child in special education*. Hackensack, NJ: Joseph Boonin.

Terminal Illness/Hospice/Palliative Care

Aldridge, D. (1995). Spirituality, hope and music therapy in palliative care. *Arts in Psychotherapy, 22*(2), 103–109.

Bailey, L. (1984). The use of songs in music therapy with cancer patients and their families. *Music Therapy, 4*(1), 5–17.

Bonny, H. L. (1989). Sound as symbol: Guided imagery and music in clinical practice. *Music Therapy Perspectives, 6*, 52–56.

Bright, R. (1981). Music and the management of grief reactions. In I. M. Burnside (Ed.), *Nursing and the aged* (pp. 137–142). New York: McGraw-Hill.

Bright, R. (1995). Music therapy as a facilitator in grief counseling. In T. Wigram, B. Saperston, & R. West (Eds.), *The art and science of music therapy: A handbook* (pp. 309–323). London: Harwood Academic.

Brown, J. (1992). Music dying. *American Journal of Hospice and Palliative Care, 9*(4), 17–20.

Brown, J. (1992). When words fail, music speaks. *American Journal of Hospice and Palliative Care, 9*(2), 13–16.

Curtis, S. (1986). The effect of music on pain relief and relaxation of the terminally ill. *Journal of Music Therapy, 23*(1), 10–24.

Dalton, T., & Krout, R. (2005). Development of the Grief Process Scale through music therapy songwriting with bereaved adolescents. *Arts in Psychotherapy, 32*(2), 131–143.

Daveson, B. (2001). Music therapy and childhood cancer: Goals, methods, patient choice and control during diagnosis, intensive treatment, transplant and palliative care. *Music Therapy Perspectives, 19*(2), 114–120.

Daveson, B., & Kennelly, J. (2000). Music therapy in palliative care for hospitalized children and adolescents. *Journal of Palliative Care, 16*(1), 35–38.

Dun, B. (1995). A different beat: Music therapy in children's cardiac care. *Music Therapy Perspectives, 13*(1), 35–39.

Fagen, T. (1982). Music therapy in the treatment of anxiety and fear in terminal pediatric patients. *Music Therapy, 2*(1), 13–23.

Forinash, M., & Gonzalez, D. (1990). A phenomenology of music therapy with the terminally ill. *Music Therapy, 8*(1), 35–46.

Gallagher, L., & Steele, A. (2001). Developing and using a computerized database for music therapy in palliative medicine. *Journal of Palliative Care, 17*(3), 147–154.

Gilbert, J. (1977). Music therapy perspectives on death and dying. *Journal of Music Therapy, 14*(4), 165–171.

Hilliard, R. (2001). The effects of music therapy-based bereavement groups on mood and behavior of grieving children: A pilot study. *Journal of Music Therapy, 38*(4), 291–306.

Hilliard, R. (2002). *The effects of music therapy on quality of life and length of life of hospice patients diagnosed with terminal cancer.* Unpublished doctoral dissertation, The Florida State University, Tallahassee.

Hilliard, R. (2001). The use of music therapy in meeting the multidimensional needs of hospice patients and families. *Journal of Palliative Care, 17*(3), 161–166.

Hilliard, R. (2003). The effects of music therapy on the quality and length of life of people diagnosed with terminal cancer. *Journal of Music Therapy, 40*(2), 113–137.

Hilliard, R. (2004). A post-hoc analysis of music therapy services for residents in nursing homes receiving hospice care. *Journal of Music Therapy, 41*(4), 266–281.

Hilliard, R. (2004). Hospice administrators' knowledge of music therapy: A comparative analysis of surveys. *Music Therapy Perspectives, 22*(2), 104–108.

Hilliard, R. (2006). The effect of music therapy sessions on compassion fatigue and team building of professional hospice caregivers. *Arts in Psychotherapy, 33*(5), 395–401.

Kerr, S. E. (2004). *The effect of music on non-responsive patients in a hospice setting.* Unpublished master's thesis, The Florida State University, Tallahassee.

Krout, R. (2003). Music therapy with imminently dying hospice patients and their families: Facilitating release near the time of death. *American Journal of Hospice & Palliative Care, 20*(2), 129–133.

Krout, R. (2005). Applications of music therapist-composed songs in creating participant connections and facilitating goals and rituals during one-time bereavement support groups and programs. *Music Therapy Perspectives, 23*(2), 118–128.

Mandel, S. (1993). The role of the music therapist on the hospice/palliative care team. *Journal of Palliative Care, 9*(4), 37–39.

Marr, J. (1998–1999). GIM at the end of life: Case studies in palliative care. *Journal of the Association for Music & Imagery, 6,* 37–54.

Maue-Johnson, E., & Tanguay, C. (2006). Assessing the unique needs of hospice patients: A tool for music therapists. *Music Therapy Perspectives, 24*(1), 13–20.

Munro, S. (1984). *Music therapy in palliative/hospice care.* St. Louis, MO: MMB Music.

Munro, S. (1993). *Music therapy in palliative/hospice care.* St. Louis, MO: MMB Music.

Munro, S., & Mount, B. (1980). Music therapy in palliative care. In I. Ajemain and B. Mount (Eds.), *R.V.H. manual on palliative/ hospice care.* New York: Arno Press.

Nguyen, J. (2003). *The effect of music therapy on end-of-life patients' quality of life, emotional state, and family satisfaction as measured by self-report.* Unpublished master's thesis, The Florida State University, Tallahassee.

O'Callaghan, C. (1996). Lyrical themes in songs written by palliative care patients. *Journal of Music Therapy, 33*(2), 74–92.

O'Callaghan, C. (1997). Therapeutic opportunities associated with the music when using song writing in palliative care. *Music Therapy Perspectives, 15*(1), 32–38.

O'Callaghan, C. (2001). Bringing music to life: A study of music therapy and palliative care experiences in a cancer hospital. *Journal of Palliative Care, 17*(3), 155–160.

Sanderson, S. (1984). *Music therapy with a terminally ill cancer patient.* Unpublished research manuscript, The Florida State University, Tallahassee.

Skaggs, R. (1997). The Bonny method of guided imagery and music in the treatment of terminal illness: A private practice setting. *Music Therapy Perspectives, 15*(1), 39–44.

Smeijsters, H., & van den Hurk, J. (1999, September). Music therapy helping to work through grief and finding a personal identity. *Journal of Music Therapy, 36*(3), 222–252.

West, T. (1994). Psychological issues in hospice music therapy. *Music Therapy Perspectives, 12*(2), 117–124.

Wlodarczyk, N. (2003). *The effect of music therapy on the spirituality of persons in an in-patient hospice unit as measured by self-report.* Unpublished master's thesis, The Florida State University, Tallahassee.

Wylie, M. E., & Blom, R. C. (1986). Guided imagery and music with hospice patients. *Music Therapy Perspectives, 3,* 25–28.

Zabin, A. (2005). Lessons learned from the dying: Stories from a music therapist. *Music Therapy Perspectives, 23*(1), 70–75.

Notes

Preface

[1] Madsen, C. K. (1979). Research and music therapy: The necessity for transfer. *Journal of Music Therapy, 23*(2), 50–55.

Part I

[1] Greenfield, D. G. (1978). Evaluation of music therapy practicum competencies: Comparison of self and instructor rating of videotapes. *Journal of Music Therapy, 15,* 15–20

[2] Prickett, C. A. (1987). The effect of self-monitoring on positive comments given by music therapy students coaching peers. *Journal of Music Therapy, 24*(2), 54–75.

[3] Alley, J. M. (1978). Competency based evaluation of a music therapy curriculum. *Journal of Music Therapy, 15*(1), 9–14.

[4] Alley, J. M. (1980). The effect of self-analysis of videotapes on selected competencies of music therapy majors. *Journal of Music Therapy, 17*(3), 113–132.

[5] Andersen, J. L. (1982). The effect of feedback versus no feedback on music therapy competencies. *Journal of Music Therapy, 19*(3), 130–140.

[6] Lathom, W. B. (1982). Survey of current functions of a music therapist. *Journal of Music Therapy, 19*(1), 2–27.

[7] Wolfe, D. E., & Hom, C. (1993). Use of melodies as structural prompts for learning and retention of sequential information by preschool students. *Journal of Music Therapy, 30*(2), 100–118.

[8] Wallace, W. (1994). Memory for music: Effect of melody on recall of text. *Journal of Experimental Psychology: Learning, Memory, and Cognition, 20*(6), 1471–1485.

[9] Rainey, D., & Larsen, J. (2002). The effects of familiar melodies on initial learning and long-term memory for unconnected text. *Music Perception, 20*(2), 173–186.

[10] Furman, C. E. (1987). Behavior checklists and videotapes versus standard instructor feedback in the developent of a music teaching competency. In C. K. Madsen & C.A. Prickett (Eds.), *Applications of research in music behavior* (pp. 73–98). Tuscaloosa, AL: The University of Alabama Press.

[11] Madsen, C. K., & Yarbrough, C. (1980). *Competency-based music education.* Englewood Cliffs, NJ: Prentice-Hall.

[12] Hanser, S. B., & Furman, C. E. (1980). The effect of videotaped feedback vs. field-based feedback on the development of applied clinical skills. *Journal of Music Therapy, 17,* 103–112.

[13] Alley, J. M. (1982). The effect of videotape analysis on music therapy competencies: An observation of simulated and clinical activities. *Journal of Music Therapy, 19*(3), 141–160.

[14] Bruscia, K. E., Hesser, B., & Boxill, E. H. (1981). Essential competencies for the practice of music therapy. *Music Therapy, 1*(1), 43–49.

[15] Braswell, C., Decuir, A., & Maranto, C. D. (1980). Ratings of entry level skills by music therapy clinicians, educators, and interns. *Journal of Music Therapy, 17*(3), 133–147.

[16] Standley, J. M. (1986). *Use of a checklist to assess music therapy group activity leadership skills.* Annual conference of the National Association for Music Therapy, Chicago.

Part II

[1] Riekehof, L. L. (1987). *The joy of signing.* Springfield, MO: Gospel Publishing House.